LEABHARLANNA CHONTAE FHINE GALL
FINGAL COUNTY LIBRARIES

Items should be returned on or before the last date shown below. Items may be renewed by personal application, writing, telephone or by accessing the online Catalogue Service on Fingal Libraries' website. To renew give date due, borrower ticket number and PIN number if using online catalogue. Fines are charged on overdue items and will include postage incurred in recovery. Damage to, or loss of items will be charged to the borrower

Date Due	Date Due	Date Due
03 JAN 20		

The Economy of Ireland

TENTH EDITION

National and Sectoral Policy Issues

Edited by

John O'Hagan

and

Carol Newman

GILL & MACMILLAN

Gill & Macmillan Ltd
Hume Avenue
Park West
Dublin 12
with associated companies throughout the world www.gillmacmillan.ie

© Editors and Contributors 2008

978 07171 4379 5

Index compiled by Cover to Cover
Print origination in Ireland by TypeIT, Dublin

A CIP catalogue record for this book is available
from the British Library.

Contents

Section II
POLICY IMPLEMENTATION

Section III
POLICY ISSUES AT A NATIONAL LEVEL

Section IV
POLICY ISSUES IN THE MARKET SECTOR

Section V
POLICY ISSUES IN THE NON-MARKET SECTOR

Preface

Overview

The Irish experience in terms of growth of employment and living standards in the period 1994 to 2007 was probably one of the most remarkable turnarounds in the economy of any country or region in Europe in the last 50 years. It is a 'story' that was observed almost with disbelief at first and is now *the* 'case study' to which most small countries refer when presenting the arguments for their own future economic transformation. In mid-2008, though, 'storm clouds' are gathering over this remarkable performance and what the future holds is hard to predict. Already, there has been a dramatic slowdown in the growth of employment and tax revenue, amid fears that things might get a lot worse.

Economic Transformation: 1994 to 2007

Nonetheless, between 1994 and 2007 the Irish economy experienced dramatic changes, the effects of which are likely to persist well into the future. In three important respects there was an exceptional economic performance (see Chapters 5 and 6 for details).

- There was a huge and sustained increase in employment throughout the period.
- Productivity continued to grow at historic rates and this, associated with the increase in employment, led to exceptional growth in total incomes, particularly in the period 1994 to 2000 when gross national income increased at 8.5 per cent per annum (by 5.1 per cent per annum in the period 2000–2007).
- There was also a remarkable increase in incomes *per head* as the proportion of the population in work increased quite dramatically, in large part due to increased female participation and the immigration of working-age individuals. In other words, there were increased incomes and these had to be 'shared' with much fewer dependants than in the past. This

demographic shift was particularly evident in the 1994 to 2000 period, when income per head increased on average by 7.4 per cent per annum (dropping to 3.3 per cent in the 2000 to 2007 period).

As a result, the concern over large-scale unemployment shifted to one about serious labour shortages, and long-term unemployment was down from over nine per cent in 1994 to less than two per cent of the labour force in 2007. The emphasis was no longer on emigration but on how to respond to immigration, especially potentially large-scale immigration of people with no ethnic connection to Ireland. Allied to the fact that an increasing proportion of the population were of working age, this meant that average incomes *per head* soared, turning Ireland into one of the highest per capita income countries in the world.

The evidence is clear for all to see: the huge increase in the number of cars and houses and major new infrastructural projects, especially road-related, have transformed the physical landscape of Ireland in a way that would have been difficult to imagine even a decade ago. There was a confidence in the country, boosted by average incomes well above those in the UK, that was palpable. For the first time, perhaps for centuries, there was and is a new and very wealthy class of Irish, living and wanting to live in Ireland.

Economic Policy Environment
There were also dramatic changes in the policy environment and the emphasis of economic decision-making, the effects of which are also likely to persist well into the future. Ireland is now a region of the euro zone, the euro having replaced Irish notes and coins in January 2002. As such, there are no chapters in this book on monetary policy or on balance of payments and exchange rate policy in Ireland. The policy emphasis now is almost exclusively on the competitiveness of the EU region, 'Ireland Inc.', and this is reflected in many chapters throughout the book (see in particular Chapters 2, 6, 8 and 9). Even in relation to this Ireland must operate within an agreed competition and regulatory environment determined, with Ireland as a voting member, at EU level. Competitiveness is a key determinant of our attractiveness to foreign direct investment: the scale of US investment has been such that Ireland might be viewed, in an industrial sense, as a region of the US economy despite the fact that in a monetary sense the country is an integral part of the euro zone.

There has also been an extraordinary change, as will be seen in several chapters, in terms of improving the competitiveness of the economy in labour and product markets (see Chapters 5, 6, 8 and 9). International benchmarking is now commonplace and the *Annual Competitiveness Reports* issued by the National Competitiveness Council each year since 1997 are some of the most talked-about reports produced. Problems remain, though, in particular in relation to physical infrastructure (see Chapter 8) and certain aspects of human capital (see Chapters 8 and 12).

Despite the industrial connection with the USA and the economic, monetary and political links with the EU, the euro zone in particular, the relationship with the UK is for Ireland still very important, for a variety of reasons (see Chapter 1). While the nature of this relationship may have altered significantly, its substance has remained the same. In terms of simple geography, Ireland is a tiny country, an island to the west of Britain, which in turn is a somewhat larger but much more densely populated island to the west of mainland Europe: its population is over 15 times that of Ireland. Ireland and the UK have a common labour market, a common language, and huge trade and tourism flows in both directions; by and large people in both jurisdictions watch the same TV programmes and follow similar key sports and cultural events. These are inescapable facts, which, as shall be seen throughout the book, are important to an understanding of the Irish economy, past and present.

Moreover, the island of Ireland consists of two political units, the larger portion of which forms the Republic of Ireland and the smaller portion Northern Ireland, which is part of the UK. This too has had an impact on economic, social and political life in the Republic. This book is about the economy of the Republic of Ireland, and henceforth the terms 'economy of Ireland' and 'Irish economy' refer to this economy, unless otherwise stated. Some reference is made to the Northern Ireland economy, but since economic policy is largely determined in London, it is difficult to devote much attention to policy there without also reviewing British economic policy in general. There has been, though, as Chapter 2 points out, greatly increased cross-border co-operation on the economic front since the Good Friday Agreement of ten years ago.

The links, economic and cultural, to Continental Europe are strengthening, something that low-cost air travel and the use of the euro has facilitated. Irish people are now much more familiar than they were even 25 years ago with political developments in Europe, and with European sporting and cultural events. Indeed, as a result of the boom in incomes many own second homes there. But Ireland and the EU have also to look at the wider world, as issues and problems that are truly global in nature must be addressed. Top of the list is the environment and the danger of serious global warming. Not far behind are terrorism, free trade, sharply increased world food prices resulting from new demands for food and land use, increased migration (legal and illegal) and international crime. As Chapter 2 points out, concerns about environmental degradation must qualify any endorsement of economic growth as a policy objective. Chapter 3, though, highlights the governance difficulties faced when dealing with environmental issues that extend beyond national boundaries. Later chapters discuss various policy measures being adopted to address such issues, both within Ireland and internationally.

The rise of China and India in particular is an economic reality that has affected not just small countries like Ireland but also the two largest trading blocs in the world, namely the EU and the USA. It has led to a huge increase in competition, for both goods and investment flows. It has also of course led to a huge increase in trade and investment opportunities. China hosts the Olympic

Games this summer, its military prowess is growing and Mandarin is the mother tongue for by far the largest number of people in the world. As such, its influence will soon extend well beyond the economic to the cultural and military spheres. Ireland, as part of the larger EU, will have to learn to adapt to such seismic geopolitical changes in the global economy.

Some Reflections
Lessons of History
Having carefully read all the chapters in this book several times, perhaps we can be excused if we indulge in a few reflections on some issues that are raised in different chapters, starting with Chapter 1. This provides an overview of the economic evolution of Ireland over several centuries, with some interesting lessons to be learned in relation to the present-day economy. Perhaps the main insight from Chapter 1 is that centuries of under-performance on the economic front might explain the enthusiasm with which the country has in the last 20 years embraced economic progress and material well-being. Related to this are the associated employment and population increases, the significance of which can only be realised in light of the country's history in relation to emigration and population decline. Moreover, the history of the economy between 1922 and the early 1990s is crucial to an understanding of the present economy; many lessons were learned from the experience of these years and several of the policies linked to the economic success since the early 1990s were put in place in this period (see, in particular, Chapters 1, 6, 8, 9 and 12).

Taking a broad look at Irish history, one can also observe, as is the case for many countries, large swings in economic fortunes, but usually over many decades. Dublin at the end of the eighteenth century, for example, was one of the great cities of Europe with magnificent Georgian buildings and at its heart Trinity College, with its fine squares and buildings, which to this day acts as a major attraction for tourists. At the end of the eighteenth century most of Ireland was dotted with stately mansions, most of which were owned by descendants of the Protestant settlers who had colonised the country in the sixteenth and seventeenth centuries. Some are still in existence to this day and in some cases are owned and lived in by some of Ireland's most successful businessmen of the last 30 years.

A century later, Dublin was in many parts a slum city, its economic and political importance greatly diminished. There are three important lessons from this period, which have resonance to this day. First, it demonstrates how things changed so adversely for Ireland (and can change for any country), after a long wave of sustained and relatively rapid economic growth. Second, what is striking is the lack of a consensus concerning the causes of the changes in economic fortunes (as there is today with regard to Ireland's boom between 1994 and 2007). Third, it was in this period that the extraordinarily close links with the USA, forged largely through emigration, were established, links that are a key, as shall be seen, to an explanation of the rapid growth between 1994 and 2007.

Despite independence in 1921, the overriding picture of the Irish economy in the period 1922 to the early 1990s is one of overall economic under-performance, continuing emigration, albeit at a reduced rate, and relative economic decline, at least compared with continental Europe. By 1992, Irish living standards had risen to 73 per cent of British levels, up from 60 per cent earlier in the century. Britain, though, experienced relative decline, also in this period, and the relative growth in living standards in Ireland was accompanied by a minimal overall increase in population: 2.97 million in 1921 to only 3.53 million in 1991, despite high birth rates throughout the period. Continuing emigration cancelled out much of the natural increase in population.

Economic Transformation: Some Qualifications
An issue covered in Chapters 2, 5, 6 and 7 relates to the question of whether or not the economic transformation in Ireland since 1994 in terms of employment and living standards was all that remarkable and, if so, whether it can be associated with an increase in the 'well-being' of Irish society. It is clear, for example, that in terms of living standards and employment levels, Ireland was simply catching up with those in countries such as Denmark, Finland and Norway (see Chapters 1 and 6). One consequence of only catching up in recent years is that while Ireland now has high per capita incomes, its levels of wealth, both private and, especially, public, still lag significantly behind those in Germany and elsewhere (see Chapters 7 and 8). The difference in the level and quality of the public infrastructure between Ireland and many Northern European countries, especially Denmark and Germany, is still striking. For example, one has only to fly from Copenhagen or Munich to Dublin to witness significantly inferior standards in Ireland in terms of airport facilities and access transport. Such public wealth takes years to accumulate and its absence in Ireland is a reflection of decades of poor economic performance prior to the 1990s.

A different issue is whether or not we, and other materially rich countries, are better off in terms of general well-being, compared either with times past or with countries with much lower incomes (see Chapters 1, 6, 7 and 12). Few people would argue that in line with the growth of material living standards in Ireland in the last decade or so their well-being has increased by a similar amount. The reason is that well-being depends on other factors such as: leisure time; friends, family and personal relationships; and 'public' goods such as the physical environment (e.g. air and other natural amenities such as mountains and rivers) and man-made public infrastructure such as roads, hospitals and drinking water supply channels. There is little doubt that for many people leisure time has decreased, especially when commuting time to work is added to the total working day. There has been no improvement in terms of distribution, with a small but significant proportion of the population experiencing 'consistent poverty' (see Chapter 7). Complaints about the public health system appear to increase with growing prosperity, despite a huge rise in health expenditure in the last ten years in Ireland (see Chapter 11).

There have also been costs associated with the growth in material living standards in terms of crowding, especially on the roads and at airports, and environmental damage (see in particular Chapters 2 and 8). One also reads reports about groups in society that feel more excluded and marginalised than was the case in the past, especially in relation to educational opportunities (see Chapters 7 and 12).

Changes that Mattered

It would be churlish, though, not to acknowledge that the changes outlined in the opening section have led to major improvements for many people, especially those in employment. The policies that impact on such change are outlined in several chapters of the book. Chapter 3 examines the role of the state, not least in establishing the rule of law and respect for private property, but also in the areas of education (Chapter 12), health (Chapter 11) and social security. Much of this expenditure has to be financed out of taxation and Chapter 4 provides a broad coverage of all the issues to which this gives rise. Part of Ireland's attraction to overseas investment is of course aspects of the tax system (see Chapter 4 and 8) and an educated labour force (see Chapter 12).

The national agreements that resulted from social partnership (see Chapters 3, 5 and 6) ensured a high degree of support from all parties and these resulted in industrial peace and wage moderation. Moreover, the resulting improvement in economic performance and the public finances allowed the government to offer tax reductions in return for further wage moderation. These tax reductions and associated changes in some social welfare arrangements resulted in a relatively low tax wedge in Ireland, where the tax wedge is the gap between what an employer has to pay to hire a worker and what the worker takes home in pay (see Chapters 4, 5 and 7). These changes had particularly beneficial effects on low-income workers, greatly boosting the financial incentive to work.

The notably increased emphasis on competition in Ireland, arising from the formation of the Single European Market in 1992, the formation of the Competition Authority in Ireland and (in subsequent years) several regulatory bodies (see Chapters 3 and 9), is particularly prominent. The age of competition, openness and reward for entrepreneurship had arrived. Whereas once entrepreneurs and business people were frowned upon in Ireland, some of the best-known and respected individuals in Ireland today are successful business people. This we like to refer to as the 'Ryanair phenomenon', namely the total change of attitude to entrepreneurship, competition, money making and the role of the state (see Chapters 1, 3, 5, 6, 8 and 9).

But it was not openness in relation to economic matters alone that changed. During the years since the early 1990s Ireland has undergone cathartic public inquiries into corruption, the role of the Catholic Church, and transparency and accountability in the private and public domains. These have undoubtedly led to more open and accountable institutions in the country, something that, as Chapter 2 highlights, is essential to a properly functioning liberal democratic market economy. Problems remain, though, especially in relation to the education and health sectors, as shall be seen in Chapters 11 and 12.

One area where competition did not apply fully was the agriculture sector (see Chapter 10), but with the changes to the EU's Common Agricultural Policy and the huge increase in world food prices in 2008, this is also about to change. Agriculture has wider implications, though, than simply for food production. It is just the first link in the chain from 'farm to fork' and highlights one key area of general policy, namely regulation in relation to health, safety and other standards (see also Chapters 3 and 9). It is also part of the environmental problem that Ireland must address in years to come. The land devoted to agricultural production accounts for 70 per cent of the total land area and hence has also a major impact on the visual and amenity value of the country as a whole.

Storm Clouds Ahead?

As this book goes to press, the storm clouds mentioned earlier are gathering over the Irish economy. A significant slowdown is expected for 2008 and 2009, with at best a return to more modest growth rates in 2010 and beyond. Given the historical experience outlined in Chapter 1, many wonder, understandably, whether the 'good times' have inevitably come to an end. The real fear is the possibility of a return to the experiences of the 1950s and/or 1980s.

There is little doubt that a large number of factors appear to have come together to Ireland's advantage, particularly in the period 1994 to 2007. This process then became almost self-fulfilling. Ireland was perceived as the 'place to be' to do business and for young people in their 20s and 30s, so even more businesses and young workers followed. They in turn established 'bases' here, like those established in the past by Irish emigrants in, for example, New York and parts of Britain, which made Ireland an even more attractive place for friends and relations. Such a process can go into reverse, though, once companies and people 'believe' that the tide is turning and when perceptions, whether well founded or not, take hold.

What could trigger this reversal? It is possible that success has already led to complacency and a *loss of competitiveness* not just to China and India but to many parts of Europe (see Chapters 1, 6, 8 and 9). People learned from the experiences of the 1980s, but how soon people forget. Besides, there is a growing body of people in Ireland who have only lived through the good times and have never experienced the presence of high unemployment and net migration and hence do not believe that such bad times could exist.

Some worry about the nature of the growth in employment, especially since 2000. In particular they worry about the huge growth of employment *in construction*, a sector that is particularly vulnerable to boom and bust cycles. Recent levels of employment and house completions are simply not sustainable, as witnessed by the huge number of unsold houses in 2008. Hence there will inevitably be a decline in numbers employed on housing construction. The concern is that the knock-on effects of this could impinge on the rest of the construction sector and – more worryingly – directly and indirectly, on the economy as a whole (see Chapters 5 and 6).

As discussed earlier, there are still major deficiencies with regard to the physical *infrastructure* of the economy. But some also doubt how good the level of *human capital* is in Ireland, certainly compared with parts of Asia and Northern Europe (see Chapters 6 and 12). The difficulty is that the view has taken hold in many quarters that Ireland has a superior education system to many competitor countries and that this was a key factor underlying the boom. It can certainly be argued that a well-educated labour force facilitated the boom, but remember, the source of much of the employment growth of the last 20 years was immigrants. Also, as levels of human capital rise in other countries, Ireland must continue to improve its levels simply to stay still. Human capital in terms of skill levels and composition is critical to the success of any economy (see Chapter 12).

Ireland's *corporation tax* regime, while recognised as being a key to the attraction of foreign companies to Ireland, is seen by many other countries to have been at the expense of employment in their countries. What such a policy does, it is argued, is lead to competitive tax cutting and ultimately very damaging outcomes for all. If other countries follow Ireland, as many of the peripheral European economies are doing, then Ireland loses its comparative advantage in this respect, and the net result is decreased tax revenues from large multinational corporations, and in the absence of compensating tax increases elsewhere decreased total taxes and hence public services. Thus, seen from a non-Irish perspective at least, there need to be some controls placed on tax competition of the sort that Ireland has engaged in over the last 40 years or more (see Chapters 1, 3, 6 and 8). As long as Ireland was relatively poor it was possible for the larger European countries to turn a blind eye, but this may not be the case in the years ahead, especially as Ireland is such an integrated and committed member of the EU 'club'. In general Ireland will have less and less influence over its tax system, given the international mobility of labour and capital and its membership of the EU. The only way to regain some 'sovereignty' in relation to some aspects of the taxation of income, savings, corporate profits, alcohol/tobacco and carbon emissions may be through co-ordinated action at EU level.

There is also concern about the growth of *public expenditure* in recent years (see Chapters 3, 4 and 11) and whether or not such growth has led to a sustainable improvement in public services such as education (Chapter 12) and health (Chapter 11). The evidence as outlined in these chapters is not encouraging. Much-needed, but painful, reform is probably required in the public sector in years to come, something confirmed by an OECD report in May 2008.

There is also the possibility of a sustained downturn in the *US economy*, to which, as argued earlier, some of Ireland's success has been inextricably linked. This would affect Irish exports to the USA but, much more important, inward investment from the USA. There is also the possibility of a sustained downturn in the rest of the global economy, but this might be just a short-term phenomenon and should not lead to any long-term stagnation in Ireland, provided the country can respond in a flexible and timely way, which it clearly did not do in the 1980s.

There are reasons to believe that it can. Changes have taken place in Ireland which will not be reversed. Attitudes to business, entrepreneurship and material success have changed quite dramatically. There is the acceptance of increased competition and openness in almost all walks of economic life, partly brought about by membership of the European Union and its inexorable moves towards a single market and partly by the increased competition from China and India in particular. There is no inherent reason why Ireland cannot remain among the high-income and high-employment countries of the world. It has well-established and stable institutions and private property in all its aspects is encouraged and protected by the rule of law. It has a liberal, democratic political system and has had stable government for many decades. These are the building blocks upon which any successful economy must be founded. Ireland has them, plus a new-found culture of entrepreneurship, hard work and openness to competition and new ideas. Given this, it is unlikely in our opinion that the successes of the last 20 years will not be maintained and built upon, especially if the deficiencies in the education and health sectors outlined in Chapters 11 and 12, and in infrastructural provision as outlined in Chapter 8, are addressed.

Structure of Book and Acknowledgements

This book has grown out of an earlier book, first published 33 years ago. The Irish Management Institute published the first six editions, Macmillan what in effect was the seventh edition and Gill & Macmillan the eighth, ninth and current editions. The broad structure and purpose of the book have remained the same over the years, but in terms of content there have been sweeping changes, even since the last edition. For example, Chapters 1 and 4 are new since the last edition and Chapters 8 and 10 have new authors. Apart from updating, major changes have also been made to the remaining eight chapters to reflect the rapidly changing circumstances and policy issues facing the Irish economy.

As mentioned, the overall structure of the book has been unchanging over the years. Section I provides the key policy background, namely the historical evolution of the economy up to the 1990s (Chapter 1) and a discussion of the key policy objectives and issues for a regional economy such as that of Ireland (Chapter 2). It is important to know what we want from the Irish economy before asking how to achieve these aims and how well we have done in so doing. These are the questions looked at in Sections II and III. Chapter 3 sets out the role of the state, in terms of rationale, levels of government and size of the state sector. This covers not just state expenditure but also state regulation and social partnership. Chapter 4 examines how such state involvement is funded and the issues to which taxes give rise. Section III consists of three quite lengthy discussions of Ireland's success or otherwise in meeting the three objectives outlined in Chapter 2, and the policy issues to which this gives rise, namely employment (Chapter 5), growth in living standards (Chapter 6) and equality (Chapter 7).

Section IV contains a detailed discussion of policy issues and performance in the market sector and builds on much of the earlier material. Chapter 8 examines the two market sectors of perhaps most importance to the success of the future economy, namely manufacturing and physical infrastructure. While the latter is largely funded by the state, the actual construction work is conducted by the private sector. Chapter 9 contains a detailed discussion of the services sector (excluding the public sector, which is the subject matter of Section V) and the issues arising in relation to competition and regulation policies with regard to the sector. Chapter 10 looks not only at the agricultural sector but also the issues of rural development, conservation and food safety. Section V concludes the book with an examination of two key areas of the public sector, namely health (Chapter 11) and education (Chapter 12).

A new innovation to accompany this edition of the book is a course website which will provide regular updates on the tables and statistics presented in this book as well as providing supplementary reading material and links to interesting media commentaries and reports as they become available. This can be accessed at www.gillmacmillan.ie.

There are many people we would like to thank who have facilitated the publication of the tenth edition of this title. We would like to thank Marion O'Brien from Gill & Macmillan for taking the initiative in this book and Emma Farrell and Aoife O'Kelly for their central role in bringing this book to publication. We would also like to thank our index compiler Yann Kelly-Hoffman and especially our copy-editor Jane Rogers for her exceptional professionalism. She was a delight to work with.

The book would not of course exist without the contributed chapters. As always, it was most enjoyable work liaising with each of the contributors, at each step of the process. In particular, it was rewarding to see chapters take shape and mesh into the overall structure of the book following comments and suggestions. We very much appreciate the input and co-operation of each and every contributor.

We would also like to thank the many lecturers and students who have used this book over the years. This has made the book both financially viable, despite the small size of the potential market, and a very satisfying experience for us. The book is also read widely outside academia, and indeed beyond these shores, and we hope that this will continue to be the case. This is the type of book, and related courses, that students seem to enjoy immensely and we are sure lecturers in other colleges have also found this to be the case. It does after all deal with the political economy of one of the most interesting case studies in recent decades in world economics!

John O'Hagan and Carol Newman
Trinity College Dublin
June 2008

Contributors

Chapters 1 and 6

Jonathan Haughton has a BA(Mod) from Trinity College Dublin and a PhD from Harvard University. He is currently Professor of Economics at Suffolk University, Boston, and Senior Economist at the Beacon Hill Institute for Public Policy.

Chapter 2

Dermot McAleese has a BComm and an MEconSc from the National University of Ireland (University College Dublin), and an MA and PhD from Johns Hopkins University. He is Emeritus Whately Professor of Political Economy, Trinity College Dublin.

Chapter 3

Philip R. Lane has a BA(Mod) from Trinity College Dublin and an MA and PhD from Harvard University. His current position is Professor in International Macroeconomics, Trinity College Dublin. He is also a Research Fellow of the Centre for Economic Policy Research, London.

Chapter 4

David Madden has a BA, an MA and a PhD from the National University of Ireland (University College Dublin), and an MPhil from the University of Oxford (Nuffield College). His current position is Associate Professor of Economics, National University of Ireland (University College Dublin).

Chapters 5 and 8

John O'Hagan has a BE, BA and MA from the National University of Ireland (University College Dublin), and a PhD from Trinity College Dublin. His current position is Professor of Economics, Trinity College Dublin.

Chapter 5

Tara McIndoe has a BA(Mod) from Trinity College Dublin and an MPhil from the University of Oxford (Hertford College). She is currently undertaking research towards a PhD at Trinity College Dublin.

Chapter 7

Sara Cantillon has a BA(Mod) from Trinity College Dublin, an MSc from the National University of Ireland (University College Dublin) and a PhD from the University of Kent (Canterbury). Her current position is Head of School of Social Justice, National University of Ireland (University College Dublin).

Chapters 8 and 12

Carol Newman has a BA(Mod) and a PhD from Trinity College Dublin. Her current position is Lecturer in Economics and Director of Research at the School of Social Sciences and Philosophy, Trinity College Dublin.

Chapter 9

Francis O'Toole has an MMangSc from the National University of Ireland (University College Dublin) and a PhD from Georgetown University. His current position is Lecturer in Economics, Trinity College Dublin.

Chapter 10

Alan Matthews has a BA(Mod) from Trinity College Dublin and an MSc from Cornell University. His current position is Professor of European Agricultural Policy, Trinity College Dublin.

Chapter 11

Anne Nolan has a BA(Mod) and a PhD from Trinity College Dublin. Her current position is Research Officer, Economic and Social Research Institute, Dublin.

Chapter 12

Colm Harmon has a BA and an MA from the National University of Ireland (University College Dublin) and a PhD from the University of Keele. His current position is Professor of Economics and Director of the UCD Geary Institute, National University of Ireland (University College Dublin).

SECTION I

POLICY
BACKGROUND

CHAPTER 1

Historical Background

Jonathan Haughton

1 WHY ECONOMIC HISTORY?

Why take the trouble to study history, and particularly the economic history of a minor European island? Five good reasons spring to mind.

History tests theory. The propositions of economics are often best tested by exposing them to historical evidence. Was Malthus right when he argued that population growth would inevitably outstrip food supply? Irish experience, even during the Great Famine, suggests not. Do farmers respond to changes in the prices they face? Evidence from late nineteenth-century Ireland confirms that they do. Does emigration serve to equalise wages between Ireland and Britain? Data for this century indicate that, broadly speaking, it does.

History gives perspective. Standard economics textbooks typically provide a short-run and partial approach to economic problems. While this may be appropriate for tracing the immediate effects of a shift in demand, or a monetary expansion, it provides fewer insights on the fundamental determinants of economic growth or of income distribution, since these may only be observed over long periods of time. The historian Joe Lee has made the point forcibly, writing that 'while contemporary Irish economics can be impressive in accounting for short-term movements, it has contributed relatively little to understanding the long-term development of the Irish economy'. He argues that most economists are 'blind to either long-term perspective or lateral linkage' and that 'with the exception of a handful of superior intelligences, Irish economists are far more impressive as technicians than as thinkers'.

An important lesson from economic history is that it provides a sense of the fragility of economic growth, and of its intermittent nature. For instance, many look back to the 1960s as a golden era of Irish economic growth. Yet Kennedy, Giblin and McHugh, in their interesting study of Irish economic development in the twentieth century, argue that 'a sense of historical perspective would have encouraged greater modesty about the achievements of the 1960s by recognising that they depended heavily on a combination of uniquely favourable external and internal circumstances'. In the same vein, it is important to recognise that the remarkable boom of the late 1990s has also passed, although not without dramatically changing the country in the process.

History fascinates. While the study of any subject may be justified on the grounds of its intrinsic worth, economic history is particularly interesting. The visible remains of the past are everywhere – ports, houses, crooked streets, abandoned fields and ruined cottages. It is natural to wonder about their origins. Less visibly, our view of history informs our view of who we are, and what our culture stands for. These roots merit exploration. History also has its share of intellectual puzzles: why was economic growth in the 1950s so anaemic? How did per capita incomes rise faster in Ireland between 1850 and 1920 than anywhere else in Europe? Was the tariff regime of the 1930s a failure?

History debunks. Ideologues of all stripes invoke history to bolster their claims. When John Mitchel argued that 'The Almighty, indeed, sent the potato blight, but the English created the famine', he was revisiting history to support his nationalist position. Marxists turn to the land question as evidence of class conflict. An appreciation of history is essential if one is to make an informed judgement about the solidity of such ideas. Once again, Lee states it well, arguing that 'the modern Irish, contrary to popular impression, have little sense of history. What they have is a sense of grievance, which they choose to dignify by christening it history'. He concludes that 'it is central to my argument that the Irish of the late twentieth century have still to learn how to learn from their recent history'. Although written only a few years ago, this view may already be outdated, prey to what F. S. L. Lyons refers to as the dilemma of the contemporary historian – recent events may still be too close in time to allow for enough historical perspective.

History instructs policy. Ireland has tried laissez-faire (1815–45); import substitution (1930–58); export promotion with foreign direct investment (1958–80). It has had budgetary discipline and chronic deficits, fixed exchange rates and floating, price controls, incomes policies, free trade zones, and public and private enterprise. Out of this varied experience there are lessons. While, in Santayana's famous words, 'those who ignore history are condemned to repeat it', the study of history is not merely to avoid making mistakes, but also to learn what works well and merits copying. The Irish experience is of particular interest to most Less Developed Countries, which are typically small open economies with a colonial past. Ireland in the twentieth century was a tardy bloomer, and a major theme of this chapter, indeed of this book, is to try to understand why.

The main focus of this chapter is on how Ireland has developed economically. Crotty defines such development as 'a situation where (a) more people are better off than formerly and (b) fewer people are as badly off'. By this yardstick it is necessary to look at population growth, since an economy whose development is accompanied by massive emigration has in some sense failed. This parallels the suggestion of the 1948 Emigration Commission, which proposed that 'a steadily increasing population should occupy a high place among the criteria by which the success of national policy should be judged'.

Economic development also requires that incomes rise (growth), including, or especially, those of the least well off (equality), and this is presumably facilitated by an efficient use of resources (notably full employment).

The starting point, arbitrarily chosen, is 1690, with the consolidation of the Protestant ascendancy. The subsequent years are divided into subperiods: growth and early industrialisation from 1690 to 1815; rural crisis between 1815 and 1850; the population decline that accompanied increasing prosperity from 1850 to 1921; and the intermittent economic development between independence and about 1960, when the story of modern Irish economic growth begins – as discussed in more detail in Chapter 6.

2 FROM THE BATTLE OF THE BOYNE TO 1815

At the time of the battle of the Boyne the Irish economy was predominantly rural, although it was no longer a woodland society. Population stood at a little under two million, roughly double the level of a century before, and was growing at an historically high rate of at least half a per cent per year. With the spread of population the forest cover was rapidly disappearing, giving way to both grazing and tillage. The largest town, Dublin, had about 60,000 inhabitants.

The country was an important exporter, especially of grain, beef, butter, wool and, to a lesser extent, linen. Presaging the situation of three centuries later, almost half of all exports went to Continental Europe, notably to France. Earnings from these exports were spent on items such as coal and tobacco, and a surplus on current account amounting to perhaps ten per cent of exports allowed for the remittance of rents to absentee landlords. Petty, visiting the country in 1672, commented on the large number of people who rode horses, and the high standard of clothing relative to France and most of Europe. He also noted the shabbiness of the houses, of which he reckoned only a fifth had chimneys. The implication was that Ireland was not significantly poorer, and was possibly better off, than most of Continental Europe at that time, although less affluent than most of England.

Income was distributed unevenly. Land was owned by perhaps 10,000 landlords, and six-sevenths of the land was held by Protestants. Much of this was let out to farmers, who in turn frequently sublet small plots to cottiers, or hired casual labour. By one estimate, a little over half of the population constituted a rural proletariat, with minimal access to land and close to the margin of subsistence. The potato had been introduced early in the seventeenth century, but was an important part only of the diet of the poor, although its spread allowed for rapid population growth throughout the eighteenth century.

Growth and Structural Change
The essential features of economic growth during the period 1690–1815 were a rapid recovery from the war, a period of relative stagnation (1700–20), 25 years of crisis that included two famines (1720–45), and a long wave of sustained and relatively rapid economic growth (1745–1815). The evidence for these is indirect, since few economic statistics were collected at the time, but trade data show a steady increase in exports, with relatively rapid growth between 1740 (£1.2

million) and 1816 (£7.08 million). The structure of exports changed, as shipments of cattle and sheep gave way to beef, butter, grain and linen.

These changes were driven in part by policy. In 1667 the Cattle Act excluded Irish cattle, sheep, beef and pork from England. The country responded by exporting wool rather than sheep, and by searching for new markets for meat, notably the important provision trade serving transatlantic ships and the West Indies, and the extensive French market. It also shifted resources from dry cattle to dairying, and butter exports grew rapidly. This process was speeded by the Woollen Acts, passed in 1699, which prohibited the export of wool from Ireland or England to other countries, and imposed a stiff duty on Irish wool entering England. More positively, the granting of duty-free access to England for linen helped that industry.

The significance of English laws for Irish economic growth is a matter of controversy. Writers in the nationalist vein have stressed the ways in which English law handicapped Irish growth, for instance by hampering the development of the woollen industry. However, Cullen has argued that the negative effects were minimal, as producers shifted rapidly and effectively into new lines of production.

The changes in the structure of production during the eighteenth century also occurred in response to an increase in the relative price of agricultural commodities, especially grain. Increasing urbanisation in Britain raised the demand for food, and Ireland was favoured as a source of supply during the Napoleonic wars. The most important effect of this improvement in Ireland's terms of trade (price of exports relative to imports) was to raise the incomes of farmers. Ireland continued to export grain until the late 1860s, when the falling costs of shipping, coupled with the opening up of the American Midwest, brought cheaper grain to Europe.

Agricultural structure was also influenced by the diffusion of the potato. An acre of potatoes could support twice as many people as an acre of grain. Moreover, potato cultivation does not reduce soil fertility, and potatoes contain substantial amounts of protein and essential minerals. Cullen argues that as the eighteenth century progressed, cottiers increasingly ate potatoes instead of butter or oats, and sold these instead, using their earnings to buy other goods; thus the shift towards the potato is seen as 'related to commercialisation and the urge to increase cash incomes ... for luxuries'.

The expansion of potato cultivation contributed to the dramatic expansion of Ireland's population, from a little more than a million people in 1600 to over eight million by 1841. It was checked briefly by a severe famine in 1740–1, which was caused by a cold summer and led to as many as a quarter of a million deaths. But population growth accelerated after 1750: better nutrition reduced the death rate, and the availability of conacre may have contributed to a reduction in the marriage age. The population rose despite substantial emigration from the northeast, which began early in the eighteenth century and became self-sustaining, and may have been as high as 12,000 annually in the difficult years of the 1770s.

5

Industry

Industrial change was dominated by the rise of the linen industry, which Cullen calls 'perhaps the most remarkable instance in Europe of an export-based advance in the eighteenth century'. From a low base in the 1690s linen exports rose rapidly, accounting for a quarter of all exports by 1731. The first linen weavers were mainly skilled immigrants, especially Huguenots who had fled France after 1685. Duty-free access to the English market helped, and in 1711 the Irish Parliament set up the Linen Board to regulate the industry, spread information and subsidise projects. Based solidly in the rural areas, an elaborate network of merchants bought the raw linen and undertook the more capital-intensive activities of bleaching and finishing. By the early nineteenth century linen was increasingly spun and woven under the 'putting-out' system; cottiers would be provided with raw materials, and paid in cash for the amount they spun or wove.

Even as late as 1841 an astonishing one person in five stated their occupation as being in textiles, and most of these lived in rural areas. Fully a third of all counties reported in 1821 that more individuals were occupied in 'manufacture, trade and handicrafts' than in agriculture. It has been argued that this type of 'proto-industrialisation' is usually a prelude to full (i.e. factory-based) industrialisation, fostering as it does entrepreneurial skills, monetisation of the economy, and commercial links. In the Irish case no such evolution occurred, although it is not clear why.

Other industries also expanded and modernised, notably those based on the processing of agricultural products, such as brewing, flour milling, and distilling. After 1800 the cotton industry flourished, albeit relatively briefly.

It is important to realise that the Industrial Revolution did in fact come to Ireland, initially. The organisation of many industries was radically changed, with the establishment of breweries, textile factories, and glass works large enough to reap economies of scale. At first these factories were located where water power was available, but steam power was introduced early too. In the eighteenth century the road network was greatly improved and expanded, at first by private turnpikes and later by local government (the 'Grand Juries'). The first canals were built.

By 1785 Pitt and others saw Ireland as a viable competitor to English industry. But by 1800 this was not the view in Ireland, and it is ironic that the areas that most favoured union were Cork and the south, with their strong agricultural base; opposition was strongest in Dublin and the north.

Distribution of Income and Wealth

The benefits of economic growth in the late eighteenth century were not spread equally. The most evident rift was that between landowners and the large rural proletariat. Rents of a third of the gross output were probably normal. In 1687 Petty estimated rent payments at £1.2 million, of which £0.1 million was remitted to absentee landlords abroad. Rents thus came to approximately double the level of exports, or almost as much as a quarter of national income. It was this surplus, and tithes paid to the Church of Ireland, that financed the magnificent country houses, churches, Dublin squares, university buildings, paintings and follies that stand as monuments to the eighteenth century.

Most farmers were tenants of large landlords, and in turn rented land out to cottiers. Frequently such plots were confined to conacre (potato land), whose quality improved because they were planted with potatoes. Cottiers also performed work for the farmers to whom they were attached. Labourers did not have even the security implied by access to a plot of land. The position of these groups did not improve in the 50 years prior to 1745. There then appears to have been a period of rising real wages, which probably stopped in the 1770s, and may never have resumed.

A second divide was between Catholic and Protestant. The Penal Laws placed restrictions on the rights of Catholics to purchase land, to worship, to run schools, to vote, to take public office, to enter the professions, to take long leases, and to bequeath property. Barred from the professions and politics, able Catholics often turned their energies towards commerce, and the expansion of trade helped create a significant Catholic middle class. By 1800 the wealthiest Dubliner was Edward Byrne, a Catholic businessman. Presbyterians and Quakers, faced with similar restrictions, also turned to commerce and industry, with some success. Over time most of the restrictions were removed or fell into disuse, and by 1793 Catholics could vote and attend Trinity College, but could not stand for office or fill certain government positions. At times the friction boiled over, as reflected in the strong sectarian component of the insurrection of 1798.

The third divide was between town and country. By 1800 Dublin had grown to be the second town of the UK, with a population of about 200,000. Cork, basing its role on the profitable provision trade, had 80,000 inhabitants, or approximately the same population as a century later. Third came Limerick, with a population of 20,000; Belfast was still a minor town. That the country was able to support such a significant urban population, and to export increasing quantities of food, reflected a growing agricultural surplus and rising agricultural productivity.

3 FROM 1815 TO INDEPENDENCE

1815 to 1850

The period 1815 to 1850 was one of rural crisis, culminating in the disaster of the Famine. The crisis was reflected in rising emigration. This was also the period when Ireland most clearly failed to participate in the Industrial Revolution that was then in full spate in Britain. The census of 1841 enumerated 8.2 million people in Ireland, a higher level than any measured before or since, and over half the level of Britain. Since 1750 the population had risen at an average rate of 1.3 per cent per year, which was well above the annual rates recorded in England (+1 per cent) or France (+0.4 per cent).

Yet by the 1830s the growth rate had fallen to 0.6 per cent, due almost entirely to massive emigration, mainly to North America; these emigrants accounted for a third of the free transatlantic migration of the period. Without emigration, the pre-Famine population would have grown at a rapid 1.7 per cent per annum, due in part to a very high rate of marital fertility. Life expectancy at birth was 37–38 years, lower than in Britain or Scandinavia, but higher than in most of the rest of Europe.

Living Standards

On the eve of the Famine, Ireland was one of the poorest countries in Europe, as the comparative figures in Table 1.1 show. Per capita income was about 40 per cent of the British level, and contemporary visitors were particularly struck by the shabbiness of people's clothing and the poor state of rural houses.

Yet if the country was poor, it was also well fed, on grain, potatoes and dairy products. Peter Solar estimates that in the early 1840s potatoes and grain alone provided a substantial 2,500 calories per person for direct consumption, two-thirds of it from potatoes. Observers at the time generally thought that the Irish were healthy and strong; they grew taller than the typical Englishman or Belgian. Also compensating for low incomes was the wide availability of cheap fuel, in the form of peat.

Table 1.1

Real Product per Capita (UK=100)

	(1) 1830	(2) 1913	(3) 1950	(4) 1992	Population growth (%) 1919–92
UK	100	100	100	100	31[1]
Ireland (South)	40[2]	53[3]	51	73	13
Ireland (North)		58	68		27[5]
US	65	119	170	142	
Denmark	61	80	99	112	57
Finland	51	47	66	96	60
Greece	39[4]	26	27	52	109
Italy	65	49	53	102	60
Portugal	68	22	23	61	54
EU-15			69	102	

Sources: Adapted by the author from K. Kennedy, T. Giblin and D. McHugh, *The Economic Development of Ireland in the Twentieth Century,* Routledge, London 1988, pp.14–15; J. Lee, *Ireland 1912–1985,* Cambridge University Press, Cambridge 1989; and R. Summers and A. Heston, *Penn World Tables Version 5.1*, National Bureau of Economic Research, Cambridge MA 1995.
[1] GB only. [2] 1841, all Ireland. [3] 1926. [4] 1841. [5] 1984.

Industry and Agriculture

It has become common to consider the 1815–50 period as one of 'deindustrialisation', during which the importance of industry in the economy fell. This is only partly correct. For the island as a whole industrial output appears to have increased. Large-scale and more efficient production methods were applied to milling, brewing, shipbuilding, rope making and the manufacture of linen, iron, paper and glass; the road system was improved and reached a good standard; banks were organised along joint-stock lines. But rural industry declined. Thus, for instance, while Bandon boasted over 1,500 handloom weavers in 1829, the number had shrunk to 150 by 1839.

The first cause of rural deindustrialisation was that the woollen and cotton industries wilted in the face of competition from Britain. This prompted Karl Marx to write, 'what the Irish need is ... protective tariffs against England'. On the other hand Ireland was not denuded of purchasing power or exports, for it could not otherwise have afforded to buy British textiles.

A second blow to rural industry was the invention of a method for mechanically spinning flax, which made hand-spinning redundant. It also led to a concentration of the linen industry in the northeast. Weaving linen was still done by hand, and was boosted by the development. In 1841 Armagh was the most densely populated county in Ireland, testimony to the importance of cottage-based textiles as a source of income.

Despite the rapid fall in prices after 1815, agricultural exports continued to rise, notably livestock and butter and, most dramatically, grain and flour. By the 1830s Ireland exported enough grain to feed about two million people annually, testimony to the dynamism of the agricultural sector, which increasingly used new technologies such as improved seeds, crop rotations, better ploughs, and carts.

The Famine

The most traumatic event of the period was the Famine. After a wet summer, blight arrived in September 1845 and spread over almost half the country, especially the east. Famine was largely avoided at first, thanks largely to adequate government relief. But the potato crop failed completely in 1846, and by December about half a million people were working on relief works, at which stage they were ended. The winter was harsh. By August 1847 an estimated three million people were being supported by soup kitchens, including almost three-quarters of the population of some western counties. The 1847 harvest was not severely harmed, but it was small because of a lack of seed. The blight returned in 1848, and in 1849 over 900,000 people were in the workhouse at some time or another. After 1847 the responsibility for supporting the poor had increasingly been shifted from the government to the local landowners who, by and large, did not have sufficient resources to cope. Noting that a few years later Britain spent £69 million on the (futile) Crimean war, Mokyr argues that for half this sum 'there is no doubt that Britain could have saved Ireland'. It is also unlikely that an independent Ireland, with a GNP of £85 million, could have done so without outside support.

As a direct result of the Famine about one million people died, representing an excess mortality of about three per cent per annum during the Famine years (and four per cent in the northwestern counties); this was well above the excess mortality rates seen in the Netherlands (two per cent) or Belgium (one per cent), but comparable to the situation in the Scottish highlands. Three-fifths of those who died were young (under ten) or old (over 60), and labourers and small farmers were hit most severely. These unequal effects have led Cullen to argue, controversially, that 'the Famine was less a national disaster than a social and regional one'.

In the course of the Famine, the output of potatoes fell by about three-quarters, the use of potatoes for animal fodder ceased, and food imports rose very rapidly. As a result the amount of calories available for direct consumption barely fell, on a per capita basis. This gives credence to Amartya Sen's contention that famines are rarely caused by an absolute lack of food, but rather by a change in the food entitlements of major groups in society. So, for instance, labourers were unable to find employment when blight reduced the need for harvesting and planting potatoes; without income they could not buy food, and so became destitute.

Distribution

Pre-Famine Ireland probably had a 'very unequal distribution of income by West European standards'. According to the 1841 census, 63 per cent of the population had access to less than five acres of land, or were 'without capital, in either money, land or acquired knowledge'. Just three per cent were professionals and rentiers, and included the approximately 10,000 proprietors, or 0.12 per cent of the population, who owned at least 100 acres.

Rent, including payments in kind, accounted for about £15 million, or almost a fifth of the national income of £80 million. Presumably the bulk of this rent accrued to the wealthiest three per cent or so of the population, implying a very great degree of income inequality. Rough calculations suggest that this group probably had per capita incomes averaging over £100 per annum, compared with a national average of £10, and an estimated £4 for poor households.

By 1845 a rudimentary welfare structure was in place, with the completion of 130 workhouses having a total capacity of 100,000. In practice the numbers living in the workhouses rarely exceeded 40,000, except during the Famine.

There is no shortage of hypotheses as to why Ireland remained poor, and hence uniquely vulnerable by European standards to the chance failure of the potato crop. Thomas Malthus, writing in 1817, considered that population growth was running ahead of food production: however, the more densely settled countries were not necessarily the poorest ones. Other writers blamed the insecurity of tenancy for low agricultural investment, although it is not clear how insecure tenancies really were. Some have pointed to agrarian violence, or the lack of coal deposits, or inadequate financial capital, or insufficient human resources (especially entrepreneurs), as barriers to economic development. None of these explanations is waterproof, and Ó Gráda wrote recently that 'exactly why comparative advantage dictated industrial decline for Ireland is still unclear'.

Fewer but Richer: 1850 to 1921

The 70 years following the Famine witnessed enormous changes in Irish society and saw the emergence of the modern economy. Over this period per capita incomes more than doubled, and came closer to the British level, while the population fell by a third. A rural middle class emerged, replacing the landlords and squeezing out the rural labourers. In agriculture, tillage declined, and the production of dry cattle increased. The northeast became industrialised.

The dominant demographic fact of the period is that population declined, from 6.6 million in 1851 to 4.2 million by 1926. Without emigration the population would have risen, by about one per cent annually in the 1860s, and by 0.5 per cent annually at the turn of the century, a decline largely explained by a falling marriage rate. Almost two per cent of the population left annually in the 1850s; the pace slowed markedly to less than one per cent after 1900. The early emigrants were drawn from all areas of the country, but in later years the bulk of emigrants came from the poorer, mainly western, districts. Over the period 1820 to 1945 an estimated 4.5 million Irish emigrated to the USA, comparable in magnitude to the flows from Italy, Austria and Britain.

Living Standards

Astonishingly, between 1840 and 1913 per capita incomes in Ireland rose at 1.6 per cent per year, faster than any other country in Europe. Where Irish incomes averaged 40 per cent of the British level in 1840, this proportion had risen to 60 per cent by 1913. From Table 1.1 it may be seen that during this period Irish incomes came from behind, and then easily surpassed, those of Finland, Italy and Portugal.

Part of the explanation is statistical. The Famine, and subsequent high levels of emigration, removed a disproportionate number of the very poor; even if those who remained experienced no increase in their incomes, average income would have been higher than before. The poor were more likely to leave because the gap between Irish and foreign wages was greatest for unskilled labour. In 1844 the wages paid to a skilled builder in Dublin were 14 per cent *higher* than in London, but the wages paid to an unskilled building labourer were 36 per cent lower. A comparable gap persisted until at least World War I.

Incomes also rose because of dramatic increases in output per worker. The northeast became highly industrialised; in the rest of the country agricultural productivity rose rapidly. Almost all the expansion of the modern industrial sector was in the northeast. While linen output increased slowly, it was increasingly concentrated in factories in Belfast and the Lagan valley: between 1850 and 1875 employment in linen mills and factories rose from 21,000 to 60,000 as power weaving replaced cottage industry. The manufacture of boilers and textile equipment needed in the mills helped diversify the industrial base, and provided the skills and infrastructure that were important for the growth of shipbuilding. Harland and Wolff, the celebrated firm that built the Titanic, grew from 500 workers in 1861 to 9,000 by 1900. The shipbuilding industry also provided an impetus for other upstream activities, including rope making, paint and engineering.

Benefiting from 'external economies of foreign trade' – regular trade links with markets and suppliers, and a financial system geared towards supporting such links – Belfast rivalled Dublin in size by 1901, when it had about 400,000 inhabitants. Londonderry became the centre of an important shirt-making industry, employing 18,000 full-time workers and a further 80,000 cottage workers at its height in 1902.

By 1907, industrial activity in Ireland as a whole employed a fifth of the work force, making the country at least as industrialised as Italy, Spain or Portugal. Half of all industrial output was exported, Ireland had a worldwide reputation in linen, shipbuilding, distilling, brewing and biscuits, and the volume of trade per capita was higher than that of Britain.

It is sometimes wondered why Ireland did not become even more industrialised, more like Clydeside than East Anglia. And, related to this question, why did the northeast industrialise while the rest of the country, by and large, did not? Put another way, why did Irish labour emigrate, rather than capital immigrate?

There was no lack of capital, and indeed from the 1880s on, Irish residents were net lenders of capital to the rest of the world, investing in British government stock, railways, and other ventures overseas. The banks may have been cautious about lending, but in this they were no different from their counterparts in England, where industrial development was rapid. Nor is there evidence that skills were lacking. The primary school system expanded rapidly, enrolling 282,000 pupils in state-subsidised schools in 1841, and 1,072,000 by 1887. Whereas 53 per cent of the population was illiterate in 1841, this fraction had fallen to 25 per cent by 1881 and 16 per cent by 1901. Enterprise may have been lacking, although clearly not in the Lagan valley. The absence of coal probably had some effect, not because this raised costs of production unduly, but because coal itself was a big business; in 1914 a quarter of the British labour force was directly employed in coal or iron and steel. Ireland was next door to, and had free access to, the world's most affluent market.

Perhaps the explanation rests largely on chance, the idea that once Belfast grew as an industrial centre, accumulating skills, capital and infrastructure, it became an increasingly attractive location for further investment – an argument that might also be made about the unanticipated growth spurt of the 1990s.

Agriculture

Between 1861 and 1909 gross agricultural output rose by a quarter: since the rural population fell sharply, output per capita in agriculture more than doubled, a performance comparable to that of Denmark, which was considered to have done exceptionally well over the same period.

This growth masks an important change in the structure of agriculture, which shifted from crops to cattle in response to a fall in the price of grain relative to cattle. Tillage, including potatoes, shrunk by two-thirds between 1845 and 1913. Farmers were not, as is sometimes supposed, slow to change or innovate. For instance, when circumstances demanded, they rapidly adopted the creamery system. Faced with changing prices and technology, wrote Hans Stahl, 'the response of the Irish agriculturalist ... was rational and normal'.

Distribution

Between 1870 and 1925 the landed proprietors 'surrendered their power and property' to an increasingly 'comfortable, educated, self-confident rural bourgeoisie', thereby effecting one of the most extensive, and most peaceful, land reforms in history.

As late as 1870, 97 per cent of all land was owned by landlords who rented it out to others to farm. Just 750 families owned 50 per cent of the land in the country. About one landlord in seven lived outside Ireland, and another third lived outside their estates; the remaining half were not absentees. Two-fifths of all landlords were Catholic.

The agricultural crisis of the late 1870s meant lower agricultural prices and this, coupled with fixed rents, squeezed tenant farmers. By now they felt confident enough to agitate for the 'three Fs' – fair rent, fixity of tenure, and free sale of 'tenant right'. Michael Davitt's Land League forged a link with Parnell and the Irish Party in parliament. Their efforts resulted in the Land Act of 1881, which established land courts to hear rent appeals. The courts reduced rents by an average of about 20 per cent, and later courts reduced rents by about another 20 per cent after 1887. In a formal sense this diluted the power of the landlord – Moody refers to it as 'dual ownership' – although it is noteworthy that during the same period real rents fell by comparable amounts in England.

Further efforts prompted legislation that provided tenants with government loans with which to purchase their land, including the Ashbourne Act of 1885 and the Wyndham Act of 1903, and paid 12 per cent bonuses to landlords who sold their entire estates. The result was that 'by 1917 almost two-thirds of the tenants had acquired their holdings'.

With rural depopulation, land holdings increased in size. The number of cottiers working less than five acres fell from 300,000 in 1845 to 62,000 by 1910. The same period saw the 'virtual disappearance of the hired labourer from Irish agriculture', as the number of 'farm servants and labourers' fell from 1.3 million in 1841 to 0.3 million in 1911.

The distribution of income can be considered in other dimensions too. Thus, for instance, Protestants maintained their share of national income. This largely reflected the growth of the industrial northeast, which was dominated by Protestant interests, and the fact that Catholics were more likely to emigrate (and more died in the Famine). Catholics did come to fill an increasing proportion of government and professional jobs, although not in proportion to their numbers. The Catholic Church itself grew rapidly, with a spate of church building between 1860 and 1900, and churchgoing became much more common. The number of

Catholic priests, nuns and other religious rose from almost 5,000 in 1850 to over 14,000 by 1900, making it one of the fastest growing professions during this period.

The small towns stagnated, and so did Dublin until late in the century. In contrast to the rest of the country Belfast grew rapidly. The zenith of its prosperity came during and immediately after World War I, with a boom in shipbuilding and engineering; as David Johnson put it, 'in economic terms the last years of the Union were the best ones'.

4 FROM INDEPENDENCE TO 1960

When it finally achieved independence, the Irish Free State could count some important assets. It had an extensive system of communications, a developed banking system, a vigorous wholesale and retail network, an efficient and honest administration, universal literacy, a large stock of houses, schools and hospitals, 3.1 million people, and enormous external assets. By the standards of most of the world's countries Ireland was well off indeed.

On the other hand the new state faced some serious problems. It had to establish a new government; the Civil War had been destructive and had helped prompt 88,000 people to emigrate in 1921–22; the dependency ratio was high – Catholics marrying before 1916 had an average of 6.0 children per family; and the post-war boom had run its course. We now document its subsequent achievements, and evaluate its performance as an independent country.

1921 to 1932: Agriculture First

The growth model pursued by the Cumann na nGaedheal government was based on the premise that what was good for agriculture was good for the country. Patrick Hogan, the Minister for Agriculture, saw the policy as one of 'helping the farmer who helped himself and letting the rest go to the devil'. This emphasis on agriculture was not surprising. In 1926 agriculture generated 32 per cent of GDP and provided 54 per cent of all employment. The government relied heavily on the support of the larger farmers. The expectation was that agricultural growth would not only raise the demand for goods and services from the rest of the economy, but would also provide more inputs on which to base a more substantial processing sector. The three major industrial exporting sectors at the time – brewing, distilling and biscuit making – were all closely linked with agriculture.

The essential elements of the policy, which has come to be known as the 'treasury view', were free trade, low taxes and government spending, modest direct state intervention in industry and agriculture, and parity with sterling. Free trade was seen as essential if the cost of farm inputs was to be kept low.

The support for free trade was perhaps surprising given that Griffith had argued that one of the main benefits of independence would be that the country could grant protection to infant industries. On the other hand, the government was cautious about making such changes, perhaps for fear of upsetting the financial community, whose opposition to protection was well known, or perhaps because they were, in the words of Kevin O'Higgins, 'the most conservative revolutionaries in history'. The government sought to deflect pressure for stiffer protection by establishing the Tariff Commission in 1926, and appointing members who were, in the main, in favour of free trade. The onus of proof was on any industry wishing to be protected, and the commission moved slowly on requests, granting few tariffs other than for rosary beads and margarine.

Government spending was kept low, the budget was essentially balanced, and revenues came to just 15 per cent of GNP in 1931. This was a remarkable achievement, given that military spending had trebled during the Civil War. One serious consequence was that welfare spending remained low, and in the absence of major government assistance, housing for the less well off remained scarce.

Ideologically the government did not favour taking a very active role in promoting economic development. Despite this it intervened pragmatically in several ways. The Department of Agriculture was greatly expanded, although the impact of this on agricultural output has been questioned. The Congested Districts Board was replaced by the Land Commission, which transferred 3.6 million acres, involving 117,000 holdings, to annuity-paying freeholders during the period 1923–37. Laws were passed to improve the quality of agricultural output, by regulating the marketing of dairy produce (1924) and improving the quality of livestock breeding by registering bulls (1925). The Agricultural Credit Corporation (ACC) was set up to provide credit to farmers. The government subsidised a Belgian company to establish a sugar factory in Carlow, and provided incentives to grow sugar beet.

A major innovation was the establishment of the Electricity Supply Board (ESB) in 1927. This, along with the ACC, represented the first of the state-sponsored bodies (SSBs) that were established during the ensuing years. The ESB successfully undertook the Ardnacrusha hydroelectric scheme, which boosted both its and the country's prestige, and was the most visible accomplishment of the first decade of independence. In due course state-sponsored bodies were set up in many fields, including air, train and bus transport, industrial credit, insurance, peat development, trade promotion and industrial development. By the early 1960s, when the most important of these bodies had been established, they employed about 50,000 people, representing about seven per cent of the total labour force. The SSBs were not the outgrowth of any particular ideology, but were rather 'individual responses to specific situations'. This, along with their ability to attract good managers, may help explain why they are generally considered to have been successful agents of economic development, especially in the first few decades after independence, when the private sector did not appear to be very enterprising.

Parity with sterling was the final ingredient in the development model pursued. Few countries at the time had floating exchange rates, and it seemed logical to peg the pound to sterling since 97 per cent of exports went to, and 76 per cent of imports came from, Britain. The Currency Act of 1927 established an Irish currency, fully backed by British sterling securities; until 1961 Irish banknotes were inscribed 'payable in London'. By linking the currency with sterling the Free State gave up the possibility of any independent monetary policy, in return for greater predictability in trade with Britain.

The economic policy of the Free State in the 1920s was comparable to the typical prescription given by the World Bank to Less Developed Countries in the 1980s: get the prices right, using world prices as a guide, reduce budget deficits, keep government 'interference' to a minimum and follow a conservative monetary policy. Did it work?

The simple answer is 'in the circumstances, yes; in most respects, eventually'. The young nation got off to a rocky start. Between 1920 and 1924 agricultural prices fell by 44 per cent; the Civil War, which only ended in 1923, arrested investment; after independence, a significant proportion of the skilled labour force left; and the recession in the UK after sterling's return to the gold standard in 1925 reduced the demand for Irish exports. However, between 1926 and 1931 real per capita GNP rose about three per cent per annum; exports rose 20 per cent, reaching a peak of 35 per cent of GNP in 1929, and a volume that was not exceeded until 1960. Industrial employment rose by eight per cent.

1932 to 1939: Self-sufficiency, Economic War and Depression

Fianna Fáil came to power in early 1932, with an economic policy that differed in two fundamental ways from its predecessor: it was ideologically committed to a policy of greater economic self-sufficiency; and it reneged on paying land annuities to Britain. It also came to power during the darkest hour of the Depression, a time when most countries were erecting tariff barriers.

Why self-sufficiency? The case for limiting economic interactions with the rest of the world is more cultural than economic, but it attracted some intellectual support. John Maynard Keynes, lecturing at UCD in April 1933, said, 'I sympathize with those who would minimize ... economic entanglement between nations. ... But let goods be homespun whenever it is reasonable and conveniently possible.' Perhaps these oft-quoted remarks are out of context, for he went on to argue that only 'a very modest measure of self-sufficiency' would be feasible without 'a disastrous reduction in a standard of life which is already none too high'.

How self-sufficiency? The main instrument used was more and higher tariffs, which rose to a maximum of 45 per cent in 1936, dipping to 35 per cent by 1938. In Europe only Germany and Spain had higher levels by then; Irish tariffs were twice as high as in the USA, and 50 per cent higher than in the UK. They were introduced piecemeal and so formed an untidy pattern that, in FitzGerald's view, had 'no rational basis'; Meenan considers that they fell more heavily on finished goods, and so provided an incentive for domestic assembly using imported raw materials. The pursuit of self-sufficiency would justify indefinite tariff protection; in this it differs from the views of Griffith, who saw a role for temporary protection to encourage infant industries to take root.

16

Self-sufficiency was also pursued by introducing price supports for wheat, which was instrumental in raising the acreage planted to wheat from 8,000 hectares in 1931 to 103,000 by 1936. Somewhat inconsistently, bounties were paid for exports of cattle, butter, bacon and other agricultural products in order to expand the volume of exports, and this resulted in a significant rise in the share of government spending in national income. To foster Irish involvement in industry the Control of Manufactures Act (1932) required majority Irish ownership, although in practice exceptions were usually granted upon request. The Industrial Credit Corporation was set up to lend to industry, and issued £6.5 million in its first four years of operation.

It is difficult to assess the effect of the policy of self-sufficiency because it became inextricably tangled with the effects of the economic war. Previous Irish governments had recognised an obligation to pay land annuities to Britain, to cover the cost of money lent under the various pre-independence land acts. These came to about £5 million annually, or about one-fifth of government spending and almost four per cent of GNP.

On coming to office in March 1932, de Valera refused to continue the annuities. In July Britain retaliated by imposing special duties, initially at 20 per cent and later at 40 per cent, on imports of livestock, dairy products and meat, and also imposed quotas, including halving the number of cattle permitted to enter the UK. The Free State countered with tariffs on British goods, including cement and coal – surprising choices for a country bent on industrialisation. After these escalations tempers cooled. Under the cattle-coal pact Irish cattle had easier access to Britain, and Ireland agreed to buy British coal. Initially agreed for 1935, the pact was extended and renewed in 1936 and 1937, and the Anglo-Irish Trade Agreement ended the 'war', with Ireland agreeing to pay a lump sum of £10 million and Britain ceding control of the 'treaty ports'. Given that the capitalised value of the annuities was close to £100 million, this was considered to be a major diplomatic and economic victory for de Valera.

The combined effects of protection and the economic war were initially dramatic. Industrial output rose 40 per cent between 1931 and 1936. Population stabilised, standing at 2.93 million in 1931 and 2.94 million in 1938 – the first period since the Famine when there had not been a substantial decline – but the amount of unemployment soared, almost quintupling between 1931 and 1934 to about 14 per cent of the labour force by 1935. In large part this reflected reduced opportunities to emigrate to the United States. Despite rapid industrial growth, agriculture stagnated, as exports fell sharply. Where exports and imports together amounted to 75 per cent of GNP in 1926, they constituted 54 per cent in 1938, although this decline pales beside the two-thirds reduction in trade which the USA faced in the early 1930s. The existing manufacturing export industries also suffered some decline. By 1936 import-substituting industrialisation had run its course, and industrial output rose only a further 4.5 per cent between 1936 and 1938. It is widely accepted that the slow growth of the economy in the 1950s was largely due to the inefficiency of the industrial sector that had developed during the 1930s.

One other event of this period merits a brief discussion. With the onset of the Depression, Britain erected tariffs on a wide range of items, including beer. This prompted Guinness to establish a brewery at Park Lane near London. Beer had been Ireland's single most important industrial export, and brewing had accounted for 30 per cent of manufacturing value added in 1926. Once the Park Lane brewery was established, there was little incentive to return to the earlier pattern of concentrating Guinness's production in Dublin. In this case British tariffs led to the establishment of an efficient new factory in England, at the expense of Ireland. It is possible that some Irish tariffs did the same in the other direction, although with a smaller internal market it is less likely to have been common. Using tariffs to promote investment and industry in this way has come under increasing scrutiny by economists in recent years, under the rubric of strategic trade policy.

Historical Debate: Was the Drive for Self-sufficiency a Mistake?
Joseph Johnston, writing in 1951, argued that but for the economic war 'our real National Income might well have been 25 per cent more in 1939 than it actually was and 25 per cent more today that it actually is. ... The process of cutting off ones nose to spite ones face is sometimes good politics, but always bad economics.' He might have noted that between 1931 and 1938 Irish GNP rose about ten per cent, compared to 18 per cent in less-protectionist Britain. He might also have questioned how many industrial jobs were really created, noting that while the 1936 census enumerated 199,000 individuals 'involved in industrial occupations', this was only 11,000 higher than the number enumerated in 1926.

Johnston's estimate of a 25 per cent decline has been sharply questioned. Recent research, which tries to recreate what might plausibly have happened in the absence of tariffs, by constructing a computable general equilibrium counterfactual, suggests that the total cost of protection might have been five per cent of GNP per year, or £7–8 million annually during the late 1930s, of which perhaps two-thirds is attributable to the economic war. Against this, Ireland gained the treaty ports and received a £90 million write-off on its foreign debt. The expansion of the industrial sector may have provided experience in business management, which was valuable in later years.

Having built high tariff barriers, Ireland was slow to reduce them later, and the average rate of effective protection of manufacturing was still an exceptionally high 80 per cent in 1966. If some of the economic sluggishness of the 1950s was the result, then the protection of the 1930s may appear more damaging; perhaps had Johnston been writing in 1960 he would have been closer to the truth. One may also wonder whether a policy of more selective protection, perhaps along the lines favoured by Taiwan or South Korea, might not have proven more valuable.

1939 to 1950: The War and Rebound
The most important economic result of World War II was that it opened a wide gap between Northern Ireland and the Republic. Between 1938 and 1947 national income grew just 14 per cent, compared to 47 per cent in the UK and 84 per cent

in Northern Ireland. Where incomes, north and south, were broadly comparable before the war, by 1947 incomes per head in the Republic had fallen to about 40 per cent of the British level, while in the north they had risen to close to 70 per cent. Why did the south perform so poorly?

Between 1938 and 1943 the volume of exports fell by a half, and imports fell even more. During this period industrial output fell 27 per cent, and industrial employment dropped from 167,000 to 144,000. The main reason was the scarcity of raw material inputs for industry, and the shortage of shipping capacity. Completely reliant on outside shippers until 1941, the government founded Irish Shipping, and moved rapidly to purchase ships, which soon proved their worth. Because of the difficulty of obtaining imports, the country built up significant foreign reserves, and by 1946 residents had external assets totalling £260 million, approximately equivalent to GNP in that year.

The total value of agricultural output fell during the war period, but net agricultural output (i.e. total output less the cost of non-labour inputs) rose, by 17 per cent, between 1938–9 and 1945. This reflected the drastic fall in the use of fertiliser and other inputs, which is generally acknowledged to have exhausted the soil significantly. The structure of agriculture changed, as the area planted in grain and potatoes almost doubled, due in part to the introduction of compulsory tillage.

During the war real GNP fell, especially initially. Living standards fell further as households, unable to find the goods they wanted, were obliged to save more. The stock of capital in industry became run down. With emigration to the USA blocked, population rose, by 18,000 between 1938 and 1946. The unemployment rate stood at over 15 per cent in 1939 and 1940, but declined thereafter to a little over ten per cent in 1945. The decrease was due to a sharp rise in migration to Britain, reaching near-record levels in 1942, as people left to work in factories and enrol in the armed forces.

The war was followed by a rebound, and per capita real GDP rose by 4.1 per cent per annum between 1944 and 1950. This occurred despite the fact that agricultural output stagnated, with gross volume falling between 1945 and 1950, and net output shrinking by five per cent. Not surprisingly, 70,000 people left agriculture between 1946 and 1951; yet during this period the unemployment rate fell and population increased. Much of this is attributable to the expansion of industrial production, which more than doubled during the same period.

Government spending rose rapidly in the early war years as the army was increased from 7,500 to 38,000 personnel. After the war, government spending grew far faster than national income, increasing its share of GNP from 23 per cent in 1945 to 39 per cent by 1951. In large measure this increase occurred as Ireland sought to emulate the 'social investment' of the Labour Party in Britain by expanding welfare spending.

1950 to 1958: Decline or Rebirth?
It had become standard to consider the 1950s as a period of stagnation and failure. This is a half truth. Between 1951 and 1958 GDP rose by less than one per cent

per year. Employment fell by 12 per cent, and the unemployment rate rose. Irish GDP/capita fell from 75 per cent to 60 per cent of the EU average. Half a million people emigrated. Yet between 1950 and 1960 real product per capita grew at 2.2 per cent per year, possibly the fastest rate recorded up to then, and industrial output expanded at 2.8 per cent per annum. Output per farmer grew at a respectable 3.4 per cent per year. Rural electrification spread, and the housing stock improved appreciably. Was the glass half full or half empty?

The key to understanding the 1950s is to note that this was the decade when Europe rebounded; Ireland's performance looks disappointing only by the standards of neighbouring countries, not by historical standards. Much of the emigration reflected the lure of improving wages elsewhere, notably in Britain.

Why did output not grow faster in the 1950s? FitzGerald believes that the key problem was a 'failure to reorientate industry to export markets', considering that 'the naïveté of the philosophy that underlay the whole protection policy was not exposed until the process of introducing protection had come to an end'. By the 1950s Irish industry was supplying as much of the domestic market as it reasonably could, and in order to expand had no option but to seek markets overseas. But since much of the industrial sector could only survive because of protection, it was too inefficient to export successfully, although it was certainly strong enough to lobby against any liberalisation.

To help provide incentives to industries to switch to exporting, export profits tax relief was provided in 1956, and in 1958 the Industrial Development Authority (IDA), which had been set up in 1949, was granted more powers to provide tax holidays for export-oriented companies. The Shannon Free Airport Development Company was set up in 1959.

One might better view the 1950s as a period of transition rather than one of failure, much as it was in Taiwan and South Korea. It has been argued that the economy was in fact in the process of reorienting itself towards export markets, but that any such change was bound to be slow. As J. J. McElligott put it in the 1920s, when warning of the dangers of protection, 'to revert to free trade from a protectionist regime is almost an economic impossibility'. Exports of manufactured goods rose quite rapidly, accounting for six per cent of all exports in 1950 but 17 per cent by 1960. Dramatic as this change was, the increase was from a very low base, and the export sector simply was not large enough to be a potent engine of growth.

An entirely different explanation comes from Kennedy and Dowling, who state baldly that 'the chief factor seems to us to be the failure to secure a satisfactory rate of expansion in aggregate demand', most notably unduly restrictive (in their view) fiscal policy in response to the balance of payment crises of 1951 and 1955. This argument provides an intellectual underpinning for the highly expansionary, and ultimately disastrous, fiscal policy experiment of the late 1970s and early 1980s.

Whatever the causes, the poor overall economic performance created a feeling of pessimism, and this in turn probably deterred investors. As T. K. Whitaker, then secretary of the Department of Finance, put it, 'the mood of despondency was palpable'. In 1958, at the request of the government, he wrote the report *Economic Development*, best remembered now for the optimistic note that it struck in pessimistic times. The report proposed that tariffs should be dismantled unless a clear infant industry case existed, favoured incentives to stimulate private industrial investment, and proposed expanded spending on agriculture. On the other hand, it warned against the dampening effects of high taxes. With such measures, it suggested, GNP could grow two per cent annually, although it stressed that this was not a firm target. These measures were incorporated in the First Programme for Economic Expansion which appeared in November 1958, but were generally not implemented.

Economic growth during the period of the first plan exceeded anyone's wildest expectations, reaching four per cent per annum instead of the anticipated two per cent. At the time much of this increase was attributed directly to the impact of the First Programme, and support for such indicative planning increased. The Second Programme, introduced in 1963 and designed to run to 1970, was far more detailed and ambitious, forecasting an annual increase in GNP of four per cent per annum; industry was to expand 50 per cent and exports 75 per cent during the plan period. When it appeared that these targets would not quite be met, the Second Programme was allowed to lapse. A Third Programme was produced, but quickly sank into oblivion, along with most of the enthusiasm for indicative planning.

5 FROM 1960 TO 1999

1960 to 1973: From Protection to Free Trade

Between 1960 and 1973 real output increased at 4.4 per cent per annum, the highest rate sustained until then. Immigration began. Per capita incomes rose by three-fifths, kept up with income growth elsewhere in Europe, and significantly outpaced growth in Britain and Northern Ireland.

This first wave of substantial economic growth has been largely attributed to the strategy of export-led growth that the government, heeding the recommendations of *Economic Development*, pursued; less publicised, but important nonetheless, were a notable improvement in the terms of trade (39 per cent better in 1973 than in 1957), expansionary fiscal policy, the boom in the nearby European economy, and the fact that solid institutional foundations had been laid in the 1950s.

The policy of export-led growth stood on two legs – trade liberalisation, and the attraction of foreign direct investment (see Chapter 8). Trade liberalisation called for reducing tariffs; these, by making inputs dearer and by drawing resources away from other sectors of the economy, had worked to inhibit exports. Foreign investment, it was hoped, would bring new skills to the country and help raise the overall investment, and hence growth, rate.

Trade liberalisation was begun in the 1960s as Ireland unilaterally cut tariffs in

1963 and 1964, negotiated the Anglo-Irish Free Trade Area Agreement in 1965 and subscribed to the General Agreement on Tariffs and Trade (GATT) in 1967. These moves also prepared for eventual membership of the European Economic Community (EEC) as it was then called.

With a panoply of tax breaks and subsidies, Ireland successfully, although at considerable expense, induced foreign companies to set up branches in Ireland, and by 1974 new industry accounted for over 60 per cent of industrial output. The ten per cent tax on profits in manufacturing also made the country something of a tax haven, although it did require at least a fig leaf of manufacturing presence.

The final thrust of government policy was wage restraint, viewed as necessary, especially with a fixed exchange rate, to help keep industrial costs at a competitive level. In the 1960s government efforts amounted to exhortation. In the 1970s wage bargaining was centralised, under the National Wage Agreements. Given the option of emigration, the scope for manoeuvre here was small. If real wages were pushed below the British level they would simply stimulate faster emigration, and so could not be sustained.

Into Europe: Trade, Investment, and Subsidies

In 1973 Ireland, along with the UK and Denmark, joined the European Economic Community (EEC, but referred to here as EU).

Membership immediately led to a reduction in trade barriers. The EU was founded as a customs union, with low internal barriers to trade and a common set of external barriers. By joining, Ireland was committed to trading freely with the other member countries, and by 1977 all tariff barriers had been removed. Many of the remaining, less obvious, restraints on trade within the European Union were dismantled as part of the effort to create a Single European Market. Officially these changes came into effect in 1992, although the full elimination of barriers remains a work in progress.

With lower trade barriers, it was recognised that some of Ireland's industry would wither under the competition, but it was also expected that Ireland would become a good platform from which companies from outside the European Community could serve the European market.

These expectations were met. While Irish exports amounted to 34 per cent of GDP in 1963, and 38 per cent in 1973, the proportion had risen to 94 per cent by 2002, one of the highest in the world (see Chapter 8). This burst of exports paralleled a similar increase in intra-EU trade that took place in the 1960s, and shows how even small reductions in the cost of trading can have a large impact on the volume of trade.

Membership of the EU also led to a net inflow under the Common Agricultural Policy (CAP), which subsidises farm prices. Higher farm prices help farmers at the expense of consumers, but as a net exporter of farm produce, Ireland was a net beneficiary (see Chapter 10).

Although about two-thirds of EU transfers to Ireland are farm-related, the remaining third consists mainly of transfers from the 'structural funds', including the Regional Development, Social and Cohesion Funds. In principle these funds might have added to investment and thereby boosted economic growth, but in practice they mainly appeared to have substituted for projects that the government would otherwise have had to finance; they thus made a more important contribution to living standards than to growth. Net receipts from the EU peaked at 6.5 per cent of GDP in 1991, and stood at 0.8 per cent of GDP in 2006.

1979 to 1986: Growth Interrupted

Between 1979 and 1986, per capita consumption in Ireland actually fell slightly and GDP rose very slowly (see Table 6.3, p. 154). What went wrong?

Membership of the EU coincided with a fourfold increase in the price of oil (from $3 to $12 per barrel) that resulted from the first oil shock in late 1973; a sharp worldwide recession followed.

The government's response was thoroughly Keynesian. The higher price of oil meant that spending was diverted towards imports, thereby depressing aggregate demand for Irish goods and services. The solution adopted was to boost government current spending, and as a consequence the current budget deficit rose from 0.4 per cent of GDP in 1973 to 6.8 per cent by 1975. For a while the policy worked: despite a difficult international situation, GDP growth during the first six years of EU membership was robust.

Then came the mistake, the source of the failure of the fiscal experiment: successive governments were unwilling to reduce the budget deficit, and continued to borrow heavily, so the ratio of government debt to GDP rose from 52 per cent in 1973 to 129 per cent by 1987, by then easily the highest in the European Union. By 1986 the cost of servicing this debt took up 94 per cent of all revenue from personal income tax (see Chapter 4). Although efforts were made to solve the problem by raising tax rates, especially in 1981 and 1983, these changes hardly increased tax revenue, suggesting that the country was close to its revenue-maximising tax rates. Much of the additional spending went to buy imports, and the current account deficit widened to an untenable 15 per cent by 1981. Partly as a result, the Irish pound was devalued four times within the European Monetary System in the early 1980s. In 1986 an estimated IR£1,000 million of private capital left the country, anticipating a devaluation; the smart money was right, and the pound was devalued by eight per cent in August.

In 1987 the Fianna Fáil government introduced a very tight budget, cutting the current budget deficit to 1.7 per cent of GDP through reductions in real government spending that made Margaret Thatcher's efforts look gentle. Capital spending was also sharply cut, especially on housing, and by 1992 the ratio of debt to GDP had fallen below 100 per cent.

The 1987 reform worked. Economic growth resumed, as confidence (and investors) returned, and exports boomed, thanks in part to the devaluation of 1986 and to continued wage restraint. But the lessons of the failed fiscal experiment are important and have been largely internalised: fiscal rectitude is important for long-term growth, and taxes cannot be pushed too high.

1979 to 1999: From Sterling to EMS to Euro

In 1979, in a move hailed at the time as farsighted, Ireland broke the link with sterling (which dated back to 1826) and joined the European Monetary System (EMS). The reasoning was straightforward. Ireland had experienced inflation averaging 15 per cent between 1973 and 1979, necessarily the same rate as in Britain, and it was believed that the key to reducing the inflation rate was to uncouple the Irish pound from high-inflation sterling and attach it to the low-inflation EMS, which was dominated by the Deutschmark. Some also argued – correctly as it turned out – that sterling would appreciate with the development of North Sea oil, and that this would hurt Irish exports. Although over 40 per cent of exports still went to the UK in 1979, about a quarter went to the other EU countries, so a change in exchange regime was considered feasible.

The adjustment to the EMS was slow and rocky. In the early 1980s inflation actually fell faster in the UK, which stayed out of the EMS, than in Ireland. The slow reduction in Irish inflation towards German levels meant that the Irish pound became overvalued, and had to be devalued within the EMS. The standard explanation is that wage demands – which often respond to recent inflation – were slow to change, so wage increases continued to be too large to be consistent with very low inflation. The lesson here was clear: economic growth and macroeconomic stability can all too easily be undermined if wage increases get out of line.

By about 1990 Ireland could boast of low inflation, a tight budget and a falling ratio of government debt to GDP, and it looked as if, after a decade of relative economic stagnation, the decision to join the EMS was finally paying off. Then in late 1992 the EMS fell apart. High interest rates in Germany, resulting from that country's need to finance reunification, caused the Deutschmark to appreciate. Sterling devalued, and the Irish pound ultimately followed, because 32 per cent of Irish exports still went to the UK, and in the absence of a devaluation, Irish competitiveness in the important British market would be too severely compromised.

After the collapse of the EMS, it became clear that a regime of 'fixed but flexible' exchange rates is an oxymoron. Without a viable middle way between floating exchange rates and a single currency, the European Union opted for the latter. The schedule was set out in the Treaty of Maastricht, signed in 1992 and ratified the following year. Ireland easily met the criteria for graduating to the euro, and the exchange rate was locked at €0.787564 per Irish pound on 1 January 1999. Ireland, like the states of the USA, no longer has the option of an independent monetary policy. This is not a radical break from the past; an independent monetary policy was not possible when the Irish pound was linked with sterling, and was severely circumscribed during the period of the European Monetary System.

The combination of macroeconomic stability and good access to the EU market – first under the Single Market Act, and then as a member of the euro zone – contributed mightily to Irish economic development. By the mid-1990s, US companies favoured Ireland as a platform for supplying the European market, particularly in pharmaceuticals and information technology. By the time this wave of export-oriented labour-using investment subsided – about 2000 – Irish consumers were able to maintain their demand, due in part to the cheap credit that arrived with the euro. This sparked a building boom that contributed to the robust expansion of output and employment until 2007. A fuller economic analysis of this period is made in Chapter 6.

6 CONCLUDING OBSERVATIONS

The significant events of Irish economic history have been marshalled to support a number of different interpretations.

Nationalists emphasise the ways in which the links between the Irish economy and Britain have worked to Ireland's detriment. Writers in this vein have stressed the damage caused by the plantations, the Navigation, Cattle and Woollen Acts, the solid growth during the years of Grattan's Parliament, the lowering of tariffs in the years after the Act of Union, the ineffectiveness of relief efforts during the later years of the Famine, and the costs of Ireland's inability to protect its industry from British goods during the second half of the nineteenth century. This approach has typically been used to lead to the conclusion that Ireland would be better off economically with independence.

Support for the nationalist interpretation waxes and wanes with the performance of the economy of the Republic. When independence did not bring a dramatic improvement in growth, and when the import substitution policy of the 1930s created an inefficient industrial base which stagnated in the 1950s, the advantages of independence came to be seen as less obvious, especially as Northern Ireland appeared to be prospering at the time. However, from 1960 to 1980, when growth in the Republic was faster, and dependence on the British market reduced, the nationalist view became respectable again despite, or perhaps because of, the dismantling of tariff protection.

Outside the Irish context, this view is comparable to the approach of *dependency theorists*, who emphasise the harmful results of links between peripheral areas and the major industrial powers. The main weaknesses of this approach is that it has tended to neglect the potentially beneficial effects of links with the metropolitan area, and has overestimated the ability of independent states to make wise decisions, as exemplified for instance by Ireland's disastrous fiscal experiment in the late 1970s.

Membership of the EU has not made the nationalist view completely obsolete, but it has been stripped of its Anglophobic character. There remains space for a nationalism, or perhaps localism would be a better term, to counteract the tendencies of the EU to regulate from the centre what would be better done at a much lower level of government.

Marxists stress the role of the conflict between different classes within the country. Thus, for instance, the Famine and subsequent emigration swept away the greater part of the rural proletariat, paving the way for the emergence of a rural bourgeoisie, which in due course wrested control over land from the aristocracy and provided the leaders of a conservative independent state. In this view the labouring class, whether agricultural or industrial, never achieved enough strength to effect significant social or economic change, and the indigenous capitalist class failed in its mission of creating a dynamic industrial base, thereby forfeiting its right to the perquisites that it continues to enjoy. The conclusion most commonly drawn is that the state needs to take a more active role in filling this entrepreneurial function. Foreign investment by footloose companies is seen as conveying few benefits.

The Marxist view fails to explain why largely non-class conflicts, such as that in Northern Ireland, can persist. It typically overstates the ability of the state and public enterprises to create sustainable jobs; once this prop falls, it is not clear what prescription for economic growth remains.

In reaction against the weaknesses of the nationalist and Marxist interpretations, most recent writers have tended to view economic events as having a significant life of their own, being 'substantially independent of political and constitutional issues'. Hence the role of the Cattle Acts, or the Act of Union, or the replacement of tenant farmers by smallholders, are seen as minor. Economic actors are believed to redirect their energies fairly quickly, and seize the available opportunities. This perspective, epitomised in the large body of revisionist writings of Cullen, could be labelled the *classical economics approach*. In the hands of a new generation of economists this approach to history has become increasingly quantitative.

This view too has its faults, in that it can go too far in neglecting political events and institutional arrangements. In the words of Douglass North, 'institutional change shapes the way societies evolve through time and hence is the key to understanding historical change'. North originally believed that inefficient institutions would be weeded out over time, but in his more recent writings he is less sanguine about this prospect. The *institutional approach* complements rather than supplants the classical economics view, and we have drawn on these two perspectives in writing this chapter.

The most interesting lessons from Irish economic history are about growth strategies. Economic growth comes from a multitude of sources, such as new technology, capital investment, education and training, land reclamation, enterprise, shifting prices, higher aggregate demand and chance. However, these are only the raw ingredients, and must be combined to sustain growth. It is easy to see these ingredients at work. The new technologies of the potato, railways, power weaving and computers have all been influential. Capital spending is essential at all times, although it rarely needs to be above a fifth of GDP. Higher levels of education and improved training have boosted labour productivity. Chance brought the potato blight and two world wars. Land reclamation helped fend off famine in the early nineteenth century. Enterprise was at the heart of the introduction of shipbuilding in Belfast. A secular increase in wheat prices radically changed agriculture in the eighteenth century. Low aggregate demand reined in growth in the 1950s.

Recognising the role of these elements is important, but holds few lessons. The study of growth *strategies* is more illuminating. The policy of laissez-faire need not guarantee growth, as experience from 1815 to 1850 demonstrates. Nor does a strategy of import substitution necessarily fare better, for while it may have been helpful in the short run in the 1930s, protection left a legacy of inefficient industry in the 1950s. An approach which favours agriculture-led development, such as that followed by the Free State in the 1920s, may succeed in raising real incomes, but given the small size of the agricultural sector (five per cent of GDP) it is no longer a realistic option. An industrialisation strategy based on attracting foreign capital also has some advantages, but is expensive to implement initially, and risks leaving a country more vulnerable to decisions outside its control.

As a practical matter Ireland has less and less room for pursuing independent economic policies. Fiscal restraint is needed because persistent expansionary fiscal policy does not work well in a small open economy, as the experiment of 1978–87 shows. With the euro in place, monetary policy is not an option. Industrial policy is increasingly circumscribed by the rules that have applied since 1993 to the Single European Market. Recognising the need for greater efficiency, the country has privatised or closed down several state-owned enterprises. Ireland now has only a little more autonomy than a typical state of the United States.

That leaves a narrower and more difficult field for local economic policy. The focus will have to be on the factors needed to maintain 'competitiveness' – what Michael Porter calls the 'microeconomic foundations of prosperity'. This includes bending to such tasks as gearing society to produce entrepreneurs, vitalising indigenous enterprise, providing adequate and appropriate education and training, evaluating public investment more thoroughly, introducing flexibility into the labour market, reducing the disincentives to do unskilled jobs, and fostering competition among firms. Affluence requires efficiency in the public arena – in the provision of services and the formulation and targeting of policy – in addition to efficiency by businesses.

Since wages in Ireland are closely linked with those in Britain (and, increasingly, Europe), once individuals have been equipped with education, economic policy has remarkably little influence on the standard of living they will enjoy in Ireland. What it can still influence, perhaps more thoroughly than was commonly believed just a few years ago, is the number who enjoy that standard of living in Ireland rather than elsewhere.

Further Reading
The literature on Irish economic history is already enormous. A few suggestions for further reading are given here, and much of the information in this chapter comes from these sources.

General History
R. Foster, *Modern Ireland 1600–1972*, Allen Lane, London 1988.
J. Lee, *Ireland 1912–1985*, Cambridge University Press, Cambridge 1989.
F. Lyons, *Ireland Since the Famine*, Weidenfeld and Nicolson, London 1971.

Economic and Social History
R. Crotty, *Irish Agricultural Production*, Cork University Press, Cork 1966.
L. Cullen, *An Economic History of Ireland Since 1660*, Batsford, London 1972.
M. Daly, *Social and Economic History of Ireland Since 1800*, Educational Company, Dublin 1981.
K. Kennedy, T. Giblin and D. McHugh, *The Economic Development of Ireland in the Twentieth Century,* Routledge, London 1988.
J. Mokyr, *Why Ireland Starved*, Allen and Unwin, London 1983.
C. Ó Gráda, *The Great Irish Famine*, Macmillan, London 1989.
C. Ó Gráda, *Ireland: A New Economic History 1780–1939*, Oxford University Press, Oxford 1995.
C. Ó Gráda, *A Rocky Road: The Irish Economy Since the 1920s*, Manchester University Press, Manchester 1997.

CHAPTER 2

Policy Objectives and Competitiveness for a Regional Economy

*Dermot McAleese**

1 INTRODUCTION

The primary policy objectives of a regional economy and a national economy are very similar. Both are concerned with achieving higher living standards, a fair distribution of income, full employment and decent environmental standards. Likewise, the secondary policy objectives, meaning by this the means of achieving the primary objectives, are broadly similar. Regions and nations both want price stability. Both worry about competitiveness. And the balance of payments has implications for both the region and the nation state, though as we shall see these implications are far more transparent in the case of a nation.

The main difference between a region and a nation is the *policy context*. A region has no independent currency and no control over its monetary policy. Its trade policy is determined by outside forces and balance of payments issues have to be radically reinterpreted. It has limited discretion in the use of fiscal policy. Seen in this context, a region's approach to policy has a dual dimension. First, it has to consider how to use its limited influence on policy developments where key policy decisions are being made. In the case of the Republic of Ireland, this might be Brussels, Frankfurt or Strasbourg depending on the issue being decided; in Northern Ireland, London would figure prominently. Second, in areas where they do possess policy autonomy, regions must ensure that this degree of policy discretion is used effectively.

As Ireland becomes increasingly integrated into the European economy, the Republic is losing many of the trappings of a national economy. The completion of the single market and the establishment of economic and monetary union constitute important turning points in this respect. Hence, the focus in this chapter is on policy objectives from the perspective of a regional economy. This perspective is of special interest at present because the Irish Republic is a comparative newcomer to regional status, unlike, say, Northern Ireland or Scotland, and it has had to acclimatise itself rapidly to the economic limitations of regional dependence. At the same time, as a nation state, the Republic can exert more power and influence at the centre of European policymaking than many European regions of much larger size.

The plan of this chapter is as follows. In Section 2 we explain why growth is regarded as the primary objective of economic policy and how it is related to employment. In Section 3 the limitations of this objective are analysed by taking account of leisure and the environment. The goal of equity and the relationship between economic growth and happiness are considered in Section 4. In Section 5 we discuss price stability and general security as objectives of policy. Competitiveness is discussed in Section 6; the search for ways of maintaining competitiveness has become the *leitmotif* of economic policy in recent years. Section 7 concludes the chapter.

2 GROWTH AND EMPLOYMENT

Introduction

Rapid, sustained growth is a primary objective of economic policy. Fast economic growth means higher living standards, and is associated with an expanding and dynamic business environment. Slow or zero growth is perceived as stagnation. Confronted with the record of a slow-growing economy, we instinctively ask what has gone wrong. Policymakers are always on the lookout for advice about ways of promoting economic growth. An advance in living standards is something that most people want, enjoy and expect to be delivered.

Economic growth is desired for many different reasons. Affluent countries see growth as an essential contributor to ever higher living standards, full employment and healthy government finances. They also perceive faster growth as a way of maintaining their economic and military positions relative to other countries. Not long ago, Americans worried about being overtaken by the Japanese; and the Japanese in turn worry about their economic standing relative to China. By contrast, governments of developing countries see faster economic growth as a means of escaping from poverty and material want, and in particular from the vulnerability and sense of inferiority that, rightly or wrongly, attaches to low economic development. For them, 'catching up' with the living standards of affluent countries is a key policy imperative. All countries appear to view growth as an indicator that resources are being employed efficiently, and faster-growing economies are often taken as models for slower-growing economies to copy and learn from.

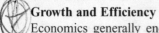

Growth and Efficiency

Economics generally endorses the idea that efficiency and growth are related. Most fast-growing economies are efficient, and most efficient economies tend to grow faster than economies of similar size and scale that are inefficient. The meaning of efficiency and growth in an economic sense is illustrated in Figure 2.1.

Imagine an economy that produces only two goods, X and Y. We set up a list of combinations of X and Y that the economy could produce if its resources were utilised in the most efficient way. In other words, for any given level of X, we find out the maximum amount of Y that can be produced in the economy. The various combinations of X and Y derived in this way are known as the *production frontier*. The production frontier is TT in Figure 2.1.

Figure 2.1

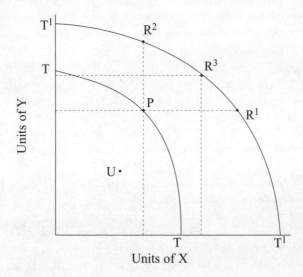

The Production Frontier

Provided production takes place on the production frontier, where resources are fully employed, more of good X implies less of good Y. In other words, in order to produce more of X, scarce resources have to be transferred from industry Y to industry X. One can go further and define the cost of X as the amount of Y that has to be sacrificed in order to produce one extra unit of X. This is called the *opportunity cost of X*. The opportunity cost concept has many practical applications and serves as a reminder of the obvious point that 'free' education, or 'free' transport and other 'free' goods offered by the state are not costless. The resources used to supply these goods and services could have been used to produce automobiles or holidays instead. Hence the well-known maxim: in economics there is no such thing as a free lunch.

An *efficient* economy is one that operates on its production frontier (i.e. at a point such as P in Figure 2.1). At any point below the production frontier, society could have more of X and Y simply by moving to the frontier. By definition, this would not be an efficient outcome. Thus point U is not an efficient outcome. At that point, some productive resources are either being used inefficiently or, worse, not being used at all. If they were mobilised, a point P could be attained which is obviously superior. In addition to *productive* efficiency as above, one must have *allocative* efficiency. This means that the goods and services produced on the frontier represented by points such as P must be distributed between consumers in an efficient manner. Allocative efficiency is achieved when there is no feasible redistribution of the fixed bundle of goods P such that one person is better off without leaving anyone else worse off. At that stage, an economy is said to have achieved Pareto efficiency. Hence, efficiency is certainly an important objective of economic policy.

Why Growth is Important

Over time, however, growth will be the main force in determining living standards. A GNP growth rate of four per cent maintained for 17 years will result in a doubling of the original GNP level. Even a more modest two per cent growth rate will translate into a doubling of living standards every 33 years. Figures such as this indicate the potential gains from raising the growth rate. In terms of Figure 2.1, outward shifts in the production frontier will over time dominate the effects of movement to a given frontier from off-frontier points, such as U. However, since countries that are efficient normally grow faster than those that are inefficient, the objectives of efficiency and growth are in practice complementary.

To illustrate the benefits of growth, we can depict it as a series of outward shifts in the production frontier, such as that represented by the move from TT to T^1T^1. The T^1T^1 frontier shows the expanded range of options growth provides to society. Economic growth is a 'good thing', in so far as it enables the consumers in the economy to enjoy:

- more of X and the same amount of Y – at a point such as R^1
- more of Y and the same amount of X – at a point such as R^2
- more of both X and Y – at a point like R^3
- any other desired combination of X and Y – on the expanded frontier.

Growth extends the range of consumption possibilities, and people choose between these different possibilities through the market system, supplemented by government intervention.

The production frontier can be shifted outwards by two forces: first, increases in the *quantity* of productive factors; and, second, improvements in the *productivity* of these factors. Since we are primarily concerned with growth per person rather than total growth, it is common to abstract from the increase in growth that is attributable solely to the increase in the population. Growth in living standards, or GNP per person, depends on (see also Chapter 6):

- the *amount* of productive factors at each person's disposal (the more machinery and the more hectares of land at the disposal of an employee the more will be produced per employee)
- the *productivity* of these factors of production (better machinery, better seeds and fertilisers, better technology)
- the knowledge, skills and motivation of the workforce (see Chapters 5 and 12).

Growth and Full Employment

Full employment means that there is work available for everyone willing to seek it at prevailing pay levels. This is obviously a desirable objective of economic policy. There is a strong empirical association between full employment and economic growth and this explains why one of the major perceived benefits of faster growth is that it provides more job opportunities and reduces the unemployment rate.

Yet in strict logic there is no reason why growth should be a necessary condition for full employment. To see this, go back to Figure 2.1. Assume a situation where TT is given (i.e. zero growth). At point U, there is unemployment. As noted above, this is an inefficient point, indicating waste of resources. The solution is to implement policies such as greater labour market flexibility that address the unemployment problem. As more people are employed, we move towards a point like P on the production frontier TT.

The necessary policies might take any of the forms outlined in Chapter 5. Hence full employment can be regarded as an indicator of efficiency. In moving from U to P, there will be an increase in output and therefore some faster economic growth will be recorded. But once attained, there is no reason why full employment should not be maintained at P. Faster growth at that stage makes no difference one way or another. Hence the 'classical' conclusion: *full employment is always attainable, irrespective of the level of output or of the growth of output*.

Intuition and empirical fact suggest that full employment is easier to attain when an economy is growing. Also when growth declines, unemployment rises. For example, Korea, long used to near zero unemployment rates, found itself facing unemployment of an unprecedented seven per cent following the 1997–8 currency crisis.

There are two main explanations why growth is positively correlated with employment. One reason is that labour productivity is increasing due to advances in technology and annual increases in efficiency. Historically the rate has been around two per cent per annum. If there were no growth, the implication is that fewer people would be needed to produce the same output and unemployment could result. A second reason is that, as tastes change and productivity rates vary, there is constant need for reallocation of the labour force between sectors. Such relocation runs much more smoothly when an economy is growing than when it is static. This explains why growth is desired not just for its own sake but for the indirect benefits it provides, such as helping to keep unemployment low.

Growth of GNP per Person as a Policy Objective

The focus on income per person rather than total income (GNP) as the policy objective has profoundly important implications.1[1] Suppose one had to choose between three growth profiles as indicated in Table 2.1.

Total GNP is increasing fastest in situation A. If total GNP were the policy objective, A would be the preferred situation. If GNP per person were the policy objective, situation C would be chosen. Ranking A and B would be more difficult. The only difference between them is that there are more people around in A to share a given GNP per person growth rate. Suppose these additional people happened to be immigrants from Africa. The economy's faster growth means that they can be accommodated without impairing average living standards of the existing population; while at the same time the immigrants' living standards are much higher in the host country than they were at home. This would suggest a preference for A over B. But there may be other effects to consider, relating to the broader social impact of immigration and effects on income distribution. An influx of unskilled immigrants, for instance, would tend to reduce earnings of native unskilled workers, but would generally tend to benefit the middle and upper classes by reducing the cost of unskilled labour that these more affluent people employ (domestic help, catering staff, gardeners and so on). Clearly, personal values and one's position in the income distribution ranking influence preferences between the various growth and population combinations.

Table 2.1

Growth: Illustrative Example

Growth profile	Total GNP (% p.a.)	Population (% p.a.)	GNP per person (% p.a.)
A	5	3	2
B	4	2	2
C	3	0	3

In the above example, population growth is treated as if it were independent of GNP growth. A crucial question is whether and how population growth interacts with GNP and the consequential effect on living standards per person. Take, for example, a country such as Nigeria with an annual population growth of three per cent. Output growth of over two per cent is needed simply to prevent living standards falling. Many argue that population growth at that rate has a negative effect on total GNP growth and hence can depress income per person. An expanding population of young people and large family size reduce national saving and consequently limit the volume of investment. Simultaneously, a burgeoning population puts pressure on a country's natural resources. If the rate of population growth interacts negatively with GNP per person, a vicious circle of economic decline can be generated. At the other end of the spectrum, excessively low population growth can be equally problematic. The 'greying' of Europe's population, for instance, has led to concerns about the financial viability of pension schemes, escalating medical costs and an erosion of social dynamism and innovation. This line of reasoning reinforces the case for GNP per person, not total GNP, as the primary policy objective.

Affluent households tend to have smaller families than poor households. Likewise, developed countries have lower population growth than poor countries. Thus, since 1980, population has grown in higher-income countries by only 0.6 per cent per annum, compared with two per cent in low-income countries. Ireland too has experienced the same phenomenon. As Chapter 5 will show, with increasing prosperity its birth rate has declined. But have we become better off because of a low birth rate, or is the birth rate low because we are more affluent? There is no definitive answer to this question, but many governments in less developed countries now believe that lower population growth would help to raise living standards and have introduced strong family planning programmes to encourage smaller family size. Irish governments have never gone as far in this direction as governments in developing countries such as India and China. One reason for this is that Irish people, unlike many in the present developing world, had the option of emigration.

Migration and Growth

The impact of emigration on living standards has long been a controversial topic. Some have argued that increased population would have raised living standards in Ireland. Patrick Pearse believed that the country could support a population of 30 million. With greater population would go larger domestic markets, greater economies of scale, higher productivity and, eventually, more growth. Higher living standards and a more dynamic local community would in turn induce skilled and talented Irish people to stay at home, thus reinforcing faster growth. This is a rather rosy view of what might have happened to living standards in the absence of emigration. Demographers, however, agree that if there had been no emigration since 1841, the population in the Republic would be in the region of 20 million instead of four million.[2] Some argued that a growing population was a good thing in itself, irrespective of its effects on material welfare. The Commission on Emigration, for example, endorsed the principle that 'a steadily increasing population should occupy a high place among the criteria by which the success of national policy should be judged'.[3]

An opposite viewpoint was that emigration acted as a welcome safety valve, enabling the amount of land and capital per person remaining in Ireland to be increased, with beneficial effects on Irish productivity. At the same time Irish emigrants were able to find more productive employment abroad. A win-win outcome for all parties, just as predicted in John Kenneth Galbraith's famous dictum that 'emigration helps those who leave, the country they go to, and the people they leave behind'.[4] Underlying this approach was the idea that the primary focus of economic policy should be the living standards of the Irish people wherever they happened to live, not just of those residing in the Irish state. Thus the policy objective should be to encourage Irish people to go where their productivity would be highest and their material rewards greatest. According to this logic, Ireland's access to the comparatively prosperous labour markets of the USA, the UK, Australia and Canada was a tremendous boon and the Irish government's main responsibility was to provide education to its citizens and equip them to make maximum use of the opportunities open to them at home *and* abroad.

Which of these differing perspectives is 'correct'? Research on this question remains inconclusive. A comprehensive NESC study found convincing evidence that emigration did not impair the long-run growth in living standards of those remaining in Ireland, but was unable to go further and assert that emigration actually improved living standards.[5] Recent developments have changed the focus of interest to the effects of immigration rather than emigration. Irish people continue to go abroad for work; but for the first time in centuries a lot more foreigners come each year to work in Ireland. At a broad level, this change in demographic pattern has been benign. Higher growth in GNP has involved both significant net immigration *and* an improvement in living standards. At one level this positive correlation between total GNP growth and growth in GNP per person suggests that in Ireland's case opting for growth in GNP per person as the primary policy objective need cause no special angst.[6] At a broader societal level, however, immigration brings special problems. The burden of adjustment to unskilled immigration falls heavily on lower-income groups in the host country population and it is unwise to ignore this (see below).

Optimal Growth, not Maximum Growth

While growth is a primary policy objective, it does not follow that the aim is simply to *maximise* growth. One reason for this is that growth involves a degree of intergenerational distribution. By cutting down on its consumption and investing more, any present generation can raise economic growth rates. Japan's average investment/GNP ratio during the period 1960–95 exceeded the investment ratio in the European Union and the United States by more than ten percentage points (31 per cent as against 22 per cent and 18 per cent respectively). Not surprisingly, Japan's growth rate of six per cent per year was twice the rate of most industrial countries. Within Europe, the faster-growing countries, such as Spain, Italy and Germany, invested more than the slower-growing countries, such as Britain. By investing so much, the early post-war generation sacrificed its material welfare in the interests of future generations. But how far to go in sacrificing this generation's living standards in order to improve those of future generations? Clearly different societies place different premiums on future relative to present living standards and, by extension, to the welfare of future over present generations. Dictatorial societies like the Soviet Union under Stalin were able to record extraordinarily rapid growth, but at terrible cost to the people who had to produce the necessary saving.

Another reason for not choosing maximum growth as a policy objective relates to its undesirable spillover effects. These have become apparent in the early 2000s in Ireland. One such effect is traffic congestion. Few fast-growing countries could hope to avoid this, unless the authorities are prepared to impose, and enforce, the type of draconian restrictions on the use of cars in urban areas that are found in cities such as Singapore. Another spillover effect is the inflow of job seekers from abroad. In the initial stages, a decline in emigration is observed and this is widely welcomed. Next comes immigration as former emigrants return to a buoyant domestic market. These immigrants help to sustain the boom by moderating pay growth and plugging vital gaps in labour supply. Generally there is no problem with immigrants of nationality and background similar to the population of the host country. Difficulties arise, however, when unskilled immigrants of more diverse background enter the picture. There are also income distribution effects to consider. Middle- and upper-income groups gain from the entry of the unskilled into the host country's workforce, but those at the lower end of the income profile can easily lose out. Finally, rapid growth and escalating property prices are inseparable bedfellows. Such asset-price inflation can cause much unease. Investors in property benefit, while those outside this 'charmed' circle miss out. Note that the latter do not lose absolutely, only in relative terms. Also, the charmed circle in a country such as Ireland can be quite inclusive; almost 80 per cent of households own their own home and thus gain from the rise in house prices. As in other areas of economic life, the gainers tend to make less of a fuss than the losers.

One important, intangible benefit of growth is the influence and power that it brings with it. We can learn from the growing dominance of the USA in the world economy how economic success and political and military power are closely linked. Economic growth since the early 1990s has dramatically shifted the balance of economic power within Ireland from the North (once the most prosperous industrial region of the island) to the Republic. There is a palpable air of self-confidence and a virtual disappearance of the grievance mentality that blighted the country in the past.

All of these advantages and disadvantages must be weighed in determining a country's optimum growth rate. Choosing an optimum growth path requires careful consideration of the broader sociopolitical factors mentioned above, as well as of the limitations of GNP as an indicator of welfare, a subject to which we turn next.

3 GROWTH AND HUMAN WELFARE

So far we have discussed economic growth as if growth, as measured by GNP in the numerator, were the sole objective of economic policy. Growth is taken to be desirable because it enlarges the range of consumption possibilities available to society. But it is well known that growth is an inadequate indicator of human welfare. As one critic expressed it:

> The Gross National Product does not allow for the health of our children,
> the quality of their education or the joy of their play. It does not include the

beauty of our poetry or the strength of our marriages; the intelligence of our public debate or the integrity of our public officials. It measures neither our wisdom nor our learning neither our compassion nor our devotion to our country; it measures everything, in short, except that which makes life worthwhile.[7]

GNP does not account for many of the things that make for the good life, and some items are included in GNP that may worsen rather than improve human welfare. Four specific criticisms of GNP have been made on this account. First, that it puts no value on leisure and the household economy. Second, that it ignores income distribution (discussed in Section 4). Third, that it takes no account of resource depletion and degradation of the environment. Fourth, some items are recorded outputs although in reality they are inputs or costs.

Leisure and the Household Economy
Leisure is a good like any other, so theoretically it should be included alongside other goods and services when choosing growth as a policy objective. The difficulty arises because of the way growth is measured. Changes in leisure hours are, for various reasons, not taken account of in the GNP statistic. Hence if GNP growth is rising but everyone is working harder and longer hours, the net improvement in human welfare may well be much lower than it appears. The average American works 1,804 hours per year; the average German works 1,437 hours per year. Americans have more goods and more GNP per head, but they have miserably short vacations.

There are various manifestations of this problem. A feature of rich societies is that employees are well paid. They are well paid because they are productive and that in turn means that the opportunity cost of leisure increases as economies become more prosperous. Hence the widely observed phenomenon that people in affluent societies tend to be more harried and harassed, have less time for talk and a chat than their counterparts in poorer countries. The process of economic growth inherently tends to accentuate this problem.

To take another example, suppose that a person takes a second job. This makes large inroads into leisure time. The GNP measure includes all the output generated but ignores the welfare cost of the loss of leisure. Human welfare has presumably increased as a result of this decision – otherwise the second job would not have been taken – but the net increase in welfare will be much less than the increase in GNP indicates. The individual is likely to be more harassed and to have less time for their family.

GNP includes only transactions that involve a monetary exchange. Hence leisure is excluded. But this is not the only excluded output. Housework done by members of a household, being unpaid, is not recorded in GNP. As members of the household enter the workforce and household tasks such as repair, maintenance, care of children are passed over to paid professionals, GNP rises. Yet all that is happening is that these functions have been shifted from the traditional realm of the household and the community to the monetised economy. Welfare has presumably increased, since the decision to work outside the home was taken voluntarily. But the increase in GNP will grossly exaggerate the increase in welfare. These examples help to explain why economic growth will bring fewer real benefits than appears to be the case.

Growth and the Environment

Conventional GNP measures do not deal satisfactorily with environmental and ecological factors. Higher GNP has implications for the environment on several levels that fail to be recorded in the statistics. Three aspects, in particular, merit attention: higher levels of pollution; depletion of natural resources; and global warming.

First, no deduction is made in GNP statistics for the higher levels of pollution and chemical waste that often accompany economic growth. Some countries have attempted to compute 'green' national accounts that allow for these negative effects, but there is as yet no consensus on how the pollution effects should be computed.

Second, depletion of a nation's stock of non-renewable resources such as oil and coal is not accounted for in GNP calculations. Even in the case of renewable resources, problems can arise if economic growth leads to their being exploited in excess of the replacement rate. For example, the serious decline in the water table caused by increased economic activity in the countries bordering on the Aral Sea, in northern China and Israel/occupied Palestine is ignored in the national accounts.

Third, economic growth is associated with deforestation, change in land use and, most notable of all, with burning fossil fuels. As a result the concentration of greenhouse gases has risen alarmingly – the current level is higher than at any time in the last 650,000 years and, as the Stern Report confirms, there has been an accompanying rise in world temperatures. Already, an increase of 0.6°C has been recorded since the mid-1970s. A change of this magnitude may appear small, but its effects over time could be enormous. The Stern Report estimates that, if nothing is done, continuation of present trends could lead to a rise in world temperatures of 2°C by 2035 and a further escalation to 5°C by the end of the century.[8] Long time lags between today's greenhouse gas emissions and future damage to climate and the environment mean that the adverse effects will not be reflected in the GNP for many years. Although Ireland might not be as badly affected by global warming as other countries, we will be expected in the interests of EU solidarity to pay wide carbon taxes (see Chapter 4), to restrain energy consumption and, in short, to become a lot more 'green' than before (see Chapters 8 and 10).

Inputs Recorded as Outputs

By a perverse quirk, the cost of moderating the adverse effects of pollution is sometimes included in GNP as an output (service provided) instead of as an input (a production cost to society). For example, the medical attention given to a victim of air pollution will be recorded in the national accounts as an addition to GNP instead of as a deduction from it. This is part of a more general criticism of GNP relating to inputs misclassified as outputs. For example, military spending is included as a positive contributor to GNP, even if that spending is undertaken at the behest of reckless political leaders and with disregard to the needs of the people. Likewise, the inclusion of expenditure on crime prevention as an output in GNP has been criticised. To be sure, such spending could represent improved living standards in so far as the community obtains greater security and more orderly traffic. But it could equally be a sign of diminished quality of the social environment and hence a cost of securing higher GNP (e.g. if more police were needed to maintain the same level of security and traffic movement).

GNP and Human Development Indicators

Making GNP per capita a primary objective is really shorthand for something much more complex. In evaluating a country's economic performance, account must be taken of the quality of the lifestyle enjoyed by the population as well as the quantity of goods and services consumed. Imagine two countries. One has a lower GNP per person than the other, but it happens to have a healthier, more literate and less crime-ridden society. In this instance, GNP is an inaccurate measure of the relative welfare of the two countries, and making GNP growth a primary policy objective may not be an appropriate response. Instead of economic growth, can we find a way of measuring human development and making it the primary policy objective?

In an effort to develop a more comprehensive socioeconomic measure than GNP, the United Nations has developed the Human Development Index (HDI). The HDI is a composite index and consists of a weighted average of data on GDP/GNP per person, income distribution, life expectancy and educational attainment of the population.

As one would expect, such exercises lead to some changes in ranking. The 2007 figures, for example, indicate an HDI ranking much higher than the GDP/GNP per person ranking for Sweden, Portugal, Greece and the UK; the opposite is the case for the USA, Singapore and South Africa.[9] Ireland is placed fifth of 177 countries in the HDI league and we come third in the GDP ranking (for well-known reasons, GDP exaggerates Ireland's welfare, as outlined in Chapter 6). By adding to the list of indicators, and measuring them in different ways, more radical alterations in ranking can be computed. Experimentation and analysis along these lines is continuing.

Yet the limitations of GNP as a measure of welfare must not be exaggerated. For all its defects, a higher output per person gives society the *capacity* to achieve a better quality of life. This explains the close positive correlation between the HDI and total output per person. There is also a strong positive correlation between GNP per capita growth and some important empirical measures of the quality of life. Countries with higher GNP per capita tend to be healthier and better educated than those with lower GNP per capita. They also tend to be better policed and are more secure in a financial and physical sense. London is safer than Lagos, Manila or Sao Paolo. Affluent Tokyo is one of the safest cities in the world. While many forms of recorded crime have increased since 1945, prosperity has tended to result in a reduction in crime and disorder. During the nineteenth century, industrial nations became less crime-ridden as they became more industrialised. Indeed, these two factors are interrelated: the rule of law and good governance are essential prerequisites of a prosperous market economy.

Faster growth makes it easier to reduce unemployment, to lessen poverty, to improve education and health services and to provide all the other good things that constitute prosperity. There are, of course, negative aspects of growth, such as damage to the environment, erosion of community life, and destruction of rural values. Since the birth of the Industrial Revolution in the late eighteenth century, economic growth has had its critics, some of the most trenchant of whom have been economists. The tradition of scepticism, verging on hostility, towards growth remains active to this day.[10] Despite these downsides, governments and those who elect them evidently believe that the positive effects of growth outweigh its negative effects, and both continue to accord it a high priority.

4 EQUITY, INCOME DISTRIBUTION AND HAPPINESS

Policy Debate

GNP per person, being an arithmetic average of total output divided by total population, reveals no information about the distribution of resources within a society. It could rise, even though the majority of the population may be getting worse off. For example, if the income of the most affluent one-third of a population rose by a total €50 billion, and the income of the poorest two-thirds fell by a total €30 billion, GNP would increase. But does it follow that society as a whole is better off?

Some argue that the long-run sustainability of growth depends on income being shared on an equitable basis. Successful policymaking requires change, and such change can only be achieved if the majority of people believe that they have a stake in the economy and will benefit from its continued growth. But this still leaves open the question of what is meant by sharing income on an equitable basis. This involves complex and long-debated issues concerning the welfare of society and the purpose of economic growth. Since Chapter 7 is devoted to this topic, a brief outline of the main parameters of this debate will suffice at this stage.

The value judgements underlying modern economics are derived from a philosophy of individualism and liberalism. *Individualism* means that what ultimately counts is the utility every individual attains and that the utility of each individual should be given an equal weight. *Liberalism* signifies that individuals should be free to decide what provides the greatest utility. Individual preferences are taken as given. The task of the economist, in this view, is to devise market structures that will enable individuals to satisfy their preferences, not to pass judgement on them.

Utility and income must be distinguished in this analysis. The standard assumption underlying economic reasoning is that the marginal utility of income is positive but decreases as income rises. Individuals always prefer a higher income to a lower one, but the intensity of this preference diminishes as income rises.[11] A systematic relationship thus links utility to income. On the face of it, the individualist principle of treating the utility of every person equally, coupled with the assumption of declining marginal utility for all individuals, would imply that the total utility in society is maximised when income is distributed perfectly evenly. But there are two reasons why even committed utilitarians do not push the argument to the extreme of total income equalisation.

First, different people derive different amounts of satisfaction from the same income levels. Material wealth does not matter equally to all. However, since utility cannot be objectively measured and compared among individuals, there is no way of finding out how much utility individuals derive from their income.

Second, the adverse effect of policies to achieve greater equality in incentives to work and enterprise may, after a point, lead to a fall in total income. Arthur Okun described the process of redistributing income as akin to transferring water from one barrel to another with a leaky bucket.[12] The more we try to increase equity by the redistribution of income, the more we reduce efficiency. In transferring income from the high-income group to the low-income group in society, the authorities levy taxes on individuals' income from employment and capital holdings. The former gives people an incentive to work less and the latter entices people to save less. Both effects lead to a reduction in the amount of income available for redistribution. The less well off in society may well lose rather than benefit from such policies in the long run.

The assumption of decreasing marginal utility implies that when we take a given amount from the rich to give to the poor, the rich will suffer less of a utility loss than the utility gain enjoyed by the poor. If asked to choose between a perfectly equal distribution of income and an unequal distribution *of exactly the same total income*, a utilitarian would favour the equal distribution. Egalitarian predispositions also emerge from other philosophies and schools of thought. Some argue that society should give the utility of the poor greater weight than the utility of the rich on grounds of need, regardless of fine points about diminishing utility. Others, such as the philosopher John Rawls, have pushed this line of judgement to the extreme, arguing that any economic change that increases inequality would be acceptable only if it also makes the poorest better off. This implies that the utility of the worst-off individual takes precedence over all others and that a fair distribution of income is one that makes the poorest person as well off as possible after taking all costs of income transfers into account.[13]

Irish policy objectives have a Rawlsian flavour. Thus governments have tended to prioritise social inclusion as a strategic objective in its own right, the primary objective being to ensure that 'the benefits of economic growth and related social improvements are shared by all sections of the Irish population'.[14] Social inclusion has been a major theme of successive agreements with the social partners (see Chapters 3 and 7).

In opposition to the egalitarian presumption, Robert Nozick argued that the idea of fairness as an outcome could not be justified. Fairness must be based on rules, not outcomes.[15] Two rules are crucial: (1) the state must enforce laws that establish and protect private property; and (2) private property may be transferred from one person to another only by voluntary exchange. Provided markets are open to competition and there are no major market 'failures', the resulting distribution of income is, by Nozick's definition, fair. It does not matter how unequally this income is shared provided it is generated by people each of whom voluntarily provided services in exchange for market-determined compensation. The entrepreneur who accepts business risks and has succeeded deserves to be rewarded. Redistribution of these earnings is unjustified. From this perspective the key issue is equality of opportunity, not equality of outcome. Indeed, given an uneven distribution of skills, motivation and willingness to work, equal opportunities will inevitably entail unequal outcomes.

So far the discussion has focused on *vertical equity*. This refers to the proposition that differently situated individuals should be treated differently. The well off, in other words, should be taxed in favour of the poor because they can afford to pay these taxes with less pain. *Horizontal equity* is also important. The underlying principle is that people with the same incomes and the same circumstances should be treated in a similar fashion. For example, families with the same number of dependants and the same income should pay the same rate of tax (see Chapter 4). Horizontal equity requires that property developers, farmers and PAYE employees should be subject to the same tax unless there is a clear demonstration of different circumstances. Perceived breaches of this equity principle can be a source of major grievance. By extension, people in different circumstances should not be asked to pay the same taxes. This principle is the motivating force of many income distribution policies. The case for regional grants and incentives, for example, is based on the idea that people in less developed regions do not enjoy the same access to infrastructure as those living in richer regions.

Equity, Economic Growth and Happiness

We have already referred to the debate about the relationship between economic growth and equity. The proposition is that to achieve income equality some sacrifice in growth is necessary because equality requires high taxes that can damage enterprise and investment. Some find this line of argument persuasive. Others doubt that such a trade-off exists. They point to the many studies showing that countries with more evenly spread income grow faster than countries with a large gap between poor and rich. Also, faster-growing economies have lower unemployment rates. Since the incidence of unemployment is highest among lower-income groups, these groups in particular will benefit. In Ireland's case, the virtual disappearance of unemployment has brought about a decline in levels of deprivation during the past decade. There is also evidence of considerable escalation of gains at the top of the income distribution. While there is general agreement that extreme income inequality is bad for growth, not all agree on how precisely 'extreme' should be defined.

The relationship between equity and growth depends ultimately on individual attitudes and culture. Income inequalities are more acceptable and financial work incentives valued more in some societies than in others. The combinations of growth and equity attainable in a competitive market economy full of individualistic materialists will be different from those attainable in a co-operative economy run by and for ascetic altruists! A poll conducted in 1994 showed that only 29 per cent of Americans thought it was the government's job to reduce income differentials, while over 60 per cent of Germans and over 80 per cent of Italians and Austrians were of that opinion.[16] In practice governments have voted with their feet on this question. Comparison of income distribution before and after tax and state benefits shows that major transfers take place from richer to poorer income groups in all industrial economies (see Chapter 7).

In recent years, the research agenda has been widened even further by tackling the much broader question of how GNP per capita is related to happiness. Do higher standards of living, whether defined on broad or narrow definitions of the term, translate into greater happiness? Economists have had a long and abiding interest in this correlation. In the light of our discussion of GNP per capita as a measure of welfare and of the importance of income distribution, the reader will not be surprised that economic research has come up with some complex findings.

A first step is how to measure happiness. The main source of information comes from large-scale citizen surveys that ask individuals to report on how happy they feel, how satisfied they are with their lives and/or with their jobs. Sometimes this is supplemented by data on suicide rates and health status as proxies for (un)happiness. Defined this way, happiness is clearly dependent on many variables other than the level of income – contrary to the much-quoted adage that 'anyone who says money can't buy happiness doesn't know where to shop'. The key methodological challenge is to identify the specific contribution of increases in GNP per capita, and by extension individuals' income level, to the happiness index.

Research over the past decade enables us to draw several broad conclusions.[17] First, for any one individual, more income leads to more life satisfaction, everything else being equal. Within a single country, at a given moment in time, those in the highest income groups are happier than those in the lowest income groups. Second, citizens of very poor countries tend to be happier as living standards increase. Studies of former Soviet Union countries, for instance, show a clear positive correlation between income per capita and reported happiness. Third, beyond a certain level of GNP per capita, the average person does *not* become significantly happier as GNP per capita increases. At an aggregate level there has been no increase in reported happiness over the past 30 years in Japan and Europe, and there has been, if anything, a decline in the USA. This is called the *Paradox of Happiness*. Fourth, *relative* income matters as much, if not more, to most people than *absolute* income levels. People's definition of what constitutes an 'adequate' level of income seems to depend as much on the level of income enjoyed by their neighbour as on the absolute value of their own income (see Chapter 6). Fifth, virtually all studies show that being unemployed has a strongly negative effect on happiness.

In Ireland, too, the relationship between happiness (measured as the percentage of the population who described themselves as 'very satisfied with their life') and material welfare is decidedly weak. The annual Eurobarometer survey showed that 40 per cent of Irish people fell into the very satisfied 'happy' category in 1980. There is no evidence of the proportion of happy people rising since then, notwithstanding the huge increase in material income. The figure in 2003 remained at around 40 per cent and has not deviated much over the past 20 years.

One element on the happiness spectrum *has*, however, changed. The number of people who are acutely *dis*satisfied with their life has declined consistently since 1990. The fall in Ireland's unemployment since that time was most likely a key factor in this development. Hence, to the extent that fast economic growth has helped us to reduce unemployment, we can conclude that economic growth in Ireland has not added much to the happiness of already happy people, but it has made those at the bottom of the happiness league feel less dissatisfied.

Archbishop Whately, who established the Chair of Political Economy in Trinity College in 1832, took an interest in a related question of whether economic growth has an impact on moral behaviour. Unlike a modern social scientist, he had to rely on deductive reasoning instead of mass opinion surveys. As a general rule, he concluded, advancement in National Prosperity, which mankind is by the Governor of the universe adapted and impelled to promote, must be favourable to moral improvement.[18] Whately championed the cause of teaching and research in economics because he believed that economic growth would lead to moral improvement, and moral improvement would in turn bring as much 'happiness' as we can reasonably expect in this life. This is an alternative perspective on the GNP/happiness correlation that would no doubt prove controversial in modern Ireland.

The literature on happiness continues to grow. It is a subject that requires cross-disciplinary research involving economics, statistics, psychology and philosophy. As yet conclusions are tentative, but the general thrust of the findings suggests two conclusions. One is that it would be a mistake for economists in the twenty-first century to focus excessively on ways to increase the level of GNP, or to accept too readily that slow economic growth necessarily indicates 'failure'. A second conclusion is that, as prosperity increases, more emphasis should be placed on the provision of public goods than on facilitating the output of more private goods and services. The 'well-being' of an individual includes much more than income: access to decent public amenities, pollution-free air, good education, a fair distribution of income and a crimeless environment contribute more to happiness than any monetary measure can adequately convey.

5 PRICE STABILITY

A regional economy has a strong interest in price stability. However, a region will experience price stability only if the centre provides it. In the Republic's case the centre is Frankfurt, the headquarters of the European Central Bank (ECB), while for Northern Ireland the relevant policy centre is the Bank of England. Policy in the regional economy must therefore focus on supporting the establishment of solid financial institutions at the centre and setting clear objectives for them.

Definition and Measurement

Price stability is a relatively new phrase in the policymaker's lexicon. But it is not a new concept. In the past, inflation was so rampant and endemic that the analysis usually proceeded in terms of the costs of inflation. Over the past 35 years, for instance, the Irish price level has increased on average by over a factor of ten; what cost the equivalent of €10 in 1972 cost more than €100 in 2007. After several years of price stability, inflation has emerged again as a source of concern. Since the launch of the euro in January 1999, Ireland has experienced cumulative inflation of over 40 per cent.

Price stability is defined as the absence of any persistent and pronounced rise or fall in the general level of money prices. The general level of prices is measured by the Consumer Price Index (CPI). This index is defined by reference to the price of a fixed 'basket' of consumer goods. In the Republic, the selection of items for the basket is made using results of the national Household Budget Survey. Every five years new weights and new items are introduced into the index. Each month some 50,000 price observations are made by the Central Statistics Office. The results are aggregated into 613 items. These include staple goods such as food, clothing, cars and petrol, and also items such as mobile telephones, medical insurance, bank charges, child-minding fees, and wedding and funeral expenses.

Three factors tend to impart an upward bias to the price increases recorded by the CPI. First, the number of goods in the sample basket is an incomplete inventory of the economy's goods. Delays in incorporating new products give rise, for technical reasons, to an upward bias (*composition bias*). Second, improvements in quality are an important feature of new goods and services, ranging from high-technology goods to medical services and drugs, and they tend to be insufficiently allowed for in CPI price data (*quality bias*). Third, the CPI may fail to take full account of people's ability to substitute low-priced goods for higher-priced goods or to shift purchases from high-priced outlets to cheaper retail outlets when prices are rising (*substitution bias*).[19] A doubling in the price of potatoes, for example, would raise the Irish CPI by over one-third of a percentage point (potatoes carry a weight in the basket of 0.33 per cent) but this takes no account of the availability of close substitutes such as rice and pasta. As time goes by, people switch their buying to products which have increased less in price: but the base weights (the CPI is a Laspeyres index) take insufficient account of this switch.

The empirical importance of these measurement biases is not known with precision. Even a bias of +1 per cent is large compared with an average inflation rate of, say, two per cent. Because of these upward biases, the objective of price stability is not defined as a zero CPI rise, but rather as CPI increases in the range of one to three per cent. The ECB defines it as year-on-year increases in the CPI of the euro zone *below but close to* two per cent, maintained over the medium term; the Bank of England adopted a similar definition in December 2003; while the central banks of Sweden, Norway, New Zealand and Canada have opted for the wider 1–3 per cent range.

The issue of whether *asset prices*, and in particular house prices, should be included in the CPI has been much debated in recent times. The issue arises because in many countries (Ireland, the UK and Spain, for example) house prices have been rising well above the CPI rate for several years. While housing costs were included in the CPI (with a weight of seven per cent in the Irish CPI), some believed that the index took too little account of the implications of escalating house prices on long-run disposable income.

The case for not making a special adjustment is based on two arguments. First, Ireland has a high proportion of owner-occupied houses, and the vast majority of them have low mortgages relative to current housing prices. Mortgage payments on average amount to only four per cent of total consumer expenditure. True, for the first-time buyer the proportion could be as much as ten times that, but first-time buyers are a small minority of the total population and the CPI strives to measure the average impact of price changes. Second, as mentioned above, while house prices are not included in the Irish CPI, the cost of *housing services* is included (i.e. rent payments on rented accommodation, the cost of housing repairs and mortgage interest payments on owner-occupied housing). The reasoning behind the focus on housing services is that what matters for living standards is not so much the price of a house per se but the cost of owning a house (i.e. interest payments) and of renting it. Imagine the case of a house costing €100,000 when the mortgage rate is ten per cent. If the buyer borrows the entire capital sum, mortgage interest payments will amount to €10,000 per annum. Now let the mortgage rate fall to five per cent. Demand for houses will rise since it is now cheaper to borrow. Suppose this leads to a doubling of house prices. The price of the house rises to €200,000, but the interest cost of the mortgage remains exactly the same as before, namely €10,000. True, annual mortgage payments will increase because of capital repayments and this may impose a strain on the borrower's discretionary income. But this effect is likely to be much less than the 100 per cent increase in house prices. The house price increase will in due course also lead to a rise in rents, but these will rise in line with total mortgage repayments. The same logic applies to other assets as well as houses (e.g. shares).

Thus, asset prices are by no means irrelevant to inflation – housing and asset prices can rise and fall for reasons other than changes in interest rates – but the CPI sticks to its task and measures prices of consumer goods, not prices of capital goods.

Why Price Stability is Important

Failure to achieve price stability impacts adversely on both economic growth and income distribution. Quantifying these adverse impacts can be difficult. But the key point is to understand why deviations from price stability are bad for economic welfare. Such deviations could take the form of inflation or deflation. Of the two, inflation is the more common and persistent danger and for this reason most of the following analysis relates to the costs of inflation.

Deflation, defined as a persistent decline in the general price level, has been a rare phenomenon in recent times. In common with most developed countries, Ireland has experienced virtually no sustained deflation since 1948. The most traumatic example of deflation was that which occurred during the Great Depression of 1929 to 1933. Another case has been the deflation in Japan after the mid-1990s.[20]

Anticipated Inflation

Suppose we focus on inflation, or upward deviations from price stability. Theories of inflation distinguish between anticipated inflation and unanticipated or 'surprise' inflation. The principal welfare costs arise only when inflation is not fully anticipated. If inflation were to proceed at a steady (or otherwise predictable) rate that the public would learn to anticipate, and if institutions adapted fully to this anticipation, people could adjust their economic behaviour accordingly. There would have to be, in effect, a fully indexed economy, implying, among other things, a comprehensive system of wage and salary indexation, indexing of tax brackets and allowances, taxation of real rather than nominal returns on assets, etc. In brief, all prices for goods and services, including labour services, would be perfectly adjustable. This would be an example of what has been called the 'flexprice' economy. In such an economy, the welfare cost of inflation involves only two types of costs: 'shoe leather' costs and 'menu' costs.

Cash balances yield an implicit social return by virtue of the convenience they afford in making transactions. Inflation can be regarded as a tax on cash balances: the negative yield on cash balances is equal to the rate of inflation. The higher the rate of inflation, the larger the negative yield and the opportunity cost of holding cash. Holders of cash balances will therefore shift into less liquid and convenient, but income-yielding, assets. This substitution involves a further loss of efficiency in so far as cash balances, which are virtually costless to produce, are economised on in favour of more frequent transactions in less liquid and intrinsically valuable assets. Anticipated inflation also imposes the so-called menu cost of actually changing prices in what have been called 'customer markets' (i.e. those markets in which prices are set and, in the normal course of events, kept unchanged for some time, such as labour markets, retail and wholesale trade, pay telephones and parking meters). Both shoe leather and menu costs increase rapidly with the magnitude of the inflation rate.

Unanticipated Inflation

The costs of anticipated inflation may appear rather theoretical. Yet research shows that they are empirically important, even at relatively low rates of inflation. Far more important, however, are the costs arising from unanticipated inflation.

First, uncertainty about the inflation rate undermines the role played by money in economising on transaction costs. Fixed-price orders, leases and other explicit long-term contracts, fixed-time schedules for price changes and the broad general commitment to continuity of offers by suppliers are important ways of assisting forward planning. Uncertainty about the future price level shortens the time horizon of such agreements, thus imposing a welfare loss on society.

Second, uncertainty about future price levels results in an arbitrary redistribution of income and wealth. A faster than expected inflation rate, for instance, will tend to discriminate against creditors in favour of debtors. It will also harm those whose incomes are fixed in nominal money terms or that are indexed only after a lapse of time (pensioners), in contrast with those whose incomes are more easily adjustable to inflation, such as unionised wage earners and owners of capital. Another effect is the redistribution of real wealth from the old (who have accumulated assets) to the young who are, in general, net borrowers. The haphazard nature of the income distribution effects can lead to social unrest and general discontent as people find it increasingly difficult to estimate the growth in their real incomes and to predict what their real earnings will be in the future. In a period of one per cent inflation, people who receive pay increases of four per cent recognise clearly that they have gained in real terms. In a world of 15 per cent inflation, those receiving pay increases of 18 per cent are likely to be much less confident about how they are faring. That loss of information is a genuine subtraction from welfare. Prices cease to fulfil their signalling function as the effects of relative shifts in prices are blurred by the general rise in the price level.

Third, inflation can have adverse consequences for economic growth. Efficiency losses, though small in any one year, can accumulate over time into a significant aggregate loss. In addition, inflation has a tendency to shorten investment horizons. It attracts capital to 'inflation hedges', such as property, at the expense of long-term investment in industry. Empirical evidence indicates that very high inflation (in excess of 40 per cent per annum) is bad for growth and that price stability is good for growth.

Inflation, Deflation and Stability

The above analysis has focused on inflation. Deflation brings similar welfare costs in its train, but for subtly different reasons. Thus, the menu costs apply in the case of anticipated deflation, with the added problem that nominal interest rates cannot be negative (the zero interest-rate constraint), an inflexibility that can lead to excessively high real interest rates. At a macroeconomic level, anticipated deflation can prolong a recession by giving consumers and investors an incentive to postpone spending. It benefits lenders at the expense of borrowers and, because downward adjustments in nominal pay are often problematic, it can lead to real wage inflexibility. Like inflation, deflation tends to be self-perpetuating and deflationary spirals are difficult and costly to reverse. Deflationary episodes have been rare and short-lived during the past 50 years. In recent times, Japan is the only major economy to experience sustained deflation. Its consumer prices have fallen by an average of 0.2 per cent per annum since 1999.

Opinion surveys suggest that the public values price stability for its own sake, apart from the economic costs outlined in this section. One could argue that stability in general, not just price stability, should be included among a region's policy objectives. Personal security (absence of crime), stability of employment (absence of fear of redundancy) and the provision of social safety nets (social welfare) all play a role in creating the good society. Sustained economic growth in a context of price stability brings with it the capacity to provide many of these benefits, just as they in turn make growth and stability more sustainable. Economic growth has rightly been defined as a process of cumulative and circular causation. No single policy objective can be pursued in isolation; each objective interacts with the others.

6 COMPETITIVENESS

Small regional economies are largely 'importers' of price trends abroad. Thus if the CPI is rising in Continental Europe and the UK at around two per cent, inflation in both parts of Ireland will also approximate two per cent. This is a valid generalisation over the long run. But it is not universally the case and significant short-run deviations between a region's inflation rate and the national/area average do occur. Since 1999, Irish prices have risen twice as fast as average euro area prices. As a result, Ireland has become one of the most expensive countries in the euro zone. Theory indicates that there will be *mean reversion* (i.e. that sooner or later the rate of price increase in Ireland will revert to the euro area average), but serious damage to the economy could be done in the interim.[21] The Enterprise Strategy Group's warning in 2004 has continued relevance: 'The cost of doing business in Ireland has risen significantly in recent years. It is eroding the relative competitiveness of our goods and services sectors, and reducing our attractiveness for new foreign direct investment.'[22]

Why do such cost divergences occur and what can or should be done about them?

Price and Cost Divergences
One reason for the divergence in price trends stems from Ireland's rapid growth relative to the euro zone. Faster growth translates into higher pay. This is non-

inflationary where productivity rises in line with pay. Thus a five per cent pay rise matched by a five per cent productivity increase leaves unit cost, and hence prices, unaffected. However, in those parts of the economy where productivity growth is relatively modest, employers will have to increase wages in line with other sectors (or else their workers will leave for better pay elsewhere). Hence unit costs and prices will tend to rise. Non-traded services are particularly prone to price inflation in such situations: restaurant meals, medical services, and building and construction. Here higher pay translates into higher prices. Prices of services have risen consistently faster than prices of goods in recent years.

A second source of inflationary pressure has been the inflationary spiral. In a booming economy the normal restraints on pay rises weaken. Employees, observing higher inflation, seek compensatory pay rises. This leads in turn to further increases in services prices and a process of self-defeating catch-up.

Third, changes in the euro exchange rate have a strong effect on domestic prices.[23] A 20 per cent decline in the value of the euro has been estimated to lead to only a one per cent rise in the average euro zone price level. However, because of the Republic's higher trade dependence and the higher proportion of trade with countries outside the euro zone, the impact of such a depreciation of the euro on the Irish CPI is far higher. The weakness of the euro for several years after 1999 imparted a strong 'imported inflation' push on Irish prices which the subsequent strengthening of the euro has been unable to reverse.

Implications of a Loss of Cost Competitiveness

When one region's prices/costs rise relative to other regions, this is termed a loss of cost competitiveness. One immediate impact of such deterioration is a decline in exports as they become more expensive to foreigners. For the same reason, domestic goods become more expensive relative to imports and the import bill rises. The balance of payments on current account then runs into deficit.

For a country with an independent national currency the next question is the effect of the deficit on the exchange rate. If the exchange rate devalues, this offers a short-run solution to the loss of competitiveness. But the resultant rise in domestic prices could set in motion an inflationary spiral, with devaluation causing domestic price increases, which lead to compensatory pay claims. This is the classic downside of devaluation as a policy response to deficits induced by cost-competitiveness problems.

In the case of a small regional economy, there are no direct exchange rate implications for a loss of competitiveness. If Northern Ireland loses cost competitiveness and runs a deficit, this will not materially affect the value of sterling. Likewise the Republic's competitiveness will have no impact on the fortunes of the euro. In each case the region is too small to affect the bigger picture. Thus the region is left with its current account deficit. When a region runs a current-account deficit, say because of a decline in competitiveness, this means that it is spending more on foreign goods and services than it is earning from exports. In this sense, a deficit signifies that a country is 'living beyond its means'. The deficit will have to be matched by foreign borrowing, and the corresponding capital inflow will eventually have to be financed and repaid. This will entail a future stream of current account surpluses spread over many years. The level of GNP available to future generations will thus be affected.

An adverse movement in a region's cost competitiveness cannot be indefinitely sustained. As regional prices increase, the region's cost structure will become more and more out of line with its competitors. It will begin to lose export markets and will become less attractive as a location for investment. Eventually growth will slow, labour demand will decline and pay pressures will ease. The speed of this process is an issue that is much debated in Ireland. Its price level is above the euro zone average. Like all booming regions, the hope is for a 'soft' landing, whereby rising costs will gradually be restrained to more sustainable levels over time. Unfortunately, the historical experience of booming regions provides many examples of 'hard' landings where adjustment takes place abruptly, property markets collapse and unemployment rises. This suggests that the major concern of any region must be to influence its competitiveness in such a way as to secure optimal growth, achieving its economic potential while moderating booms and avoiding busts along the way. It must do so without two major policy instruments to which a nation state might have recourse: commercial policy and an independent exchange rate. That leaves domestic competitiveness policy as an instrument of major importance.

Broad Definition of Competitiveness

Competitiveness has become something of a global preoccupation since the 1990s. Every region worries about it and governments everywhere feel compelled to do something to improve it. Practically every country in Europe has set up competitiveness councils. The *World Competitiveness Report*, and its rival, the *Global Competitiveness Report*, are published annually and attract worldwide publicity. Their findings are scrutinised with a fine-tooth comb by development agencies and government commissions. In short, maintaining competitiveness can now be described as a key secondary policy objective, with improvements in competitiveness seen as crucial to achieving growth and full employment.

Competitiveness has been a well-established theme in economic debate in Ireland. In the Republic, the National Competitiveness Council was set up in 1997. Its *Annual Competitiveness Report* is a rich source of information on competitiveness indicators (see Chapter 8 for example). The Council's remit is to examine key competitiveness issues and to make recommendations on policy actions required to improve Ireland's competitive position. Attention has also focused on business competitiveness in Northern Ireland. The Economic Research Institute of Northern Ireland has published several reports on this topic, drawing on a comprehensive set of UK regional competitiveness indicators and other data.[24]

Competitiveness can be defined in a narrow sense or in a broad sense. The narrow definition focuses on trends in pay, productivity and unit costs. These components are aggregated into a cost competitiveness index and movements in the index are tracked over time and compared with trends in competing countries. For many years, emphasis was placed on this narrow definition partly because of data limitations (information on the components of the broader definition has only recently become available) and partly because Ireland's performance on the cost competitiveness definition was poor and it has to be given priority.

The broader definition includes price and non-price factors such as product quality, reliability of supply, back-up marketing services and taxation, and extends to consideration of human resource development, business services, infrastructure and public finance and administration. A country's long-run competitive position can also be profoundly influenced by its policy towards research and development (R&D), and by its success in product innovation and technology. Innovation and R&D are key ingredients of a region's infrastructure (see Chapters 6 and 8). Competitiveness authorities in both parts of Ireland currently use the broader definition of competitiveness. In this they are in line with international practice. For instance, the World Economic Forum defines competitiveness as 'the ability to achieve sustained high rates of growth in GDP per capita'. Thus competitiveness measures the degree to which a nation or a region can, under free market conditions, produce goods and services that meet the test of international markets while simultaneously expanding the real income of its citizens.

Note that competitiveness is a relative concept. Success in the competitiveness league depends on how well an economy is progressing relative to others. It is possible for all countries to grow faster, to generate more employment, to export more; but by definition only some countries can become more competitive. In other words, the process of striving to be more competitive, in so far as it improves economic growth and efficiency, is a positive-sum game. But in terms of ranking in competitiveness leagues it is a zero-sum game: one region advances in the ranking order only if some other region declines. Failure to recognise this point can lead to competitiveness becoming what has been called a 'dangerous obsession' instead of a stimulus to improved performance.

Strategy to Improve Competitiveness

Policies to improve competitiveness constitute the theme of many chapters of this book. These policies change over time and according to circumstances will differ across region and nation. To date the policy objective in both parts of Ireland has focused on creating an environment that would encourage:

- the growth of export-oriented firms, especially Irish-owned firms
- the retention and attraction of foreign direct investment in knowledge-based sectors and activities such as electronics, pharmaceuticals, biotechnology and software
- the development of linkages between existing and new green-field firms
- a balanced location of economic activity within the island.

This ambitious programme has involved several policy dimensions and instruments, which will be analysed throughout this book.

The context of Ireland's competitiveness challenge has changed markedly in recent years. First, in the past Ireland has benefited significantly from the Structural and Cohesion Funds. With rising prosperity, however, the Republic's net receipts from Brussels are diminishing. According to Department of Finance estimates, in 2011 Ireland will become for the first time a net contributor to the EU.

Second, policy measures taken at the centre (Brussels/Frankfurt/London) are becoming increasingly important. Monetary and exchange rate policy is the obvious example. The centre also exerts major control over fiscal, competition, transport and agriculture policy as well as state aids and taxation. The European Commission is concerned about competitiveness at the EU-wide level, and action taken to improve it will have important implications for both parts of Ireland.

Finally, the scope for regional policy initiatives, though declining, remains of crucial importance. A key fiscal incentive in the Republic is the 12.5 per cent tax rate for all corporate income from 2003 and the Brussels-approved 'grandparenting' of the ten per cent rate up to 2010 for all companies already in operation. In addition, domestic authorities on both sides of the border have some degree of discretion in the payment of capital grants, training grants, R&D support and so on. The extension of these fiscal and financial concessions to internationally traded service industries has proved to be a significant incentive to the development of the Irish Financial Services Centre and the attraction of major multinationals to Ireland (see Chapter 6 and 8). Provision of a good physical environment and human capital structure (education) is also an intrinsic part of a strategy for improving competitiveness (see Chapters 8 and 12).

7 CONCLUSION

The first priority of economic policy is to ensure high and rising standards of living. In practical terms, this means that most governments' economic performance is judged by reference to changes in GNP per person. People want economic growth because of what it can do for them in terms of higher purchasing power and also because of the other good things that often accompany growth, such as full employment, generous safety nets for the poor and greater security.

Growth is a primary objective, but there are limits to what it can deliver. Growth at any price is not a sensible objective, nor is the attainment of maximum growth, particularly when this would involve a large increase in immigration. In setting medium-term targets, rather than asking what is the maximum growth an economy can reach and then working out the implications of this for policy, we should instead be asking what growth we wish to obtain and work backwards from there. There is need for a more active debate in Ireland about the optimal sustainable growth rate, as distinct from the maximum rate of growth.

GNP per capita has many limitations as an indicator of human welfare. It leaves out of account leisure, the environment and global warming, and misclassifies many inputs as outputs. Another limitation is that GNP per capita neglects important indicators of human welfare such as education and life expectancy. Despite its many failings, however, the GNP per capita statistic serves as a remarkably good proxy for more sophisticated measures of human welfare, as comparisons between rankings based on GNP per head and the UN Human Development Index demonstrate.

Equity in the sense of a fair distribution of income and an adequate level of income for all individuals is an important policy objective. The issue of equity is indeed a central aspect of most economic problems. In the Irish political domain concerns with equity and income distribution often outweigh concerns with economic efficiency in discussion of policy alternatives. Policymakers seek to reduce the evils of social exclusion and long-term unemployment by widening opportunities for education and work. Care should be taken, however, when deciding on the degree of redistribution to avoid penalising the achievers and stifling economic growth. Despite much research there is still no scientific way of determining what is an 'equitable' or 'fair' distribution of income.

It is also important to consider the 'well-being' or happiness of the community in the broadest sense when formulating economic policy. Beyond a certain income level there is little association between GNP per person and happiness and none at all between growth and spiritual development. This reinforces the need for policies that will seek to maximise societal welfare and that will deliver a pollution-free, low-crime and safe society.

Price stability is a policy objective that is both desired for its own sake and as a means to the end of attaining growth. There is now more conviction among politicians of the electoral advantages of running an economy in a way that maintains price stability. As a population ages, it is likely that the constituency in favour of price stability will grow. Politicians seem increasingly content to leave monetary policy to independent central banks. This new approach is helpful for price stability and good for the overall economy, since low inflation and output growth complement one another in the long run.

Has the adoption of price stability as a policy target been associated with a demonstrable improvement in economic efficiency and social stability? Many argue that it has. They would agree with Keynes that deviations from price stability, whether in the form of inflation or deflation, have inflicted great injuries; 'both evils are to be shunned'.[25] Hence the importance of ensuring that price stability, once restored, is thereafter maintained.

As we advance into the twenty-first century, we can expect competitiveness to occupy the high ground as a major secondary policy objective for the economy. Competitiveness covers a wider spectrum of economic variables. Irish policymakers used to focus on standard comparisons between cost and price indicators here and those in competitor countries. These indexes continue to be relevant. Within the space of a few years, the Republic has become a comparatively expensive location for visiting or doing business, and prices and pay rates have converged towards the higher end of the European spectrum, without any obvious detrimental effect on growth to date. So far so good. But in the longer run, it clearly will be necessary to justify these higher earnings by higher productivity. It is here that the broader definition of competitiveness comes into play. Competitiveness in this broader sense includes R&D, education, quality improvement, marketing and physical infrastructure – the intangible and often difficult to measure aspects that impact crucially on an economy's ability to perform well.

Endnotes

* The author wishes to thank the editors for their percipient and helpful comments. He has drawn on Chapters 2 and 12 of D. McAleese, *Economics for Business*, Financial Times Prentice Hall, London 2004.

[1] See Chapter 6 for a discussion of the difference between GNP and GDP, an issue of particular importance in Ireland. In most countries they give the same numbers but in the case of Ireland GNP (income) is around 15 per cent less than GDP (output), so we will use GNP for the remainder of this chapter.

[2] Estimated from data in National Economic and Social Council (NESC), *The Economic and Social Implications of Emigration,* Stationery Office, Dublin 1991.

[3] Department of Social Welfare, *Commission on Emigration and Other Population Problems,* Stationery Office, Dublin 1954, para. 473.

[4] J. K. Galbraith, *The Nature of Mass Poverty*, Harvard University Press, Cambridge MA 1979.

[5] NESC, *The Economic and Social Implications of Emigration,* Stationery Office, Dublin 1991.

[6] In the words of the Whitaker Report, 'emigration will not be checked nor will unemployment be permanently reduced until the rate of increase in national output is greatly accelerated', Department of Finance, *Programme for Economic Expansion,* Stationery Office, Dublin 1958, p. 7.

[7] R. Kennedy, quoted in *Finance and Development*, Washington, December 1993, 20.

[8] N. Stern, *The Economics of Climate Change: The Stern Review,* Cambridge University Press, Cambridge 2007.

[9] United Nations Development Programme, *Human Development Report,* Oxford University Press, New York 2007.

[10] Economic texts of this genre include E. Mishan, *The Cost of Economic Growth*, Penguin, Harmondsworth 1967; S. Linder and F. Hirsch, *The Social Limits to Growth*, Routledge, London 1977; R. Doubtwaite, *The Growth Illusion*, Lilliput, Dublin 1992; R. Frank, *Luxury Fever: Why Money Fails to Satisfy in an Era of Excess,* Free Press, New York 1999.

[11] This assumption excludes extreme cases such as Ascetics, who are happiest with a minimal income, and Scrooges, for whom income becomes more important the more they have of it.

[12] A. Okun, *Equality and Efficiency: The Big Trade-off,* Brookings Institution, Washington DC 1975.

13 J. Rawls, *A Theory of Justice*, Harvard University Press, Cambridge MA 1971.

14 NESC, *Opportunities, Challenges and Capacities for Choice*, Stationery Office, Dublin 1999, p. 51.

15 R. Nozick, *Anarchy, State and Utopia*, Basic Books, New York 1974.

16 *Economist*, London 5 November 1994.

17 Seminal contributions have come from R. Easterlin, 'Does economic growth improve the human lot? Some empirical evidence', in P. Davis and M. Reder (eds), *Nations and Households in Economic Growth*, Academic Press, New York and London 1974; and A. Oswald, 'Happiness and economic performance', *Economic Journal*, November 1997. See also D. Blanchflower and A. Oswald, 'Well-being over time in Britain and the USA', *Journal of Public Economics*, Autumn 2004. A readable and enlightening overview of the literature is provided in R. Layard, *Happiness: Lessons from a New Science*, Penguin Books, New York and London 2005.

18 R. Whately, *Introductory Lectures on Political Economy*, London 1831.

19 The upward bias in the US CPI has been estimated at 1.1 percentage points per annum, 0.5 of which is due to substitution bias. The substitution bias in the Irish CPI appears to be much smaller, 0.02 per cent, but we have no comparable Irish estimates for the other sources of bias. See also R. Somerville, 'Changes in relative consumer prices and the substitution bias of the Laspeyres Price Index: Ireland 1985–2001', *Economic and Social Review*, Spring 2004.

20 Deflation brings serious problems in its train and it is important to keep these in mind in evaluating policy options for the European Central Bank. Because it is a new institution, many feared that its urge to establish sound price-stability credentials might lead it to give too much weight to inflation and pay too little attention to the dangers of deflation. The ECB asserts that its commitment to price stability is 'symmetric'; deviations on either side of its price target are equally undesirable.

21 See P. Lane, 'Ireland and the deflation debate', *Irish Banking Review*, Winter 2003, and D. McAleese, *Economics for Business*, Financial Times Prentice Hall, London 2004, Box 12.1.

22 Enterprise Strategy Group, *Ahead of the Curve: Ireland's Place in the Global Economy*, Forfás, Dublin 2004, p. 21.

23 P. Honohan and P. Lane, 'Divergent inflation rates in EMU', *Economic Policy*, October 2003. An update of the data in 2007 confirms the original findings of this paper.

24 Economic Research Institute of Northern Ireland (ERINI), *Business Competitiveness in Northern Ireland*, Belfast January 2008.

25 J. M. Keynes, 'Economic consequences of the peace', *Collected Economic Writings*, Macmillan, London 1971, p. 149.

SECTION II

POLICY IMPLEMENTATION

CHAPTER 3

Role of Government: Rationale, Levels and Size

Philip R. Lane

1 INTRODUCTION

Chapter 2 established economic policy objectives for Ireland. The government, on the premise that it indeed cares about national welfare, is responsible for the attainment of these goals, either directly or in tandem with its international counterparts. The government's ability to achieve its policy goals is facilitated by the special powers assigned to the state, most notably its powers of compulsion. In this chapter, the role of government in pursuing these policy objectives is addressed.

The rest of the chapter is organised as follows. Section 2 reviews the theoretical basis for government intervention in the economy. The allocation of responsibilities across different levels of government is described in Section 3. In Section 4, the central role played by public expenditure and taxation policies is analysed. Section 5 addresses other policy instruments available to the government, while Section 6 discusses the economic and political factors determining the size of the government sector. Section 7 concludes the chapter.

2 RATIONALE FOR GOVERNMENT INTERVENTION

There are a number of classic arguments that provide a rationale for government intervention in the economy. The starting point is to recognise the absurdity of a no-government economy. A central authority and a *legal system* are necessary to permit the (implicit or explicit) contracts that govern all economic activity, for example through the design and enforcement of corporate and labour laws. Cross-country evidence and historical examples show that anarchy and the absence of a 'rule of law' result in very poor economic performance (and the emergence of private contract enforcement systems, such as Mafia-style organisations): the evidence from 'failed states' lends considerable support to these concerns.[1] Put another way, we can interpret economic activity as an elaborate game: as with any other game, a set of rules and a referee are required. The government is responsible for designing and enforcing the rules that determine permissible behaviour on the part of firms and consumers: the anarchic alternative would be unstable and highly deleterious for economic performance.

A second function relates to the efficient allocation of resources. A laissez-faire economy will not efficiently provide *pure public goods* (e.g. national defence). A public good is non-rival (it can be collectively consumed) and non-excludable (its benefits cannot be easily withheld from individuals): examples include the provision of national security and basic scientific research (a new mathematical formula can be used by everyone and, once published, is non-excludable). Non-excludability prevents market provision, since no one has an incentive to pay for a good if it can be freely consumed. The state must step in to provide such public goods and raise the resources required by levying taxation.

Similarly, market prices do not reflect *external effects*, with the result that activities generating positive externalities are under-produced and those generating negative externalities are overproduced. A good that produces a positive externality is similar to a public good, in that some of its benefits are non-excludable and accrue to others than just the direct consumer. However, such goods may be rivalrous and may be partially excludable, so that some private provision occurs even if the level of production is inadequate.

The road network is a good illustration of a positive externality: the gain to building an extra kilometre of motorway increases the productivity of other parts of the road network that become more accessible. One obvious example of a negative externality is environmental pollution. A second example is provided by commonly held resources such as fisheries, whereby individuals are not responsible for the maintenance of a sustainable stock. To promote goods that generate positive externalities, the state may engage in direct provision or offer subsidies. In contrast, it may impose quotas or taxes on goods that generate negative external effects.

Other sources of market failure include *monopoly power* and *imperfect information*. The former means that prices will be too high and output too low relative to the competitive outcome. The latter means that many credit and insurance markets are missing or incomplete, since it is impossible for private firms to adequately evaluate projects, accurately calculate default risks and monitor the behaviour of individual agents. Such market failures provide a prima facie case for some kind of government intervention, either by direct provision or through subsidisation.

However, the desirability of actual intervention is tempered by 'government failure': it is not clear that, in many cases, governments can deliver a more efficient outcome than that generated by even imperfect markets. Electoral pressures, interest group lobbying, perverse incentives in administration; corruption, restrictive practices and inflexible procedures in the public sector, and poor management skills may all lead to welfare-decreasing interventions in the economy. Accordingly, the optimal degree of government intervention must balance the prospective gains against potential implementation problems.

Even if free markets delivered a perfectly efficient outcome, *distributional considerations* would still justify government intervention. The income distribution attained by a market economy is conditional on the initial distribution of endowments (both monetary and individual characteristics such as intelligence, good health and family background). Being lucky in one's choice of parents is an important determinant of success in a market economy: for example, in Ireland and elsewhere, educational attainment levels are highly correlated with family income levels and social background (see also Chapter 12). Moreover, economic outcomes have a random element. The weather influences the success or failure of many agricultural projects and many entrepreneurs recognise the role played by fortune in creating viable new businesses.

Accordingly, voters typically demand that the government redistributes income in order to protect the poorly endowed and the unlucky. However, the ability of the government to redistribute income is constrained along two dimensions. First, excessively high taxation depresses incentives, reducing the level of income and growth rates. Second, mobile factors (capital, highly skilled workers) will leave jurisdictions that impose harsh tax burdens.

3 LEVELS OF GOVERNMENT

Different levels of government can intervene in the economy. Although the traditional focus has been on national governments, global, European and local levels of government are increasingly important.

Global Governance

For some issues, global levels of government are better placed. Ireland also participates in the World Trade Organisation, is a member of the International Monetary Fund and World Bank and subscribes to various international policy agreements, such as the Kyoto Protocol on climate change.

The driving force behind global levels of governance is that the globalisation of many economic activities enhances efficiency and is facilitated by a common set of international rules. For instance, it would be an extremely tedious procedure for each country to negotiate bilateral agreements with all its potential trading partners: the World Trade Organisation and the various regional trade agreements greatly reduce the transaction costs in ensuring trade liberalisation.

Similarly, in tackling problems that are fundamentally global in character, non-co-ordinated national policy responses make little sense.[2] The most obvious example is the climate change problem: carbon emissions in each country symmetrically affect the global climate. However, similar considerations apply in the domain of public health: high levels of air travel mean that a virus that emerges in one area can quickly be transmitted around the world (the SARS crisis in East

Asia in 2002–2003 is one example). To the extent that some security threats are global in nature (for example, the control of nuclear weapons and the risks posed by dissident groups that seek to disrupt global economic and social systems), there is also a global level to defence policies. Finally, large international income inequalities, especially the extreme poverty of the 'bottom billion' of the global population (primarily in sub-Saharan Africa) constitutes a global problem across many dimensions.[3] In addition to the ethical issues, it is in the self-interest of advanced economies to promote international development, in view of the interconnections between extreme poverty, political instability, mass migrations and public health.

Moreover, the globalisation of economic activity also makes national or regional policy actions less effective: for example, high tax rates or excessive regulation will prompt mobile factors to relocate to more business-friendly regimes. Conversely, national subsidies or tax breaks distort international location decisions, since a firm may opt to produce even in an inefficient location if it receives sufficiently high compensation from the host government. For these reasons, co-ordination of international policies can potentially restore the ability of governments to tax mobile factors and avoid undesirable 'subsidy auctions' in competing for footloose firms.

That said, the difficulty with international policy co-ordination is that there is not always consensus on the correct policy. Preferences may legitimately differ across countries on important issues such as: the appropriate level of taxation; the ideal level of social protection; and the optimal degree of risk aversion in food regulation. Accordingly, global governance arrangements are more easily achieved on technocratic issues such as world trade and financial systems, with less progress made on social issues. For this reason, it is sometimes argued that the development of global governance has been unbalanced: much progress has been made on co-operation in economic policy but with less effective co-ordination of labour or environmental regulations. However, in the absence of a directly elected 'world government', it is unlikely that much progress can be made on controversial issues that are the subject of much disagreement both within and across countries.[4]

These factors mean that global levels of governance are likely to remain quite circumscribed in the absence of sufficient consensus on various issues across sovereign nations. In terms of new initiatives, the main area where global action may occur is in relation to climate change, in view of the emerging consensus on the nature and urgency of the problem. Even in that domain, the capacity to forge a global agreement that tackles global warming in an efficient yet equitable manner is open to question. One basic problem is that a fair global solution plausibly involves a significant transfer of funds from the advanced economies to the developing world, to compensate for the fact that the accumulated stock of carbon emissions has been primarily generated by high-income countries over many decades of industrial activity: achieving agreement on the scale of such redistribution will be difficult. A second problem is that it is difficult and costly to impose sanctions on non-compliant nations, so any global initiative must rely on softer methods of promoting compliance – for example, peer pressure across member governments, plus monitoring by national and international 'civic society' groups such as Friends of the Earth, Greenpeace and other activist organisations.

EU Governance

EU membership is the most important international commitment of the Irish government. Although the scale of intergovernmental co-operation at the EU level faces many of the difficulties encountered at global levels of governance, the scope for establishing common policies is much greater at the EU level. This reflects the very close economic and social ties across the member countries, plus the elaborate institutional structure that has been developed (European Commission, Council of Ministers, European Parliament) to promote and sustain policy making at the EU level. Moreover, since member states bargain over many issues, decision making is facilitated by the multi-dimensional nature of political relations among the member states: for instance, some undesirable regulation in one area may be accepted in exchange for a concession on another issue. In other cases, the level of disagreement may be so strong that co-ordination is not possible, with countries retaining independent national policies. Although a national veto still remains on some policy issues (e.g. taxation), majority voting now applies in many areas. This trend will be reinforced over the next few years, if the Lisbon Treaty, which extends the scope of qualified majority voting, is ratified.

In order to create a single market, EU law guarantees the 'four freedoms': the free movement of goods; the free movement of services and freedom of establishment; the free movement of persons (and citizenship), including free movement of workers; and the free movement of capital. In addition, EU competition law also now sharply restricts national autonomy in industrial policy. For instance, EU governments can now only invest in state-owned enterprises on a commercial basis: rescuing loss-making firms for non-economic reasons is no longer permitted. In addition, large public contracts must be advertised at an EU-wide level, rather than directly allocated to domestic firms. In these ways, the EU can be interpreted as an international 'agency of restraint' that promotes more efficient allocations and depoliticises many economic decisions.

That said, the difficulty with international policy co-ordination is that there is not always consensus on the correct policy. Preferences may legitimately differ across countries on important issues such as: the appropriate level of taxation; the ideal level of social protection; and the optimal degree of risk aversion in food regulation. Since member nations bargain over many issues, some undesirable regulations may be accepted in exchange for concessions on other issues. In other cases, the level of disagreement may be so strong that co-ordination is not possible, with countries retaining independent national policies.

A common criticism of international policy co-ordination is that it leads to a 'democratic deficit', with decisions made at a level that is too far removed from ordinary voters. The EU has traditionally suffered from this objection, since policy decisions have been made at intergovernmental Council of Ministers meetings that are held in private with no review by national parliaments.

The new Treaty of Lisbon seeks to redress this imbalance in several ways. First, the design of the treaty was extensively debated in a highly participatory Constitutional Convention before the final articles were agreed. In Ireland, this debate was further widened through the activities of the National Forum on Europe that held a large number of public meetings to improve awareness and permit debate on European policy issues. Second, the treaty is intended to improve democratic accountability. For instance, major EU policy decisions will now be reviewed by national parliaments, in addition to the European Parliament. In addition, the European Council of Ministers will conduct more of its business in public session and it will have a 'public face' in that the President of the European Council will be elected for a term of two and a half years and cannot hold any national mandate. Democratic accountability is further improved by the closer alignment of national population sizes and relative voting power in the Council of Ministers under the new treaty.

As indicated, many decisions concerning government spending and taxation remain at the national level, providing scope for significant variation in the level and nature of government intervention across member countries. Following the earlier discussion, harmonisation of tax rates on mobile capital is advocated by some member countries. However, there is little agreement on the appropriate tax rate: a high capital tax rate may be progressive and reduce pressure on other parts of the tax base but has a negative effect on growth performance. Ireland has opted for a low-tax strategy and resists pressure to harmonise rates at a higher level. Indeed, the gains to a low-tax strategy have been augmented by the persistence of higher rates in other EU countries, as capital shifts to Ireland from other locations. Moreover, the further widening of EU membership to encompass the lower-income countries from Central and Eastern Europe makes it unlikely that significant further EU-wide harmonisation of fiscal policies will be agreed in the near term.

In 1999, a subset of 11 EU members adopted the euro as a single currency. By 2008, 15 EU members had joined the euro area, with further members expected to join over the next decade. A monetary union offers microeconomic efficiency gains and facilitates the development of a deep, liquid capital market. Moreover, a large bloc is plausibly insulated from destabilising speculative attacks on its currency, permitting lower average interest rates. A core feature of European Monetary Union is that the member governments have delegated the operation of monetary policy to an independent agency – the European Central Bank. Perhaps the most important advantage is that a supranational central bank may be more effectively insulated from political pressures than are national monetary authorities.

The delegation of technocratic forms of government intervention, such as the conduct of monetary policy, to semi-autonomous institutions can be interpreted as a useful agency of restraint that ties the hands of political leaders who face enormous short-term pressures to adopt populist policies that may damage the economy in the long term. Democratic accountability is ensured through several mechanisms: the mandate of the ECB is fixed by treaty; the President of the ECB testifies before the European Parliament on a regular basis; and the ECB is in regular dialogue with the European Commission and the Euro Group of finance ministers.

However, a 'one size fits all' monetary policy may itself be a source of instability for member countries with business cycles that are not highly correlated with the core of the euro zone. In the early years of EMU, Ireland fell into this category: in view of our high growth rates, interest rates were inappropriately low and excessive inflation was the result. In the other direction, countries such as Germany, Portugal and Italy may have preferred a looser monetary policy at various times, in view of poor domestic performance in these economies. For Ireland, the open question is our capacity to adjust to a major domestic contraction inside the EMU framework.

Local Government

At the other end, some policy issues are being devolved from national to local and regional levels of government. Local government plausibly has an information advantage in designing and implementing policies that better reflect the preferences and needs of local residents. A closer relationship with the electorate may also improve the responsiveness and accountability of government. However, decentralisation also brings risks, especially if fiscal and functional responsibilities are not clearly allocated between the centre and periphery. In Ireland, local government has traditionally played a very limited role. However, with the switch towards greater local financing and autonomy in the provision of services (e.g. waste collection, water services), the trend is for greater diversity in local government in Ireland. The application of the subsidiarity principle is also more evident at the EU level: there is greater recognition that the EU should focus its energies on those policy areas where co-operation is most effective, with the return of some policy issues to national governments. For instance, with the move to direct payments in subsidising the agricultural sector, it is predicted that responsibility for the agricultural sector will be shifted from Brussels to national levels of government (see Chapter 10).

Finally, in light of the improved political climate since the 1988 Good Friday Agreement, progress has been made in improving policy co-operation between the Republic of Ireland and Northern Ireland, with considerable scope for yet further integration. Significant scale economies can be achieved in areas such as tourism (e.g. with the creation of the all-island Tourism Ireland marketing organisation) and network externalities can be better exploited by more efficiently integrating the transport and energy networks between the two jurisdictions. Moreover, the economic success of the Republic of Ireland has led to some reorientation of activity in Northern Ireland, with a greater focus on pursuing cross-border business opportunities. Under the Good Friday Agreement, a number of intergovernmental agencies have been established to facilitate enhanced policy co-operation in areas such as the environment, agriculture, education, health, tourism and transport.

4 PUBLIC EXPENDITURE AND TAXATION

There are three types of government spending: public consumption, transfers and public investment. The first category incorporates the provision of government services such as the civil service, education, health, the justice system and defence. The second includes social welfare payments, payments to the EU central budget and debt interest payments. The third refers to spending on infrastructure (e.g. the road network) and on the buildings and equipment associated with the provision of government services.

Public Consumption

Education and healthcare are the major items of public consumption. We only briefly review these sectors, since they are covered in more detail in Chapters 11 and 12. Spending on education and healthcare is in part motivated by redistributive considerations, to ensure access for all to at least a minimal level of services. At an efficiency level, private financing of education is plagued by credit problems and the healthcare sector suffers from myriad asymmetric information problems. Finally, promoting education arguably confers positive externalities and is necessary to a healthy democracy, since political participation is positively related to education levels. Although these arguments justify public financing of the education and healthcare sectors, this need not involve monopoly public provision of these services: for instance, the state could provide vouchers to parents that could be used to pay fees at private schools or insurance premiums to private healthcare companies.

Transfers

The welfare budget is the largest component of transfer spending. Some transfers can be justified by imperfections in insurance markets. For example, private insurance schemes are unlikely to provide fairly priced protection against the risk of unemployment. However, the stronger motivation behind transfers is redistribution: voters are unwilling to allow the incomes of the unemployed, the sick or the old to fall below a minimum level. In designing a welfare system, there is a clear trade-off between the level of benefits and the need to provide incentives to seek employment (in the case of unemployment benefit) or to save privately for retirement (in the case of pensions).

Producer subsidies are another kind of transfer. Although these have been declining in recent years, subsidies are still used to attract multinational corporations and support local start-ups. One problem with producer subsidies is that behaviour is distorted: rather than focusing on innovation and maximising profitability, entrepreneurs may divert resources to lobbying the government for subsidies. However, the worst excesses of this kind of behaviour have been sharply circumscribed by stricter EU regulations on the allocation of state aids to industry. Most notably, the European airline industry has historically been a major recipient of state subsidies, but the European Commission now regularly prohibits the protection of 'national champions'. A second problem with producer subsidies is that Ireland competes with other EU countries for footloose firms: this bidding war may result in the successful country suffering a 'winner's curse', having to offer a subsidy larger than any potential benefits. With the rapid decline in unemployment, the structure of Irish producer subsidies has shifted from targeting job creation to encouraging strategic sectors with the potential for high growth.

Public Investment

Public investment has two economic functions: the provision of (a) public inputs that directly raise the productivity of the economy; and (b) public amenities that improve the quality of life and are valued by the community (see Chapter 8). Of course, the same project may contribute to both objectives. For example, an improved road network not only improves economic performance but the elimination of traffic jams is to be welcomed for its own sake in terms of reducing stress levels. Conversely, cultural projects and sports facilities not only improve the quality of leisure time but may indirectly improve economic performance by making Ireland a more attractive location for internationally mobile workers.[5]

The state plays a central role in ensuring the provision of infrastructure, such as the transport network or the planning framework for housing and urban development. Infrastructure is fundamentally characterised by external effects: the value of a network is greater than the sum of its parts. For this reason, the state plays a leading role in the planning and design of networks in transport, utilities, housing and urban development.

In addition to its planning role, the state also directly provides much infrastructure. For instance, although privately funded toll roads and bridges can make a contribution to the overall transport network, public good and equity considerations mean that much infrastructural investment is financed by the state. Direct provision also solves severe co-ordination problems: for instance, a laissez-faire system may see wasteful duplication in those areas likely to generate the highest toll revenues.

In recent years, infrastructural investment has been high in Ireland, in a bid to redress the severe infrastructural deficit that emerged from a combination of low investment during the 1980s and early 1990s and rapid economic and population growth (see Chapter 8). The *National Development Plan 2007–2013* sets out an ambitious programme, with the objective of both improving the physical infrastructure (new roads, Luas extension, Dublin metro project, capital projects in the health and education sectors, new social housing) and the 'knowledge' infrastructure (government investment in human capital and scientific research).

However, it may have been more effective to adopt a more gradual rate of increase in public investment. The pro-cyclical timing of the acceleration in public investment can lead to high inflation in the construction sector, especially if it is already under pressure due to rising private investment activity. The scale of the increase in public investment may also run into administrative, planning and legal bottlenecks that further reduce returns. Over the medium term, it is certainly the case that a stable level of public investment is far preferable to the 'stop-go' cycle that has historically characterised Irish public investment dynamics.

The healthy state of the public finances means that much of the investment has been met by tax revenues. However, some of the investment takes the form of public-private partnerships (PPPs), while tolls have partly financed some road and bridge projects. Although private sources of finance are typically more expensive (since the government can borrow at lower rates than private firms), PPPs do enable the use of scarce private managerial talent to achieve social goals. Moreover, the PPP contract typically includes appropriate penalty clauses, such that the risk of cost overruns or time delays is potentially transferred to the private operator. There have been only a few PPP projects in Ireland, and the UK experience has been that the transfer of risk to the private operator is not always successfully executed. However, the pressure to increase public investment is sufficiently strong that the PPP route may become more widely used in the future.

An important element in efficient provision of public infrastructure is that all projects are subjected to a comprehensive cost-benefit analysis. Economic analysis has a large part to play in such evaluations. However, especially with respect to the provision of public amenities, variation in individual preferences between private goods and public amenities means that evaluation of such projects also has to take into account social and political factors in addition to the economic dimension. In Ireland, full cost-benefit analyses have not been applied to all projects in a transparent manner, such that the rationale for some investment decisions is not always clear.

Taxation

Chapter 4 will focus on taxation and the public finances, so we will only briefly discuss the role of taxation as a policy instrument. At one level, the main impetus for taxation is to finance public expenditure and the design of the taxation system is accordingly targeted at collecting revenues in a manner that least distorts economic decisions. However, there is a secondary role for tax policies in order to correct market distortions – such tax interventions can be made 'revenue neutral' by rebating the revenues collected through a reduction in other taxes.

In relation to environmental protection, the role of taxation as a method of altering behaviour is widely recognised. For instance, Ireland has been a pioneer in reducing usage of plastic shopping bags, through the introduction of a small levy in 2002 that quickly converted most of the population to re-usable bags. Similarly, bin charges have induced households to recycle more and avoid unnecessary packaging. At a wider level, it is broadly recognised that a carbon tax has a key role to play in reducing carbon emissions, both domestically and internationally. The design of a suitable carbon tax is one of the primary goals of the new Commission on Taxation that was established in 2008 to propose reforms of the Irish taxation system.

Along another dimension, user charges may be required to ensure efficient use of congested networks. In Ireland, there has been traditional resistance to charges for utilities such as the water network or waste collection. However, it is likely that such charges will have to be extended over time to include even traffic taxes to relieve pressure on limited road networks, especially in the Dublin area. Designing a scheme that retains access for low-income households is a difficult challenge.

Another form of tax intervention is the deployment of tax breaks to encourage certain types of activity. In Ireland, tax breaks have been widely used to promote construction in certain areas and industries. In addition, tax breaks have been also used to promote the arts (income from artistic activity is tax free up to a generous threshold limit), the film industry and the bloodstock industry. In general, it is difficult to make the case for tax breaks – if an activity is evaluated as deserving of a subsidy, it is more transparent to offer a direct subsidy rather than to provide indirect support through the tax system. Moreover, tax breaks are of most value to high-income households, so the exploitation of tax breaks can lead to a regressive element in the tax system in relation to the highest earners. For such reasons, there is considerable political momentum to restrict the use of tax breaks.

5 OTHER POLICY INSTRUMENTS

State-Owned Enterprises

State-owned enterprises, ranging from Aer Lingus to the ESB, have historically played a major role in the Irish economy. Government ownership in the commercial sector may be explained by a number of factors. First, underdeveloped capital markets prevented private entrepreneurs from raising the finance required to build profitable firms in capital intensive sectors such as transport. Second, rather than implement regulation of monopolies (as in the USA), European countries tended to favour government ownership of utilities such as electricity production and telecommunications. Third, state ownership was seen as facilitating the pursuit of social goals such as regionalisation and access to cheap services. Finally, in many countries, state-owned enterprises have facilitated political patronage, with decisions concerning employment and investment being manipulated for electoral purposes.

In recent years, there has been a global shift towards the privatisation of such state-owned firms (see Chapter 9). The development of sophisticated capital markets now allows private entrepreneurs to finance efficiently even large-scale ventures. Market liberalisation, sometimes mandated by EU law, has reduced fears of monopoly power in many sectors. Moreover, as indicated earlier in the chapter, the EU prohibition on state aid to rescue non-viable firms means that such firms can no longer be protected for political reasons. Finally, technological innovations, such as in the telecommunications sector, now make it more feasible to have multiple competitors even in 'network' industries.

Where monopoly power is likely to persist, governments typically now prefer to regulate private firms as an alternative to direct state ownership (see Chapter 9). Similarly, social goals (such as the provision of cheap postal services to remote areas) can be achieved by a combination of subsidies and regulation, without requiring actual government ownership. Finally, with accumulating evidence on the performance of privatised industries in other countries, ideological resistance to private ownership has weakened over time.

Another reason for the shift towards privatisation is that government ownership may actually be detrimental to performance. Managers and workers in a state-owned enterprise know that they need not seek to maximise profits, since there is no threat of loss of control to outside investors, and hence have a weak incentive to behave efficiently or control costs.

In addition, as indicated earlier, the government may direct state-owned enterprises to pursue non-commercial objectives, such as providing employment for supporters of the government or locating in disadvantaged areas.[6] A decline in clientelism and an improvement in the transparency of the political system have weakened the incentive of the government to manipulate the semi-state sector to achieve such non-economic goals. Even in the absence of privatisation, there are benefits to depoliticisation of these enterprises. Commercialisation of many Irish state-owned enterprises occurred in the 1980s, with significant improvements in performance. More recently, the privatisation process gained pace, with the disposal of the government interest in firms such as Eircom, Aer Lingus, ICC and ACC. The privatisation process may also extend to health insurance (sale of VHI) and parts of the public transport system.

In designing a privatisation process, the government faces several conflicts. To maximise revenues, the government should seek the highest issue price or permit a concentration of ownership among large shareholders, but this may conflict with a social goal to broaden the shareholder base. To secure the co-operation of powerful unions, the government may feel compelled to offer sharply discounted shares to incumbent workers in the state-owned firms and insert worker protection clauses into the privatisation contract, even if this reduces the value of the firm. Of course, the privatisation process should be fully transparent, to prevent state assets being sold at artificially low prices to politically connected business interests.

Privatisation generates a one-time cash windfall for the government. However, it is important to understand that the net impact on the government's balance sheet is much smaller: by transferring ownership, the government no longer receives dividends from the firm, reducing future government revenues. That said, to the extent that the firm is worth more in private hands and the buyout of incumbent workers is not too costly, the net financial gain of privatisation to the government will be positive.

Regulation and Competition Policy

The privatisation of firms with considerable monopoly power (such as Eircom), together with the principle of operating the remaining state-owned firms (such as the ESB and Bord Gáis) on a commercial basis means that the role of regulatory agencies has taken on new prominence in recent years (see Chapter 9). Ireland has a large number of sectoral regulators (such as the Commission on Energy Regulation, the Commission on Communications Regulation and the Commission on Aviation Regulation) that seek to prevent abuses of monopoly power by monitoring market conduct and retaining powers of approval over the prices charged by firms in these industries. While regulators rely heavily on economic theory to identify instances of market abuse or excessive price mark-ups, it is not always straightforward to establish the scope for greater competition in certain sectors or the best methods to encourage the entry of new firms. Moreover, especially in network industries, incumbent firms may frustrate efforts to reduce barriers to entry, especially by making it difficult for new entrants to obtain access to key distribution channels.

An important problem in the Irish context is that regulatory decisions are subject to judicial review, such that much regulatory energy is diverted to legal battles with regulated firms that seek to overturn decisions through submissions to the courts. The considerable resources of highly profitable firms are also deployed in public relations campaigns that may have the intent of placing pressure on regulators to favour the interests of producers over consumers.

Even in sectors with many suppliers, market inefficiencies may arise if mergers and acquisitions lead to a reduction in the number of firms or if incumbent firms collude (explicitly or implicitly) to raise prices or erect barriers to entry. Accordingly, the Competition Authority has an important role to play in ensuring that open competition is preserved. In recent years, the Competition Authority has received more powers to enforce competition and the rate and intensity of investigations into anti-competitive practices have increased. Moreover, the Competition Authority has been pro-active in researching and analysing the level of competition in many important services sectors (Ireland scores poorly in international comparisons in relation to the level of competition in sheltered services sectors), which has led to reforms in the legal profession and other sectors.

In addition to preventing abuses of monopoly power, the government also regulates many spheres of economic activity in order to redress other perceived failures of a laissez-faire system. Informational asymmetries justify safety regulations, since individual consumers are ill-equipped to evaluate products that potentially carry high risks (air travel, processed foods and machinery, to name just three examples) – accordingly, the markets for such goods can only operate effectively under the assurance of government-approved safety regulations (see

Chapter 9). Of course, the trade-off faced in such regulatory systems is ensuring that such standards are not distorted in order to discourage innovation, restrict entry by new firms or act as a barrier to international trade. Regulation is also employed in pursuit of social goals, through the establishment of agencies, such as the Equality Authority and the National Disability Agency, that act to ensure that businesses do not operate in ways that are prohibited under the relevant social legislation.

Finally, regulation plays an important part in environmental policy. For asymmetric information reasons, a market system may not be able to ensure that all firms produce using environmentally responsible techniques – accordingly, firms are monitored to ensure that production does not violate environmental standards. In relation to managing climate change, the allocation of carbon quotas is widely used as an alternative or a complement to a carbon tax. The relative merits of 'quantity' regulation (quotas) versus 'price' regulation (taxes) depend on the precise scenario, but a hybrid system that employs both tools may be the prudent choice when faced with a very uncertain economic environment, which is surely the case in relation to the climate change phenomenon (see Chapter 4).

Social Partnership

The role played by the social partnership process in contributing to the success of the Irish economy has been widely debated.[7] While there were various forms of national agreement during the 1970s, these were unstable and had fallen into abeyance by the early 1980s, with the depressed economy characterised by poor industrial relations and a high incidence of employer-worker disputes in both the private and public sectors. By the mid-1980s, the severe economic crisis had generated a widespread desire for radical reform. One possible route was to adopt the UK reform model (a decentralisation of pay setting, accompanied by a reduction in the power of trade unions). However, using the foundations of the National Economic and Social Council (NESC) *Strategy for Development 1986–1990* report, a consensual approach to reform was adopted. Since 1987, there has been a succession of national agreements that are negotiated between the government, trade unions, employer federations and a host of other representative groups. Although this approach has been criticised for diminishing the role of elected politicians in formulating policies, it can be argued that it simply acknowledges the reality that many policies are likely to be ineffective without the co-operation of employers and trade unions; moreover, ultimate decisions remain the responsibility of the elected government. Social partnership in Ireland is related to the 'corporatist' tradition of collective bargaining between unions and employer federations in a number of Continental European countries but the scale of government involvement and the range of topics covered under the social partnership agreements is unusually extensive.

While the main focus of these agreements has been on establishing national guidelines on wage increases, the remit of social partnership has also extended to the negotiation of labour protection regulations and a range of social policy initiatives. In recognition of the long-term nature of such reforms, a ten-year framework agreement *Towards 2016* was agreed between the social partners in 2006, although detailed negotiations on pay and implementation issues continue to occur at higher frequency (every two to three years). A particular innovation in this agreement was the introduction of a lifecycle framework, in order to target the appropriate social and developmental policies for individuals at different life stages (children, young adults, people of working age, older people) and people with disabilities.

In relation to the core pay agreement, the social partnership process is clearly important in determining public sector pay – although the baseline pay increases are further adjusted via two mechanisms that are exclusive to the public sector (the benchmarking process and the Review Body on Higher Remuneration in the Public Sector). It is not so clear that the national pay agreements are very important in determining pay in the private sector, since firms and workers deviate from the national agreements in line with sectoral requirements: in a market-based economy, pay and conditions in the private sector are ultimately determined at the firm level.

However, especially in the context of EMU, there may be occasions under which a collective approach to pay determination may be helpful in dealing with macroeconomic problems. In particular, there are scenarios in which workers may accept that a loss of competitiveness requires a collective fall in wages: it is less disruptive to achieve this via a co-ordinated agreement than through decentralised pay negotiations. For this reason, there may be considerable value in retaining the social partnership framework, even beyond its role in the determination of social policies, labour market regulations and public sector pay.

A State Investment Fund

A recent innovation in Ireland has been to establish the National Pensions Reserve Fund (NPRF) in order to finance future state pension liabilities. Rather than exclusively using budget surpluses to pay down the public debt, one per cent of GNP each year is allocated to the NPRF to invest in a portfolio of financial assets. The dividend income and capital gains on these assets can then be employed to finance pension expenditures, as a partial alternative to raising future taxation.

However, the precise design of such a fund is critically important for its success and political acceptability. A major concern is the politicisation of investment decisions. At the extreme, this might involve discriminating between domestic projects on the basis of the political connections of entrepreneurs. Less obviously, it may induce the allocation of an excessive portfolio share to domestic over foreign assets, with lobby groups pressing the state fund to support domestic firms and workers.

This is a very difficult problem. On the one side, it is desirable to minimise political interference in the operation of the fund. On the other side, in a democratic society, the operators of a state fund must be politically accountable.

Much of the international debate concerning the delegation of public tasks to independent agencies, such as central banks and industry regulators, is relevant here. An important principle is that the government defines the objectives of the agency but the agency is given wide scope in the pursuit of these objectives, subject to the issuing of regular public reports justifying any deviations from targeted outcomes.

It should be clear that the correct investment approach for a state pension fund is to overwhelmingly hold overseas assets. First, this strategy minimises the politicisation problem. Second, it is a sensible hedge. Imagine if the state pension fund held domestic assets: in the event of a domestic downturn, the public finances would be hit not only by a decline in tax revenues but also by a contraction in investment income. By holding foreign assets, in contrast, 'tax base risk' is offset. Third, the state pension fund would be large relative to the domestic market but tiny in global terms such that investing overseas improves flexibility and liquidity in portfolio management.

The initial investment strategy of the NPRF has largely respected these principles. Its equity and bond holdings are overwhelmingly international, with only modest holdings of domestic securities. However, it has announced plans to play a larger role in funding domestic infrastructural investment, which increases the risk that the fund's strategy will be subject to political pressure.

6 SIZE OF GOVERNMENT: ECONOMIC AND POLITICAL FACTORS

In evaluating tax and expenditure policies, a fundamental question is the optimal size of government. If the government is too large, it makes sense to prune expenditure and cut taxation; conversely, increases in spending and taxation are required if the government is too small to achieve desired policy outcomes. Of course, determining the optimal size of government is a difficult challenge and involves both economic and political dimensions.

Trends and International Comparisons

Although the government can also exert much influence through legislation, regulation, social partnership and moral suasion, measures of public expenditure and taxation are most widely employed as imperfect proxies for the size of government. However, there has been much interest in recent years in measuring other dimensions of government intervention in the economy. For instance, the World Bank's *Doing Business* survey ranks countries on many dimensions of government regulation and bureaucracy while the OECD maintains a comprehensive database on regulation in its member countries. As shown in Table 3.1, Ireland scores quite well along some dimensions of these indices but its rank is quite low in areas such as the regulations concerning the ease of employing workers and enforcing contracts.

Table 3.1

Business Environment[1]: Ranking of Selected Countries

	Doing business	Starting a business	Employing workers	Protecting investors	Enforcing contracts
Singapore	1	9	1	2	4
New Zealand	2	3	13	1	13
USA	3	4	1	5	8
Hong Kong	4	13	23	3	1
Denmark	5	18	10	19	30
UK	6	6	21	9	24
Canada	7	2	19	5	43
Ireland	8	5	37	5	39
Australia	9	1	8	51	11
Iceland	10	14	42	64	4

Source: World Bank, *Doing Business Survey* (www.doingbusiness.org).
[1] In terms of government regulation and bureaucracy.

In relation to levels of public expenditure, Table 3.2 shows that the share of total government spending relative to GNP in Ireland has declined dramatically since its peak in 1985. However, recent years have seen some reversal in this trend. In terms of the composition of public expenditure, a dramatic decline in debt-interest payments as a share of GNP has been a major driver of the shrinkage in government size. Other factors have also contributed to a decline in the size of government spending. First, Ireland's relatively young population means that public expenditure on pensions is naturally lower, which is reinforced by the relatively greater role played by the private sector in financing pensions in Ireland. Second, lower unemployment in Ireland means that social benefit payments are a smaller burden. Third, Ireland has fewer defence commitments than the major countries, so military expenditures are lower. These factors are reflected in international comparative data, which show that Ireland has the lowest ratio of

Table 3.2

Composition of Public Expenditure[1] (as a proportion of gross national income)

	Total	Consumption	Investment	Interest	Social security
1980	54.6	19.9	4.2	6.3	11.1
1985	58.6	20.1	4.2	10.8	15.8
1990	46.7	17.9	2.3	8.5	12.8
1995	45.6	18.1	2.5	5.9	13.0
2000	36.6	16.0	4.1	2.3	9.3
2005	40.1	18.6	4.0	1.2	10.7

Source: OECD, *OECD Economic Outlook Database*, OECD, Paris 2007.
[1] The category 'other' is not included in the table.

total government spending to gross national income among the advanced European countries, even if it is high relative to the ratios in countries such as the United States and Japan. For example, in 2006 the percentage for Ireland was 39.6, similar to those for Canada and Spain, above that for Japan (35.6) but well below those for Denmark (50.5), France (52.9), Italy (50.2) and Sweden (55.3). The figures for Germany, Netherlands and the UK were all around 45 per cent.

Causes of Variations in Size of Government
Wagner's Law
Many factors contribute to variation across countries and over time in government spending. First, across countries and over time, there is a clear positive correlation between the level of income per capita and the share of public expenditure in national income: this tendency is known as Wagner's Law. One reason is that public subsidies to health care, education and pensions may be interpreted as luxury items, with an income elasticity of demand greater than unity.

As incomes grow, voters demand more of these services, placing upward pressure on public spending. However, the damaging costs of excessive taxation place an upper bound on the sustainable level of spending on these items. The fiscal reforms attempted by many countries in recent years may in part be a result of having approached this upper bound. The increasing mobility of capital and skilled labour also places limits on the feasible size of government, by placing a cap on sustainable tax rates.

Baumol's Disease
Another driving force behind upward pressure on public spending is the so-called Baumol's Disease, named after the American economist who proposed the hypothesis.[8] Baumol's hypothesis is that an economy can be divided into progressive and non-progressive sectors. Productivity gains in the progressive sector drive up wages, which must be matched by the non-progressive sector if it is to attract labour. This phenomenon has clearly been operating in Ireland in recent years: strong productivity improvements in the manufacturing, software and financial services sectors have led to rapid wage growth.

Provision of education and healthcare services plausibly falls into the non-progressive sector, on the basis that productivity growth in such labour-intensive sectors is limited. It follows that the implicit relative price of these services must rise, as wages increase without a compensating improvement in productivity. If the income elasticity of demand for these services exceeds the price elasticity of demand, the ratio of public spending to national income will increase, even if the volume of services provided is unchanged. In order to retain labour, it has been necessary to significantly raise the salaries of teachers and health workers. For this reason, the rapid increase in education and healthcare spending in Ireland in recent years has mostly been absorbed by rising wages, with a much smaller improvement in the level of services (see Chapters 11 and 12).

It is wrong to assume, however, that productivity growth in publicly financed sectors is impossible, as another factor in slow improvement is the lack of competitive pressure to produce efficiently. Improved management, stronger cost controls and the outsourcing of some services may help force more rapid productivity growth in these sectors. Moreover, recent technological change may enable new productivity gains. For example, Internet-based courses and learning aids may be feasible in many education sectors, while the electronic transmission of X-rays and other medical information permits the remote provision of medical expertise. An important challenge for policymakers is to ensure such new technologies are exploited, even in the face of resistance from traditional suppliers, such as public sector unions.

Demographic Factors
Demographic factors are also important in determining the level of public spending. In the 1970s and 1980s, Ireland had an unusually large cohort of children, placing pressure on the education budget. At the other end of the life cycle, many countries now face an increase in the proportion of old people in the population, with attendant growth in healthcare and pension expenditures. Currently, Ireland enjoys an unusually favourable demographic profile, with the vast bulk of the population in the working age bracket, which allows either a decline in government spending or an improvement in the quality of services and pension levels. The problems associated with the greying of the population is not expected to significantly hit Ireland until 2010–25 (see also Chapter 5).

Automatic Stabilisers √
Welfare spending fluctuates over the economic cycle, as the number of unemployed falls during expansions and rises during recessions. Such 'automatic stabilisers' induce a natural countercyclical pattern in government spending: however, this may be attenuated by pro-cyclical shifts in the level of benefits: during booms, the level of benefits tends to improve.

Political Economy of Public Spending
The preceding analysis generally assumes that the government acts to maximise social welfare. While the bulk of public expenditure may be usefully interpreted in this way, a substantial component is influenced by a more overtly political process, in which public expenditure allocations are the outcome of a struggle between interest groups, public sector workers and politicians. This process may produce outcomes that are contrary to social welfare: government failure may be as important as market failure in deviating from optimal outcomes.

Public Choice Theory
One reason why social welfare is not maximised is voter ignorance of the true costs of public expenditure. The Downs paradox (individual votes have no influence on the result of an election) suggests that it is not individually worthwhile for the electorate to learn much about the costs of different public

spending programmes. In contrast, some groups have vested interests in specific areas of public expenditure (e.g. farmers and agricultural subsidies) and will act collectively to promote these specific public expenditures. In a famous book, the late Mancur Olson pointed out that such interest groups are easier to organise in a rich society and hence this problem will increase over time.[9]

The characteristics of the civil service bureaucracy can also contribute to government failure. Civil servants act as agents for the government in evaluating and monitoring the effectiveness of public spending. An influential hypothesis is that bureaucrats like to maximise the size of their departmental budgets, as this is associated with power and status. With each department seeking to promote its own expenditure programmes, the net result is to place upward pressure on the level of public spending. An exception is the Department of Finance: arguably, its focus is on holding back the overall level of spending.

Design of the Political System
Much current research is devoted to analysing the impact of the structure of the political system on public expenditure decisions. For instance, it is suggested that governments that are coalitions of parties with significantly different political philosophies and short tenures in office are less able to control public expenditure. Each party in a coalition has a veto on reductions in its favoured areas so that a prisoner's dilemma results – it is in the collective interest to control spending, but no single party has the incentive to accept unilateral spending reductions. Short tenures make it unfeasible to implement spending controls as there will not be time to enjoy the benefits before the next election.

In such circumstances, it seems that fiscal control can only occur under 'crisis' conditions, with the public debt so high that there is no alternative to reform. Often, this requires suspension of normal political rivalries and the formation of a government of national unity. Elements of this story ring true for the Irish experience during 1977–87. Once fiscal control is established, fear of a return to instability may restrain expenditure for a long period. However, memories eventually fade and the pressure for a relaxation on public spending may resume. Looking forward, it will be a challenge for the coalition-based Irish political system to maintain control on fiscal spending, in the absence of binding external constraints on the budgetary position. However, the EU Stability and Growth Pact does place some limit on the potential for fiscal excess (see Chapter 4).

Another manifestation of politically driven fluctuations in public spending is the impact of the electoral cycle on public spending: in the run up to elections, there is a tendency for public spending to increase (especially on visible projects) and taxes are reduced. The timing of these fluctuations suggests such spending has little basis in terms of social welfare but rather is directed at winning favour for the incumbent government.

International evidence suggests that fiscal control is better achieved by a transparent system that places ultimate responsibility for fiscal policy on the finance minister than by a collegial and secretive system in which lines of responsibility are not clearly designated.[10] Improving transparency in the fiscal process can also help eliminate perceptions of a 'democratic deficit' in the discussion, analysis and evaluation of alternative policy proposals.

7 CONCLUSION

The central theme of this chapter is that the state is a major economic actor. A well-functioning and effective government is necessary to achieve economic efficiency and redistributional objectives. The maximisation of social welfare requires that the government chooses the optimal mix of policy instruments to attain its desired policy objectives.

The analysis in this chapter gives some clues as to the likely evolution of the government's role in the economy in the coming decades. One global trend is a shift from the government as provider to a greater use of private inputs to achieve social goals. Another trend is towards ever greater internationalisation of the policymaking process, as trade and financial linkages bind countries closer together. In the opposite direction, further decentralisation of some government functions to local levels of government is also likely to occur.

Public expenditure policies remain the primary method by which the state intervenes in the economy. With the economic boom, the decline in the public debt and an extremely favourable demographic structure, the government now has much more freedom in making spending decisions. Accordingly, it has never been more important that rigorous evaluation procedures are employed to ensure that the state obtains value for money and delivers public services in an efficient and equitable manner. In particular, an important priority is to ensure that the public investment programme operates in an effective manner and avoids disruptive stop-go cycles.

Finally, it should be clear that government performance is an important determinant of international competitiveness. An efficient government enhances the ability of domestic firms to compete in international markets, by reducing the taxation and other costs of attaining policy objectives, in international empirical studies, an efficient government is highly correlated with strong growth performance.[11] For this reason, and for the others discussed in this chapter, the analysis of government intervention in the Irish economy remains a primary task for those interested in maximising Ireland's national welfare.

Endnotes
1   See A. Shleifer and R. Vishny, *The Grabbing Hand: Government Pathologies and Their Cures*, MIT Press, Cambridge Mass 1998.
2   See J. Sachs, *Common Wealth: Economics for a Crowded Planet*, Penguin Press, New York 2008.

3   See P. Collier, *The Bottom Billion*, Oxford University Press, Oxford 2007.
4   See D. Rodrik, 'How far will international integration go?', *Journal of Economic Perspectives*, Winter 2000.
5   E. Glaeser, J. Kolo and E. Saez, 'Consumer city', *Journal of Economic Geography*, 1, 2005.
6   See Shleifer and Vishny, op. cit.
7   See P. Sweeney, *Ireland's Economic Success: Reasons and Lessons*, New Island Press, Dublin 2008.
8   W. Baumol, 'Macroeconomics of unbalanced growth: the anatomy of urban crisis', *American Economic Review*, June 1967.
9   M. Olson, *The Logic of Collective Action: Public Goods and the Theory of Groups*, Harvard University Press, Cambridge MA 1965.
10 See J. Poterba and J. von Hagen, *Fiscal Institutions and Fiscal Performance*, University of Chicago Press, Chicago 1999.
11 See R. Barro and X. Sala-i-Martin, *Economic Growth*, MIT Press, Cambridge MA 1995.

CHAPTER 4

Taxation, Debt and the Public Finances

David Madden

1 INTRODUCTION

This chapter examines the issues of taxation, debt and the public finances. It complements the topics covered in Chapter 3 and also serves as a useful backdrop to some of the sectoral issues addressed in Section IV. In Section 2 of the chapter the broad features of the Irish tax system are discussed and compared with other OECD countries. Section 3 examines the rationale for taxation, and discusses the desirable features of a tax system. It will be seen that in some cases there may be trade-offs between different optimal features of the tax system and also that policymakers are frequently the prisoners of history. The tax changes that can feasibly be implemented may be quite different from the sort of tax system designed from scratch. This section also discusses the role of taxes as a corrective device to influence individual behaviour and suggests that this role for taxation is likely to expand in future, particularly in the area of carbon taxes. Using this as a framework, the base for taxation in Ireland is discussed in Section 4, noting the distinction between the nominal and effective incidence of taxation.

Section 5 discusses the issue of the public finances. Recent discussion of this topic has been in the context of the fiscal rules applying to membership of the European Monetary Union. While these rules, as outlined in the Stability and Growth Pact, appear to impose tight constraints on the operation of fiscal policy, in reality the situation is somewhat different. The revised version of the pact, introduced in 2005, implies that application and interpretation of the rules is effectively at the discretion of elected politicians who are unlikely to impose harsh sanctions upon themselves.

2 STRUCTURE OF THE IRISH TAX SYSTEM

In this section the broad features of the Irish tax system are examined using as a benchmark for comparison the other members of the Organisation for Economic Co-operation and Development (OECD) and EU member states.

International Comparisons

We start by examining the overall level of tax revenue in Ireland compared to the rest of the OECD and the EU and then examining its composition. Table 4.1 shows general government receipts as a percentage of GDP/GNP for Ireland, the EU-19 countries and the OECD for a number of selected years.[1] In general it does not matter whether GDP or GNP is used as the denominator as they are typically quite close. In Ireland, however, GDP can exceed GNP by up to as much as 15 per cent so we use GNP as the numerator as it arguably gives a better idea of the resources available to the country. The table shows Ireland's tax ratio to be slightly below that of the EU but slightly above that of the OECD. It also shows that there has been little discernible trend in the last 15–20 years.

Table 4.1

General Government Tax Revenue as a Percentage of GDP/GNP

	1990	1995	2000	2005	2006[1]
Ireland (% GNP)	37.4	36.2	37.2	36.4	37.1
EU 19[2]	38.0	38.7	39.2	38.7	n.a.
OECD[2]	33.9	34.9	36.2	36.2	n.a.

Source: OECD, *Revenue Statistics 1965–2006*, OECD, Paris 2007.
[1] Estimates.
[2] Unweighted average.

Any perception that Ireland has relatively high taxes probably stems from the relatively high percentage of tax on personal incomes. Table 4.2 shows the composition of tax revenue for Ireland and the OECD from 1985 to 2005. Over this period Ireland has generally followed the trends elsewhere in the OECD, with lower taxes on personal income, higher taxes on corporate income, and a switch from specific indirect taxes such as excise duties to general indirect taxes such as VAT. The proportion of tax revenue accounted for by taxes on personal income has followed the downward trend elsewhere in the OECD but the level still remains above the average. It is also noticeable that in Ireland the decline in specific indirect taxes has been much steeper than elsewhere in the OECD with the consequence that overall indirect taxation in Ireland as a percentage of total revenue has fallen from 43 per cent to 36 per cent, whereas in the OECD it has remained fairly constant (though the composition has switched towards general taxes). The relative decline in the importance of indirect taxation in Ireland has been offset by increases in corporate taxation and property tax. The increase in property tax has been quite pronounced since 1995, reflecting the property boom over that period (under the OECD definition property taxes includes stamp duties on property transactions). As property prices level off and decline the relative importance of stamp duties and consequently property taxes in overall taxation is likely to decline also.

The key features of the main taxes are now examined. As Table 4.2 shows, the principal taxes in Ireland are personal income and social security contributions (both employer and employee), consumption taxes (both general and specific) and corporate income taxes. Between them these taxes account for around 90 per cent of tax revenue in Ireland. The concentration of tax revenue in these areas has diminished slightly in recent years, owing to the growing importance of stamp duty.

Table 4.2

Composition of Tax Revenue (Percentage of Total)

	1985		1995		2005	
	Ireland	OECD	Ireland	OECD	Ireland	OECD
Corporate income taxes	3	8	9	8	11	10
Personal income tax	31	30	31	27	27	25
Social security and payroll taxes	17	23	16	26	16	27
Specific consumption taxes	22	16	16	13	11	11
General consumption taxes	21	16	22	18	25	19
Property taxes (including stamp duty)	4	5	5	6	8	6
Other tax	2	2	1	2	2	2

Source: OECD, *Revenue Statistics, 1965–2000*, OECD, Paris 2007.

Personal Income Taxes

Dealing first of all with personal income tax, all taxpayers have a personal tax credit. For couples, if both partners are working outside the home the married couple's credit is twice that of a single person's credit. There is also a further PAYE credit and other credits related to circumstances such as the presence of a dependent relation or incapacitated child, etc. There has also been a substantial increase in recent years in the value of tax credit assigned to the employment of a home carer. It seems fair to suggest that the changes in the tax credit system over the last eight to ten years have been directed at increasing labour supply, in particular the labour supply of those who might otherwise have been engaged in home duties. This direction of policy has not been without controversy, as will be explained below. Taxable income will also be affected by various reliefs such as mortgage interest relief, relief on health insurance contributions, etc. (the rationales for these reliefs are discussed in more detail below).[2] There is then a standard tax rate of 20 per cent and a higher tax rate of 41 per cent.

The combination of credits and allowances permits the tax authorities to introduce a degree of tax progressivity (i.e. the average tax rate rises with income) even though there may only be one or two actual tax rates. The degree of tax progressivity will depend upon the interaction of the actual tax rates, the magnitude of tax credits and the width of the tax bands (i.e. the range of income over which the particular tax rate applies). As incomes are generally increasing over time it is typical for tax authorities to adjust tax credits and tax bands to reflect this increase. If credits and bands are not adjusted (or are only adjusted to a limited degree) then what is known as bracket creep may occur, whereby a number of taxpayers find themselves paying an increasing proportion of their income at the higher tax rate. Table 4.3 provides a rough indication of the extent to which bracket creep may have been a factor in recent years, showing the percentage change in the value of tax credits, tax bands and average industrial earnings (we choose 2003 as our starting point as 2002 was the first year tax credits were introduced). The figures for tax credits and tax bands are for a single person, while the earnings figures are average industrial earnings for all industries. Clearly average industrial earnings do not cover all workers, and the figures are for single workers only, so the table should be regarded as indicative rather than conclusive.

Table 4.3

Percentage Change in Tax Credits, Tax Bands and Average Industrial Earnings

	Tax credits	Tax bands	Average industrial earnings
2003	0	0	6.4
2004	0	0	5.0
2005	3.9	5.0	3.8
2006	6.3	8.8	3.1
2007	4.8	6.3	4.1[1]
2003–2007	15.8	21.4	24.6

Source: Department of Finance, *Income Tax Statistics: 1975–2007* (available at www.finance.gov.ie/documents/publications/Taxation/Taxstats.pdf 2007).
[1] First six months only.

Table 4.3 suggests that bracket creep may well have been an issue in the early years following the adoption of tax credits. More recent budgets, particularly those of 2006 and 2007, saw relatively generous indexation of both credits and tax bands, so the degree of accumulated bracket creep over the five-year period 2003–2007 has been relatively modest.

Another useful indicator of the degree to which the income tax system is progressive is to examine the evolution of the percentages of tax units who are in different bands from 2000 to 2004 (the most recent year for which data were available at time of writing) (see Table 4.4). Note that these figures exclude tax units who are exempt from tax because they do not exhaust their tax credits

(Revenue Commissioners reports only provide this data from 2004, when approximately 35 per cent of tax units were exempt). The figures for this table broadly mirror those of table 4.3, with a significant proportion of tax units 'creeping' up from the standard to the higher rate in 2004, reflecting the non-indexation of credits and bands. Given the indexation which has taken place since then it is almost certain that the fraction of tax units paying tax at the higher rate decreased in the 2005–2007 period. Despite this indexation it is still likely that in the region of 40–45 per cent of tax units were paying tax at the higher rate (or about 27–30 per cent if exempt tax units are included).

This table will clearly be influenced both by tax changes introduced in various budgets and by the evolution of incomes over the relevant period. Even allowing for the extent of tax cuts over the period, and the attempts to direct these tax cuts at the lower paid, it is still noticeable that in excess of one quarter of Irish tax units still pay tax at the higher rate. It is probably this fact that gives rise to the perception among taxpayers that Ireland is a heavily taxed country.

Employee social insurance payments are usually regarded as a personal tax since the contributions do not cover the cost of the associated social provisions. Since public servants pay contributions at a rate below non-public employees this is particularly true of state pensions. For non-state employees the rates of social insurance payments vary according to circumstance and earnings, with different weekly and annual ceilings. The relationship is quite complex but broadly speaking it is progressive.

Table 4.4

Percentage of Tax Units in Different Bands (excludes exempt tax units)

	Marginal relief	Standard rate	Higher rate
2000	0.9	53.1	46.0
2001	0.3	65.3	34.3
2002	1.0	59.8	39.2
2003	1.6	55.1	43.3
2004	1.7	49.1	49.1

Source: Revenue Commissioners, *Statistical Reports 2006* (available at: www.revenue.ie/pdf/statistical-report/2006/income_distribution_statistics.pdf 2006, Table IDS17).

Consumption Taxes

Taxes on consumption, both specific and general, account for about 36 per cent of tax revenue in Ireland. The breakdown between them has varied over the years with a fall in the share of revenue accounted for by specific consumption taxes (mainly taxes on tobacco, alcohol and petrol) from about 22 per cent in 1985 to 11 per cent in 2005. This partly reflects the overall trend in the OECD area but the reduction in specific taxes also reflects a form of 'tax competition' whereby it was believed there was widespread smuggling of various goods from the relatively low-taxed Northern Ireland to the Republic. This reached such a stage by the mid-to late 1980s that despite the precarious state of the public finances certain excise duties were actually cut to offset smuggling.

Consumption taxes share one feature with income taxes in Ireland in that the base is relatively narrow, due to the zero-rating or exempting of certain goods and services for VAT purposes, most notably food. The rationale for the non-taxation of food is of course that food constitutes a higher percentage of total expenditure for lower-income households and taxation of food would represent a greater burden on such households. As shall be seen below, however, this is despite the fact that in many respects food is an ideal good upon which to levy a tax.

Corporation Tax

Probably the most striking feature of corporation tax is its substantial rise over time. However, this reflects the expansion of the corporate tax base owing to the economic expansion of the last ten years and the relatively high tax elasticity of corporation tax compared to other taxes. The OECD calculate that in Ireland a 1.0 per cent rise in GDP leads to a 1.2 per cent rise in corporation tax receipts as opposed to increases of only 0.5 per cent for indirect tax and 1.0 per cent for direct tax. Corporation tax now accounts for a higher share of tax revenue in Ireland than the OECD average.

The high share for corporate taxation in Ireland may also reflect a degree of tax competition: countries are reluctant to increase corporate taxation for fear of deterring international investment. It is this desire to attract foreign investment that lay behind the dual nature of corporation tax in Ireland for so long, whereby there was a standard rate ranging from about 50 to 28 per cent accompanied by a preferential rate ranging between zero and ten per cent on manufacturing and certain internationally traded service activities. Corporation tax is now levied at 12.5 per cent on trading income: the ten per cent rate is being phased out and is likely to be completely gone by 2010. How much of a role this low tax strategy has played in attracting foreign direct investment and promoting employment in Ireland is difficult to assess, but some recent OECD research suggest that its impact may be significant (see Chapters 5 and 8).[3]

3 PRINCIPLES OF A GOOD TAX SYSTEM

This section of the chapter explains why taxation is a necessary evil, and what sort of features are desirable in a tax system. It will be seen that designing the 'best' tax system is a formidable task and probably beyond the scope of any tax authority. Indeed, it is unrealistic to expect economic analysis to come up with optimal tax recommendations along the lines of 'the optimal tax on lawnmowers is 22.5 per cent'. Rather, as Frank Hahn has put it, the aim is to explore 'the grammar of arguments about policy'.[4] However, there are more modest and attainable objectives. For example, it may be possible to identify, from a given starting position, directions of tax reform that will improve welfare.

When trying to design the best tax system or identify tax reforms, the policymaker will invariably be forced into trading off various factors, such as equity and efficiency. How precisely this trade-off is resolved is a thorny issue of policy and one which ultimately involves value judgements. In this case the role of the economist is not to make specific recommendations but rather to highlight the trade-offs as clearly as possible. It is then left to the policymaker, who is presumably accountable to the public at large in some way, to make the decision. Frequently economists employ the tool of a *social welfare function* to mimic the decision-making process. Optimal policies are then chosen to maximise the value of the social welfare function. Of course, the precise specification of the social welfare function is crucial and it is essential that the sensitivity of results to this specification are tested.

Broadly speaking, the type of issues that will figure significantly in any social welfare function and that consequently are the principles which should form the basis of any good tax system are efficiency, equity and simplicity. These are discussed in turn, bearing in mind the conflicts and trade-offs that often arise between them.

Efficiency
Efficiency in a tax system arises because, in general, taxes create distortions. They create distortions because they drive a wedge between the producer price of a good or service and the consumer price of that good. For example, suppose a baker is happy to sell 100 loaves of bread at €1 a loaf, and consumers are happy to buy 100 loaves at this price. If the government then decrees that a tax of ten cents per loaf must be paid, this drives a wedge between the price at which the producer is willing to supply, and the price at which the consumer is willing to purchase. (The precise effect of the ten cents tax on the final selling price is a separate issue, discussed below.) The existence of the ten cents wedge implies that both producer (and consumer) are producing (and consuming) away from the optimum they would freely choose in the absence of taxation. Thus, the tax has had two effects on their welfare. First, between them they are ten cents per loaf worse off than before the tax was imposed. This is the *income effect* of the tax and it must arise for any tax revenue to be collected. As long as a certain amount of revenue has to be collected this income effect will arise, regardless of what goods are taxed. However, since the revenue collected for the tax will presumably be spent on some worthy project, it can be argued that the income effect does not impose any net welfare loss on society as a whole. Of course, it has implications for the welfare of the producers and consumers of bread, but if the revenue raised goes towards providing more teachers or nurses, for example, it will also have positive implications for the welfare of these groups. However, when examining efficiency the distributional aspect of taxes is ignored (this is addressed by the equity aspect of taxes). How the revenue is spent is also usually ignored.

Decisions regarding the collection of taxes and how to spend them are assumed to be made separately, an assumption which is not always too far from reality (an exception to this principle is the case of *earmarked taxes*, which will be discussed in more detail when we examine corrective taxes).

However, because both producer and consumer are away from their optimum quantities of loaves produced and consumed there is a separate loss to them arising from the *substitution effect*. This loss is often known as the *deadweight loss* or *deadweight burden* of the tax. While a need to raise revenue of, say, €10m will always give rise to an income effect of €10m regardless of where the tax is levied, it is not the case that the extent to which agents are moved away from their pre-tax production and consumption levels is independent of where the tax is levied. Thus different taxes give rise to different deadweight losses and from an efficiency point of view the best tax is the one, or combination, that raises a given revenue with the smallest deadweight loss. Thus ideally we want a tax that raises revenue but does not cause people to behave differently from how they would in the absence of the tax (i.e. it has a zero substitution effect). An extreme example of this is what is known as a *lump-sum* tax. This is a tax which is imposed on agents regardless of their behaviour. It is lump-sum because it does not depend upon how much they consume or produce of a commodity. Unfortunately it is very difficult (if not impossible) to devise a lump-sum tax which does not have some implications for people's behaviour. One example which has been suggested in the past is a *poll tax*, i.e. a tax which is levied upon every individual in the state (it has to be individual rather than household, since otherwise it would have implications for household size and formation) regardless of their financial circumstances. While such a tax may be desirable from an efficiency point of view it can be argued that it is not desirable from the perspective of equity or fair play, since rich and poor will pay the tax alike (this is related to the concept of ability to pay, which we discuss in the next section). This can have severe implications for people's willingness to pay, since a tax that is considered a blatantly unfair tax is likely to give rise to protest. From an administrative point of view such a tax also creates a headache. For example, if records of those liable for tax are kept on, say, the electoral register, there is an incentive for people to keep their names off the electoral register, and they will thus lose their vote. The experience in the UK in the early 1990s with a poll tax is a salutary reminder of just how difficult it is to impose a truly lump-sum tax.

If a lump-sum tax is not feasible, what is the next best alternative? As outlined above, the extent of the deadweight loss is related to the amount by which agents' behaviour differs from their behaviour in a no-tax situation. Since the imposition of a tax is equivalent to changing the price of the good or service, ideally taxes should be imposed where a change in price gives rise to the smallest change in behaviour. Sensitivity of behaviour to price changes is measured in terms of *price elasticity*. Hence, in general, relatively higher taxes should be imposed on those goods or services where price elasticities of supply and demand are lowest. What this implies is that a *uniform* tax system, where all goods and services have the same tax, is rarely optimal, unless elasticities are the same across goods, though as discussed below such a tax may be attractive from an administrative point of view. Note this refers not just to own-price elasticities but also cross-price elasticities. For example, a high tax on petrol is likely to have an impact on motor purchases. Ideally, in trying to minimise the deadweight loss, all relevant elasticities should be taken into account, which imposes significant informational requirements.

Uniformity and Corrective Taxes

In concluding this discussion on efficiency there are two further points worth discussing. These are the case for uniform indirect taxation and the role of corrective taxes.

As outlined above, efficiency arguments tend to point away from uniform indirect taxes, since substitution effects for goods will differ. However, uniformity has attractions from an administrative viewpoint and it presumably reduces the scope and motivation for tax evasion. There is also pressure at EU level towards indirect tax harmonisation. There is relatively little empirical work on the relevant costs and benefits, but it can be argued that a compromise, whereby there is a considerable degree of uniformity supplemented by surtaxes on a selected subset of goods, may be the best approach.[5]

One set of goods where a persuasive case can be made for surtaxes are goods where there are negative consumption (or production) externalities. Take, for example, the case of tobacco. Were tobacco to be untaxed then presumably the market price would be that price where the marginal cost and marginal valuation to the individual would be equal. However, it can be argued that in the case of a good such as tobacco there is a divergence between actual private cost and perceived private cost, and also a divergence between private and social cost. Thus private individuals may not fully discount the future health problems associated with tobacco consumption. They are also unlikely to take on board such costs as the costs associated with passive smoking (these are known as *external* costs). The imposition of a corrective (or *Pigovian,* after the economist Arthur Pigou) tax will ensure the equality of private and social cost. Thus there is a case for taxation of tobacco above and beyond the rate which equity and efficiency considerations suggest should be applied. Similar arguments can be made for goods such as alcohol and petrol. The precise calculation of such external costs can be a tricky business and probably the best we can hope for is to arrive at a reasonable range of figures.[6]

In general, it seems likely that the role of corrective taxes, in terms of influencing individual behaviour, is likely to expand in the future. There has been speculation in some countries (including Ireland) concerning the introduction of a tax to combat obesity (the so-called 'fat tax'). Such a tax would in principle be applied to foods in proportion to the quantities of saturated fats therein. Research carried out in the UK has suggested that such a tax could save in excess of one thousand lives per annum, though there are non-trivial difficulties involved in the practical implementation of such a tax.[7] A tax on food with high saturated fat could, however, create difficulties from an equity viewpoint, as these foods are disproportionately consumed by low-income households.

It is noticeable that in the case of a fat tax there is no obvious externality to be corrected, unlike, say, the case of tobacco or alcohol. What appears to be happening here rather is that the corrective tax is being used as a form of self-control device. Recent research in economics and psychology suggests that many individuals may not be time-consistent in their preferences and hence there is a market failure in the sense that their short-run behaviour is not consistent with their long-run preferences. Government intervention, in the form of a corrective tax, can address this market failure.[8]

It is possible to criticise such fiscal interventions on the basis that they represent undue interference by government in individual decision-making and that it is a case of the 'nanny state' gone mad. However, a feature of many such interventions is that they do not impose any penalty upon those individuals *without* self-control problems who choose to become smokers (or fatty food addicts or whatever). Interventions can be designed so that there is no coercion involved whereby committed smokers are forced to pay more for their cigarettes. These are examples of what has been labelled *liberal paternalism* where it is recognised that in some cases '... individuals make inferior choices, choices which they would change if they had complete information, unlimited cognitive abilities and no lack of willpower'.[9]

Finally, it is likely that taxation will have a major role to play in addressing environmental issues and climate change in particular. This is such a substantial issue that we will hold back discussion of it until the section on specific types of taxation.

Equity

The discussion above showed how considerations of efficiency have to be balanced by those of equity. This principle of taxation is now explored in more detail. Equity is one of those terms that is often used in casual conversation but is sometimes difficult to define precisely. In the context of taxation it can usefully be explained via the concept of *ability to pay*. Suppose a tax authority is trying to decide how much tax should be levied from each household. Leaving aside for the moment the size or composition of households, assume that they differ in one respect only: their economic resources. The application of the ability to pay principle then implies that the tax levied on each household should be related to their economic resources, i.e. their ability to pay the tax in question. What is known as *horizontal equity* implies that families with identical economic resources should pay equal taxes. People who are alike from the point of view of taxation (in terms of the level of their resources) should pay equal tax. A related concept is that of *vertical equity*. It indicates that different agents (from the point of view of taxation) should pay different tax. Of course, the extent to which different agents pay different tax will dictate the *progressivity* of the tax system.

In general, agents with more resources will pay more tax, but exactly how much more will be a matter of debate. For example, one approach could be that individuals pay the same proportion of their resources in tax, thus implying that people with greater resources pay a greater absolute amount of tax. Alternatively, it could be argued that those with greater resources should pay not only a greater absolute amount of tax, but also a greater proportion of their resources in tax.

Thus in applying the concept of horizontal equity the essential principle is that agents who are alike in all relevant characteristics should be treated equally from the point of view of taxation. While this appears to be a relatively straightforward principle to apply, in practice it can be quite tricky. For example, what are the relevant characteristics? Most people would agree that characteristics such as race, religion or gender should not be taken into account when assessing tax liability. Yet even this apparently simple principle can run into trouble. For example, in the case of social security tax most people would probably agree that the rate of tax should not differ according to gender. Yet this implies discrimination in favour of females, since the actuarial benefits of social security pensions are greater for women, because on average they live longer. This is a case where, while agents may be equal *ex ante*, they are not equal *ex post*. The extent to which marital status should affect tax treatment is also problematic and has changed significantly through the years.

Principles of equity also come to the fore when analysing changes in taxation. This is because people adjust their behaviour in response to an existing tax system and changes (particularly large changes) can cause windfall gains and losses for different groups. Take for example the fact that the returns to owner-occupation of housing are not taxed. Suppose now there is a change whereby these returns are taxed. This will affect the underlying value of the asset and will bring about a loss for house owners. Since these house owners bought their houses under a tax regime that they may reasonably have expected to remain unchanged, it is arguable that the loss conferred on the buyer by the tax change is 'unfair', even if it satisfies other criteria of equity and efficiency. Thus any tax change runs the risk of contravening *transitional equity* and it is difficult to see ways around this, bar the signalling of such changes well in advance in order to give agents the time and opportunity to adjust their actions.

Even when the thorny problem of what is meant by equity is overcome, trade-offs with efficiency will almost inevitably arise. For example, the efficiency principle suggests applying high tax rates to goods and activities that have low elasticities, in other words goods that are not price sensitive. Typically these will be necessities such as food and shelter, which people have to consume, regardless of their price. However, these are precisely the goods that constitute a larger share of the budget of less well-off households, so high taxes on these goods and activities will place a greater burden on the poor and contravene principles of equity.

This simple example shows how tax authorities face difficult trade-offs in trying to design the best tax system. It also indicates that the optimal tax system could be quite complex with a myriad of different tax rates on different goods and activities. But a complicated tax system will be costly to run and will itself absorb substantial administrative resources. This brings us to the last of our desirable features of a tax system: simplicity.

Simplicity

The principal argument in favour of a simple tax system is that it is less costly to run. The costs of a tax system usually come under two headings: administrative costs and compliance costs. Since the object of taxation is to raise revenue for the provision of services by government, there is little point in having a tax system so complex that its administration absorbs considerable quantities of the resources it is trying to collect.

But it is easy to forget that much of the cost of running a tax system falls not just on the tax authority, but also on those paying the tax. For example, in many countries the tax burden for the self-employed is self-assessed. Thus the individual in question calculates their tax liability, taking into account all the allowances and exemptions for which they are eligible. The more complicated the tax system the greater will be the resources involved in accurately assessing tax liability. This may give rise to agents devoting considerable resources to arranging their affairs so as to minimise their tax liabilities (where this is done legally it is known as *tax avoidance*, where illegally it is *tax evasion*). To the extent that the same amount of revenue could be collected by a simpler tax system where such rearranging is not necessary, this is a waste of resources. In the extreme, an exceptionally complex tax system will give rise to incentives (and opportunities) for widespread tax evasion, which in turn implies further resources devoted to pursuit and prosecution of tax evaders. Since the opportunities for tax evasion are usually greater for the well off, a system which has or is believed to have a high level of tax evasion will lose the confidence of the majority of middle- and low-income taxpayers. Thus a tax system that is simple and transparent, in terms of who is liable for what tax, is likely to reduce the cost to government for a variety of reasons.

How precisely to deal with tax evasion itself gives rise to trade-offs in terms of commitment of resources. Generally, the simpler the tax system the less opportunity and incentive there will be for evasion. A low tax rate applied to a wide range of goods and activities will also encourage compliance, since the return to evading any one tax will be relatively small. But of course these features may conflict with equity and efficiency. The incentive to evade tax will also be affected by the expected cost of detection, which in turn is influenced by the probability of detection and the sanctions imposed upon those who are caught. But, of course, after a certain point there may well be diminishing returns to the amount of resources devoted to detecting tax evasion, indicating that the tax authorities may have to choose some 'optimal' level of evasion.

As an alternative to devoting more resources to the pursuit and prosecution of tax evaders, the authorities may try the carrot rather than the stick. For example, the belief that there was widespread tax evasion in Ireland in the course of the 1970s and 1980s led to a tax amnesty being declared in 1988, with a further tax amnesty announced in 1994. The first amnesty was successful in the sense of bringing in large quantities of previously uncollected tax and also presumably in bringing agents into the tax net who had previously been outside it. The second amnesty raised major misgivings, however, owing to the conflicting incentives it offered tax evaders. On the one hand, it may have brought more tax evaders into the tax net. On the other hand, however, it may have discouraged tax evaders from coming clean, since they may have felt that further tax amnesties might be declared in the future. This problem is known as 'time-consistency' and it can arise in many aspects of government policy. Governments may state that they intend to follow a certain policy line, but subsequently may find it optimal to change this line. They then have to trade off the benefits of making the switch in policy against the costs of the lost credibility in not sticking to their original plans.

Conclusions

This section has outlined some of the issues involved in designing a 'good' tax system. Such a task will often be an exercise in compromise, since typically efficiency must be balanced against equity, while also bearing in mind the advantages of a simple, transparent tax system. The section has also emphasised the degree to which taxation can play a role in correcting market failures. The next section moves away from the broad principles of tax design to some of the more practical issues of implementing a tax system, giving examples from the Irish situation where applicable.

4 ISSUES IN IRISH TAXATION

Given the desirable features of a tax system referred to above, what sort of goods or activities should be taxed, and who ultimately pays the tax? The first question refers to the appropriate tax base. Two primary candidates for the tax base are income and consumption. Apart from the obvious consumption and income taxes there are also taxes on corporate profits, upon wealth and so on. What are the rationales for these taxes and what is the relevant base? Without going into too much detail it will be seen that the issues involved can be quite complex. Not the least of the difficulties involved is the fact that the agent from whom the tax is collected may not bear the full, or indeed any of, the real burden of the tax. This is the question of *tax incidence* and, in many cases, who ultimately pays any given tax is not an easy matter to ascertain.

Choice of Tax Base

Broadly, the two most popular candidates for the tax base are comprehensive income and consumption. The most commonly used definition of comprehensive income is that of Simons, who defines it as: 'The amount which may be spent on consumption without adding to or subtracting from real wealth in the process.'[10] The principal difference between comprehensive income and consumption lies in the treatment of savings. If the base for taxation is income, savings will be doubly taxed, once when they are earned and again when the return is paid. With a consumption base they are taxed only when consumed.

A further distinction between income and consumption taxes is that income taxes are typically progressive, i.e. the marginal tax rate exceeds the average tax rate. Consumption taxes are rarely progressive and so arguably are less well designed to address equity goals. Of course it is possible to levy higher taxes on goods that are consumed disproportionately by better-off individuals, but in general it seems fair to say that while consumption taxes may score high on efficiency grounds, they are not as effective in pursuing aims of equity.

Despite the distortion between savings and consumption that arises when an income base is used, pure consumption taxes are relatively rare worldwide. Only India and Sri Lanka have adopted them and they have found that, from an administrative point of view, they left much to be desired. However, it must be pointed out that a truly comprehensive income tax is also practically impossible to implement, since it requires that the return to all forms of capital, including human capital, be taxed. There is also the problem of switching from a predominantly income base to a consumption base. In general large-scale tax changes cause problems of their own, so much so that it can be argued that the administration of the cure is worse than the disease.

In practice, virtually all countries apply a direct tax system that is effectively a compromise between a comprehensive income tax and a consumption tax. This is because, while financial asset income is typically taxed, many other forms of asset income are not taxed (e.g. the return to human capital). Even in those cases where asset income is taxable, the tax rate may differ, thus influencing the after-tax rate of return and presumably altering the composition, if not the overall level, of savings. Research for Ireland and other countries has indicated that the tax system can exert a major influence on the after-tax rate of return and it is far from clear that this is a benign influence.[11] While the lower rates of inflation since the early 1990s removed much of this distortion, we are still some way off a 'level playing field' for the tax treatment of different forms of saving.

The Irish personal income tax base is also narrowed by a significant quantity of exclusions, reliefs and exemptions. Examples of these are the exclusion of the imputed income from owner-occupancy of housing. There is also tax relief for interest payments on mortagages, not to mention pension and health insurance contributions. Finally, certain forms of income (e.g. child benefit, rental income from certain sources) are exempt from tax. Clearly, the greater the range of exemptions and reliefs, the narrower is the tax base and the higher must be the effective tax rate on that portion of income which is taxable. It is difficult to obtain precise estimates of the cost of these various exemptions in terms of revenue foregone as even the figures provided by the Department of Finance regarding the cost of some schemes are listed as 'extremely tentative'. However, some idea of the orders of magnitude can be obtained from the estimated cost of income tax relief arising from pension contributions in 2001. The Department of Finance estimated the cost of this to be about €1,400m.[12] Given the increase in numbers employed and pay rates since then it does not seem unreasonable to suggest that this cost could approach €2,000m. While income tax relief for pension contributions is undoubtedly one of the more costly forms of relief, it is clear that were these reliefs/exemptions not present the structure of the personal tax system (or indeed other branches of the tax system) could look radically different. Of course there may be valid reasons for the presence of at least some of these reliefs/exemptions, but it seems difficult to justify the current extent, not to mention the fact that many of them introduce arguably unnecessary and arbitrary market distortions.

Finally, it is worth pointing out that not all forms of income face tax at the same marginal rate. Capital gains are taxed at a rate of 20 per cent, compared to a top income tax rate of 41 per cent. While capital gains had previously been taxed advantageously (with a tax rate of 40 per cent compared to a top marginal rate of 46 per cent) its relative position has improved in recent years. This is consistent with an approach whereby investment income has been by and large favourably treated with other reliefs directed at various types of investment. Once again, while a case can be made for some of these reliefs in isolation, it is difficult to argue that the combined effect has been beneficial.

Unit of Taxation
Another basic issue in taxation is the choice of unit of taxation. When dealing with personal income or consumption tax the choice is between the individual and the family. This issue has attracted much heated debate in Ireland in recent years, not least because shifting demographic conditions means that the nature of the family has changed over the years. The issue becomes particularly thorny when dealing with the case of married couples, where in some cases both spouses are 'working', and in the other case where one spouse is 'working' and the other is on 'home duties'. Take the case of two families, where in Case 1 only one spouse works outside the home and earns, say, €80,000. In Case 2, both spouses work outside the home and earn €40,000 each (additionally we suppose that both families are identical in all other respects). In both cases family income is €80,000. Does this imply that they both have an equal ability to pay, and that principles of horizontal equity indicate that they should have the same tax liability? The 1999/2000 budget introduced changes which implicitly answered 'No' to this question. The widening of tax bands at the standard rate of income tax was greater in the case of the two-earner family (Case 2), implying that after the budget their tax liability would be lower. Essentially this was presented as a move towards 'individualisation' since tax liability was being calculated more on the basis of the individual than of the family. Equivalently there was less than 100 per cent transferability (of allowances and tax bands) between the two spouses in the one-earner family.

Did this 'reform' go against the principle of horizontal equity? The answer to this question lies in what are regarded as the relevant characteristics when comparing families for their tax liability. If earned income is to be the only relevant characteristic the families are equal before tax, and then according to horizontal equity should be equal after tax. However, in the case of the one-earner family, if some value is to be put on the home duties carried out by the non-earning spouse, the one-earner family is in some sense better off, and thus according to principles of vertical equity should have a higher tax liability. Opponents of this viewpoint argued that the proposed changes would leave those families where one spouse chose to remain at home at a disadvantage and that it was in some sense 'anti-family' (since in many cases the at-home parent is minding children). Part of the rationale for the move towards individualisation may also have been the incentives it offered to increase labour supply at a time when the country was at full employment. Whether this initiative would have been proposed at a time of high unemployment is open to speculation.

In the immediate aftermath of the 1999/2000 budget an additional widening of the tax band for spouses at home was introduced so that both families would have had the same tax liability. Since then, the combination of tax credits and tax bands have led to a system involving a mixture between full individualisation and a pre-1999 aggregation system. Implicitly, the position appears to be that, in terms of the example above, the two families are not entirely equal in terms of relevant characteristics and so some differential tax treatment is warranted. Of course precisely how different the treatment should be (or equivalently how much vertical equity should be applied) will ultimately boil down to a value judgement.

The individualisation controversy vividly illustrates the complex and often emotional issues that can arise when choosing the appropriate unit of taxation. It also shows the difficulty of introducing tax changes, even in cases where there are no losers in absolute terms. Overall, the trend in Ireland, as in other EU countries, appears to be towards taxing the individual rather than the family.

Corporation Tax and Incidence

Aside from the obvious taxes on consumption and income, there are also taxes on corporate profits. As seen in Section 2, corporation tax has become increasingly important in recent years in Ireland, both as a source of revenue and as an instrument of industrial policy. What is the rationale for such a tax? Before answering this question it is helpful to introduce the notion of the incidence of a tax. This is best explained by the following example. Suppose the government introduces a tax on firms. The firm owners now see their profits reduced. Presuming firms will attempt to minimise the impact of the tax on their profits, they then may choose to (a) pay their workers less or (b) increase their prices to consumers, or maybe they will do a combination of both. In this case who has really paid the tax? Nominally the tax authorities collect it from the firm, but in effect it seems as if the tax is really paid by the workers and/or consumers. Thus, while the nominal incidence of the tax is on the firm, the effective incidence is on the workers/consumers. How do we know how much of the incidence of the tax is passed on to the workers and how much to the consumers and how much is left for the firm to pay? This broadly depends on the state of the relevant markets involved. For example, if the firm has a monopoly in the production of the good in question, or if market demand is very inelastic, a considerable portion of the tax can be passed on to the consumer. However, if the market for the good is very competitive, with close substitutes available, the firm will not be in a position to burden the consumers with the tax. In the case of taxing firms, the situation where the burden of the tax is mostly borne by workers is known as *backward shifting*, while the case where it is consumers who bear the burden is known as *forward shifting*. A final difficulty is that there is little compelling empirical evidence on who exactly pays the corporation tax.

The difficulty in assigning the incidence of corporate taxation has led to suggestions that there is little point in taxing the firm. The tax can always be passed on to other agents and in any event the firm is ultimately owned by people (shareholders). Even if the incidence of the tax falls on the firm, why not tax the income/consumption of the owners directly? Why tax them via the firm?

A number of arguments have been put forward to answer these questions. Space constraints prevent us from going into too much detail, so we will keep the discussion brief. The first argument is that the corporation benefits from various publicly provided goods. Among the more obvious of these are roads, bridges and airports, but firms also benefit from highly trained workers who have been educated at public expense. Ideally, the corporation could be charged for these benefits at point of use, but this would create major administrative problems. So the corporation tax is an imperfect mechanism for achieving the goal of enforcing the corporation to pay for the publicly provided goods it consumes and benefits from.

The second reason for taxing corporations relates back to the definition of comprehensive income. If the tax authorities use comprehensive income as their tax base, probably the most difficult portion of this income to tax is accrued capital gains (i.e. the increase in the value of assets). When these gains are realised they can be taxed according to the normal personal tax system. But someone could choose not to realise such gains while their wealth (in the form of the value of shares of untaxed companies) can increase. Taxing companies is once again an imperfect way of taxing such accrued capital gains. Of course not all income from shares comes in the form of capital gains. Dividends may also be paid. In this case taxing the firm and then taxing the individual on their dividends may be seen as double taxation. To avoid this, most tax regimes have some method of adjusting personal tax liabilities to take account of the tax paid on their behalf by companies.

Carbon Taxes

Perhaps the taxation issue which has received most attention in recent years and is likely to remain of critical importance in the medium term is the area of so-called 'green taxes', i.e. interventions to further environmental goals. These are sometimes referred to as carbon taxes, since they are typically taxes designed to affect carbon emissions, and the term may also refer to fiscal initiatives to control emissions which do not directly involve taxes on carbon products. To a certain extent such taxes exist already with the high rates of motor tax and taxes on petrol. However, the high tax on petrol almost certainly arose as a means of correcting the external costs of pollution, while the high tax on motor cars (and petrol) could also have been justified on equity grounds, given that consumption of such goods (in terms of both the number of vehicles per household and vehicles' engine capacity) is disproportionately concentrated in higher-income households.

More recent proposals to introduce green taxes have been designed to address the issue of global warming and climate change. While some controversy over the precise causes of global warming may still remain, the consensus at inter-governmental level is that carbon emissions are a cause of global warming and that some form of control of these emissions is warranted to avoid the adverse consequences of climate change.

It is not possible to provide a comprehensive review of the issues concerning climate change policy in this chapter, so we will just concentrate on those aspects that have relevance for taxation policy. Broadly speaking, we can regard climate change policy as having three core components: the targets, the institutional structure and the instruments.[13] Regarding targets, Ireland is committed under the EU burden-sharing agreement associated with the Kyoto Protocol to have an average level of emissions over the 2008–2012 period which is 113 per cent of their 1990 value. It has been argued that such a target is unrealistic for Ireland, given that 1990 represented a relatively low point in the recent economic cycle. The most recent projections suggest that Ireland will come in at about 0.5 per cent below its target but only via the purchase of 'Kyoto credits' and the use of 'carbon sinks' (i.e. forests which soak up carbon dioxide).[14] However, it must be remembered that there is a huge degree of uncertainty surrounding the optimal level of target emissions or indeed what the time path of these targets should be, so should Ireland miss its target by a small amount this is unlikely to be of grave consequence.

In terms of institutional structures, by definition global climate change is a global policy, so ideally some form of global response is required. The experience so far has been mixed, with the US (the greatest single source of carbon emissions) and developing countries opting out of the Kyoto Protocol. However, the emissions trading system introduced by the EU shows that some level of multilateral action is possible and it seems highly unlikely that the US would not be involved in some way in future multilateral action.

Regarding policy instruments, it is here that taxation may have a key role to play. Climate change can be regarded as a clear case of a market failure where intervention can be justified. The classic 'problem of the commons' refers to a common resource which is in limited supply (in this case the common resource is the extent to which the earth's atmosphere can absorb carbon emissions without an undue effect on world climate). The impact of each individual user on the stock of the resource is effectively zero, hence individuals do not take this into account in their decisions of how much to use the resource. In the aggregate, however, over-usage of the resource will have implications for all the population and thus social costs exceed private costs. In this instance some form of regulation is justified. But what form of regulation is optimal?

There are a variety of policy options available in order to obtain a target level of emissions. Given that the target level is by definition a quantity, then at first glance a quantity-based instrument seems attractive. In terms of obtaining some form of international agreement it may also be easier to negotiate in terms of quantities rather than prices (as would be the case with a carbon tax). Hence we have the emissions trading system introduced by the EU where each participating state is endowed with a quota of emissions and trading of these quotas is permitted. However, there are reasons to believe that price-based systems (i.e. tax) may be superior on pure efficiency grounds to quantity-based instruments. Any given carbon tax will inevitably imply a certain quantity target of emissions (depending upon the supply and demand curves for emissions). While there may be some uncertainty regarding what this target will eventually be, the area of climate change policy in general is riddled with uncertainty and so this should not be regarded as a major obstacle. Price-based systems in general also economise on the gathering of information. An appropriately set carbon tax should simultaneously affect both supply and demand for emissions and bring about a greater congruence between the private and social costs of emissions.

A further attractive aspect of a carbon tax is that it can simultaneously correct a market failure and also provide tax revenue which in turn can be used to either lower taxes elsewhere or provide subsidies for the adoption of environmentally friendly technologies. This is the so-called 'double dividend' of corrective taxes and while in principle a similar effect could be obtained from a tradeable permits system (if the permits were auctioned), in practice quantity based systems do not offer this advantage. In general, it is also typically more straightforward to alter a tax than a quantity.

There can also be pitfalls with tax-based policies, especially when they are applied in conjunction with emissions permits and where some form of international tax co-ordination is required. For example, suppose Ireland were to unilaterally introduce a carbon tax which would apply in conjunction with the current EU-based tradeable permits system. Since the carbon tax would increase the price of emissions in Ireland it would reduce the demand for such emissions. As Ireland is a net importer of emissions in the EU this would reduce Irish imports of emissions from the rest of the EU and consequently reduce emissions exports from the rest of the EU to Ireland. However, since the total amount of EU emissions is capped, the reduction in Irish emissions would be exactly offset by an increase elsewhere (presuming the emissions constraint is binding). Thus a unilaterally imposed tax in Ireland would not affect the total amount of EU emissions, but only the distribution of such emissions within Europe. There are clear similarities with the issue of tax competition in the context of corporation tax discussed earlier.

Recent budgets in Ireland have introduced some initiatives designed to address climate change. For example, the structure of motor taxation has been altered specifically to address the emissions issue. While in the past higher rates of tax have applied to larger engines, as outlined above, this was generally justified on the basis of correcting the social costs of pollution (aside from the climate change effect) and also to introduce a form of progression into the tax. However, from mid-2008 the motor tax system will now be explicitly structured to address climate change, with motor tax rates applied on the basis of emission levels rather than engine size. There is also a commitment to introduce a specific carbon budget each year in conjunction with the traditional budget in order to meet the target level of emissions referred to above. It is also noteworthy that the 'new' Commission on Taxation whose establishment was announced in February 2008 is specifically mandated to address the issue of the introduction of measures to further lower carbon emissions.

Wealth Taxes

Finally, what about taxes on wealth and bequests? These differ from the taxes discussed above in that they tax a *stock* – in this case wealth or else a gift, or inheritance of wealth – as opposed to a *flow,* such as wage or profit income or consumption. But why should wealth be taxed when presumably tax has been applied to the income that generated this wealth? Recall from our discussion above that one of the problems of applying a comprehensive income tax is that it may be difficult to tax the return on certain forms of wealth, or on unrealised capital gains. Taxing the underlying wealth may partially remedy this. The taxation of wealth may also reduce the *concentration* of wealth (i.e. the extent to which it is unequally distributed) and so a case can be made on equity grounds. It can also be argued that since wealthy people benefit to a greater extent from one of the primary services provided by government (law and order and the protection of property), they should be taxed accordingly.

Attempts to apply a wealth tax in Ireland have met with little success. In 1975 a wealth tax was introduced essentially to replace existing estate duty, but was subsequently abandoned due to a variety of problems. These related primarily to the excessively high administrative and compliance costs, not to mention opposition from a variety of powerful interest groups. To compound the situation, in 1977 rates on domestic property were abolished. While there were undoubted problems with establishing accurate valuations of property, not least at a time of relatively high inflation, the abolition of rates, as opposed to their reform, represented an unfortunate narrowing of the tax base. In 1983 a residential property tax was introduced, but once again it fell foul of the problems typically encountered by taxes of this nature. Since the tax was to be applied only on property valued above a certain threshold, once again there were issues regarding valuation. The low yield from the tax was indicative of problems with its application and in 1997 it was abolished.

Taxes on bequests or gifts are very similar in spirit to taxes on wealth. However, instead of an annual tax on wealth, they represent a tax on wealth at irregular intervals occasioned perhaps by the death of the wealth holder (an *estate tax)*, or when a gift is being made. Currently in Ireland there is an exemption threshold for such taxes (which varies according to the relationship between the donor and recipient, with higher thresholds for 'closer' relationships) and a tax rate of 20 per cent. There may also be exemptions for family homes. Note that the administrative costs associated with valuation of wealth for an estate tax are likely to be much lower than for an annual wealth tax. This is because such a valuation will typically be carried out anyway on the estate of the deceased. Overall, there is relatively little accord on the incentive and incidence effects of estate and gift taxes, and they receive comparatively little attention since they rarely constitute a substantial percentage of overall government revenue.

Tax Base Revisited

Before concluding this section it may be worthwhile to revisit the issue of the appropriate tax base. Is there an optimal mix, in terms of direct and indirect taxes or in terms of personal versus corporate taxation? When the problem is couched in these terms optimal taxation is limited in what it has to say, primarily owing to issues such as nominal and effective incidence discussed above. Claims along the lines that the corporate sector should increase its share of tax revenue are essentially meaningless unless there is knowledge of the effective incidence of the tax. Similarly, the incidence of income tax reductions will fall on both employer and employee. And reductions in income tax rates are of limited benefit to wage earners if accompanied by offsetting consumption tax increases.

However, this begs the question of why there is such an extensive range of taxes. If all taxes are ultimately paid by individuals then why not simply have a single rate of tax applied to the relevant base? There are essentially two answers to this question. First, since taxes have simultaneously to try to satisfy principles of equity, efficiency and simplicity it is difficult to find a single tax that scores well on all of these criteria. Some taxes will have strengths in one department and some in others. In this case a (limited) mix of taxes may be preferable to a single tax. And since uniform indirect taxation is only optimal under very specific conditions, why should only one form of taxation be optimal? The second reason for having a range of taxes is simply because that is the current situation. This answer is not as trite as it seems. As outlined above, the introduction of large-scale changes to the tax system will typically cause windfall gains and losses in ways that may not be entirely predictable. In this sense it may be the case that 'an old tax is a good tax'.

In this case, probably the best rule of thumb is to generally concentrate relatively higher tax rates on the less elastic goods and services, provided the distributional consequences are not adverse. What tentative forecast can we make regarding the likely evolution of the tax base in the medium term? Since the mid-1970s probably the most glaring anomaly in the Irish tax system has been the absence of any comprehensive form of taxation of property and the reluctance of the tax authorities to confront this issue. One corollary of this is the (by international standards) high number of taxpayers whose marginal tax rate is the higher rate of tax. A further consequence has been that local authorities (whose revenue source has traditionally been local property taxes) have had to rely, to an arguably excessive degree, on central government for revenue, which may have undermined local democracy. However, experiences regarding the introduction of property (or wealth) taxes have been such that governments are unlikely to risk the potential political fall-out of such an initiative.

Probably the most reliable forecast that can be made regarding the tax base concerns the introduction of some form of carbon tax, the justification for which was discussed at length above. It is ironic that the major development in terms of the expansion of the tax base in Ireland in the near future is likely to arise not from any optimal tax perspective but instead as a response to external events (in the form of climate change).

5 GOVERNMENT SPENDING, DEBT AND THE PUBLIC FINANCES

Fiscal Policy: The Background

The dark days of the 1980s, with chronic public debt and concerns over the financial solvency of the state, now seem a distant memory. In more recent years, primarily owing to the strong economic growth since the mid-1990s, measures reflecting the state of Irish public finances have been far healthier. Table 4.5 gives an idea of the evolution of general government lending for Ireland and the OECD since 1990, while the bottom part of the table shows how the national debt (using the Maastricht definition) has evolved for Ireland and the euro area since 1997.[15]

Table 4.5

General Government Financial Balances and Debt as a Percentage of GNP/GDP

| | Government financial balances | | | |
	1990	1995	2000	2007[1]
Ireland (% of GNP)	-3.2	-2.4	5.5	2.6
OECD[2]	-2.9	-4.0	0.2	-1.6
	Gross public debt (Maastrict definition)			
	1997	2000	2005	2007[1]
Ireland (% of GNP)	62.9	44.4	32.6	29.2
Euro Area[2]	73.3	68.9	70.5	66.9

Source: OECD, *OECD Economic Outlook No. 82*, OECD, Paris 2007.
[1] Estimates and projections.
[2] Unweighted average.

The table shows that in the early 1990s Ireland was still suffering somewhat from the hangover of the 1980s. However, following the onset of strong growth in

1995 general government financial balances turned positive, and even though there has been a slight deterioration in recent years Ireland still shows healthier financial balances than the rest of the OECD. In terms of public debt the figures are presented in conjunction with those for the euro area as it is public debt with regard to the criteria laid down in the Maastricht Treaty and consequently in the Stability and Growth Pact which are of most relevance. They show once again that Ireland has a low ratio of gross public debt as a fraction of GDP relative to the euro area. Of course, one of the primary reasons why Ireland's fiscal position has been so favourable in recent years is owing to the high rates of economic growth. High rates of growth automatically tend to increase government surpluses as expenditure on income support payments typically fall while tax revenues simultaneously increase.

We next turn to discuss Irish fiscal policy in the context of European Monetary Union. Ultimately, Ireland's fiscal policy must be evaluated against the backdrop of its participation in monetary union and the conditions on fiscal policy laid down in the Maastricht Treaty and the Stability and Growth Pact. We discuss the constraints which membership of a monetary union must place on fiscal policy and we evaluate the attempts by the European Union to devise and impose rules to enforce these constraints.

Maastrict Criteria and the Stability and Growth Pact
Since the mid- to late 1990s, probably the most important background influence on Irish fiscal policy has been the set of rules and conditions which have applied arising from Irish participation in European Monetary Union (EMU). These rules were initially known as the Maastricht criteria and later became refined as the Stability and Growth Pact (SGP). We will first outline the reasons why binding fiscal rules are desirable in a monetary union. We will then discuss the optimality or otherwise of the rules put in place for EMU, followed by a discussion of how they have operated since EMU started. We conclude by examining what lessons have been learned and how fiscal rules are likely to operate in the medium term.

The Need for Fiscal Rules in a Monetary Union
The first issue to be aware of when examining fiscal rules is the increased importance of fiscal policy when in a monetary union. In general, compared with the high point of the mid-1960s, fiscal policy has not been held in high regard as an instrument for the government to smooth business cycles. It has generally been held that monetary policy is superior as it is less subject to time lags and unpredictable side effects. However, in a monetary union, no individual country has control over its monetary policy. Thus fiscal policy is the only stabilisation instrument available, and this is especially true for small countries, which are likely to have the least influence on the joint monetary policy of the monetary union. A further argument in favour of fiscal policy in a monetary union is that, since the 1950s, fiscal policy has generally been held to be more effective in a regime of fixed exchange rates. For each individual country in a monetary union

the exchange rate is given and hence the policy environment closely corresponds to that of a fixed exchange rate.

Thus there are strong incentives for active fiscal policy for members of a monetary union. However, there are also market failures, which suggests that some form of rules is necessary to ensure a greater congruence between the cost of irresponsible fiscal policy to an individual country and the cost to the union as a whole. Take for example the case of what can be termed the deficit bias. Suppose one individual country engages in excessive spending leading to government deficits which it wishes to finance by borrowing. If the country were not part of a monetary union, then any sign of irresponsible fiscal policy would be penalised by an increase in the cost of borrowing. In a monetary union, however, the interest rate is set centrally, and so the impact of any one country on the cost of borrowing may be negligible. There is no automatic market discipline imposed on irresponsible fiscal policy. Essentially there is a 'free ride' for each individual country. However, if *all* (or even a sufficiently large number of) member countries avail of this free ride then irresponsible fiscal policy will be penalised by higher interest rates. Hence, what is individually rational for each individual country (to engage in low-cost irresponsible fiscal policy) leads to a sub-optimal outcome for the union as a whole.

The above is perhaps an exaggerated account of the problem and it could be argued that international financial markets would discriminate between borrowing by different member states and that the price of government bonds for irresponsible countries would reflect this. In particular the 'no bail-out' clause in the European Community Treaty explicitly prohibited governments from availing of overdraft facilities in the European Central Bank or domestic central banks and was intended to convey the message that irresponsible fiscal behaviour would be penalised. However, the experience has been that despite poor fiscal conditions in countries such as Greece and Italy there has been relatively little increase in the spread between government bonds issued by these countries and those issued by other more prudent countries.[16]

However, even if one individual country engaged in sustained irresponsible fiscal policy to the extent that there was a danger of default on its debt, there would very likely be significant cross-border effects. Although most agents obey to some extent the laws of portfolio diversification there can still remain what is known as 'home currency bias' and the evidence suggests that 'EMU member countries disproportionately invest in one another relative to other country pairs'.[17] Thus a strong case exists for fiscal rules to ensure that some form of fiscal discipline is maintained.

Before moving on to discuss the rules in detail, it is worth noting the situation in the USA regarding the extent to which different states have constraints upon their fiscal sovereignties. Here there is a much greater degree of economic and monetary union than in Europe, yet there are still different risk premiums attached to the bonds issued by different states. It should also be pointed out that the degree of fiscal federalism in the USA (the process whereby a downturn in activity in one state is automatically followed by transfers of funds into that state from other states) reduces the scope for excessive deficits. We now turn to discuss the rules the European Community initially imposed and how they worked in practice.

What Rules were Applied and Did They Work?

Before discussing the actual rules and their application it is worth pointing out that, unlike the case of taxation, there is little consensus on what are optimal fiscal rules. One suggestion which has been put forward is the so-called 'golden rule of public sector investment', i.e. that over the fiscal cycle government borrowing should not exceed government capital formation (or, more simply, governments should only borrow for investment purposes). Such a rule has a superficial attractiveness since it implies a degree of 'prudence' on behalf of governments. However, it suffers from serious difficulties in application. For example, many items of public spending do not fit comfortably into the definition of either 'current' or 'capital', e.g. is a public vaccination programme current spending or an investment in the health of the nation? It is also not clear why, if it is optimal for private individuals to smooth their consumption over time and over different situations, it is not for the public sector as well.

The first version of the Stability and Growth Pact (SGP) provided a medium-term target of close to balance or in surplus for the public finances of each member country. The general government deficit-to-GDP ratio was not to exceed three per cent and there was to be a 60 per cent limit for the gross debt-to-GDP ratio. This last figure was not necessarily binding, provided member states could show that their debt-to-GDP ratio was at least 'approaching' the 60 per cent limit. There was also some acknowledgement that the three per cent target might be difficult to meet in times of recession. Thus the three per cent rule would be dropped if GDP were to fall by more than two per cent, while if it fell by more than 0.75 per cent countries could apply for suspension of the rule. If the rule was broken, there was a prescribed sequence of events whereby, if no corrective action was taken, a fine could ultimately be imposed upon the errant member. This fine started at 0.2 per cent of GDP and rose in line with the actual size of the deficit. This whole process was known as the Excessive Deficit Procedure (EDP).

One of the more innovative aspects of the SGP rules was that the *ex-post* fines imposed for excessive deficits outlined above was accompanied by *ex-ante* assessments of fiscal plans. The idea was that each country would submit three-year fiscal plans and that these plans should adhere to the Broad Economic Policy Guidelines (BEPG). If the plans did not adhere to the BEPG, warnings would be issued and countries were expected to take action. The idea was that the EDP would only be invoked in extreme conditions and that adherence to the BEPG would ensure that prevention would be better than cure.

It is clear that the rules were open to criticism on a number of grounds. First, the target figures of three per cent and 60 per cent were clearly arbitrary – why not targets of four per cent and 80 per cent respectively? On the other hand, some form of quantitative target may have been deemed necessary, so whatever figures were adopted were going to face this criticism. Second, and perhaps a more substantive criticism of the rules, was their asymmetric nature. While the medium-term goal was for countries to move to fiscal balance, penalties were to be imposed only on those countries with excessive deficits, yet no penalty was to be imposed for excessive surpluses. Finally, if countries were eventually to achieve fiscal balance over the medium term this would imply that the debt to GDP ratio would eventually approach zero, with no clear justification that this was an optimal level.

How did the SGP rules fare in the early years of monetary union? It can be argued that the SGP rules had a limited impact in terms of fiscal discipline. In the early years of EMU general government balances deteriorated and by 2003 the non-cyclically adjusted general government financial deficit stood at over three per cent of GDP, with Germany and France recording deficits of over four per cent. Such deficits should have led to the imposition of fines. Instead the European Union's Council of Ministers voted to suspend enforcement of the fines, which in turn led to the European Commission bringing a case in the European Court of Justice against the decision of the Council of Ministers. The Court voted that the Council did not have the right to suspend enforcement but despite this no penalty was paid by the offending countries. It was also noted that some countries used various loopholes in the European system of accounts to reduce the deficit reported to Eurostat, reflecting the fact that in general there can be quite a degree of discretion in terms of the definition of fiscal 'stance'.[18] It is also arguable that the SGP did little to either improve growth or stability in the euro zone.

So why was the SGP relatively unsuccessful in the early years of EMU? Some of the possible reasons, such as the concentration on headline as opposed to cyclically adjusted fiscal targets, have been listed above; and some commentators have argued that the extraordinary circumstances under which the EDP could be suspended were defined too loosely. But perhaps the biggest problem the SGP faced was that when growth slowed down and the EDP dictated that fines should be imposed on two of the largest and most powerful countries in the euro zone, France and Germany, the Council of Ministers backed down. This contrasted with the cases of Portugal in 2002, when the EDP procedure was applied, and the warning issued to Ireland in 2001 over breaches of the BEPG. The perception was created that there was one rule for the big countries and another for the small. Thus by 2003 the SGP, as originally devised, was effectively in crisis.

In response to this crisis the SGP was revised in 2005. The three per cent and 60 per cent ceilings for deficits and debt ratios were retained but the medium-term targets and adjustment paths were altered. Medium-term targets were redefined on a cyclically adjusted basis and could differ by country depending upon potential growth rates and debt levels. The definition of the exceptional circumstances under which a country was permitted to breach the three per cent ceiling was relaxed. It now corresponded to a negative GDP growth rate or a protracted period of low growth relative to potential. This effectively extended the deadline allowed to correct excessive deficits. When the deficit exceeded three per cent marginally, the Commission was permitted to take into account various extenuating circumstances whereby certain types of expenditure such as research and development or development aid might be considered exempt.

Is the revised SGP likely to be more effective in credibly imposing fiscal discipline than its predecessor? On the positive side it could be argued that the newer version has retained the best elements of the old SGP (in particular the deficit and debt ceilings have remained unchanged) while being more realistic in terms of extenuating circumstances. If it is more acceptable to member states it is more likely to gain support and countries are more likely to adhere to the rules.

However, a more negative assessment of the new SGP is also possible.[19] The new rules effectively give more discretion to the Council of Ministers in terms of interpreting the rules. The wording of the rules give a wide scope to the Council to declare extenuating circumstances and to extend deadlines for deficit correction. Thus, instead of the sanctions applying automatically (as was originally envisaged in the first SGP), they may now be imposed effectively at the discretion of the Council. Since it is in all Council members' interests for the conditions to be interpreted leniently this creates a bias towards a watering down of the SGP conditions. In effect the SGP rules become endogenous rather than exogenous.

Despite the reservations listed above concerning the new SGP, it is noteworthy that since 2005 it appears that financial markets believe the new rules to be credible, as there have been no signs that investors are unwilling to invest in euro-denominated assets. However, since 2005 Europe has generally experienced benign economic conditions and it is only when the economic cycle turns down and government balances come under pressure that the true test of the new rules will apply.

In truth, it is difficult to envisage how the SGP could realistically be reformed. At present the rules are being applied by the players in the game rather than by an external referee and there is little chance that the Council of Ministers would delegate the interpretation and application of the rules to an external body. Already monetary and exchange rate policy are outside the control of sovereign governments so it is highly unrealistic to expect them to surrender their one remaining sphere of influence. It should also be pointed out that many people would view it as desirable that at least one branch of economic policy should be under the control of elected and accountable representatives. Thus the SGP is most likely to carry on in its present guise until the next crisis, which will probably occur when the euro zone experiences the next sharp economic downturn.

6 CONCLUSION

This chapter has given an overview of the basic issues involved in taxation, government spending and the level of public debt. It has tried to illustrate how they apply to Ireland and has given a brief account of the main features of the Irish tax system and how it compares with the rest of the OECD. The main conclusion reached here is that while it is untrue to regard Ireland as a heavily taxed country, there has been relatively little progress in expanding the tax base. In terms of future developments in taxation the main area of activity will almost certainly be in taxes designed to address climate change. There is also scope for initiatives in other forms of corrective taxation.

The chapter also examined the broad thrust of fiscal policy and the issue of the public finances and concluded that, on a cyclically adjusted basis, Irish fiscal policy has been relatively prudent. However, the very strong rates of growth in the last ten years complicate the calculation of cyclically adjusted balances for Ireland.

The last part of the chapter examined the operation of the Stability and Growth Pact. It discussed the rationale for fiscal rules in a monetary union and reviewed the operation of the pact so far. It concluded that despite the 'reforms' introduced in 2005, the problems in the operation of the pact which arose in 2003 are likely to recur as soon as the euro zone experiences a sharp economic downturn.

Endnotes

1. The OECD classification of taxes is confined to compulsory, unrequited payments to general government. They are unrequited in the sense that benefits provided to taxpayers from government are not normally in proportion to their payment. The EU-19 countries are Austria, Belgium, Czech Republic, Denmark, Finland, France, Germany, Greece, Hungary, Ireland, Italy, Luxembourg, Netherlands, Poland, Portugal, Slovak Republic, Spain, Sweden and the United Kingdom.

2. For a useful summary see NESC, *Opportunities, Challenges and Capacities for Choice,* Stationery Office, Dublin 1999.

3. See D. Hajkova, G. Nicoletti, L. Vartia, and K. Yoo, 'Taxation, business environment and FDI location in OECD countries' (Economics Department Working Paper No. 502), OECD, Paris 2006.

4. See F. Hahn, 'On optimum taxation', *Journal of Economic Theory*, Vol. 6, 1973.

5. N. Stern, 'Uniformity versus selectivity in indirect taxation', *Economics and Politics*, Vol. 2, No. 1, 1990.

6. D. Madden, 'Setting the appropriate tax on cigarettes in Ireland', in T. Callan, D. McCoy and D. Madden (eds), *Budget Perspectives*, Economic and Social Research Institute, Dublin 2002.

7. See T. Marshall, 'Exploring a fiscal food policy: the case of diet and ischaemic heart disease', *British Medical Journal,* Vol. 320, 2000; and A. Leicester and F. Windmeijer, 'The fat tax: economic incentives to reduce obesity' (Briefing Note 49), Institute for Fiscal Studies, London 2004.

8. For a more detailed review of these issues see D. Madden, 'Health interventions and risky behaviour' (UCD Centre for Economic Research Working Paper), University College Dublin, Dublin 2007.

9. See R. Thaler and C. Sunstein, 'Libertarian paternalism', *American Economic Review*, Vol. 93, No. 2, 2003.

10. H. Simons, *Personal Income Taxation*, University of Chicago Press, Chicago 1938.

[11] See R. Thom, 'The taxation of savings' (Research Report No. 2), Foundation for Fiscal Studies, Dublin 1988.

[12] See Department of Finance, *Budget 2006: Review of Tax Schemes*, Stationery Office, Dublin 2006.

[13] For a more comprehensive discussion of these issues see D. Helm, 'The assessment: climate change policy', *Oxford Review of Economic Policy*, Vol. 19, No. 3, 2003.

[14] See R. Tol, 'Irish climate policy for 2012: an assessment', *ESRI Quarterly Economic Commentary*, Winter 2007; Commission of the European Communities, *Progress Towards Achieving the Kyoto Objectives*, COM, Brussels 2007; and Chapter 10.

[15] Government net lending is defined as current general government tax and non-tax receipts less general government current outlays. Gross debt is specified according to the criteria set out in a protocol to the Maastricht Treaty (see EC Council Regulation No. 3605/93 of December 1993).

[16] See B. Coeure and J. Pisani-Ferry, 'Fiscal policy in EMU: towards a sustainability and growth pact', *Oxford Review of Economic Policy*, Vol. 21, No. 4, 2005.

[17] See P. Lane, 'Global bond portfolios and EMU', *International Journal of Central Banking*, Vol. 2, No. 2, 2006.

[18] See V. Koen and P. Van den Noord, 'Fiscal gimmickry in Europe: one-off measures and creative accounting' (OECD Working Paper No. 417), OECD, Paris 2005.

[19] See L. Calmfors, 'The revised Stability and Growth Pact – a critical assessment', Institute for International Economics Studies, Stockholm University, Stockholm 2005.

SECTION III

POLICY ISSUES AT A NATIONAL LEVEL

CHAPTER 5

Population, Migration and Employment

John O'Hagan and Tara McIndoe

1 INTRODUCTION

The experience with regard to employment and unemployment has been the truly remarkable 'story' of the Irish economy in the last 15 years. Table 5.1 illustrates clearly the dramatic changes that have taken place since 1993. Who could have predicted the scale of the change in the intervening years? Employment in 1993 was just 130,000 higher than in 1961; the only period in which there was a significant increase in employment up to this was during the 1970s, when just over 100,000 net new jobs were created. Between 1993 and early 2000, however, over 475,000 net new jobs were created, quite a phenomenal increase in employment in such a short period. It did not stop there, though, as a further 420,000 jobs were created between 2000 and 2007, bringing to almost one million the total number of net new jobs created between 1993 and 2007. The decrease in unemployment during the same period, as seen in Table 5.1, was equally remarkable. This extraordinary economic performance has changed the economic and physical landscape of Ireland in quite a remarkable way in just over a decade.

The increase in employment was the main force behind the extraordinary increase in output in the economy in this period. Definitionally:

$$(1) \qquad\qquad Q = (Q/E) \cdot E$$

That is, the output of an economy (Q) can be expressed as the product of the average productivity of those in employment (Q/E) and the level of employment (E). As we will see later, the level of employment in Ireland in some years increased by over six per cent; this alone would have pushed up Q by six per cent, assuming no change in productivity. Thus, increases in E were the main factor explaining the exceptional growth in Q in the period 1993–2007 (especially the increase in the skilled labour supply). These continue to raise Ireland's potential growth rate above that of its neighbours. Productivity, though, was also increasing during this period, hence ensuring a much faster increase in Q than in E; the causes of this growth in productivity are the subject matter of Chapter 6. The growth in productivity, however, in the 1990s and 2000s was lower than that in the 1960s and not much higher than that in the 1970s and 1980s. The remarkable thing is that the huge increase in employment was not accompanied by any decrease in the growth of productivity. In some senses the increase in E was feared to be a temporary phenomenon as increases in E in Ireland are constrained by the supply of suitable labour; however in the last nine years there has been an exceptional increase in labour supply (see below), which could continue for some time with the aid of net immigration.

Table 5.1

Employment: The Success Story 1993 to 2007

	Employment (millions)	Unemployment rate (%)
1961	1.053	5.0
1971	1.049	5.5
1980	1.156	7.3
1986	1.095	17.1
1990	1.160	12.9
1993	1.183	15.7
1996	1.329	11.9
2000	1.671	4.3
2004	1.836	4.4
2007	2.095	4.5

Sources: 1961–2003, J. O'Hagan and T. McIndoe, in J. O'Hagan and C. Newman (eds), *Economy of Ireland*, Chapter 4, Gill & Macmillan, Dublin 2005; 2004–2008, CSO, *QNHS: Quarter 2 2007*, Stationery Office, Dublin 2007, Table 16.

Sections 2 and 3 examine the issues of population and labour supply and emphasise the critical role that migration plays in this regard, a factor that sets Ireland apart from other OECD countries. Section 4 looks at the issue of employment, its growth and composition, and compares Ireland's performance to that of a number of other countries. The huge reliance on employment growth in the construction sector in the 2000s is highlighted. Section 5 does likewise in relation to unemployment. The rest of the chapter examines the various factors that may influence the level of employment, and hence the level of unemployment, in a small open economy such as that of Ireland. Section 6 examines three factors that impinge on job creation, arising from the single European market and globalisation: namely increased competition for goods, increased mobility and migration of labour across national boundaries, and technological change. As the section highlights, the adaptability and skill levels of the labour force are the key issues in responding to these global pressures.

A major reason for the different responses in different countries to the phenomena of migration, technological change and the globalisation of trade perhaps relates to the *flexibility* of the labour market, and this is the subject matter of Section 7. Issues such as the wage-setting process and the effects of employment legislation on employment creation are discussed in some detail. The effects of prolonged payment of unemployment and related benefits and the effectiveness or otherwise of active labour market policies in dealing with unemployment will also be examined in Section 7. Section 8 concludes the chapter.

2 POPULATION

Population Change and its Components

The size of the population has major emotive significance in Ireland; not surprisingly given the huge reduction in population in Ireland following the Famine (see Chapter 1). As a result, the size of the population has in a sense become an objective of policy in itself (for a discussion of this see Chapter 2). Table 5.2 outlines the trends in population dating back to 1841. The population of the Republic of Ireland in pre-Famine days was over 6.5 million. The decline in this population size in the post-Famine period is all too obvious: a fall of over two million in 20 years despite a high birth rate. Population continued to decline up to 1926; almost 50 years later there was no increase on the 1926 level, when the population in 1971 still stood at only 2.978 million. Since then population size has increased by almost 1.5 million with most of this increase occurring between 1991 and 2007, and the population in 2007 approaching 4.4 million for the first time since 1861. This is seen by many as a very positive development and reflects a reversal of a demoralising decline that had persisted for almost a century and a half.

Table 5.2

Population, Republic of Ireland, 1841–2007 (millions)

Years	Population	Years	Population
1841	6.529	1926	2.972
1851	5.112	1951	2.961
1861	4.402	1961	2.818
1871	4.053	1971	2.978
1881	3.870	1981	3.443
1891	3.469	1991	3.526
1901	3.222	2002	3.917
1911	3.140	2007[1]	4.346

Source: CSO, *Statistical Yearbook 2007*, Stationery Office, Dublin 2003, Table 1.1, and CSO, *Population and Migration Estimates,* Stationery Office, Dublin 2007, Table 1.
[1] Preliminary.

The total population of a country depends on three factors: the number of births, the number of deaths and the level of net migration. The difference between the number of births and deaths is known as the natural increase and in most countries the natural increase translates directly into a population increase. This has not been the case in Ireland, where in the past the change in population has 'tracked' much more closely the trend in migration than that of the natural increase.

As seen in Table 5.3, the number of births per annum reached a peak in the 1970s and declined significantly after that; it increased again in the 2002–2006 period, but this was more a reflection of the increase of the population than of any increase in the birth rate. As a result, from having one of the highest birth rates in Europe only 20 years ago, Ireland now has a birth rate little above the levels pertaining in Northern Europe. This means that the natural increase in the population is averaging around 30,000+ per annum, the same as in the 1970s, despite the large increase since then in the population of child-bearing years.

Table 5.3

Components of Population Change, Selected Intervals
(annual average in thousands)

	Total births	Total deaths	Natural increase	Population change	Estimated net migration
1926–36	58	42	16	0	- 17
1951–56	63	36	27	- 12	- 39
1956–61	61	34	26	- 16	- 42
1961–66	63	33	29	13	- 16
1966–71	63	33	30	19	- 11
1971–79	69	33	35	49	14
1981–86	67	33	34	19	- 14
1986–91	56	32	24	- 3	- 27
1991–96	50	31	18	20	2
1996–2002	54	31	23	49	26
2002–2006	61	28	33	81	48

Source: CSO, *Statistical Yearbook 2007*, Stationery Office, Dublin 2003, Table 1.2.

Migration

While there have been significant changes in the natural increase, they are slight compared to the huge swings in net migration that can occur: 40,000 per annum in some years in the 1980s to net immigration of 2,000 in the early 1990s, around 25,000 in the late 1990s and almost 48,000 in the 2000s. The number of births also increased in the 2000s but this, as mentioned above, was more a reflection of an increase in the population of child-bearing years than of any change in the birth *rate*. The picture that is emerging in the late 2000s is that on average the natural increase will be about the same as in the past, but, because of the downturn in the economy in 2008, and probably beyond, a significant reduction in net in-migration is likely over the next ten years.

The *net* immigration figure is the balance between two flows: *gross* outflows, and gross inflows of people. Looking first at gross inflows (Table 5.4), it can be seen that immigration increased steadily, up from 40,000 in 1996 to almost 110,000 in 2006 and 2007. Initially the increase was due primarily to returning Irish nationals, who accounted for around half of total gross immigration between 1996 and 2000. In absolute terms the immigration of Irish nationals continued after 2000 at the levels of the period 1996 to 2000, but there was also a large inflow of non-Irish nationals, initially from 'Rest of the World' (mainly Africa, Nigeria in particular) and, since the enlargement of the EU in 2004, a further huge increase of non-Irish nationals from 'Rest of EU', mainly Poland. The increasing number of non-Irish nationals who currently make up the country's population and labour force is the most obvious change in Irish society over the past five years. The evidence for this is clear to see, not only in Dublin but across the country, including many small rural towns. The employment implications will be discussed in Section 6.

Table 5.4

Estimated Immigration Classified by Nationality, 1996–2007 (thousands)

	Irish	UK	EU[1]	Rest of USA	World	Rest of Total
1996	17.7	8.3	5.0	4.0	4.2	39.2
1998	24.3	8.6	6.1	2.3	4.7	46.0
2000	24.8	8.4	8.2	2.5	8.6	52.6
2002	27.0	7.4	8.1	2.7	21.7	66.9
2004	16.7	7.4	13.3	2.3	18.8	58.5
2006	18.9	9.9	62.6	1.7	14.7	107.8
2007[2]	20.0	5.8	63.1	2.8	17.8	109.5

Source: CSO, *Population and Migration Estimates*, op. cit., Tables 2 and 3.

[1] From 2005 this column includes migrants from the ten accession states and from 2007 includes Bulgaria and Romania.

[2] Preliminary.

As can be seen in Table 5.5, there was also substantial out-migration over the period 1996 to 2007. It was of course less than gross in-migration, and substantially so in some years, but nonetheless the persistence of out-migration during the boom years is noteworthy, especially the large rise between 2004 and 2007. While there is no breakdown of this out-migration by nationality, data are provided by the CSO by country of destination. Given these data, is seems reasonable to assume that most of the out-migration to the UK and the USA would have consisted of Irish nationals. Some of the outflow to 'Rest of EU' and 'Rest of World' would also consist of Irish nationals but it is likely that much of the out-migration to Rest of World, especially in recent years, has been that of non-Irish nationals. Thus, Table 5.5 would seem to indicate that substantial out-migration by

Irish nationals persisted during 1996 and 2007, but at what precise level cannot be ascertained. Nonetheless, should in-migration fall off in years to come, and out-migration remain at the levels that obtained in the decade up to 2007 – and perhaps increase as non-Irish nationals return home following a downturn in the economy – it is conceivable that *net* out-migration could result over the next few years.

Table 5.5

Estimated Emigration Classified by Country of Destination, 1996–2007 (thousands)

	UK	Rest of EU[1]	USA	Rest of World	Total
1996	14.1	5.1	5.2	6.8	31.2
1998	11.8	5.9	5.3	5.6	28.6
2000	7.2	5.5	4.0	10.0	26.6
2002	7.4	4.8	4.8	8.5	25.6
2004	7.1	5.0	3.9	10.5	26.5
2006	8.8	8.0	3.3	15.8	36.0
2007[2]	10.1	10.2	2.9	19.0	42.2

Source: As for Table 5.4.

[1] From 2005 this column includes migrants from the ten accession states and from 2007 includes Bulgaria and Romania.

[2] Preliminary.

Table 5.6 provides an age breakdown of immigrants over the period 2002 to 2007, which is of relevance to our later discussion. The most remarkable feature is the huge proportion of total immigrants in the active age-groups of 15 to 24 and in particular 25 to 44. This means that the vast bulk of immigrants came here for work, and have few young dependents. Most of the dependents were probably attached to Irish nationals returning home, with tiny numbers associated with the immigration of non-Irish nationals. This means that, unless they have had children since they arrived in Ireland, many immigrant workers have no family ties to Ireland and hence are still highly mobile, reinforcing the point made earlier that many of the immigrants could go elsewhere if and when employment prospects turn down, as they have already, in Ireland.

3 LABOUR SUPPLY

Labour supply in any country depends on three factors: the total size of the population, the proportion of that population of working age, and the proportion of the working age population seeking or in work. This is illustrated by the identity:

(2) $$L = (P) . (Pa /P) . (L/Pa)$$

where L is the size of the labour force, P the size of the population, and Pa the size of the population of working age. The labour force, in turn, consists of those in employment (E) and those unemployed (UE). Hence:

(3) $$L = E + UE$$

Two further identities of interest to this discussion are the following:

(4) $$Q/P = (Q/E) . (E/P)$$

(5) $$E/P = (E/L) . (L/Pa) . (Pa/P)$$

Equation (4) links the demographic factors back to (1). It states that output per person employed and the proportion of the population employed determine output per head of population. We saw in Equation (1) that increases in E were the most important factor accounting for record increases in Q in Ireland in the last ten years; E/P has also increased at a record rate, thereby pushing up Q/P (our measure of living standards, as seen in Chapter 2) to record levels. E/P (the proportion of the population in employment), as can be seen from Equation (5), is influenced by three factors, all of which increased in the 15 years up to 2007; E/L (the proportion of the labour force in employment) has increased as unemployment decreased, Pa/P (the proportion of the population of working age) has increased because of demographic factors (as shall be seen later) and L/Pa (the proportion of the working population in the labour force) has increased, principally because of increased participation by married females in the labour force. These very favourable demographic trends, in terms of their impact on living standards, have become known as Ireland's 'demographic dividend' in the 1990s and 2000s.

Working-Age Population
As a result of the fall in the birth rate in the last two decades, there has been a large fall in the population aged 15 and under. The decline in the population aged under 15, now stabilised, clearly has had major implications for the economy in, for example, the area of education. However, because of the high birth rate prior to this, and, more important, the trends in migration observed above, there has been a large increase in the population aged 15 to 64, and especially in the prime working-age population, 25–64. As seen above, a large proportion of the immigrants were of prime working age, thereby pushing up the population in this age group disproportionately. The number of people aged 25 to 64 rose from 2.18 million in 1991 to over 2.91 million by the year 2006; this is a very large increase in such a short period and had a marked effect on Ireland's age dependency ratios.

Table 5.6
Estimated Immigration Classified by Age Group, 1996–2007 (thousands)

	0–14	15–24	25–44	45–64	65 and over
2002	7.0	19.8	35.2	4.2	0.8
2004	6.1	18.7	28.8	4.2	0.7
2006	11.5	31.6	57.2	6.1	1.4
2007[1]	11.7	30.3	59.8	6.9	0.9

Source: As for Table 5.4.
[1] Preliminary.

Table 5.7 highlights these changes in the composition of the population. In 1981, those aged under 15 years accounted for 51.4 per cent of those aged 15 to 64, but in just over 20 years this had dropped by almost 21 percentage points. At the same time, the population aged 65 and over, expressed as a proportion of the 15–64 population, also declined, albeit slightly. As Table 5.7 illustrates, these favourable demographic trends have now run their course; importantly, though, there will be no worsening of the demographic situation until after 2011, when the percentage classified as 'old' begins to rise significantly. These projections, however, depend very much on what happens with regard to migration over the next decade or so. A return to significant out-migration could dramatically alter these projections.

Table 5.7
Age Dependency Ratios,[1] 1981 to 2021

Year	Young	Old	Total
1981	51.4%	18.2%	69.6%
1991	43.4%	18.5%	61.9%
1996	36.5%	17.6%	54.1%
2002	29.3%	16.4%	45.7%
2006	29.7%	16.1%	45.8%
2011[2]	31.5%	17.8%	49.3%
2021[2]	30.5%	23.5%	54.1%

Sources: O'Hagan and McIndoe, op. cit.; CSO, *Census 2006 – Principal Demographic Results*, Stationery Office, Dublin 2007, Table 2; and CSO, *Population and Labour Force Projections 2006–2036*, Stationery Office, Dublin 2007, Table S.
[1] The ratios in the first two columns are obtained by dividing the population aged 0–14 and 65 years and over by the population aged 15–64. The final column is the sum of these two.
[2] Forecasts, assuming immigration continues at moderate levels and fertility decreases to 1.85 by 2011 and remains constant thereafter.

Participation in the Labour Force
An important factor when examining the employment situation in any country is the proportion of the working population that actually seeks work. This is known as the labour force participation rate.

Table 5.8 provides data for Ireland, a number of other small EU countries, two countries of particular interest to Ireland (the UK and the USA) and the OECD group; where possible these will also be used as the comparator countries in the other tables in this chapter. As can be seen in Table 5.8, the labour force participation rate for males in Ireland is about average for most other countries listed; but for females it is considerably less. The figure for females for Ireland is 61.3 per cent, compared to a figure of 55.0 per cent in Greece (the lowest rate), 70.3 per cent in the UK, and 76.7 per cent in Denmark (the highest rate).

Table 5.8

Labour Force Participation Rates[1] in Selected OECD Countries, 1994 and 2006

	Males		Females	
	1994	2006	1994	2006
Belgium	72.0%	72.7%	51.2%	58.9%
Denmark	83.7%	83.4%	73.8%	76.7%
Greece	77.0%	79.1%	43.2%	55.0%
Ireland	*76.2%*	*81.0%*	*45.8%*	*61.3%*
Netherlands	79.6%	81.9%	57.3%	69.4%
Norway	81.6%	81.4%	70.9%	74.8%
OECD	81.4%	80.4%	57.8%	60.8%
UK	85.1%	83.2%	67.1%	70.3%
USA	84.3%	81.9%	69.4%	69.3%

Source: OECD, *Employment Outlook*, OECD, Paris 2007, Table B.
[1] Ratios refer to persons aged 15 to 64 years who are in the labour force divided by the total population aged 15 to 64.

A noteworthy feature, though, is that female participation rates are increasing in most countries, and Ireland is no exception. Following a substantial increase up to 1994, the rate has increased further in Ireland, up from 45.8 to 61.3 per cent, a large rise in such a short period. By 2006 the rate for Ireland exceeded the OECD average but, as discussed above, it is still well below some key comparator countries, in particular the UK. It is difficult to predict how much further this participation rate will grow in Ireland, but with the much lower birth rate, and improved employment prospects, it could increase to the UK level if not to that of Denmark or Norway. If this happened, it would lead to a large increase in the labour force arising from this factor alone. The increase in the female participation rate is primarily due to the increase in the participation rate of married females. The dramatic changes in this regard can be seen in Table 5.9.

There have been huge changes in the participation rate for all the age groups shown and it is predicted that these increases will continue for the next decade, bringing Ireland into line with other EU countries in this regard. The really striking increases are in the age groups over 35, with a large increase also in the 25–34 age group; up from 31.7 per cent in 1986 to 73.2 per cent in 2007. The participation rate for married females in the 45–54 age group, though, increased from just 18.7 per cent in 1986 to 64.8 per cent in 2007, reflecting a quite dramatic economic and social change.

Table 5.9

Labour Force Participation Rates, Married
Females by Age Group, 1986–2007

Age group	1986	1996	2002[1]	2006	2007
25–34	31.7%	62.6%	65.9%	71.3%	73.2%
35–44	19.5%	52.1%	62.2%	64.0%	66.2%
45–54	18.7%	37.2%	55.3%	62.4%	64.8%
55–59	13.1%	25.1%	35.4%	47.1%	46.1%

Source: CSO, *Labour Force Survey,* various issues, Stationery Office, Dublin ·1987/1997, Table 8B; CSO, *Quarterly National Household Survey* (*QNHS*), various issues.

Conclusion

A consideration of migration trends is central to any discussion of labour supply in Ireland. Migration, more than any other factor, determines changes in the size of the population increase and the growth of the labour force. As seen in Table 5.3, more than half of those added to the Irish population on an annual average basis between 1996 and 2007 were as a result of net inward migration. The decline in the birth rate and the rise in the labour force participation of females aged 25 to 64 may have been dwarfed by the changes in net migration, but in themselves they are very significant changes which, after the effects of net migration are removed, will have a marked bearing on the growth of the labour force in years to come.

4 EMPLOYMENT: GROWTH AND COMPOSITION

Overall Employment

The first point worth noting from Table 5.10 is the tiny size of the workforce in Ireland: around 2 million in 2005, as opposed to 8.2 million in the Netherlands, 28.7 million in the UK and 141.7 million in the USA. Given that there is an effective common labour market between Ireland and the UK, it is very important for labour policy purposes to bear in mind the relative sizes of the two labour markets.

The most striking fact in relation to employment in Ireland has been its growth relative to other countries. In the ten years to 2004, employment grew on average by 4.1 per cent per annum in Ireland compared to less than one per cent growth in many countries; only the Netherlands, at 1.6 per cent, had a rate of growth comparable to that in Ireland. This is remarkable given that employment in Ireland had actually declined in the 1980–86 period and had not managed to rise significantly over the entire decade spanning the years 1980–90 (see Table 5.1).

Table 5.10

Employment and Employment Growth in Selected OECD Countries

	2005 millions	1994–2004	2006	2007[1]	E/Pa % (2006)
		Annual percentage change			
Belgium	4.251	0.8	1.1	1.1	65.9
Denmark	2.767	0.5	1.9	1.2	80.1
Greece	4.625	0.9	2.4	1.6	67.0
Ireland	*1.952*	*4.1*	*4.4*	*3.4*	*71.3*
Netherlands	8.191	1.6	0.9	1.4	75.7
Norway	2.289	1.1	3.2	2.3	78.2
OECD	523.021	1.1	1.6	1.3	70.5
UK	28.730	1.1	0.8	1.0	76.7
USA	141.715	1.2	1.9	1.1	75.5

Source: OECD, *Employment Outlook*, OECD, Paris 2007, Table 1.2 and Table B.
[1]Forecasts.

The growth of employment since 2005 has continued to outpace all the countries listed in Table 5.10. This means that for 15 years Ireland has managed to outperform the smaller European countries as well as the UK and the USA in the employment growth stakes. While this extraordinary performance may be coming to an end in Ireland (the ESRI has predicted zero growth in employment in 2008), the period 1994 to 2007 was truly remarkable, in terms of employment growth both in an absolute sense and even more so in a comparative sense.

Ireland of course had a much greater increase in potential labour supply than any of the other countries, hence unemployment would have remained at a very high level and the position of net immigration might have been translated into substantial net emigration without this growth in employment. Much of the early immigration, after all, was due to the return of people who had emigrated in the depressed labour market conditions of the 1980s. As seen earlier, much of the immigration in the 2000s was due to immigration of non-Irish nationals, and since 2004 especially from the Eastern European states who became EU members in that year.

These points are well borne out by the last column in Table 5.10; this shows the ratio of total employment to population size aged 15–64 years for each of the countries listed. Despite the rapid growth of employment in Ireland, just 71.3 per cent of the population aged 15–64 were in employment in 2006, similar to the figure for the entire OECD in the same year; the figure for the USA was 75.5 per cent, for the UK 76.7 per cent and those for Denmark and Norway as high as 80.1 and 78.2 per cent respectively. These figures reflect what was seen earlier in Table

5.8: the low labour participation rate for men and the low figure for females compared to these countries, albeit (as seen earlier) increasing rapidly.

It could be argued therefore that the employment increase in Ireland in the last 15 years is strongly associated with a huge increase in the labour force, an increase that is simply bringing Ireland up to the international norm in terms of the proportion of the total working age population in employment.

Part-time Employment

An important issue relating to the growth of employment in some countries, including Ireland, is the extent to which it consisted of part-time employment. The available data suggest (Table 5.11) that the level of part-time employment as a proportion of total employment is low throughout the countries examined. In this regard Ireland is not out of line with its OECD counterparts. Similarly, there appears to have been no significant increase in part-time employment, especially among males, in recent years.

There is a marked gender difference in relation to part-time employment, as may be seen in Table 5.11. Only 7.7 per cent of total male employment in Ireland is part-time, whereas 43.8 per cent of female employment is part-time. These percentages vary considerably from country to country, but on balance the position in Ireland is not unusual. More striking, as evidenced by the figures in the last column of Table 5.11, is the very high share in total part-time employment accounted for by females. In Ireland this is above the OECD average, and well above that for Denmark, Greece, and the USA.

Table 5.11

Incidence and Composition of Part-time Employment[1]
in Selected OECD Countries, 2006

	Part-time employment as a proportion of total employment (%)			Share in part-time employment (%)
	Men	Women	Total	Women
Belgium	6.7	34.7	19.3	81.1
Denmark	11.4	25.6	18.1	66.2
Greece	4.0	12.9	7.5	67.0
Ireland	*7.7*	*43.9*	*19.9*	*78.7*
Netherlands	15.8	59.7	35.5	75.5
Norway	10.6	32.9	21.1	73.5
OECD	8.1	26.4	16.1	72.1
UK	9.9	38.8	23.4	77.6
USA	7.8	17.8	12.6	67.8

Source: OECD, *Employment Outlook*, OECD, Paris 2007, Table E.
[1]Part-time is defined as usual hours of work of less than 30 hours per week.

What is perhaps more important is the extent to which part-time employment is involuntary, i.e. chosen by the individual only because they could not get full-time work. The evidence suggests that involuntary part-time employment has not grown significantly as a proportion of total employment in the countries for which data exist, with, if anything, a decrease in this proportion in the case of Ireland.[1]

There is little evidence therefore that the increase in employment in Ireland and other countries was not 'real', in the sense that it took place in involuntary part-time employment. In other words, where the increase in employment was due to an increase in part-time employment, this reflected a desire for such employment; largely, it seems, from female employees entering the labour force and with a preference for part-time work as it fits better with family and other commitments.

A different but related issue is the extent to which the increase in employment was in temporary work. This is a much debated topic in labour market economics as some economists believe that an increasing proportion of jobs will have to be temporary if labour markets, especially in Europe, are to be sufficiently flexible to cope with an employment crisis, a topic to which we shall return below.

Although experiences across the OECD vary, it does appear that younger and less well-educated workers disproportionately fill temporary jobs. On the other hand, temporary workers are a diverse group who work in a wide range of occupations and sectors. Other characteristics of temporary employment include the tendency for temporary jobs to pay less than permanent ones as well as sometimes offering less access to paid vacations, sick leave, unemployment insurance, and other fringe benefits including access to training. Temporary workers are generally less satisfied with their jobs and more often report inflexible work schedules and monotonous work tasks than their permanent employment counterparts.[2] There is no evidence, though, that this is a particularly acute problem in the Irish context, at least not yet: 85 per cent of employees are on secure contracts, and this percentage has increased since the mid-1900s. This may be due to the weakness of employment protection laws in Ireland, allowing employers sufficient flexibility not to need to resort to temporary contracts.

Sectoral Composition of Employment

Table 5.12 outlines the composition of employment in Ireland from 1994 to 2007. While the data are not strictly comparable, the table shows some broad trends in this composition in the period. One striking feature is the relatively small size of the agricultural sector; many more people now, for example, are employed in education and health, financial and business services or the wholesale and retail trade than in agriculture.

The once central position of the agriculture sector has truly diminished (see Chapter 10) and now accounts for just 5.5 per cent of total employment (down from over 12 per cent only 15 years ago). There are now more people employed in hotels and restaurants than in the total agricultural sector, reflecting the increased importance of tourism to the Irish economy and the marked trend towards eating out by Irish people. The services sector as a whole is now almost three times the size of the industrial sector and five times that of the manufacturing sector (other production services). As can be seen in the final column in Table 5.12, the growth areas have been the wholesale and retail trade, hotels and restaurants, health, transport and financial and other business services. The most striking growth, though, has been in construction, especially since 1998. The level of employment in construction more than trebled between 1994 and 2007, with most of the increase occurring since the late 1990s. It is considered that the reliance on such a high level of employment in construction is not sustainable and could lead (and indeed already has led, in early 2008) to a major cut-back in such activity with very serious consequences for the broader economy.

Table 5.12

Employment by Sector: Ireland

	(thousands)			
	1994	1998	2007	2007/1994
Agriculture, Forestry and Fishing	*147.0*	*135.9*	*114.7*	*0.78*
Industry of which:	*343.3*	*428.5*	*571.8*	*1.67*
Other production services	251.8	302.4	291.5	1.16
Construction	91.5	126.1	280.3	3.06
Services of which:	*730.2*	*929.1*	*1,409.0*	*1.92*
Wholesale and retail trade	169.2	211.1	293.5	1.73
Hotels and restaurants	68.4	97.8	124.8	1.82
Transport, storage and communication	55.9	87.0	122.4	2.18
Financial and other business services	114.3	171.0	287.6	2.52
Public administration and defence	66.4	70.9	104.6	1.58
Education	80.5	93.3	141.5	1.76
Health	101.0	113.9	213.0	2.11
Other	74.5	84.1	121.6	1.63
Total	*1,220.6*	*1,494.0*	*2,095.4*	*1.72*

Sources: O'Hagan and McIndoe, op. cit., and CSO, *QNHS – Quarter 2 2007*, op. cit.

Despite the continuing decline in the share of total employment accounted for by agriculture in Ireland, this proportion is still six times higher than in the UK and more than double that applying in Denmark. In contrast, Ireland has a higher share of total employment in industry than these countries, partly of course due to the high proportion of total employment in construction.

Turning now to services, we can see from Table 5.13 the share of total employment in Ireland accounted for by services is around the EU average but still well below the rates applying in Belgium, Denmark and the UK. Services now account for almost two-thirds of all employment, however, and it is instructive to look at the breakdown of this total by subsector (see Table 5.13). Ireland has a higher share of total employment than the EU average in hotels and restaurants and financial and other business services. The UK, though, as one would expect, has a considerably higher proportion of total employment in the financial and business services sector than Ireland. Ireland has a lower percentage of employment than the EU average in education and a considerably lower proportion than in Belgium and the UK. The same applies in relation to the health sector. The sector with the lowest relative percentage of employment in Ireland, however, is public administration and defence (5.1 per cent in Ireland compared to an EU average of 7.3 per cent).

Table 5.13

Employment in the Services Sector: International Comparison 2005

	Proportion of total employment (%)				
	Belgium	Denmark	*Ireland*	UK	EU-25
Overall	*72.3*	*72.4*	*65.1*	*76.2*	*66.4*
Wholesale and retail trade	13.4	14.6	*13.8*	15.3	14.6
Hotels and restaurants	3.5	2.2	*5.8*	4.3	4.2
Transport, storage and communication	7.8	6.4	*6.1*	6.9	6.1
Financial and other business services	12.0	12.6	*13.3*	15.7	12.4
Public administration and defence	10.2	6.0	*5.1*	7.1	7.3
Education	9.2	7.4	*6.4*	9.1	7.2
Health	12.4	17.9	*9.7*	12.3	9.8
Other	3.8	5.3	*4.9*	5.5	4.8

Source: European Commission, *Employment in Europe 2006*, Office for Official Publications of the European Communities, Luxembourg 2003, Table 12.

5 UNEMPLOYMENT: EXTENT AND FEATURES

International Comparisons

Table 5.14 provides the key information on recorded unemployment rates in Ireland and selected OECD countries, including some small EU countries, since 1994. The unemployment rate is given by $E/(E + UE)$ and the picture is fairly clear. In 1990 Ireland had an unemployment rate that was almost double the rate applying in every other country listed. By 1994 the unemployment situation in Ireland had improved only marginally, whereas for all of the other countries shown it had deteriorated, in Belgium by as much as three percentage points.

Between 1994 and 2004, all countries bar Greece experienced significant declines in unemployment, with the OECD average declining from 7.6 per cent in 1994 to 6.9 per cent in 2004. The most dramatic decline of course was for Ireland, down from 13.4 per cent to 4.5 per cent in the same period. The Irish figure remained around 4.5 per cent until late 2007 and could rise above 5.5 per cent in 2008. In the meantime, the OECD average dropped to 6.0 per cent in 2006, with a likely further decline in 2007 due to strong employment performances in France and, in particular, in Germany. Thus by 2008 the Irish unemployment rate will probably be around the OECD average and well above the rates applying in Denmark, the Netherlands and Norway.

Table 5.14

Standardised Unemployment Rates in Selected OECD Countries[1]

	As a percentage of the labour force			
	1994	1999	2004	2006
Belgium	9.8	8.5	8.4	8.2
Denmark	7.7	5.1	5.5	3.9
Greece	8.8	12.0	10.5	8.9
Ireland	*14.3*	*5.7*	*4.5[2]*	*4.4[2]*
Netherlands	6.8	3.2	4.6	3.9
Norway	6.0	3.3	4.4	3.5
OECD	7.6	6.6	6.9	6.0
UK	9.3	5.9	4.7	5.3
USA	6.1	4.2	5.5	4.6

Source: As for Table 5.8, op. cit., Table A.

[1] All series are benchmarked to labour force survey-based estimates and have been adjusted to ensure comparability over time.

[2] Figure differs from that in Table 5.1 where the CSO was the data source.

Comparison/Measurement Problems

Standardised Unemployment Rates

The discussion above is based on the assumption that the data can be used for valid comparison both across countries and over time. Is this the case? There are three main issues of concern here. The first is whether or not all countries are using the same methods of defining and compiling data on unemployment; the second is whether or not there is a consistent series over time for Ireland; the last is whether or not there are certain categories of persons that are not, and perhaps cannot be, included by any country but which should be included in any discussion of labour market slack (i.e. where labour demand is less than labour supply) in an economy.

International comparison of unemployment rates is fraught with difficulty, despite the best efforts of the OECD and the EU. Nonetheless, there are reasonably reliable comparative data for the EU member states, if not for most of the OECD countries, and these are the data that inform comparative studies and international policy debate.

In relation to Ireland, there are two main sources of data on unemployment: the Quarterly National Household Survey (QNHS) and the Live Register. The QNHS gives two measures of unemployment: the International Labour Office (ILO) measure and the Principal Economic Status (PES) measure. The first of these is the internationally recognised measure of unemployment and defines somebody as 'unemployed' if their response in the survey makes clear that they did not work even for one hour for payment or profit in the previous week, that they actively sought work in the previous four weeks, and are available to start work within two weeks. This is a strict measure of unemployment, much stricter than the Live Register measure. The latter counts each month all those in receipt of unemployment benefit or unemployment assistance, plus those who, though entitled to no payment, wish to have social insurance contributions 'credited' to them; in addition, casual and part-time workers who work for no more than three days in the week may be entitled to register on account of the days they do not work. There is little doubt therefore that it gives an overstatement of the number unemployed in the normal sense of the term.

It is the ILO data, therefore, that are used for international comparison, as the methods used in arriving at these data are considered to give the more accurate indicator of the underlying level of unemployment in a country. These data are also used in this chapter, unless indicated otherwise. It is important to remember that the ILO definition is quite a restrictive measure of unemployment and perhaps gives the most favourable picture of the unemployment problem in a country. It excludes, for example, many who are in involuntary part-time work and also those described as discouraged and marginalised workers.

Invalidity/Disability Benefit Issue

There are also many people unable to work through invalidity or disability. The proportion of the working age group in this category has grown significantly in some EU countries in recent years, with some commentators suggesting that some of the decrease in unemployment, in the Netherlands and the UK in particular, could be linked to this development. For example, in the UK in late 2007 there were more people aged under 35 on disability benefit than on unemployment benefit and a major programme has been put in place to get many of these people back to work, on the lines of the policies used to bring the long-term unemployed back into the labour force both in the UK and Ireland, and more recently Germany.[3]

Helping disabled people find and keep jobs is a major challenge for all OECD countries, including Ireland, especially given that the potential personal, social and financial benefits are huge. An OECD report in 2003 found that in most countries once a person entered a disabilities-related programme they remain a beneficiary until retirement; on average only one per cent of benefit recipients find a job each year. Although it is costly to leave disabled people outside the labour force, no country has so far been successful in crafting policies that will help disabled people return to work. The OECD suggests various broad areas for improvement, including: individual benefit packages with job search support, rehabilitation and vocational training; new obligations for disabled people including, for those who are capable, a requirement to look for work; involving employers and trade unions in reintegration efforts; and more flexible cash benefits, depending on job capabilities and changes in an individual's disability over time.[4]

Long-Term Unemployment
Apart from the level of unemployment, its composition is also of considerable interest to economists, for reasons already alluded to. The most important consideration in this regard relates to its composition in terms of short-term (less than 12 months) and long-term (12 months or more) unemployment.

Long-term unemployment (LTU) in Ireland rose significantly between 1980 and 1994. The long-term unemployment rate was only 2.8 per cent of the labour force in 1980, rising to 8.3 per cent in 1988 and rising again in the early 1990s to 9.0 per cent of the labour force. Table 5.15 shows the marked decline that has taken place in LTU since 1994. The reductions on all three counts are remarkable: the numbers in absolute terms are down to nearly a fifth of their level in 1994; the drop in the LTU rate is even more dramatic; and the share of LTU in total unemployment dropped from over 60 per cent in 1994 to around 29 per cent by late 2007. As a result, the LTU rate (1.3 per cent) in late 2007 was below the level pertaining in 1980.

Table 5.15
Long-Term Unemployment in Ireland, 1994–2007

	Number ('000s)	Unemployment rate	Long-term unemployment rate
1994	128.2	14.8%	9.0%
1998	63.6	7.8%	3.9%
2002	21.7	4.2%	1.2%
2007	28.4	4.5%	1.3%

Source: O'Hagan and McIndoe, op. cit., and CSO, *QNHS – Quarter 2 2007,* op cit., Table 16.

What has brought about these reductions? There were probably three factors at work: very favourable aggregate demand conditions; the effects of special labour market programmes (in particular the Community Employment Programme and Back to Work and Back to Education Allowance Scheme); and the effect of tighter social welfare control measures (see below).

6 ADAPTING TO NEW TECHNOLOGY, AND INCREASED TRADE AND MIGRATION

The increase in unemployment in the 1980s and early 1990s was not unique to Ireland, but affected almost every country in Europe, including, as seen earlier, the

Nordic countries. What caused the rise in unemployment in Europe? More specifically, why did high unemployment rates persist into the 2000s in most of Europe, especially in France, Germany, and Italy, and why are they beginning to fall again, in the case of Germany quite dramatically?[5] A number of causes have been suggested, which can be grouped into two broad headings. First, there are arguments relating to global factors such as increased competition in international trade, technological change and greater freedom of movement of labour, especially in the EU, and hence a large increase in migration. These are factors that would have affected every country in Europe, but some to a greater extent than others. How each country fared depended largely on the skill level and adaptability of their labour forces in the new circumstances. These issues will be discussed in this section. Second, there are structural arguments relating to such issues as the role of unions and wage bargaining/setting, employment protection legislation and the taxation and social welfare systems. These issues will be discussed in Section 7.

The Single Market, Trade and Technological Change

Given the extent of Ireland's trade, and factor and corporate links with the world economy, it is inevitable that the increasing globalisation of economic activity has, and will continue to have, a major effect on economic activity and employment in Ireland (see later chapters). Added to this is the deepening of the single European market and the removal of barriers to free trade in services, mergers and acquisitions and capital flows, with the consequential implications for economic activity, competition and employment in Ireland. Ireland's entry into the euro zone in the late 1990s was a further major commitment to the benefits and challenges of the single market.

It is generally believed by economists that an increasing intensity of trade and integration will lead to higher incomes, but that it will also lead to the displacement of labour in some activities and the expansion of labour in others. The net impact on employment should be negligible as long as labour and product markets function well and wages are reasonably flexible. Thus, if decreased overall employment should result from increased trade intensity and competition it is not trade or competition per se that is causing the problem but the functioning of the labour and product markets, a topic that will be returned to in a later section. The evidence, according to the OECD, supports such an argument. This, indeed, is the reason why Ireland has adopted such a pro-trade liberalisation, pro-competition stance in the last 30 years.

Increasing international trade and economic integration may also have an impact on innovation and the absorption of technological change. It is argued by some that labour-saving technologies are, at least in part, introduced in anticipation of and/or in response to the greater competition both on domestic and foreign markets that arises from the increased globalisation of trade and European integration. As such, the effect of increased international integration and technological change are difficult to separate in practice.

Technology is central to the process of growth (see Chapters 6 and 8): it allows increases in productivity and thereby in real incomes. But does it destroy jobs and in the process create unemployment?

Fears about widespread job losses associated with the emergence of new technology are not new and are in the aggregate largely unfounded. They date back to at least the time of the Industrial Revolution in the early nineteenth century when the Luddite movement in England destroyed new machinery for fear of job losses. It is true that technological change involves a process of job destruction in some older occupations, firms and industries, but it also involves a parallel process of job creation in new and emerging sectors and occupations. There are many historical examples of predictions of large-scale technological unemployment being followed in fact by large net expansions of jobs, the experience in the last two decades or so with regard to the IT sector in the USA being the most recent striking example.

While Ireland's adoption of new technology will be discussed in later chapters, particularly Chapter 8, it is worth noting here that there are four key technology areas that will influence the country's success in IT: infrastructure; competitive market conditions; education and training; and access for all. It has been, and will be, the country's ability to take appropriate action on all four fronts that will allow us to absorb and adapt to the new technology: our ability to do this in turn will be the key to employment, not only in manufacturing but also, and more important perhaps, given its scale, in the services sector (see Chapters 8, 9 and 12).

Labour Market Integration
Labour market integration is a highly contentious aspect of economic integration in Europe. Popular opinion holds immigrants responsible for high unemployment, abuse of social welfare programmes, street crime and the deterioration of neighbourhoods. Economic theory predicts that in a world of no unemployment there will be both winners and losers resulting from labour migration. Without migration, however, the worldwide allocation of productive factors is inefficient. Improving the overall efficiency of the world economy through migration then leads to a net gain which must be split between the home and foreign country.

In a situation where there is no unemployment and workers initially earn better wages in the domestic economy than in the foreign economy, migration will result in labour flowing from the foreign to the domestic economy. This may push down wages at home, harming domestic workers while benefiting domestic capital owners. The opposite happens in the foreign economy. Wages there tend to rise as some foreign labour moves to the domestic economy; thus, remaining foreign workers are better off while capital owners are made worse off. The net outcome is positive for the efficiency reasons outlined above.

Complements and Substitutes
For most European economies labour is comprised of both highly skilled and low-skilled workers. Recognising this distinction allows a more nuanced

understanding of the dynamics of labour market integration under net-inward or net-outward migration. Highly skilled labour can then be defined as 'human capital' which introduces the idea of economic complements and substitutes when discussing labour market outcomes. The basic theory of labour market integration outlined above assumed two factors of production, labour and capital; assigning highly skilled workers to the productive factor 'capital' is important when extending this discussion to the Irish or broader EU context. In this way unskilled workers are seen as complements to skilled workers and capital: as the supply of unskilled workers increases and their price falls demand for skilled workers and capital rises.

Immigrants often have a skill mix that is different from that of domestic workers. In the EU this means that many domestic workers can be thought of as belonging to 'capital'. In line with the discussion above, migration of relatively unskilled labour then results in net gains for domestic human capital. Even where immigrants have a higher skill level than the average native worker there can be a win-win outcome for both domestic and imported labour. Instead of shifting labour from the foreign to the domestic economy, *capital* is effectively being imported. This is because increased supply of skilled workers raises the productivity of the unskilled workers and thus increases their relative wage level. So immigrants with skills that complement the skill mix in the receiving nation are typically less likely to create losers in the receiving nation.

The empirical evidence for Ireland suggests that although the skill make-up of immigrants is higher than that of the native population, immigrants tend to fill low-skilled jobs and thus act as complements to the high-skilled Irish workforce, even if this means that migrants achieve a low occupational attainment relative to their educational attainment.[6] The evidence shows that immigrants occupy a lower proportion of the higher-skilled occupations relative to the native population. This holds over time, and is thus not merely reflecting the fact that newly arrived immigrants often experience downward occupational mobility.

Estimating the impact of migration on the wages of domestic workers has been undertaken for Ireland. For example, the net immigrant inflow between 2003 and 2005 is estimated to have added between 2.3 and 3.0 per cent to GNP. 'The route through which this was achieved was to lower high-skilled wages relative to where they would have been and to facilitate the increased employment of high-skilled labour. The effect of this was to increase demand for low-skilled wages (or reduce low-skilled unemployment, depending on how this is modelled).'[7]

Unemployment
Immigration can also interact with the domestic labour market by directly altering the level of unemployment. Taking into account migration's effect on unemployment is important in the European context of relatively inflexible labour markets and in Ireland due to the historic association between outward migration and high domestic unemployment and more recently the association between low domestic unemployment and very high inward migration. These issues are also

pertinent when considering the likelihood of significantly slower growth in Ireland in the next few years as well as the concern that employment growth is set to slow significantly or indeed stop altogether, as predicted by the ESRI (see earlier discussion).

In a situation where unemployment exists (i.e. there is a mismatch between supply and demand in the labour market), theory suggests the following on entry of net immigration. In Europe this mismatch almost always means excess supply, due in part to national labour market institutions that are typically biased in favour of workers who already have jobs. First, if immigrants can be hired at lower wages to perform the same jobs as locals, the demand for local workers will decline as cheap immigrants fill jobs before the market turns to the native market to fulfil any remaining demands. Thus domestic wages and native employment fall. Note, however, that the drop in native employment (even in this extreme case) will be less than the number of immigrants. This dampening is due to the drop in wages that occurs, thereby increasing demand for labour, and means that overall employment increases in the economy. Second, there may be no increase in overall unemployment. Immigration affects unemployment only to the extent that it affects the structure of the labour market. For example, as wages are lowered fewer domestic workers will be prepared to offer their labour services at the going wage and hence will withdraw from the labour force; if this matches the decrease in native employment there will be no net increase in unemployment.

In the preceding discussion we have assumed that natives and immigrants are substitutes rather than complements. If instead immigrants are complements to native workers, immigration will raise the demand for native workers, resulting in higher wages, higher employment, and an unambiguously favourable impact on unemployment.

It remains to be seen whether the favourable impact of migration on the Irish labour market as evidenced above will continue as the Irish economy experiences slowing growth. Preliminary evidence suggests (see Table 5.5) that recent immigrants are still highly mobile and that some have started to return to their home countries as the growth in construction work begins to slow. In this way the ease of movement between Ireland and the new European member states may help to mitigate adverse employment impacts of a global economic downturn.

Education, Training and Skills Adaptability

Over the last 20 years the structure of work in the industrialised world has, for the reasons mentioned above, been changing. There has been a shift in demand away from low-skilled, low-wage jobs towards high-skilled, high-wage jobs. The change in the nature of work arises not only from the transformation of jobs by technology and international trade but also from the 'natural' sectoral changes that have occurred with regard to employment (see Table 5.13). Allied to this, because of immigration, there has been a marked transformation in labour supply in many sectors.

The skills required in services are different from those needed for industry,

133

hence the declining industrial workforce cannot be automatically transplanted into services jobs. The new wave of employment creation leads, as mentioned earlier, to a transformation of the competencies required from the workforce. Not only do they need different qualifications and skills but the continuously changing nature of work also requires them to have a high degree of flexibility that was not necessary in the past when permanent, stable positions were the norm.

The skills of the labour force, then, have to be altered to take account of the changing environment and nature of work that accompany this. In the absence of this adjustment, mismatch can, and may have, become a serious problem in the labour market in Ireland. Evidence for this is reflected in repeated statements of serious skills shortages in the Irish economy and other parts of the EU.

It is for these reasons that the EU has placed special emphasis on upgrading the skills and competencies of the labour force, as part of the search for a solution to maintaining and increasing employment. Not all persons have acquired adequate initial education and training before they enter the labour market and these are the people most likely to experience long-term unemployment in Ireland and elsewhere in Europe. The first priority, then, must be to reduce through preventive and remedial measures the number of young people who leave school without some qualification (see Chapter 12).

The next concern is to ensure that those who have acquired satisfactory initial qualifications make the transition to employment, and this may be assisted by a more employer-led approach to education, particularly vocational education. Last, and perhaps of most relevance in relation to the issues discussed in this section, is the need to emphasise continuing education and training (see Chapter 12), as individuals need the opportunity to upgrade their knowledge and competencies to prepare themselves for the changes brought about by increasing international trade, migration and technological change. For similar reasons the Irish government slightly altered its policy on work permits and visas for immigrants seeking work: it actively recruits suitably qualified people intended for designated sectors where skills shortages are particularly acute. In addition, FÁS proactively dealt with skills shortages via its skills training for the unemployed and redundant.[8]

7 FLEXIBILITY IN LABOUR MARKET

It has been mentioned already that structural rigidities in labour markets, especially in those of many countries in Europe, may largely explain why unemployment until very recently was at such high levels in these countries. Putting it more positively, it is argued that it is the countries with flexible labour markets that have experienced the lowest rates of unemployment in the 2000s. There are several dimensions to the structural rigidity and labour market flexibility arguments and some of the key ones are looked at here.

First, wage and price adjustments are examined, with attention devoted to industrial relations and product market competition. Second, quantity adjustments (which refer to barriers facing the movement of people in and out of jobs) are analysed. Policies to enhance quantity adjustment include reforms of employment protection legislation and active labour market policies. Last, the effect of the tax and social welfare systems on the working of the labour market will be examined briefly.

Wage Adjustments

Price formation in the labour market is, by necessity, different from that in other markets. This is because wages are not simply a price of one type of product among others, but determine to a large extent the well-being of the majority of people in modern society. Societies' concern about social justice and the distribution of income therefore becomes integrally linked to wage setting. Because of this, distinct social arrangements and institutions intervene in every country in the market-clearing role of wage adjustments. However, even if the operation of the price system for labour is different from that for products, the effects of prices being too high are the same, i.e. wages above market-clearing levels will result in excess supply and therefore lower levels of employment than would otherwise be the case.

Industrial Relations

As mentioned previously, the response of wages to market conditions has to be seen against the background of the institutional arrangements, particularly those relating to industrial relations and the role of trade unions, in the labour market in each particular country. These arrangements have been partly designed to encourage stable employment relationships and to avert the income insecurity that can accompany rapid price adjustments in the market for labour, as happened in the USA in the 1980s. However, in so doing, these arrangements may encourage anti-competitive behaviour in the labour market and, as in all markets, this will result in lower demand because prices are not set at their clearing rate. This of course must be set against the advantages for employees of the protective industrial relations arrangements and the potential advantages for employers, in that these arrangements may strengthen co-operation by workers and prevent the harmful behaviour that may be inherent in a more atomistic wage-setting environment (see Chapter 3 for a further discussion of this issue).

Given the above, it is generally recognised that income restraint by trade unions and individual workers is essential to employment creation in Ireland and that there *is* a trade-off between pay and employment. In the multinational high-tech sector of the economy, pay moderation can lead to more employment in the medium to longer term, through increased profitability and its effect on investment location decisions. In the more traditional labour-intensive parts of the traded sector there is likely to be a substantial trade-off between pay and employment, as in many cases pay moderation is essential in this sector, simply to retain existing jobs. In the sheltered private sector, pay moderation is necessary to underpin the competitiveness of the traded sector and also to generate increased employment in this sector. Last, in the public sector, given a fixed budget, there is a very direct and almost immediate trade-off between pay and employment.

While the unionisation rate in Ireland fell in the 1990s, in line with many other countries, the rate in Ireland was still above that in the UK and way above that in the USA, although well below the Scandinavian countries. In relation to the wage-bargaining process, there is a degree of corporatism in the Irish labour market with a large proportion of wages being determined by national wage agreements (see Chapter 3). Ireland therefore appears to have adopted in recent years the preferable system of wage bargaining (i.e. centralised) for such a small country where participants are more likely to take wider economic interests into account.[9] The OECD, though, warned in general against too little differentiation of relative wages by skill, region, or other dimensions. It also acknowledges that it might be best to accept the variation in national industrial relations and practices evident across member states and concentrate instead on 'identifying policies that increase wage flexibility in the presence of such structures ... and that greater allowance be made for the potential contribution of centrally co-ordinated bargaining to achieving aggregate wage restraint, at least in those countries whose histories and structures are compatible with such an approach'.[10] Presumably foremost in their minds in this regard was Ireland.

Competition in Product Markets
Imperfect competition in the product market can also affect the wage level and thereby the level of employment and unemployment. If there is an absence of competition in the product market, firms have an option of choosing 'supra-normal' profits ahead of increased employment. They also have the option of retaining the entire surplus for themselves or sharing it with existing employees. The latter will happen if the workers have bargaining strength, or the rents may be willingly shared with workers to encourage efficiency and to boost work motivation, i.e. the employers may be prepared to pay what are called 'efficiency wages'. Whatever the rationale for rent sharing with workers, such arrangements favour the 'insiders' at the expense of the 'outsiders' and create a united lobby between unions and employers to oppose the removal of the imperfect competition in the product market that is giving rise to the rent. The solution to reducing the distortional effects of imperfect product market competition on labour market outcomes is clearly to remove the opportunity for producers to earn rent, and this calls for a strict and tough competition regime, a topic that is covered at some length in Chapters 3 and 9. More important, the opening of the EU market to increased competition, internal and external, has greatly reduced the potential for such imperfect competition. Besides, entry into the euro zone has removed the exchange rate option for dealing with excessive wage rises: employers and employees must now 'live' with the euro exchange rate, which is in turn determined by market conditions and not by direct Central Bank intervention. The

potential benefits of course are reduced exchange rate risk, more transparency of prices, less transactions costs and increased employment levels overall.

The OECD, while recognising the strengthening of product-market competition since 1998, emphasised that 'additional measures to significantly strengthen competition in most countries will ... have to involve reductions in regulatory and administrative opacity, administrative burdens on start-ups and statutory barriers to entry in certain sectors' (see Chapter 9).[11] Nonetheless, regulatory impediments to product market competition declined throughout the OECD between 1998 and 2003 and Ireland, along with the UK and the USA, has one of the most liberalised environments in this regard.[12]

Minimum Wage

A national minimum wage (NMW) was introduced in Ireland in 2000 (see also Chapter 3). Although the ESRI predicted that this would decrease employment and increase unemployment and inflation, 95 per cent of firms surveyed a year later viewed the NMW as having had no impact on the numbers of employees they had subsequently hired. Those paid less than the NMW are concentrated in sales and personal services, which reflects a wider concern that younger female and non-national workers are most likely to experience low pay.[13] Ireland's minimum wage is relatively high, though, compared with 19 other OECD countries. However, by 2004 only 3.1 percent of full-time employees were on the minimum wage in Ireland, thereby mitigating its potential adverse impact on employment. Besides, it was lower than that in the UK, the main comparator country for Ireland in this regard.

Many studies have shown that the adverse impact of minimum wages on employment is modest or non-existent. This, however, depends on the level of the minimum wage and how it interacts with the tax system. The important thing in this regard is to ensure that work pays better than remaining on social welfare benefits and also that high rates of labour taxation do not apply at low income levels (see Chapter 7). An employer considering hiring a low-skilled or inexperienced worker is likely to compare the worker's expected productivity with the *sum* of the minimum wage and employer-paid social security contributions when deciding whether or not to hire. In the case of Ireland the evidence shows that the minimum cost of labour, as a percentage of labour costs for the average employee, is one of the lowest in the EU, and thus the adverse labour effects of a minimum wage are likely to be minimal.[14]

Employment Protection Legislation

Employment protection relates to the 'firing' and 'hiring' rules governing unfair dismissal, lay-off for economic reasons, severance payments, minimum notice periods, administrative authorisation for dismissals and prior discussion with labour representatives. A number of benefits are alleged to justify employment protection legislation: encouraging increased investment in firm-specific capital; reducing contracting costs by setting general rules and standards; and early notification of job loss to allow job search prior to being laid off. As against this, employment protection legislation imposes constraints on firms' behaviour that can raise labour costs and adversely affect hiring decisions. It may also provide strong incentives for employers to use forms of employment (e.g. short-term contracts) that do not involve high firing costs. Labour security legislation does not only affect the actions of employers, it also influences the bargaining power and, hence, strategy of the insiders (see above). With the legislation in place, workers' fear of job loss will be greatly diminished and they will push for higher real wages. This will then have an impact on labour demand. Labour security legislation could therefore cause labour demand to be inflexible both directly (i.e. through employers' immediate decisions) and indirectly (i.e. through its promotion of higher real wages). In fact, employment protection laws are thought by many to be a key factor in generating labour market inflexibility.

It appears, though, that a certain level of employment protection is justified to protect workers from arbitrary or discriminatory dismissals. However, the OECD believes that dismissals that are required on economic grounds must be allowed and that the provision of more explicit, long-term commitments to job security should not be imposed on all firms but decided on a firm-by-firm basis. Whether and to what extent reform is required clearly depends on the country-specific circumstances. A related issue is that the emphasis is now increasingly on employment security rather than job security, that is on guaranteed employment rather than employment in a specific job. The best way to ensure this is to increase adaptability and employability, as discussed earlier.

Attempts have been made to construct various summary indicators to describe the 'strictness' of employment protection in each country, including Ireland. Given the complexity of constructing such indicators, they are inevitably somewhat arbitrary, but nonetheless are indicative. An OECD study ranking EU countries according to 'strictness' of protection in the areas of individual dismissals of regular workers, fixed-term contracts and employment through temporary employment agencies showed in 2003 that employment protection was ranked relatively low as a problem in Ireland.[15]

However, employment protection legislation in the EU is much more rigid than it is in the USA. Using a measure of rigidity of employment index, a World Bank survey showed that the employment framework in Ireland is in fact more rigid than the OECD average and significantly more rigid than in economies such as Denmark and the UK. Ireland had in 2006 a score of 33 (minimum 0 and maximum 100, with higher values indicating more rigid regulation), compared to figures of zero in the USA, 14 in the UK, 17 in Denmark, an OECD average of 26, 44 in Germany and figures of over 50 in France and Italy.[16]

Taxation
Payroll taxes, such as employers' social security contributions, raise the costs of employing labour over and above the wage paid. Income taxes and employees' social security contributions reduce the return to working. These taxes, therefore,

are important because they directly affect the rate of return from decisions to enter the labour market and thereby affect the supply of labour (see Chapter 5). They may also influence the choice between working in the black economy and in declared paid employment. These taxes may have an even greater impact on employment and unemployment through their influence on wage determination and therefore on the demand for labour. In a perfectly competitive labour market these effects would be minimal, but as seen earlier most labour markets are far from perfectly competitive. Hence, cuts in real wages through the imposition of increased personal income taxes or social security contributions may be resisted by workers and compensated for by higher nominal wages – but at the cost of higher unemployment. Likewise, an increase in employers' social security contributions can also result in unemployment when workers resist offsetting wage cuts. In the light of increased competition, both within the EU single market and globally, though, the scope for such resistance by trade unions and workers is significantly reduced, as discussed earlier.

Reductions in average tax rates at low levels of earnings are clearly an important way of increasing the income differential between being in and out of work, for the groups for which this is the most serious problem (see above). It appears that particular attention needs to be devoted to social security contributions in this regard, not just to the level of these contributions but also their structure: employers' taxation not only influences the amount of people who are employed but may also influence the type of worker who is hired.

The rate at which social benefits are withdrawn, as seen in Chapter 4, is also another important aspect of the problem. A feature of many tax and benefit systems, including that in Ireland, is that they can embody very high marginal tax rates for those on low incomes, especially those with large families, as benefits are reduced and earnings are taxed. There have been some successful attempts to address this problem in Ireland in the last decade. As OECD evidence shows, tax cuts on average incomes were particularly striking in Ireland in the period 1994 to 2004, with targeted reductions for low incomes very prominent.[17] As a result, by 2006 Ireland's tax wedge (i.e. the gap between what the employer pays and what the employee receives) was the lowest in the OECD.

Unemployment Payments
The rationale for unemployment insurance payments is 'to relieve people who have lost a job through no fault of their own from immediate financial concerns, and thus allow efficient job search. Insurance benefits, therefore, have an economic efficiency as well as a social equity objective'.[18] In relation to unemployment assistance payments, which apply in Ireland after 12 months and effectively for an indefinite period, the social or equity role, in reducing poverty among unemployed people and cushioning the adverse effects of high and rising unemployment, becomes paramount. As a result of the above, there would be strong political objections to resist any cuts in unemployment benefits or assistance and this clearly flavours any debate on the causal connection between

unemployment benefit/assistance and unemployment. However, the possibility of such a causal connection, and its extent, must be addressed, as it has been recently in countries such as France, Germany and Italy, where unemployment persisted, at high levels, for more than a decade and led to a build-up of large-scale long-term unemployment and a 'handout' dependency.

Few economists question the fact that there *is* a link between the benefit system and unemployment. At the simplest level, unemployment payments may create an option of leisure and low income, which some people might choose in preference to full-time work and a higher income. However, such payments could affect employment in many other ways. First, receipt of such payments may prolong intervals between job searches, even for those who want to work. Second, because unemployment payments reduce the cost of becoming unemployed, employed people may take a tougher stance in industrial relations disputes or in collective bargaining over wages (see earlier), thereby exacerbating the high real wage problem. Last, payments may increase employment in high-turnover and seasonal industries, by subsidising these industries relative to those that provide long-term contract jobs.

The adverse effects of unemployment payments may, however, result not so much from the existence and level of these payments, but more from the entitlement conditions, the administration of the system and other institutional background factors. For example, payment of unemployment benefits is conditional upon the claimant being available for, and willing to take, full-time work. If this condition is not effectively implemented, people *not* in the labour force (i.e. not available for or not seeking work) may register as unemployed simply to collect unemployment payments. If this condition is strictly enforced and payments stopped if it is not met, then many of the distortional effects of unemployment payments could be substantially reduced. This problem has been tackled with some success in Ireland in the last 15 years. A related issue is that the employment agency must not only enforce this condition but must also facilitate effective job search, the final topic to which we now turn.

Active Labour Market Policies[19]
The OECD, as far back as 1994, was unequivocal concerning the changes that needed to be effected in benefit administration. They suggested, for example, much more in-depth verification of eligibility, much better matching of workers to job vacancies and fieldwork investigation of concealed earnings and related fraud. A more fundamental problem, they claimed, was making unemployment payment, especially to the long-term unemployed, effectively conditional on availability for existing vacancies. In particular, they stressed that the long-term unemployed should be expected to take, and unemployment payments made conditional on taking, even low-status jobs. As the OECD noted, much may depend upon achieving a social, political and analytical consensus on this, rejecting the opposite idea that modern economies should be able to afford to make work optional. The real concern here is that if people are allowed to drift into

long-term unemployment, as happened in Ireland in the 1980s and early 1990s, that the problem becomes more difficult to overcome. At an individual level long-term unemployment may lead to significant de-skilling and demotivation. At a macroeconomic level, and partly as a result of this, the long-term unemployed may not be regarded as 'employable' and in a sense may cease to be part of the labour market.

A similar problem has arisen in recent years in relation to groups receiving *non-employment* benefits (see earlier discussion in relation to invalidity and incapacity benefit). As discussed earlier, despite the improved employment conditions in many OECD countries and the greatly reduced numbers on unemployment payments, the numbers on some non-employment benefits have grown. These benefit recipients represent a large share of the potential workforce and if their numbers are not reduced employment rates will remain low for years to come in many OECD countries. The pattern in relation to non-employment benefit recipients 'suggest that there could be a high pay-off to extending activation measures, currently available to the unemployed, to persons receiving these non-employment benefits'.[20] Recent experience demonstrates that there is considerable scope to apply activation strategies to persons receiving non-employment benefits, albeit with appropriate modifications for the specific characteristics of each group.

What was being suggested above was effectively a much more active approach to labour market policy on behalf of the employment service in each country. The purpose of active labour market policies is threefold: first to mobilise labour supply, second to improve the quality of the labour force, and third to strengthen the search process in the labour market. They are particularly appropriate for those experiencing long-term unemployment (and many of those on long-term disability benefit), because, as mentioned, many of them are effectively not participating in the labour force. Because of the de-skilling and demotivation that has taken place, they need assistance with education and training, and because of demotivation and the indefinite nature of unemployment and related payments the search for jobs may not be as active as might be desired.

Active labour market policies can be classified into four categories: first, state employment services (e.g. placement and counselling); second, labour market training (i.e. for unemployed and employed adults); third, youth measures (e.g. remedial education, training or work experience for disadvantaged young people); and last, subsidised employment (i.e. subsidies to increase employment in the private sector, support for unemployed persons starting their own enterprises and direct job creation in either the public or non-profit sector).

In the last decade or so many countries, including Ireland, increased both the number and variety of instruments used to activate jobseekers. Job placement efforts have been enhanced, there is a greater emphasis on testing and monitoring work availability, there is earlier intervention in the unemployment spell and participation in programmes is compulsory, and there is more efficient administration of public employment services. There is considerable evidence that these measures have made a significant impact on the numbers in long-term unemployment in several countries, including Ireland. However, such measures are costly, and ongoing evaluation of the cost-effectiveness of each programme needs to be undertaken.

8 CONCLUSION

The outstanding economic policy failure in the last 40 years in Ireland was the inability to increase employment in the 1980s, despite the huge increase in the potential labour force in this period. The result of this failure was a dramatic increase in the unemployment rate and emigration of almost 200,000 people. More seriously, perhaps, the sustained failure to increase employment meant not only that the high level of unemployment persisted into the mid-1990s, but also that an increasing proportion of that total drifted into long-term unemployment and in many cases, therefore, effectively left the labour market.

The outstanding policy success of the last 40 years on the other hand, indeed of the whole post-independence era, was the increase in employment between 1993 and 2007, and the corresponding huge reductions in unemployment and the dramatic switch from large-scale emigration to significant immigration. In a very short period the disastrous failures of the 1980s had been turned around into one of the most remarkable success stories in terms of employment growth in the Western world. A variety of explanations for this have been looked at in this chapter, with further insights to follow in Chapter 6. There are no simple explanations, though. The policy of attracting foreign investment, much of it in the high-tech sectors, allowed Ireland cope with the trade and technological effects of globalisation (see Chapter 8). The positive policy stance to trade in general, and the EU and the euro in particular, may have helped in this regard (see Chapters 1, 6 and 8). The advent of the 'borderless' economy meant that Ireland's peripheral location mattered much less than before (see Chapter 8). The increased emphasis on competition in the non-traded sector of the economy added to Ireland's competitiveness (Chapters 3 and 9), while the centralised wage bargaining process appears to have delivered on competitive wage setting and a good industrial relations climate (Chapter 3). Past policies on education also appear to have been a factor (see Chapter 12) and the relatively flexible employment protection environment that was in place would have assisted in the huge employment increase that the above facilitated. Ireland also appears to have a relatively 'entrepreneur-friendly' climate, as measured by relative cost, length of time and minimum charter capital required to form a private limited liability company.[21] Finally, changes in taxation and the increased emphasis on active labour market policies made inroads into the most intractable unemployment problem that Ireland faced in the mid-1990s, namely that of long-term unemployment.

Ireland's success on the employment front in the last 15 years must, though, be set in context. It followed decades of failure to provide jobs for Irish people, the result being large-scale emigration in the 1950s and again in the 1980s. This also resulted in extraordinarily high unemployment levels in the decade 1985 to 1995. Potential labour supply had been increasing rapidly in Ireland since 1980 and a large employment increase was required to absorb this growth in supply; without it there was initially, and would have continued to have been, large-scale emigration and high levels of unemployment. The country, in other words, for the first time in its history provided employment to those who needed it. This has been the norm in other small European countries such as Denmark, the Netherlands, and Norway for decades. Indeed, the unemployment rate in Ireland is still higher than in these three countries and the proportion of those of working age in employment in Ireland lags well behind that in these countries.

Much progress has been made, but more has to be achieved and the failures of the past on the employment front must not be repeated. One failure of recent origin was the over-reliance on employment growth in the construction sector, the consequences of which, while becoming evident in the first half of 2008, may only come into fuller focus in the years ahead: by mid-2008 the unemployment rate had climbed to 5.2 per cent, the highest for a decade. The other major concern on the horizon is what the impact will be on migration of any significant slow-down in the labour market. To date it appears that in-migration has been a 'win-win' situation for Irish employment, but will this continue to be the case and, perhaps more important, will this continue to be perceived to be the case?

Endnotes

[1] See P. Sweeney, *Ireland's Economic Success: Reasons and Lessons*, New Island, Dublin 2008, p. 156.

[2] OECD, 'Taking the measure of temporary employment', *Employment Outlook*, OECD, Paris 2002.

[3] See 'Sickness claims rise in stressed-out south', *Financial Times*, 22/23 March 2008. See also OECD, *Employment Outlook: Boosting Jobs and Incomes*, OECD, Paris 2006, which expresses concern that the rise in non-employment benefit dependency has, if anything, increased in some countries despite the strong recent gains in employment.

[4] OECD, *Annual Report 2004*, OECD, Paris 2004, p. 35.

[5] The OECD provides outstanding work in relation to data on employment and related matters, and employment policies, both in general and by member country. Its key publication is the annual *Employment Outlook* with its overall general chapters, detailed research reports and detailed statistical tables. Three landmark *Jobs Study* reports were produced in 1994 and a major reassessment of the strategy recommendations in these reports carried out in 'General policies to improve employment opportunities for all', in OECD 2006, op. cit.

[6] A. Barrett and D. Duffy, 'Are Ireland's immigrants integrating into its labour market?' (IZA Discussion Paper Series, No. 2838), Bonn 2007.

7   A. Barrett and A. Bergin, 'The economic contribution of immigrants in Ireland' in B. Fanning (ed.), *Immigration and Social Change in the Republic of Ireland,* Manchester 2007.

8   Department of Enterprise, Trade and Employment, *National Employment Action Plan 2003–2005*, Stationery Office, Dublin 2003, Chapter 3.

9   See OECD 2006, op. cit., pp. 80–8, for a good review of wage-setting institutions and policies in OECD member states. Table 3.7 in this report illustrates the huge variation in practice in terms of both the level of centralisation and co-ordination.

10 OECD 2006, op. cit., p. 88.

11 Ibid., pp. 106–7.

12 National Competitiveness Council, *Annual Competitiveness Report 2007*, National Competitiveness Council, Dublin 2007, Table 4.16.

13 NESC, *An Investment in Quality: Services, Inclusion and Enterprise,* Stationery Office, Dublin 2003, Chapter 8.

14 OECD 2006, op. cit., pp. 86–8.

15 OECD, *Employment Outlook*, OECD, Paris 2004, Chart 2.1.

16 *Annual Competitiveness Report 2007*, op. cit., Table 4.18. See also, 'EU told to transform social security rules', *Financial Times*, 25 March 2008. The Director of the European Department of the IMF was quoted as stating that Ireland was one of four European countries (the others being Denmark, the Netherlands and the UK) which 'were prompted by a clear sense of crisis and had succeeded because visionary governments had introduced a comprehensive package of long-term structural and fiscal reforms'.

17 OECD 2006, op. cit., Table 3.11.

18 OECD, *Jobs Study: Part II,* OECD, Paris 1994., p.171.

19 A comprehensive review of these policies is contained in OECD, 'Activating the unemployed: what countries do', *Employment Outlook*, OECD, Paris 2007.

20 OECD 2006, op. cit., p. 75.

21 *Annual Competitiveness Report 2007*, op. cit., particularly Table 4.20.

CHAPTER 6

Growth in Output and Living Standards

Jonathan Haughton

1 THE CELTIC TIGER

As measured by gross domestic product (GDP) per capita, Ireland was the fourth richest country in the world in 2005, behind only Luxembourg, the United States and Norway.[1] Twenty years ago, nobody would have predicted this outcome; Ireland was then one of the poorer members of the European Union, perceived at home and abroad as something of an economic laggard.

The dramatic Irish growth spurt of the 1990s and 2000s – although it has now run its course – has attracted the attention of researchers and would-be emulators, especially among the new EU members of Eastern Europe. How did Ireland become so rich? What were the keys to the recent success of the Celtic Tiger?

We address these questions here, beginning with the numbers. To anticipate the argument: Ireland's economic growth in the late 1990s and 2000s was real and impressive and the country is indeed very rich, if not quite as affluent as the GDP per capita numbers imply. Taking a long view, most of Ireland's recent growth may be thought of as an overdue catch-up; but there remains the suspicion that Irish economic performance has now gone beyond what would be expected, so there may be something exceptional to explain.

Why is Ireland rich? And what underlies the growth that propelled Ireland to the ranks of the most affluent nations? It is helpful to address these questions in two steps. First, we use the Solow growth model to identify the proximate determinants of growth and living standards: how much is due to high levels of investment, long hours of work, or more technology. This then guides us in our search for the more fundamental explanations, which are likely rooted in policy decisions, demographic changes, and the evolution of the world context over the past generation – essentially since Ireland joined the European Economic Community in 1973. The narrative in this chapter thus picks up where the story in Chapter 1, on Irish economic history, left off.

It is argued that Ireland's growth spurt in the late 1990s and 2000s was due to a fortunate confluence of events – the opening of the economy and society to trade and the flow of ideas, the arrival of the EU single market that made Ireland an attractive platform for US investors, a boom in the US economy that provided a supply of investment, an improvement in the educational level of the Irish labour force, transfers from the EU, a highly credible macroeconomic stance, fiscal discipline, improved labour relations, and relatively modest taxes. This created a virtuous circle: as jobs were created, well-educated and experienced workers immigrated (or did not leave); an entrepreneurial 'can do' attitude took root; and financing remained available.

Now that Ireland has caught up, there are signs of complacency: fiscal discipline has weakened; one of the world's highest minimum wages limits the creation of entry-level jobs; Ireland is now a net source rather than destination of foreign investment; and the relatively high investment rate is now associated with rather slow growth in output per worker. Other countries have faltered after rising close to the top of the affluence league – Sweden and Japan come to mind. It follows that maintaining and consolidating its new-found affluence will be a challenge for Ireland over the coming generation.

2 HOW AFFLUENT IS IRELAND?

Output and Income

Since 1995, Ireland has caught up economically with its peers in Western Europe. This is shown clearly in Figure 6.1, which compares the evolution of Irish per capita output since 1975 with those of the USA, Denmark and the UK. Denmark is included here because it is, like Ireland, a small open economy, and has often been held up as a role model for Ireland to emulate.

Figure 6.1

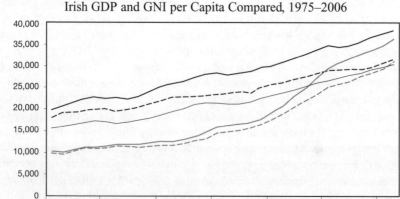

Irish GDP and GNI per Capita Compared, 1975–2006

Sources: Central Bank of Ireland, *Bulletin*, Dublin, various issues; World Bank, *World Development Indicators*, www.worldbank.org [accessed April 2008].

Two measures of Irish affluence are shown in Figure 6.1. The first is gross domestic product per capita, which measures the money value of goods and services produced and marketed in the economy in a year; it represents the value added by economic activity within the geographic borders of a country, and is the most commonly used indicator of economic activity. There was a clear acceleration in the growth of Irish GDP/capita starting in about 1994, with slower but still robust increases after 2000.

In order to compare output across countries, the measures of GDP/capita in Figure 6.1 are shown in 'international dollars' in the prices of 2000. A serious problem in cross-country comparisons of this sort is that prices differ substantially from one country to the next: a euro in Ireland barely buys a cup of coffee, but converted into rupees and spent in India, it would buy a whole meal. So if the exchange rate were used to convert India's GDP into euros, it would understate the true purchasing power of India's GDP. The standard solution is to recompute every country's GDP using a common set of 'international' prices, giving a measure of purchasing power parity (PPP) GDP that is reasonably comparable across country. By this measure, GDP per capita in Ireland in 2007 was approaching the US level and was well above the level of the UK or Denmark.

However, in the Irish case, GDP is not a particularly good indicator of affluence. Not all of the goods and services produced in Ireland accrue to Irish citizens or residents; for instance, profit that is repatriated does not contribute to local incomes. A more satisfactory measure of the output that stays in Ireland is gross national income (GNI), which starts with GDP and adds net factor income from abroad (NFIA) – this gives Gross National Product (GNP) – and then includes net transfer payments from abroad (NTPA). In 2007 these amounts, in billions of euros, were as follows:

GNI	=	GDP	+	NFIA	NTPA
155.6	=	184.8	-	-27.9	-1.3

The most striking feature of these numbers is the uncommonly large value of transfer payments out of Ireland, mainly the repatriation of profits by foreign firms operating in Ireland. An unknown, although no doubt significant, part of the factor income flows may be attributable to profit outflows that reflect transfer pricing, as some corporations overstate their exports and understate their imports in order to book their profits in low-tax Ireland. As a result of this measurement error, reported GDP may overstate 'true' GDP by as much as ten per cent. In 1960, Irish GNI was six per cent higher than GDP; by 2007 it was 16 per cent lower.

This makes a difference: in 2007, 15 countries had levels of GDP per capita that were higher than Ireland's GNI per capita, making the Irish case look far less exceptional. Using GNI rather than GDP per capita, Ireland passed the UK level in 2006 and is very close to the Danish level, but still remains well below the level in the USA, as Figure 6.1 shows.

Other Measures of Living Standards

We have seen that Ireland has caught up with its European peers, as measured by GNI per capita. This is now true of most other measures of living standards, although in most of these cases the improvements lagged behind the rise in GNI per capita by a few years. The most striking feature of Table 6.1, which shows a selection of measures of living standards, is how similar Ireland now looks to the rest of the European Union.

Table 6.1

Indicators of the Quality of Life

	Ireland					EU-25	USA	EU-25 extreme
	1960	1970	1980	1990	2005	2005	2004	2005
Health								
Infant mortality rate	31	20	12	8	4.0	4.3	6.8	2.4
Life expectancy, F	72	74	75	77	81.8	81.9	80.4	83.9
Life expectancy, M	68	69	70	72	77.1	75.8	75.2	78.4
Crime[1]								
Crimes/1,000	..	..	..	..	21	65	41	131
Prisoners/100,000	..	..	..	..	72	87	682	131
Homicides/millions	..	..	..	6	13	17	56	113
Environment								
CO2/capita, t	4	6	7	9	10.6	7.9	19.6	24.8
Municip. waste, kg/cap	..	..	..	..	740	518	750	740
Smoke, mg/m3	..	..	211	269	41[2]	..	..	..
Connectivity								
% hh, Internet	..	..	..		50	51	60	80
Airline pass, m	..	1.5	1.8	4.8	24.3	704.6	..	..
Fixed lines/1000	..	..	142	281	390	480	886	670
Mobile phones/1000	0	0	0	7	1030	950	488	1580
Assets								
Houses/1000	..	280	300	330	420	450	..	..
Cars/1000	..	..	216	227	507	553		..

Sources: Central Bank of Ireland, *Bulletin*, Central Bank, Dublin, various issues; World Bank, *World Development Indicators*, www.worldbank.org [accessed April 2008]. Eurostat News Release 161/2007.
[1] 2002
[2] 2002. Smoke figures are for Dublin only.

Ireland's life expectancy continues to rise, and has surpassed the EU average for men (but not yet, quite, for women). The infant mortality rate – defined as the number of deaths of infants up to six months old per 1,000 population – is very low by historical standards, and is now below the EU average. These measures, considered to be good indicators of health outcomes in general, show that Ireland has now caught up with the standards that prevail in Western Europe (see also Chapter 11).

GNI represents an annual flow of final goods and services; even when GNI rises, it can take time to build up a good stock of assets – cars, houses and fine roads. This helps explain why Irish visitors to France, for instance, are often struck by the high quality of the infrastructure, in a country whose consumption per capita is now appreciably lower than that of Ireland (see Chapter 8). However, Table 6.1 shows evidence of catch-up: car ownership per capita rose by an astonishing 123 per cent between 1990 and 2007, a measure that goes a long way towards explaining the increasingly high levels of congestion on Irish roads. House building rose above the long-term sustainable level after 2001; where Ireland had 330 houses per thousand people in 1990, this figure had risen to 440 by 2007, despite a 22 per cent increase in the population over the same period, and bringing Ireland close to the EU average of 450 houses per thousand people.

Ireland is also connecting fast. The stock of telecommunications assets has risen remarkably, with a trebling in the number of mainline phones between 1980 and 2002; there is high mobile phone penetration, although home use of the Internet, at 50 per cent, is essentially at the EU-25 average (51 per cent), and well below the 80 per cent rate seen in the Netherlands. There has also been an explosion in airline traffic.

By European and US standards, Ireland has a low level of reported crime, although recently the homicide rate has risen to close to the EU-15 norm. The incarceration rate remains relatively modest, with an average of 3,151 prisoners in custody on any given day in 2005.

Tourism operators boast of Ireland's wild and open beauty – the woodlands were cleared by the sixteenth century! – and its clean air and water. While water is relatively clean, and smoke levels in Dublin have fallen dramatically since 1990, emissions of CO_2, the main greenhouse gas, now exceed the EU-15 average. Besides, Irish firms and households generate 740kg of municipal waste per person per year, the highest level in the EU, and close to the 750kg level of the United States.

There is another interesting way to evaluate Irish levels of affluence. The United Nations Development Programme annually constructs its *Human Development Index*, which combines measures of life expectancy, educational achievement (literacy and school enrolment rates), and GDP per capita into a single index. The most recent figures refer to 2005, and rank Ireland fifth in the world with a score of 0.959 (out of a maximum possible 1.000). Ireland scores especially well on GDP per capita (and thereby its position is overstated, for reasons seen earlier) and education. Ireland's Human Development Index has risen rapidly since 1975, when it was first measured, as Table 6.2 shows.

An unsurprising consequence of the increase in real incomes and consumption has been a drop in absolute poverty, particularly over the past decade. Using a poverty line set at 60 per cent of average income in 1987, the proportion of the population in poverty was then 16 per cent, falling to 15 per cent by 1994, eight per cent by 1998 and five per cent by 2001 (see Chapter 7). By then, those most likely to be poor were parents living alone (24 per cent), the unemployed (18 per cent), and children (seven per cent).

Table 6.2

Human Development Index for Ireland

1975	1980	1985	1990	1995	2000	2005
0.810	0.825	0.844	0.869	0.893	0.926	0.959

Source: United Nations Development Project, *Human Development Report 2007/2008*, http://hdr.undp.org/en [accessed April 2008].

It appears that income inequality did not change substantially during the economic boom – incomes at the top of the distribution may have risen rapidly, but the increase in the labour force participation rate helped raise the incomes of those near the bottom of the distribution – but this conclusion is somewhat tentative given the difficulties inherent in comparing data from household surveys with different designs.[2] The most important implication is that the gains of rising incomes were spread widely, rather than accruing to any single group. Inequality in Ireland appears to be similar to that found in the UK and Italy, but is greater than in the Nordic countries, and lower than in the United States.

Employment and Population

An economy's success could also be measured by its ability to provide employment for those who want it, and to sustain a larger population. Between 1960 and 1986 the rise in employment was negligible, from 1.05 to 1.09 million. Then came a remarkable, and historically unprecedented, burst of job creation, pushing employment up to 2.12 million by 2007 (see also Chapter 5). Between 1986 and 2007, employment rose from 31 per cent to 49 per cent of the total population.

Migration flows have mirrored the changes in employment, albeit with a lag of a few years. There was immigration in the 1970s, when Irish economic growth was higher than elsewhere in Europe. Emigration resumed in the early 1980s, peaking at 44,000 (1.3 per cent of the population) in 1989. In due course the pendulum swung back, and about 150,000 people migrated into Ireland in the course of the 1990s, with a further 200,000 net arrivals between 2000 and 2005. By then, foreign-born residents numbered 585,000 and represented 14 per cent of the total population, a proportion that is higher than in most other high-income countries including the USA (12 per cent), but lower than in Australia or Canada (19 per cent each).

The importance of the inflow of migrants can hardly be understated. Between 1997 and 2006 the total population rose by 609,000; during this same period a total of 575,000 people moved to Ireland. With out-migration essentially offsetting the natural increase of the population from births (less deaths), recent population growth is essentially entirely due to the wave of in-migration. There were similar waves of immigration into France and Germany when they grew rapidly in the 1960s, but the welcome mat has worn thin in recent years as economic growth rates there have faltered.

Figure 6.2

Labour Force and Employment, 1960–2007

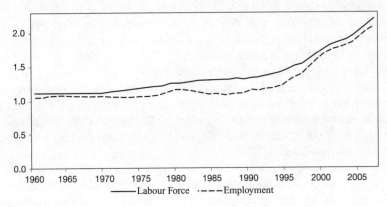

Sources: Central Bank of Ireland, *Bulletin*, Dublin, various issues; World Bank, *World Development Indicators*, www.worldbank.org [accessed April 2008].

The unemployment rate, five per cent in 1960 and seven per cent in 1980, surged to 17 per cent by 1986, remaining in double digits for a decade before falling very rapidly in the late 1990s to a low of 3.7 per cent in 2001, after which it edged up again slightly, reaching 4.5 per cent in 2007 and 5.5 per cent by early 2008. The high unemployment rate of the 1980s was a consequence of slow economic growth, coming at a time of diminished employment opportunities abroad (particularly in the UK), a rapid increase in the working-age population, and a system of taxes and subsidies that made working unremunerative for many low-skilled workers.

One consequence of Ireland's poor track record in creating employment prior to the early 1990s was to keep many women out of the labour force completely. As recently as 1987 the labour force participation rate for women was 40 per cent, one of the lowest in the EU, although by 2006 it had risen to 64 per cent, somewhat above the EU average (see Chapter 5).

An Obsession with Output per Capita?
It is clear that most measures of living standards are correlated, if not perfectly, with GNI per capita. That is one of the reasons why economists and others tend to use GNI per capita as their primary measure of welfare.[3]

Is this an unhealthy obsession? In an oft-quoted speech (see also Chapter 2),

Robert Kennedy said in 1968, 'we will find neither national purpose nor personal satisfaction in an endless amassing of worldly goods ... the gross national product measures neither our wit nor our courage, neither our wisdom nor our learning, neither our compassion nor our devotion to country. It measures everything, in short, except that which makes life worthwhile.'

Perhaps the only way to respond to Kennedy's challenge is to ask people how satisfied they are with their lives, and then to determine whether these subjective evaluations are linked to GNP per capita. In a recent study in which a sample of adults were asked whether they felt excluded from society, ten per cent of Irish respondents answered 'yes', slightly below the 12 per cent response for the EU-15 countries. Fully 92 per cent of Irish households reported that they were 'fairly' or 'very' satisfied with their lives, somewhat above the EU-15 average of 88 per cent; this lies below the level in Denmark (97 per cent) but well above the level in Greece (71 per cent). Commenting on the findings, Alber and Fahey write, 'the comparisons of countries across Europe ... [show that] the level of GDP per capita in the country in which the individual lives turns out to be the best predictor of individual life-satisfaction'.[4]

A more recent study ranked countries based on responses to surveys of (subjective) happiness that were administered to 80,000 people around the world. Ireland was ranked 11th, behind Denmark (1), Austria (3), Finland (6) and Sweden (7), but ahead of the UK (41), the US (43) and France (62). Interestingly, only one of the top ten countries in this study was poor (Bhutan), and it appears that individual happiness is strongly correlated with health, wealth, and access to education. A particularly strong (negative) correlation was found between happiness and unemployment; this is a likely channel by which the economic growth of the 1990s may have influenced well-being in Ireland.[5]

In short, Robert Kennedy overstates the case: GNI may not measure personal satisfaction, but it is closely correlated with it, in which case it is indeed a useful guide to happiness!

We are left with the conclusion that Ireland is indeed a rich country. The interesting question, then, to which we now turn, is: how did it get there?

3 DETERMINANTS OF IRISH AFFLUENCE

We have established that Ireland has closed the gap with Western Europe by almost all measures of affluence, and that most of the catch-up occurred since the mid-1990s. We now need to ask what explains this recent success, and why, by 2008, the episode of rapid growth has come to an end.

The immediate cause of the increase in the output of the Irish, or any other, economy is a rise in the inputs – the factors of production – used to generate output. The relationship between output (Q) and inputs of labour (L), capital services (K) and 'human capital' (H) may be summarised as a *production function* of the form

(1) $$Q = A.F (L, K, H)$$

where the function F(.) is increasing in its arguments. The constant A is usually taken to represent 'technology', but this should be interpreted broadly to include everything that enhances the productivity of inputs, including such things as better managerial techniques and regulatory changes that spur competition. Economic historian Douglass North won a Nobel Prize largely on the strength of his work emphasising the importance of institutional change – such as the development of private property rights, or patent law – in enhancing economic growth over time.

A first cut at the determinants of Irish growth may be determined from Table 6.3, which summarises Irish economic performance since 1960, starting with the 'golden age' of growth in the 1960s, the period of the first oil shock in the mid-1970s, the dismal period of the early 1980s (when per capita consumption declined), the early recovery that began in the late 1980s, the growth spurt of 1994–2000 when real GNI rose by 8.5 per cent per year, and the echo of the boom, which maintained solid economic growth until 2007.

The surge in economic growth in the late 1990s was associated with very rapid increases in the amount of labour used: employment rose by a remarkable 5.8 per cent per year. Employment growth slowed to an annual rate of 3.3 per cent between 2000 and 2007, still a high rate by any standard, but enough of a reduction to be reflected in sharply lower growth in output.

Properly measured, there was also a surge in capital services since 1994, so in some sense the growth spurt was also a marvel of capital. The capital stock of an economy changes over time as capital is added (investment) or subtracted (depreciation and scrappage). Prior to 1994, total additions to the capital stock barely matched subtractions, which explains the very slow growth rate – for instance, the capital stock rose by just 0.2 per cent per year between 1986 and 1994.

There is a further wrinkle: not all investment is equally productive in the short run, so a €1,000 investment in software should raise output by about €375 in the next year, while an equivalent investment in housing would raise output by perhaps €36 per year.[6] These reflect the flow of *capital services* that result from investment. In the 1994-2000 period, although the total capital stock rose by 2.4 per cent annually, capital services rose by 6.2 per cent per year; the explanation is that investment during that time was flowing disproportionately into capital with a quick payoff. This is in contrast with the period 2000-2007, when capital services rose less quickly than the capital stock, due mainly to the surge in investment in housing (which has a long slow payback) relative to other investment.

Between 1960 and 2000, GNI (and GNP) consistently grew faster than either inputs of labour ('employment') or capital, which means that by any measure, productivity rose. This effect was particularly strong in the late 1990s, confirming as seen earlier that the growth spurt was also a marvel of productivity. To see this, it is helpful to work with a growth version of equation (1); using g to denote a growth rate, we have

(2)
$$g_Q = \alpha_L \cdot g_L + (1 - \alpha_L) \cdot g_K + g_A$$

which says that the growth of output (Q) may be decomposed into a weighted average of the growth of effective labour (L) and the growth of capital services (K) plus the growth of technology (A).[7] The weight α_L is typically taken as the share of labour income in national income. The last term is a residual that cannot be observed directly, but it measures that component of growth in Q that cannot be attributed either to growth in labour or to growth in capital services, and so gives the *growth in total factor productivity*.

Table 6.3

Measures of Recent Performance

	1960–73	1973–79	1979–86	1986–94	1994–2000	2000–2007
			(annual growth rates, %)			
Output						
Real GDP	4.4	4.2	1.8	4.7	9.7	5.4
Real GNI	4.2	4.2	1.1	4.6	8.5	5.1
Inputs						
Employment	0.0	1.3	-0.7	1.3	5.8	3.3
Capital services			-5.2[1]	1.1	6.2	6.1[2]
Capital stock			0.3[1]	0.2	2.4	7.2[2]
Output per capita						
Real GDP/capita	3.7	3.3	1.5	4.6	8.5	3.6
Real GNI/capita	3.5	2.6	0.4	4.5	7.4	3.3
Productivity measures						
Real GDP/worker	4.3	3.5	2.9	3.4	3.7	2.1
Real GNI/worker	4.2	2.8	1.8	3.2	2.6	1.8
Real GNI/capital services			6.1[1]	3.5	2.2	-1.2[2]
Real GNI/capital stock			0.2[1]	4.4	6.0	-2.2[2]
Consumption						
Real consumption/capita	3.2	2.7	-0.1	3.3	5.8	4.1
Real full consumption/cap	3.5	3.0	0.3	2.5	5.4	3.3
			(levels in end year)			
Employment (millions)	1.06	1.15	1.09	1.20	1.69	2.12
Population (millions)	3.07	3.37	3.54	3.57	3.81	4.29
Unemployment rate	5.9	7.1	17.2	14.8	4.3	4.5

Sources: as for Table 6.1; and M. Keeney, *Measuring Irish Capital* (Research Technical Paper 13/RT/06), Central Bank of Ireland, Dublin 2006.
[1] 1981–86. [2] 2000–2004.

Some relatively recent figures on the growth of Irish total factor productivity (TFP) are displayed in Table 6.4. The pattern they show is quite remarkable, although somewhat exaggerated because they are based on GDP figures that are subject to measurement error. That said, the figures show that between 1975 and 2001 Irish TFP rose by a total of 98 per cent (or 75 per cent if GNI is used rather than GDP), far outstripping the EU-15 mean of 39 per cent, and well above the total TFP growth of 32 per cent seen in the USA and Japan over the same period. There is nothing pre-ordained about TFP growth: since 1975 it also rose rapidly in Finland and Portugal, but hardly changed in Greece. The increase was particularly rapid during the last part of the 1990s.

Table 6.4

Total Factor Productivity Growth, 1975–2001

	1975–85	1985–90	1990–95	1995–2001	1975–2001
		(annual growth rates, %)			(total % rise)
Ireland	*1.8*	*2.9*	*2.6*	*4.0*	*98*
EU-15	1.4	1.5	1.1	1.0	39
USA	1.0	0.9	0.9	1.5	32
Japan	1.4	2.8	-0.3	0.2	32
Finland	1.5	2.0	1.8	3.3	70
Portugal	1.9	3.6	1.3	1.8	71
Greece	-0.2	-0.1	0.1	1.9	10

Source: Spring Singapore, www.spring.gov.sg, July 2004.

Since 2000, the growth of total factor productivity in Ireland has fallen almost to zero. Between 2000 and 2007, real GNI rose by 5.1 per cent annually; during the same period employment rose by 3.3 per cent and capital services by about 6.1 per cent annually, increases that almost entirely 'explain' GNI growth and leave little room for any contribution from technological improvement.

In short, the nature of economic growth changed fundamentally between the late 1990s and the first years of the twenty-first century. We return to this point in more detail below.

4 FROM OUTPUT PER PERSON
TO OUTPUT PER WORKER

Decomposing GNI per Person[8]

In one important respect, 1994–2000 stands out from the periods both before and after it: GNI per capita rose by 7.4 per cent annually, or about twice as quickly as at any other time. Yet GNI *per worker* did not grow especially quickly during this period. This apparent anomaly calls for an explanation.

The answer lies in the fact that about half of the rise in GNI per capita since 1994 is attributable to an increase in the share of the population that is working: even if these newcomers were no more productive than other workers (so GNI per worker remains unchanged), they would add to total output and, for a given population size, this would boost GNI per capita.

A more detailed decomposition is set out in Table 6.5. The identity shown there breaks down annual real GNI per capita *growth* into its component parts, and also shows the annual (log) percentage growth rate of each component for two time periods – the growth spurt of 1994–2000 and the subsequent period of consolidation between 2000 and 2007.[9]

Table 6.5

Decomposition of GNI/capita growth

$\dfrac{\text{GNI}}{\text{population}} =$	$\dfrac{\text{GNI}}{\text{hour}}$.	$\dfrac{\text{hour}}{\text{worker}}$.	$\dfrac{\text{worker}}{\text{labour force}}$.	$\dfrac{\text{labour force}}{\text{adults 15–64}}$.	$\dfrac{\text{adults 15–64}}{\text{population}}$
1994–2000					
7.1	3.1	-0.6	1.9	1.7	0.9
100%	44%	-8%	27%	24%	13%
2000–2007					
3.2	1.8	0.0	-0.0	1.1	0.4
100%	54%	0%	-1%	35%	12%

Sources: as for Table 6.1.

It is clear from Table 6.5 that the single most important contributor to the rise in GNI per capita in both periods was increases in output per hour worked, which is the part of economic growth that the Solow model is designed to explain.

This decomposition shows that an eighth of the growth in Irish GNI per capita was due to an increase in the proportion of working-age adults in the population (whose output was therefore not diluted as much by the presence of children or retirees). Even more important was the increase in the proportion of working-age adults in the labour force (the labour force participation rate). In the boom period of the late 1990s, but not since then, the rise in GNI per person was helped considerably by a rise in the proportion of the labour force that was actually working (which is the mirror image of the unemployment rate).

These factors, which were unusually favourable in the late 1990s, are sometimes referred to as the 'demographic dividend', although in earlier years the need to create jobs was seen as a demographic drag! Together they accounted for over half of the rise in GNI per capita during Ireland's growth spurt, and for almost half of the (much slower) increase during 2000–2007. The important point is that these factors are not expected to contribute much to growth in the years ahead, as the population ages, labour force participation reaches a plateau, employees reduce the hours they work per year, and the unemployment rate nudges back up (as it had already done by early 2008).

Explaining Output per Worker: the Solow Model

The demographic dividend has largely come and gone, which returns the focus to the determinants of changes in output per worker ('labour productivity'). To organise our ideas, it is helpful to return to the production function of equation (1). If inputs are doubled, it is reasonable to suppose that output would also double; more generally, this implies that equation (1) is linearly homogeneous in labour, physical capital and human capital. So we may write:

(2)
$$\frac{Q}{L} = A.F\left(1, \frac{K}{L}, \frac{H}{L}\right)$$

or

(3)
$$q = Af(k,h)$$

Used creatively, Equation (3) can be illuminating. It implies that output per worker (q) will rise if:

- the capital stock rises – via investment, mainly financed by savings – since this boosts k. Note that by investment is meant the acquisition of more physical capital such as machinery, buildings or infrastructure, and not financial 'investment', which merely amounts to a transfer of ownership of existing wealth;
- workers acquire education, training and experience, and enjoy good health, since this raises h;
- technical advance, innovation and institutional change occur, since these increase A.

These are useful, if rather obvious, conclusions. However, it is possible to make the analysis much more interesting.

Solow Growth model

The 'workhorse' for understanding the role played by investment and other factors of production in economic growth is the model developed by MIT professor and Nobel laureate Robert Solow. Here we develop the model graphically and apply it to the Irish case.

The production function in (3) may be graphed as the curve 0–q in Figure 6.3. It curves because of the 'law' of diminishing marginal returns: as the amount of capital per worker (k) rises, output per worker (q) also rises, but less and less quickly.

Now assume that a constant fraction, s, of output is invested. This gives the investment supply curve 0–s.q, which has the same shape as the production function but is only s per cent as high.

157

Figure 6.3

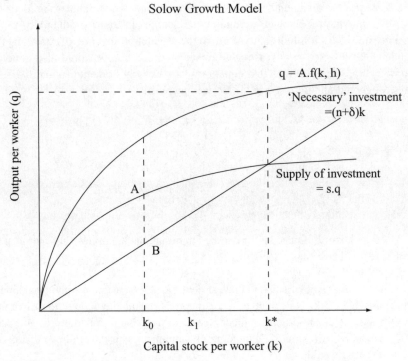

Solow Growth Model

Capital stock per worker (k)

To complete the story we may add a line that reflects the investment that would be necessary to prevent k (and therefore q) falling. Simply to maintain the capital stock per worker, we need to:

- invest enough to replace the wear and tear ('depreciation') of the capital stock; represented by δ, this is of the order of five per cent per annum in most economies;
- invest enough to equip newcomers to the labour force; otherwise their arrival would dilute the capital stock and capital per worker (k) would fall. An n per cent rise in the labour force thus requires n per cent more capital for this purpose.

Taken together, 'necessary' investment per worker thus represents $(n+\delta).k$, and is shown by the straight line in Figure 6.3.

A poor country will have a low stock of capital per worker, such as k_0. At this point, the supply of investment (s.q) exceeds necessary investment $((n+\delta).k)$, leaving an investment surplus that will serve to deepen the stock of capital. Thus by the next year, the stock of capital will rise to k_1, and so on.

There is an important implication. Poor countries should be able to grow faster than rich ones, because their investment 'surpluses' are larger relative to Q/L.

Note that the process stops at k*. In other words, investment alone can raise k to k*, and therefore output per worker to q*, but then growth stops – unless, of course, other influences can be brought to bear.

This has an immediate and interesting implication: economies should experience (conditional) convergence. For a given savings rate (s), technology (A.f(.)), employment growth rate (n) and depreciation rate (δ), all countries should converge on the same k* and hence the same level of output per worker.

Has Ireland Converged?

It is natural to ask whether recent Irish economic growth follows the predictions of the Solow model, in effect causing the Irish economy to converge to those of the rest of the EU.

This question may be addressed with the help of two graphs. Figure 6.4 shows GDP per worker in 1960 (in 2000 international PPP US dollars) on the horizontal axis and the annual percentage growth rate of GDP per worker from 1960 to 2006 on the vertical axis (GNI for Ireland, for reasons discussed earlier). In 1960

Figure 6.4

Initial Income and Subsequent Growth: OECD, 1960–2006

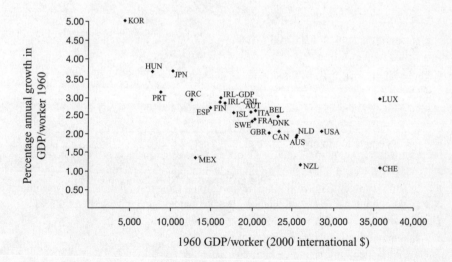

Sources: Central Bank of Ireland, *Bulletin*, Dublin, various issues; World Bank, *World Development Indicators*, www.worldbank.org [accessed April 2008].

Ireland was relatively poor, grouped with Greece, Spain, Japan and Mexico. The Solow model predicts that poorer countries should grow faster than richer ones, until they have caught up: thus South Korea (initially poor) should grow faster than Switzerland (initially rich). It follows that we would expect the observations in Figure 6.4 to fall along a line that slopes downwards to the right, which is what we see, with a correlation coefficient between the two series of –0.69. Viewed this way, it would appear that Irish economic growth was no more than one would have expected. Taking the 1960–2006 period as a whole, then, it makes sense to use the Solow model to try to identify the proximate causes of Irish growth (in output per worker).

Figure 6.5 is similar to Figure 6.4 except that it takes 1980 instead of 1960 as the starting point. It is more difficult to see any clear pattern in these observations; again, only Luxembourg and South Korea stand out from the other observations, suggesting that growth in these countries was higher than would have been predicted by Solow-type conditional convergence. The correlation in this case is – 0.35, not significantly different from zero.

Figure 6.5

Initial Income and Subsequent Growth: OECD, 1980–2006

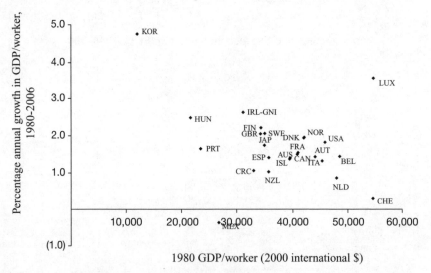

Sources: Central Bank of Ireland, *Bulletin*, Dublin, various issues; World Bank, *World Development Indicators*, www.worldbank.org [accessed April 2008].

Ireland is at the upper edge of these observations, suggesting that its economic growth (per worker) was somewhat higher than one would have expected, given the Solow framework. This is more evident if a larger sample of countries is used – which is actually more appropriate than confining the sample to countries that have already become rich: most countries poorer than Ireland have not grown as rapidly as Ireland did over the past two, or four, decades.

In short, Ireland appears to be a relatively rapid converger. This calls for an explanation.

Applying the Solow model

We now use the Solow model to help understand, in more detail, the factors that have influenced the growth of GNI (or GDP) per worker over the past decade or so, remembering of course that this growth in labour productivity was not particularly high during this period (as Table 6.6 shows).

Investment

In the Solow model, a higher savings rate, by allowing more investment, would cause an acceleration of economic growth in the short run, and allow growth to continue longer *but not indefinitely*. In other words, even if Ireland were to invest a higher proportion of its GNI, it would not permanently grow faster than other countries.

Since 1997, Ireland's investment rate has been slightly higher than the EU-25 average of about 20 per cent of GDP/GNI. Table 6.6 shows that the Irish investment rate was particularly high in the 1970s and early 1980s, falling sharply for almost a decade before recovering somewhat after 1994.

Table 6.6

Gross Investment and Economic Performance, 1960–2007

	1960–73	1973–79	1979–86	1986–94	1994–2000	2000–2007
	(average for period, as % of GDP)					
All investment	20.1	25.0	23.0	17.1	21.3	25.4
Housing investment					5.5	10.7
	(annual growth rates, %)					
Real GNI/worker	4.2	2.8	1.8	3.2	2.6	1.8
Capital services			-5.2[1]	1.1	6.2	6.1[2]

Sources: as for Table 6.1.
[1] 1981–86. [2] 2000–2004.

All of the increment in the investment rate after 2000 is attributable to a surge in investment in housing. The housing market is highly cyclical: this is clear from Figure 6.6, which graphs the number of new houses completed annually from 1970 to 2007. Given current population growth and other demographic changes such as the trend towards smaller households, there is a demand for about 50,000 new houses annually; in 2006, completions were almost double this level, clearly an unsustainable situation.

Figure 6.6

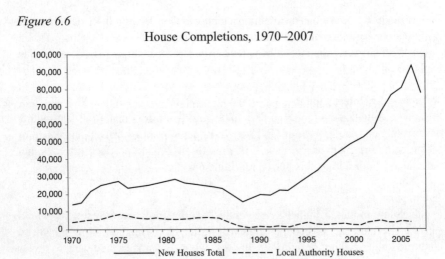

House Completions, 1970–2007

New Houses Total ———— Local Authority Houses ------

Source: Department of Environment, Heritage, and Local Government, *Housing Statistics*, April 2008.

It has been argued that the provision of capital services actually fell between 1980 and 1989, in part due to the accelerated obsolescence of equipment (especially for transport) that resulted from high oil prices. This situation is shown in Figure 6.7, where the light line measures the evolution of the value of the

Figure 6.7

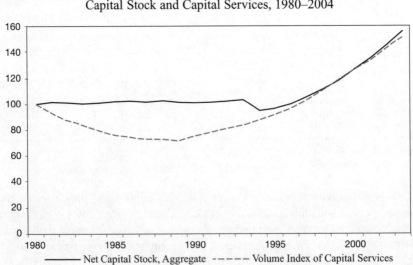

Capital Stock and Capital Services, 1980–2004

Net Capital Stock, Aggregate ———— Volume Index of Capital Services ------

Source: M. Keeney, 'Measuring Irish capital' (Research Technical Paper 13/RT/06), Central Bank of Ireland, Dublin 2006.

capital stock, while the heavy line tracks the evolution of capital services (i.e. the capital stock weighted by its annual productivity). In the early 1990s, as seen previously, investment went disproportionately to high-return activities (machinery, software, equipment); after 2000, investment was directed to long-lived assets, most notably housing.

With the end of the housing boom the investment rate has fallen. This need not be fatal: the United States has had an investment rate lower than the Irish rate for over half a century, but this has not prevented the US from maintaining its position of affluence. The trick is to use the investment productively, and this requires complementary inputs of skilled labour and technology – topics to which we now turn.

Labour Force Growth

The growth in total output (Q) consists of the growth in output per worker (Q/L) plus the growth of employment (n). Clearly, if employment grows more slowly, this will directly reduce the rise in output (for a given level of output/worker).

But there is an additional effect. The Solow model implies that slower growth in the labour force (n), by reducing the number of new workers who need to be equipped with capital, will delay, again not indefinitely, the time when economic growth *per worker* (i.e. Q/L) stops. Formally, when n falls, the line $0-(n+\delta).k$ swivels down, and k^* moves to the right (see Figure 6.3).

Between 1994 and 2000, as seen earlier the period of most rapid growth, employment in Ireland grew by a remarkable 5.8 per cent annually, significantly faster than the 1.1 per cent annual rise in the population over the same period (see Chapter 5). The rapid rise in employment was due to a large inflow of young people into the labour market, a resumption of immigration, and a substantial rise in the proportion of adults employed (with an associated dramatic fall in the unemployment rate). After 2000, employment grew only half as quickly, but still expanded by a fifth by 2007. By 2005, 67 per cent of the working-age population – defined as those aged from 15 to 64 – were employed, up from 52 per cent in 1994, and higher than the EU-27 mean of 63 per cent. Both the male and female employment rates are still rising.

Table 6.7

Employment Rates, 1994–2005

	Ireland		EU-27	Denmark[1]
	1994	2005	2005	2005
% of population 15–64 employed	52.2	67.1	63.4	75.9
Male employment rate (%)	64.6	76.2	70.8	79.8
Female employment rate (%)	39.6	58.3	56.6	71.9

Source: CSO, *Measuring Ireland's Progress*, Stationery Office, Dublin 2007, Table 3.2.
[1]The Danish figures are shown here because they were the highest in the EU-27.

The rapid growth in employment helped raise Ireland's total GNI, but the new workers had to be equipped with capital, which one would expect to restrain the growth of GNI per capita (q), for any given investment rate. Yet the growth of GNI per worker continued to expand at its historical trend rate.

This is a remarkable case of the dog that did not bark. Employment grew by 1.3 per cent annually between 1986 and 1994, and 5.8 per cent annually in the period 1994–2000. Simply equipping these additional workers to the standard of existing workers would typically require investment equivalent to about 14 per cent of output, or over a half of total investment.[10] Normally this would have halved the growth of GNI per capita, yet this did not happen.

In other words, the growth in GNI per worker was maintained in the late 1990s despite an unusually rapid increase in employment, a phenomenon that also characterised the Asian Tigers, including Singapore and Taiwan, during the periods of their most rapid growth.

This requires an explanation. One possibility, still within the framework of the Solow model, is that the services of the capital stock expanded, and we saw above that this was indeed the case. Another possible explanation is that human capital improved, a point to which we return below.

Human Capital

Education, training, experience and good health make workers more productive, and more employable. Thus increases in 'human capital' can boost economic growth. There are likely to be diminishing returns to additional human capital, which means that the effect, at the margin, on economic growth will eventually become negligible. Formally, an increase in human capital (h) will shift the curves 0–q and 0–s.q in Figure 6.3 upwards, pushing the steady state capital-labour ratio (k*) to the right.

Universal secondary education was only introduced in Ireland in 1968, and older workers are not particularly well educated by Western European standards (see Chapter 12). However, the recent expansion of higher education has created a well-educated cohort of young people; in 2006, 40 per cent of those aged 25–34 had some third-level education, up from 27 per cent in 1999, and well above the EU-27 rate of 29 per cent. In passing it is worth noting that women are substantially more likely than men to go on to tertiary education in Ireland, as in all other countries of the EU, but the gap is especially wide in the Irish case, where 47 per cent of young women, but only 34 per cent of young men, have received higher education.

The improvement in the quantity of higher education does coincide substantially with the growth spurt of the late 1990s and 2000s, and undoubtedly played a significant role, although Ireland is by no means the European leader in this area. In 2004 Ireland produced locally 0.6 PhDs in mathematics, science and technology per thousand of population, in line with the EU-27 average (also 0.6), but well below the levels of Sweden (1.8), Portugal (1.0) and the UK (0.9).

On average, the Irish educational system provides a solid, if not spectacular, base. A standardised test administered to 15-year-olds in OECD countries in 2003 found that Irish students scored 515 in reading literacy (compared to an OECD average of 494), 503 in mathematics, and 505 in science (compared to OECD averages of 500). Only Finnish students performed consistently better at reading – perhaps Ireland is a literary society – but Irish students were in the middle of the pack when judged by their performance in mathematics and science (see Chapter 12).

Technological and Institutional Change
Logically, within the framework of the Solow model, the only potentially persistent source of growth is technological change, including institutional progress. Formally, this raises the A parameter year after year, which shifts upwards the 0–q curve (see Figure 6.3) and hence also the 0–s.q curve. That technological change is the only durable source of economic growth is not surprising; 'modern' economic growth, with its concomitant rise in popular living standards, only began with the Industrial Revolution in the late eighteenth century.[11]

Technology may be created or acquired. A narrow view of technology would focus on the creation and application of technology through spending on research and development (R&D). The numbers in Table 6.8 show that Irish spending on R&D, as a proportion of GDP, is low by EU standards, and rising but slowly.

Table 6.8
Research and Development Spending as a Proportion of GDP, 1991–2005

	Ireland				EU-27	EU maximum: Sweden	EU minimum: Romania
	1991	1996	2001	2005	2005	2005	2005
R&D/GDP (%)	0.93	1.32	1.17	1.26	1.84	3.86	0.39

Source: CSO, *Measuring Ireland's Progress*, Stationery Office, Dublin, December 2007.

This level of spending is too low to explain much of Ireland's economic growth. But until recently, Ireland was a 'follower' country that, like China, could still acquire technology that had been created elsewhere.

The acquisition of technology is helped if a society and economy is highly open – to trade (making it easy to import goods, including investment goods, that incorporate improved technology); to ideas (so managerial, organisational and institutional changes can be learned and copied); to foreign direct investment (so that international firms can bring best-practice technology and skills); to allowing labour-market flexibility (so resistance to technological change is low); and to competition (forcing firms to stay on their toes).

By such measures, Ireland has become a truly open society. Exports in 2005 were equivalent to 81 per cent of GDP, similar to the situation found in most of the smaller economies of Eastern Europe. Irish exports rose by 125 per cent between 1995 and 2000, and increased by just 29 per cent in the following five years. Indeed, Ireland's share of world exports peaked in 2001–2002 when it reached 1.35 per cent; two years later, its share of world services exports peaked, at 2.39 per cent of the global total. The period of frenetic export-led growth is now over.

Ireland is very receptive to foreign investment, which as recently as 2002 flowed in to the tune of 20 per cent of GDP. Now the net flows have reversed, and Ireland has become an important source of investment abroad: in 2006, outflows of direct investment amounted to $22.1 billion, equivalent to 10.1 per cent of GDP; this was partly offset by $12.8 billion worth of inflows (5.9 per cent of GDP). Among EU countries, only Luxembourg, which is also an important financial centre, has flows of a comparable order of magnitude.

Ireland's march towards openness is not new. It began in earnest in the 1960s with the Anglo-Irish Free Trade Agreement, and was boosted by EU membership (1973) and the advent of the European single market (1992). The Irish growth spurt of the late 1990s and 2000s may have required such openness, but Ireland was not unique among European countries – including those that grew far less quickly – in this respect.

The contribution of technological change may be measured as the growth in output per unit of input, or total factor productivity (TFP); for instance, if inputs (labour, capital, land) each rise by two per cent and output rises by five per cent, then total factor productivity – which we conventionally attribute to 'technology' – rises by about three per cent.

5 GROWTH IN OUTPUT: A SYNTHESIS

Let us now return to the central puzzle of this chapter: what accounts for Ireland's growth spurt of the late 1990s, the continued strength of the economy after 2000, and the sharp slowdown by 2008? This is a puzzle that is all the greater because, as we have just seen, Ireland in the 1990s had almost no scope for changing fiscal, monetary or exchange rate policy.

The simple version of the story runs something like this: with relatively low taxes and macroeconomic stability, Ireland by the early 1990s was an attractive destination for US companies wishing to serve the European market. Investment flowed into export-oriented manufacturing, where it had a quick payoff, raising output and employment very rapidly. As more households could count on steady earnings, the demand for consumer durables (especially cars) and housing increased, but with a lag.

This consumer demand was fuelled by cheap credit, made possible after Ireland switched to the euro in 1999 – the real interest rate essentially fell to zero, and consumers responded by taking out mortgages and expanding their use of credit (which rose by more than 15 per cent both in 2005 and 2006). The adoption of the euro also boosted Ireland's financial services sector. Over-exuberant developers built excessive numbers of houses, and the inevitable correction began in 2008 as the construction sector contracted; meanwhile, high wages, a strong euro and high prices have cost Ireland its competitive edge in many export markets. Having converged to European levels of output per worker (or per capita), Ireland is now converging to European levels of economic growth, much as the Solow model would lead one to expect.

Growth Environment
There are, however, four areas where Ireland, wittingly or not, has espoused pro-growth strategies, or has been just lucky – in the role of the state, attitudinal changes, social protections, and the US factor.

Role of the State
Like the USA, UK and Japan, but unlike most of the richer EU countries, the government sector in Ireland is relatively small (see Chapter 3). The low tax burden helps limit distortions to the choices that households make about work, consumption and investment (see Chapter 4). More specifically, Ireland's regime of low tax rates on corporate income makes the country attractive to foreign investors: the effective marginal tax rate on the profits generated by foreign investments in Ireland is estimated at 13 per cent, well below the OECD mean of 21 per cent;[12] formally, the corporation tax rate is just 12.5 per cent, compared with an EU average of 31 per cent and a US rate of 39 per cent. Ireland also has the lowest restrictions on inflows of foreign direct investment of any OECD country.[13]

The relatively light weight of the state sector is possible in part because of low military costs and health and education systems that are inexpensive relative to their outputs (see Chapter 3). But one might point to 1987 as the turning point: in national discussions, the government promised to lower taxes if wages were restrained and labour peace restored. Thus began a dynamic that has been maintained since, and that differs sharply from the European norm where governments typically promised more welfare payments, rather than lower taxes, in return for wage restraint. This is reflected in the structure of personal income taxes: an 'average' production worker who is married with two children would have disposable income equal to 103 per cent of gross pay in Ireland, compared with 96 per cent in the US and 83 per cent in the EU (see Chapters 3 and 4). The comparatively modest size of the public sector – civil servants are not numerous, but they are comparatively well paid – has also kept in check the proportion of the public with a vested interest in raising taxes.

Some argue that much of the credit for the rise in employment in the 1990s and 2000s should go to national wage agreements that kept labour costs low and bought labour peace; they point to a reduction in strikes since 1987 – there were only six industrial disputes in 2007 – as evidence of the success of these efforts. However, this argument is not entirely compelling: labour unrest abated in most of Western Europe at the same time, without a corresponding rise in employment;

and in practice, actual wage increases bore little relation to the rates negotiated in national agreements – hardly surprising given that Ireland's labour market is integrated with that of the UK and, increasingly, the rest of the EU.

One may also measure the weight of government by the extent of rules and regulations. Like the UK and USA, but in contrast with most of Continental Europe, Irish rules protecting employment and product markets are relatively light, again a feature that endears the country to investors (see Chapters 3 and 4). The 1990s also saw a new government commitment to fostering competition (see Chapters 3 and 9), with changes that were particularly successful in the airline industry but have yet to affect some expensive and cosseted groups, such as lawyers.

Every year the World Bank publishes an 'Ease of Doing Business' ranking (see Chapters 3 and 8); in the 2008 version, Ireland was ranked eighth out of 178 countries, behind Denmark (fifth) and the UK (sixth), but ahead of France (31st) and Greece (100th). The average rank for the EU countries was 34. Although Ireland was among the top twenty countries in seven of the ten dimensions that are used to compute this ranking, it scored relatively poorly in its rules for property registration and, to a lesser extent, its procedures for enforcing contracts.

Attitudes

Although it is hard to quantify, there appears to have been a change in attitudes over the past three decades, a change that favours economic growth. In the 1970s, college students tended to aspire to jobs in the Foreign Service, or as employees in well-established firms. Now they are more likely to want to be entrepreneurs. In 2007, 8.2 per cent of Irish adults were either thinking of setting up a business or had just started one; this was lower than the rate in the USA (9.6 per cent), but substantially higher than in France (3.2 per cent), Japan (4.3 per cent) or the UK (5.5 per cent).[14] There is no better metaphor for the transformation than the relative decline of staid, state-owned Aer Lingus and the rise of tough, profitable, private and entrepreneurial Ryanair, although this story has a twist because Aer Lingus has responded by re-inventing itself as a budget carrier.

By the 1990s Ireland's fertility rate, once the highest in Western Europe, had fallen to the same level as a number of other EU countries, again a symptom of changing attitudes, including an increasing disregard for some of the teachings of the Catholic Church. In the 1970s, over 90 per cent of Roman Catholics went to Mass every Sunday; by 2005 this number had been halved.

It is difficult to account for the change in attitudes, but a case can be made that high unemployment in the UK and the USA made emigration less attractive in the early 1990s; forced to stay at home, but unable to find wage-paying work, many young people started to improvise, learned to like the change, and began to succeed. With greater opportunities for success, attitudinal change was strengthened. At the same time Ireland became better informed about, and more closely attuned to, attitudes prevalent in Continental Europe.

Social Protection

The comparatively small government sector has a price, too – less social protection, including relatively modest spending on health, education and pensions, and fewer national cultural institutions. Government pensions and transfers (such as unemployment assistance) do reduce income disparities in Ireland, but less markedly than in almost any other EU country.

On the other hand, this relatively hard-nosed attitude towards social protection has probably helped economic growth. A decade ago, the structure of taxes and subsidies was such that, for low-skilled workers, it did not pay to go to work. This structure has now been rationalised, unblocking a serious barrier to employment; equivalent changes have been much slower to arrive in countries such as France and Germany.

US Factor

If the USA did not exist, Ireland would not have experienced a growth spurt in the 1990s, although since 2000 most of the economic growth has been home-grown. In the 1990s, four-fifths of foreign direct investment originated in the USA, and US firms now account for a quarter of manufacturing employment and about a half of manufacturing output and exports (see Chapter 8). The high-tech wave that lifted the US economy in the 1990s and 2000s washed over Ireland too, but not over most of the rest of Europe. The point is not that US investors raised the Irish investment rate, but rather that the investments they made, and the associated learning and external economies of scale, had a large and immediate effect on output, and employment.

It may now be more realistic to think of the Irish economy not as a region of Europe, but as an outpost of the USA attached to the edge of the EU.

We still need to ask why US investors steered so much of their investment to Ireland rather than, say, Scotland or Greece or Portugal or India. In part the answer is because Ireland made them welcome, with low taxes and other benefits. But Ireland has historically had close links with the USA; there are strong cultural similarities between the two countries; and they share a common language.

By 2006, foreign investors owned assets in Ireland equivalent to $41,700 per capita, four times the level in the EU countries ($10,980). Irish companies have begun to return the favour, and in the same year they held assets internationally to the tune of $29,110 per capita, well above the EU mean of $12,990 and higher than the US level of $7,960 (see Chapter 8).[15]

The Combination

In a nutshell, the Irish growth spurt occurred because all the economic planets came into alignment at the same time. The key elements: a booming US economy providing firms there with the profits to invest abroad; a ten per cent tax on manufacturing profits to attract them to Ireland, coupled with relatively light regulation of labour and product markets; the lure of a pool of well-educated and English-speaking workers; the creation of a single European market that could be served efficiently from Ireland; a credible and conservative macroeconomic stance; wage restraint due to the inertia built into early rounds of national agreements; and a new-found attitude favourable to entrepreneurial activity (see also Chapter 5, in which a similar conclusion is reached).

Once the boom began, it led to a virtuous circle, raising the demand for housing and other construction, as well as for a wide array of services such as restaurants, banks and accountants. Although manufacturing employment peaked (at 318,000) in 2001, over 400,000 jobs were created between 2000 and 2007; perhaps surprisingly, given the attention that the sector has received, only a quarter of these new jobs were in construction (whose share of jobs rose from eight to 13 per cent between 1998 and 2007). Large numbers of jobs have also been created in recent years in finance, health care and public administration.

A recent book on spatial economics presents a model of 'punctuated equilibria' that matches the Irish case rather well.[16] Consider a region that exports some good. Part of the export earnings are spent and re-spent locally; the computer exporter pays local workers, who buy restaurant meals from chefs, who spend their money buying haircuts, and so on. Now suppose that as the region grows, the proportion of export spending that goes into local purchases rises, which is plausible. Then it can be shown that as exports rise, local income will rise too, at first fairly slowly, then increasingly quickly, and then it will suddenly jump from one equilibrium path to another, before resuming a slower and steadier rise. Ireland has just jumped.

6 WILL GROWTH CONTINUE?

The period of rapid economic growth is now over. The relevant question for the future is whether Ireland will be able to maintain its position as one of the most productive and affluent countries in the world. Sweden, once one of the most affluent countries in Europe, has in recent years slipped in the rankings. So has Japan, still struggling for an encore after its spectacular growth prior to 1989. Can Ireland expect the same?

'Forecasting is difficult,' wrote Nobelist Neils Bohr, 'especially about the future.' Even so, some things are clear.

On the positive side, an interesting feature of the 'punctuated-equilibria' model is that if exports fall, the economy will not decline as quickly as it grew. Having reached a higher plateau, the economy will be able to remain there relatively easily. This helps explain why the OECD still expects Irish economic growth to continue to exceed the OECD average over the next few years.[17] Moreover, corporate income tax rates remain low, entrepreneurialism is alive and well, and anticipated improvements in infrastructure and the regulatory environment are likely to help sustain growth.

Against this, the decomposition of Section 4 indicates that the 'demographic dividend' is essentially over: the unemployment rate is rising again, the share of prime-age adults in the population is nearing its peak, and the increase in labour force participation rates cannot continue indefinitely.

Second, the Solow framework predicts that the *growth* in GNI per worker will eventually fall, although continued external economies and ongoing improvements in human capital and technology could postpone this somewhat. Perhaps the fall has already occurred: labour productivity grew by 3.1 per cent annually from 1994 to 2000, but since then has risen by just 1.8 per cent per year. This slowdown has occurred despite an upturn in the proportion of output devoted to investment.

Third, some of the economic planets discussed in Section 5 are going out of alignment: in early 2008 the USA began to slide into recession; wage restraint is not in evidence; government spending has been expanding; and a number of Eastern European countries, particularly new EU members, are quite explicitly trying to emulate the 'Irish model' and now provide cheap entry points to the EU market, much as Ireland did a decade ago.

And fourth, Ireland has become a victim of its own success. It is now a high-cost destination for investors. This is to be expected; with a tighter labour market, wages have risen; and with rising incomes, the demand for housing and land has increased, pushing up their prices. Here we have a textbook case of a boom running its course.

Even staying near the top of the GNI per capita ranking will be challenging. Irish education is good, not extraordinary; the investment rate is solid, but is no longer delivering the expected increases in labour productivity growth; government regulatory policies are fairly light, but the public sector is not universally honest, transparent or efficient (as the OECD points out in a recent report).[18] The World Economic Forum ranks Ireland 22nd worldwide in 2007 in its 'global competitiveness index', and the *World Competitiveness Yearbook* ranks it 14th: whatever one may think of rankings of this nature (see Chapters 2 and 8), these do not point to overwhelming international confidence in the growth prospects of the Irish economy.[19]

Moreover, if investment and jobs can flow rapidly into Ireland, they can leave quickly too. In 2007, there were 292,000 jobs in industry; yet since 1970 an estimated 274,000 industrial jobs have been lost.[20] Given the rapidity of turnover of industrial jobs, the sector could shrink rapidly.

The biggest danger to long-term growth is complacency. The government sector could expand too quickly. Individuals could lose their work ethic; in Norway, the average worker is absent from work for an average of 4.8 weeks per year (not counting regular holidays).[21]

Meanwhile there is a more immediate challenge: after 14 'fat' years, the long-postponed downturn has arrived, and the government will now have to rediscover how to counteract the effects of economic contraction.

Endnotes

[1] World Bank, *World Development Indicators*, www.worldbank.org [accessed April 2008].

[2] See B. Nolan, *Trends in Income Inequality in Ireland*, ESRI, March 2006. Combat Poverty Agency Research Seminar.

[3] In measuring living standards, it might make more sense to use gross national income (GNI) rather than gross domestic product (GDP). However, for most countries, GNI and GDP are very similar; and GDP data are published more promptly than GNI figures (which require measures of international flows of factor payments and transfers).

[4] J. Alber and T. Fahey, *Perceptions of Living Conditions in an Enlarged Europe*, European Foundation for the Improvement of Living and Working Conditions, and European Commission, Luxembourg 2004, p. 51.

[5] A. Oswald, 'Happiness and economic performance', University of Warwick, April 1997.

[6] These measures of the rental cost of capital are the averages, over the period 1980 to 2004, as estimated by M. Keeney, 'Measuring Irish capital' (Research Technical Paper 13/RT/06), Central Bank of Ireland, Dublin 2006.

[7] For a derivation of equation (2), see D. Perkins, S. Radelet and D. Lindauer, *Economics of Development* (6th edn), Norton, New York 2006.

[8] As discussed earlier, GNI relates to income and GDP to output and it was argued there that in most countries both of these are approximately the same. This is not the case in Ireland, with the earlier statistics indicating that GDP exceeds GNI in some years by 16 per cent or more. It is likely also, though, that much of this discrepancy is due to the fact that GDP is not an accurate measure of output either, due to the transfer-pricing practices of multinational companies. While the true measure of output for Ireland is likely to lie between the GNI and GDP measures, we believe that it may lie closer to the GNI measure and as such GNI, not GDP, will be used in this subsection.

[9] This table shows logarithmic growth rates, which is why they differ slightly from those given in Table 6.3.

[10] This assumes a capital-output ratio of three.

[11] The term 'modern economic growth' was coined by Nobel laureate Simon Kuznets, whose *magnum opus* traced the growth of the UK and USA over the past two centuries.

[12] K. Yoo, 'Corporate taxation of foreign direct investment income 1991–2001 (OECD Working Paper UnECO/WKP(2003)19), OECD, Paris 2003.

[13] S. Golub, 'Measures of restrictions on inward foreign direct investment for OECD countries' (OECD working paper ECO/WKP(2003)11), OECD, Paris 2003.

[14] N. Bosma, K. Jones, E. Autio and J. Levie, *Global Entrepreneurship Monitor: 2007 Executive Report*, Babson College and London Business School, London 2008.

[15] UNCTAD, *World Investment Report 2007*, www.unctad.org/wir [accessed April 2008].

[16] M. Fujita, P. Krugman and A. Venables, *The Spatial Economy*, MIT Press, Cambridge MA 1999.

[17] OECD, *Economic Outlook*, OECD, Paris 2007.

[18] OECD, *Economic Surveys: Ireland*, OECD, Paris 2003.

[19] World Economic Forum, www.weforum.org [accessed April 2008]; *World Competitiveness Yearbook*, Lausanne, Switzerland 2004.

20 Based on information from the Department of Enterprise, Trade and Employment, as reported in Department of Finance, *Budgetary and Economic Statistics*, Dublin, March 2004. The lost jobs refer to notified redundancies.

21 L. Alvarez, 'In Norway, a nation calls in sick: oil money affecting work ethic', *New York Times*, 25 July 2004.

CHAPTER 7

Equality: Distribution, Poverty and Income Supports

Sara Cantillon

1 INTRODUCTION

The relationship between good economic performance and high incomes, on the one hand, and quality of life and individual and societal well-being, on the other, is an increasingly topical concern in public policy. Sachs attributes to modern economic growth 'higher living standards than were imaginable two decades ago' while at the same time acknowledging that 'it has also brought phenomenal gaps between the richest and the poorest'.[1] Increases in inequality, both within countries and between countries, the persistence of poverty, especially child poverty, in wealthy countries and the widening gap in income and wealth between developed and developing countries have sparked renewed interest by academics, and a sense of urgency by policymakers, in the issues of distribution and equality. There is also a growing recognition of the economic costs of inequality in terms of ill health, crime, educational underachievement and social exclusion. Issues of global inequality and poverty have moved back to centre stage within the international development institutions such as the UN and the World Bank in increasing recognition of the failed development project of the last 25 years. Within the EU, the issues of social exclusion and poverty were the distinct focus of the European Summit in Lisbon and objectives on how to combat them were agreed at the European Council in Nice. The development of commonly agreed and defined EU social indicators to enable co-ordination and progress assessment in poverty eradication and social inclusion are acknowledgements of the central, rather than residual, importance of distributional issues in promoting 'a competitive and dynamic knowledge-based economy'. In Ireland, the economic boom of the past decade has made the issue of defining what is meant by poverty more pertinent. It is against this background that this chapter is set. While the debate surrounding equity as a policy objective and its interaction with growth objectives is covered in detail in Chapter 2, this chapter addresses the issues of equality and distribution, focusing in particular on income, poverty and social welfare in the form of income supports.

Section 2 gives a brief overview of the scale and the patterns of existing inequalities in Irish society and globally. It is a relatively easy task to demonstrate inequality; it is more difficult to specify what we mean by equality, and harder again to put any consensus on equality objectives into practice. Section 3 provides a framework for thinking about equality in economic and other dimensions. It identifies four generative dimensions of equality – economic, political, cultural/social, and affective – and highlights the key equality issues that arise within each dimension. Clearly, a central area is inequality in economic resources, both in its own right, and in terms of its implications for the other dimensions of equality discussed. Sections 4 and 5 address inequality in economic resources by looking at poverty and the distribution of income and wealth. They provide an overview of the conceptual and measurement issues raised in relation to poverty, income and wealth, examine recent trends and some of the factors underlying those trends and present some international comparisons. Section 6 examines the extent to which the state achieves redistribution of income objectives through the social welfare system. Section 7 concludes the chapter.

2 EXTENT OF GLOBAL INEQUALITY

The annual reports from the United Nations Development Programme (UNDP), the World Bank and the Organisation for Economic Co-operation and Development (OECD) all demonstrate that poverty is widespread and deep-rooted and illustrate the stark contrast between the life prospects of the rich and the poor across the globe.[2] Figures for the Human Development Report for 2007/2008 show that life expectancy ranges from 39 years in Zambia to 82 years in Japan. Of every 1,000 children born in Sierra Leone 282 die before their fifth birthday compared to 3 in Iceland and fewer than 10 in OECD countries as a whole. The OECD estimates that 2.7 billion people subsist on less than $2 a day; that over one billion people have no access to clean water; and that over two billion have no sanitation services. Recent OECD studies report that the richest two per cent of the world's adults own more than half of the global wealth. Within OECD countries, disparities have also grown: between 1994 and 2003, earnings inequalities increased in 17 out of the 20 countries for which there is information. These statistics are blunt reminders of global inequality but even within countries the better off have longer and healthier lives than the worse off. For example, manual workers in the UK are four times as likely to die from lung cancer as professionals, while in the USA African Americans are eight times more likely than whites to die from homicide.

These differences in how people's lives turn out reflect a range of inequalities in their circumstances – in the conditions of their lives. The most researched inequalities of condition are those to do with income and other economic resources. Global income inequality is reflected in the widening gap in average incomes between the richest and the poorest countries. The per-capita income gap between them has progressively increased over the past 200 years from a ratio of 3:1 to 40:1. Global per capita income trebled between 1960 and 2000, with the most marked increases in Eastern Asia and China in particular, but there are also over 100 countries whose per capita income has declined since the 1980s.[3] Assessing data from 73 countries, the UNDP estimated that 53 countries, containing over 80 per cent of the world's population, experienced rising inequality. A narrowing of inequality occurred in only nine countries, containing four per cent of the world's population. The sharp increase in income inequality between countries has been reflected in the majority of industrialised countries from the mid-1980s, with the increase in income inequality most conspicuous in the UK and the USA.

Income inequality has several recognisable patterns. The most obvious is that income reflects social class. The wealthiest belong to a class whose income is derived almost entirely from investment. Within paid employment there is a marked difference between the incomes of executives and workers. This gap has increased significantly since the 1960s. There is also a difference between the income of men and women. Even in the more egalitarian countries, like Denmark and Sweden, women's share of incomes is estimated at 82 per cent of men's. Another common pattern of income inequality is its connection to 'race' and ethnicity. In the USA, African American families receive on average less than two-thirds the income of non-Hispanic white families. Income inequality also reflects disability. The incomes of severely disabled people in Britain are only about half of average income. Further, within the paid workforce, women, disabled people, ethnic minorities and other marginalised groups are disproportionately represented among casualised workers. While the proportion of women in professional jobs has increased, women are still disproportionately represented among part-time and low-paid workers. This trend is particularly evident in Ireland, where 23 per cent of all women employees work part-time compared with five per cent of men.

It is argued that 'the stubborn persistence of poverty and the increasing inequality both between and within developed and developing countries help create the conditions for the expansion of terrorism, armed conflict, environmental degradation, cross-border diseases and organised crime'.[4] The adoption of eight Millennium Development Goals (MDGs) by the UN, and the project of monitoring the progress in achieving these, represents some recognition at a global level that gross forms of inequality between nations and regions in the world, and between women and men, is detrimental to the survival and well-being of humanity. In the Millennium Declaration, governments acknowledged the growing realisation of global interdependency, especially in relation to the environment, and agreed that globalisation should become a positive force for all. The issue of climate change is one of controversy and debates about its reality and what measures to take are slowing a global response. It is generally accepted, however, that the impact of global warming, and other predicted changes, such as extreme weather, shifts in global ocean circulation, decreases in crop yields and sea-level rises, on our natural systems and lifestyles will be considerable. From an equality perspective the issue is the distribution of the impacts of these changes and that some countries will suffer more than others. Already climate change in Africa has brought about increasingly prolonged droughts and more unpredictable rainfall patterns. With crops dying and seeds being washed away, those dependent on agriculture for their livelihood are being forced to survive through increasingly desperate measures such as selling their assets, migration and further degradation of the environment.

The year 2007 represented a midway point between the adoption of the UN Millennium Goals in 2000 and their target date of 2015. Yet, in 2007 sub-Saharan Africa was not on target to achieve any of the eight goals. Even the reduction in extreme poverty is moving at such a slow pace that the goal of halving such poverty will not be achieved by 2015. Moreover, where poverty has been reduced, it has been accompanied by rising inequality. The poorest fifth of the population in developing regions of the world consumed less in 2004 than in 1990, despite rising economic growth. This pattern is not unique to poorer regions such as sub-Saharan Africa; it also applies in the 'developed' world, in the Commonwealth of Independent States, and in Eastern Asia, where the consumption of the poorest people declined dramatically between 1990 and 2004. For poorer countries to develop, it is recognised that there is a need for a more open, legally binding, predictable, non-discriminatory trading and financial system throughout the world. At the World Trade Organisation meeting in Doha in 2001, promises were made to engage in trade negotiations that would focus on improving prospects for developing countries. By 2007, however, there was no agreement on what measures would be adopted. As for development aid, donors will have to increase aid-flows faster than any other public expenditure in order to fulfil their commitments to increase aid to $130 billion and double aid to Africa by 2010. The likelihood of this happening is slim. Ireland's net official development assistance in 2007 amounted to 0.47 per cent of GNI. While this represents a substantial increase on previous years it is well below the previous commitment to the UN target of 0.7 per cent of GNI by 2007. This commitment has since been extended to 2012.

3 IDEA OF EQUALITY

Definitions
At a very general level, equality can be described as a relationship between two or more people regarding some aspect of their lives.[5] What this relationship is, who it is about and what aspect of their lives it concerns is not straightforward. Once the idea of equality is explored more deeply its complexity begins to emerge. A key question, raised by Sen, is equality of what? What is it that should be distributed equally? For example, is the concern overall well-being or 'welfare'? Or are the aims

more tangible, like equality of income or wealth? Should the focus be on outcomes such as educational attainments, or on the opportunities people have for achieving these? Needless to say economists and political theorists give very different answers to this distribution question – Rawls talks about primary social goods, Sen talks about the distribution of capabilities to achieve valued functionings, while Atkinson focuses on the right to a minimum level of resources. Another key issue is whether to apply the idea of equality to individuals or to groups. In other words, equality between whom? When the Universal Declaration of Human Rights, Article 1 states that 'All human beings are born free and equal in dignity and rights', it is referring to each and every individual person. But equality also matters in terms of groups, such as women or ethnic minorities. An important factor determining individuals' lives is the way social structures work to privilege the members of some groups over others. For example, there are inequalities structured around religion, race, gender, etc. In addition, there are many different and overlapping groups, even in relatively homogeneous societies. Equality between men and women, for example, does not necessarily involve equality between social classes, or equality between disabled and non-disabled people.

Equality, then, can be defined in terms of both individuals and a wide variety of groups; it can relate to many different dimensions of people's lives; and it can refer to many different types of relationship. All of these differences have some kind of basis in the idea of treating people as equals. It follows that far from being a single idea, equality refers to countless ideas, which may have very different implications and in particular may conflict. The conflict between equality and other societal objectives, and in particular the relationships between equality and economic growth and equality and efficiency, is an area that has generated a vast literature within economics (see Chapter 2).

Different Dimensions

Table 7.1 identifies some of the key factors that affect well-being or quality of life. These are identified as four core contexts in which the generative causes of inequality may emerge: namely, the economic, the political, the cultural and the affective, all of which in turn impact on each other. These dimensions do not necessarily pick out every aspect of equality and inequality that may be of economic, sociological or political interest, but the categories are sufficiently broad to cover most of the contemporary equality issues.

Table 7.1

An Equality Framework

Dimensions of Equality	Key Issues of Each Dimension
Economic	Distribution of resources
Social/cultural	Recognition and respect
Political	Representation/power relations
Affective	Care and solidarity

The economic sphere is concerned with the production, distribution and exchange of goods and services; the social/cultural sphere is concerned with the production, transmission and legitimisation of cultural practices and products, including various forms of symbolic representation and communication; the political sphere refers to all activities where power is enacted, including decision-making procedures within all types of organisations and institutions, policymaking procedures, and decision making within political life generally; the affective domain connotes those activities involved in developing bonds of solidarity, care and love between human beings. It refers to the socio-emotional relations that give people a sense of value and belonging in their personal, community, associational and working lives.

The focus of the framework is on identifying the major contexts for generating inequality and the key inequalities relating to these contexts. It is important to keep in mind that the dimensions overlap and that the key inequalities identified as correlating with a particular dimension are present in each of them. For example, in the political system there are certainly inequalities of power, but there are also inequalities of politically relevant resources, of recognition, of income and other material resources, and of prospects for solidarity. Furthermore, the contexts that generate inequality vary for different groups. While the economic context may be the principal one generating inequality among those groups whose most defining status is an economic one (the homeless, low-income workers or those who are welfare dependent) other groups may experience economic inequality or poverty as a derivative of either sociocultural and/or political factors. So, for example, while the primary generative cause of inequality for gays, lesbians and bisexuals may be generally defined as sociocultural, arising from the lack of recognition and respect for sexual difference, the implications of this extend beyond the sociocultural sphere. For example, they may feel vulnerable in educational, health and other employments that are controlled by religious organisations. Not only does the lack of recognition impact on employment opportunities in particular areas, it also affects such issues as pension entitlements, taxation issues (e.g. transferring of standard tax credit), and property rights (e.g. inheritance). The focus of this chapter is on the issues of inequality that arise in the economic sphere, but before moving to these in terms of outcomes such as poverty and income inequality, the liberal and radical perspectives on issues of economic equality and distribution are outlined.

Distribution of Economic Resources

The first dimension identified in Table 7.1 is economic, which concerns the distribution of resources. The most obvious resources are income and wealth, and these are the resources that economists typically concentrate on. A wider view of economic resources, however, would also consider non-financial conditions that affect access to goods and services, such as the right to public services and the right not to be excluded from goods and services by discriminatory treatment, as well as environmental factors such as a safe and healthy environment, the geographical arrangement of cities, the accessibility of buildings, etc. Time, particularly leisure time, is another important resource. Also to be included in a broader view of economic resources is what Bourdieu calls social and cultural capital. Social capital consists of the durable networks of social relationships to which people have access, while cultural capital includes both people's embodied knowledge and abilities and their education credentials.[6]

Assuming that significant inequality in the distribution of resources is inevitable, the objective can be either to regulate this inequality by combining a minimum floor or safety net with a principle of equal opportunity, or to aim at what can best be described as equality of resources. The minimum floor is a logical extension of a basic needs approach and is an intrinsic part of the modern welfare state. Quite where the floor should be and how it should be defined are continuing issues, as will be illustrated later in the chapter, when looking at the debates about whether poverty is 'absolute' or 'relative' and whether it can be defined entirely in terms of income or should include other resources. The key point is that the objective is often primarily concerned with eliminating poverty rather than promoting equality of resources. The central concern is to ensure that the competition for advantage is as fair as possible and that it is governed by equal opportunity. The persistence of major social and economic inequalities, however, inevitably undermines all but the thinnest forms of equal opportunity. Within the education system the introduction of free fees at third level, for example, has not produced a significant change in the socio-economic profile of those attending university, with about 20 per cent of children with fathers in 'unskilled manual' occupations entering third level compared with 80 per cent of children with fathers in 'higher professional' occupations (see Chapter 12).

The more radical view of equality accepts the urgency of satisfying basic needs and providing a safety net against poverty, but recognises a wider range of needs and tends to take a less market-oriented view of how these needs should be satisfied. For example, people with physical impairments may not only need higher incomes than those without these impairments, but also may need changes in the physical environment that promote their inclusion in the activities that others take for granted. Because of the multi-faceted and disputable nature of well-being and the complicated relationship between resources and prospects for well-being, it is very difficult to define equality of resources. It is certainly not the idea that everyone should have the same income and wealth, because people make different choices in relation to work and have different needs, and because there are other important resources to consider. However, if differences in need, or choosing to work harder or longer, were the only reasons that justified inequality in income, it should follow that people who have similar needs and who work in similar occupations for similar amounts of time should have similar income. This implies, for example, that there should be no significant differences in income between men and women, between people of colour and whites or between migrant workers and Irish workers. The empirical evidence for Ireland, and elsewhere, confirms that this is not the case. In 1996, women's earnings were 79 per cent of men's. By 2005 this proportion had increased to 91 per cent, a greater improvement than for the EU-27 as a whole, which increased from 83 to 85 per cent over the same period. However, persons working 15 hours a week or less, the majority of whom are more likely to be female and on lower incomes, are excluded from this indicator.[7]

Policy

There have been several important policy and legislative changes to progress equality in Ireland over the last number of years. These include the adoption of equality legislation, namely the Employment Equality Act 1998 and the Equal Status Act 2000, and the establishment of equality institutions: the Equality Authority and the Office of the Director of Equality Investigations. Taken together with the establishment of the Disability Authority and the Human Rights Commission, these are all developments with potential to contribute to reducing poverty, inequality and discrimination. With the launch of the National Anti-Poverty Strategy in 1997 Ireland became the first European Union member to adopt a national poverty reduction target. From an equality perspective, this represented a significant step forward in terms of political acceptance of a definition of poverty; of explicit recognition of the responsibility of government for reducing the extent of poverty; and of the need for a systematic, institutionally based strategy for combating poverty. In the affective domain there have been a number of legislative provisions addressing the regulation of the care of children in particular, such as the Parental Leave Act 1998 and the Education (Welfare) Act 2000. The development of increased maternity and parental leave, albeit unpaid, also signifies a growing recognition of the importance of care for infant children. However, the overall lack of support for childcare, the inadequate support for home carers of adults and dependent disabled persons suggest that affective relations generally have not been a political priority to date. There has also been an attempt to promote greater equality of power through the social partnership system, although the extent to which the system has achieved substantive, as opposed to symbolic, gains is a topic of debate. While the partnership agreements do have the potential to promote greater equality in the distribution of economic resources this has not been an explicit objective, with the outcome described as 'solidarity without equality'.[8] The following sections look at the area of equality in relation to distribution, poverty and social welfare.

4 INCOME AND WEALTH

The concept of income is more complex than it appears. The simplest way to think of income is as a flow deriving from a stock of wealth which, on an individual basis, can arise broadly in three forms: physical wealth such as houses, cars, paintings and other consumer durables; financial wealth such as stocks and shares, government bonds and bank deposits; and human wealth, which is primarily embodied in individuals as a result of education and training (i.e. human capital) but which can also arise from 'natural talent'. Each of these forms of wealth produces money and non-money income. Money income, being easier to quantify, receives most attention, but also deserving are non-money income flows from the different forms of wealth. These include such intangibles as job satisfaction (or dissatisfaction), enjoyment of leisure, and non-money income in the form of your own production such as housework, childcare and other caring functions. Conventional economic analysis defines 'work' as paid employment. This view is increasingly contested as producing a one-sided picture from which distorted and inefficient outcomes result. Economic life depends on both paid work and on the unpaid activities undertaken in the private/domestic sector. The issue of non-market work features prominently in feminist economics, an important contribution of which has been to explore the interface between feminist theory and political economy with particular emphasis on caring and other forms of non-market work.[9] For example, in recent years, data collection on unremunerated work, currently outside most national accounting systems, has been undertaken in several countries with a view to explicitly recognising and incorporating the economic contribution of unpaid work into income measures.

Measurement of Income
The income of individuals or households is not easy to measure. Usually it is gauged at an individual level through tax and social security records and at a household level through household surveys. While surveys are the main data source used in Ireland these can be problematic because of issues of coverage and accuracy. Household income surveys collect data on income from the following sources: employee earnings, self-employment, farming, secondary jobs, casual employment, state training or work schemes, social welfare transfers, child benefit, the renting of land or property, interest or dividends, retirement pensions, pensions from abroad, annuities, covenants or trusts, sick pay, maintenance from outside the household and educational grants. Not all income, however, is included in the data collected. For example, it does not cover imputed rents, capital gains, fringe benefits or the value of publicly provided goods and services. This last omission is particularly relevant when making cross-country comparisons, in which, for example, comparisons in income distribution between the USA and the UK fail to take into account the availability of free education and health in the latter. The reliability of responses, especially in relation to self-employment and income from property, also raises difficulties, as does the very low response rate of people at the top of the income range.

Other measurement issues that arise include the definition of income used; the time period chosen; the recipient unit; and the use of equivalence scales. Three types of income are separated for analysis: direct or market income; gross income, which includes both market income and social welfare transfers; and disposable income, i.e. after income tax and social insurance contributions are deducted. The appropriate definition of income must be based on what you want to evaluate, and disposable income is the one most used in welfare analysis. The time period chosen is also of importance: while income is a flow on a weekly, monthly or annual basis, people cannot freely borrow on the basis of future or expected income. If income did not fluctuate or if you could borrow and lend freely on the basis of expected income it would not matter which time period was chosen for comparison purposes. As financial markets do not perfectly accommodate the smoothing of incomes, weekly income is usually used for poverty analysis, annual income for income distribution and lifetime income for differences in age groups.

The recipient unit refers to whose income is being measured, which raises questions as to how it should be defined, whether on an individual or household basis, and how different size units should be compared. Using individual income would greatly distort the actual welfare of women working in the home and of children who have no independent income. On the other hand, any household-based comparison between, say, a single person and a couple with children needs to take account of the differences. What is at issue is not income per se but what it means in terms of welfare or living standards, i.e. how far an income has to be stretched within a family or household unit. While we can easily calculate income on a per capita basis this does not take into account different needs within households or economies of scale, which implies the costs for two people living together is expected to be less than two living separately, e.g. heating a room or bulk buying. So instead of dividing the total income by each individual, equivalence scales are used for each adult dependent and child. The scales range considerably, and as such, depending on which scale is used, will lead to differences in the results obtained. What is referred to as the OECD scale gives the first adult a value of 1, each additional adult a value of 0.7 and each child a value of 0.5.

The difference in needs between various household members is thus identified through differences in the value of the equivalence scales used for adults and children. However, this principle is not extended to other types of need, for example, health or disability issues, childcare needs or caring for an elderly person at home. This is a key issue from an equality perspective. A final point to consider in relation to the recipient unit is the implicit assumption that income, and other resources, are shared equally within it. This is an area to which increasing attention is being paid and on which the evidence to date suggests that the processes of intra-household resource allocation should be studied rather than assumed a priori. For example, a number of studies suggest that resources are not shared equally and that there may be hidden poverty within non-poor households or that some members of poor households may be worse off than others. As a result the risk of poverty for certain household members, in particular women and children, may be underestimated. If living standards within households are not equivalent this could have implications for income-support policies aimed at eliminating poverty.

Measures of Income Distribution

Having collected the data at household level, the most common way of summarising and presenting the data is to rank households from lowest income level to highest. Decile shares identify what share of total income is held by each decile so that the percentage share of total income held by the bottom ten per cent can be compared with other income deciles. This can be illustrated graphically by what is called the Lorenz curve, which shows the share of total income going to the bottom ten per cent, 20 per cent, etc. (Figure 7.1). The position of the Lorenz curve relative to the diagonal gives an indication of the extent of inequality in a given distribution of income. The Lorenz curve is constructed by plotting the percentages of national income received by different percentages of the population when the latter are ranked by income level. That is, it plots the percentage of income received by the bottom 20 per cent, the percentage received by the bottom 40 per cent, and the bottom 60 per cent and so on. If there is full equality such that the bottom 60 per cent receive 60 per cent of total national income or the top 20 per cent receive 20 per cent, the Lorenz curve would lie along the diagonal of the diagram. As such, the further the curve is from the diagonal, the further is the distribution from full equality and therefore the greater the inequality.

Figure 7.1

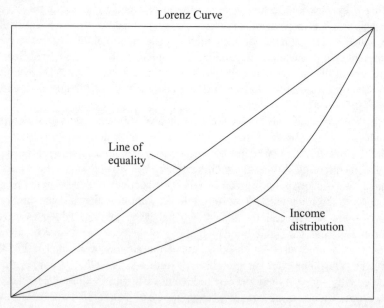

A summary measure of the amount of inequality implicit in a Lorenz curve can be obtained by use of the Gini coefficient. This is calculated by dividing the area between the Lorenz curve and the diagonal by the area of the triangle formed by the diagonal and the axes. As the Lorenz curve moves further from the diagonal, the Gini coefficient approaches a value of one, indicating a greater degree of inequality. As the Lorenz curve moves closer to the diagonal the Gini coefficient approaches a value of zero, indicating greater equality. Using the Gini index, which is the Gini coefficient expressed in percentage terms (i.e. Gini coefficient multiplied by 100), a country with a perfectly even distribution of income is assigned a value of zero and a country where one individual possesses all income is assigned a value of 100. According to the UNDP, the world's three most egalitarian countries, with scores under 25, are Japan, Denmark and Hungary. The most unequal, with scores over 60, are Brazil, Nicaragua, Botswana and Sierra Leone.

Another summary measure often used is the decile (semi-decile or quintile) ratio, which compares the proportion of income attributable to the top ten or 20 per cent of the income distribution to the corresponding proportion for the lowest ten or 20 per cent. In egalitarian Japan, the poorest 20 per cent receive 11 per cent of total income while the richest quintile receives 36 per cent. In Brazil and Botswana, the poorest 20 per cent receive just over two per cent of total income and the richest 20 per cent account for over 70 per cent of income.[10]

Caution should be exercised in interpreting summary measures of this kind as they conceal distributional judgements. For example, the welfare of different groups is not apparent from the Gini coefficient. Lorenz curves allow income distributions to be unambiguously ranked provided they do not intersect. This is seldom the case in practice. If they do cross, the ranking will depend on which part of the income distribution is considered. It may be the case that if the focus is on the very poor, country X might rank higher than country Y, whereas if the focus is on the middle-income bracket it may be the other way around for the same two countries.

Distribution of Income in Ireland

Ireland has a high degree of income inequality. The distribution of disposable income has not changed greatly since the 1970s with the top ten per cent of the income distribution having approximately 25 per cent of total income and the bottom ten per cent having approximately two per cent of total income. However, there have been changes in the share of total income accruing to different decile groups. Between 1973 and 1994 there was an increase in the proportion of total income going to the bottom income decile (from 1.7 per cent to 2.1 per cent (based on Household Budget Survey (HBS) data produced by the Central Statistics Office (CSO)) but since 1994 there has been a decrease in the proportion of income going to the bottom decile. These reversing trends were reflected in the Gini coefficient, which showed a decrease in inequality between 1973 and 1987 and an increase thereafter. Using the HBS for 1994/95 and 1999/2000 the share of the bottom 20 per cent declined by half a percentage point and the share of the top ten per cent rose by 1.5 percentage points. However, differences in data sources, and income definitions and measurement, can impact greatly on both the levels of, and trends in, income inequality. The HBS data, for example, do not account for differences in household size. When equivalence scales are applied, the bottom decile still loses out but the share going to the top decile increases by 0.3 percentage points (rather than 1.5), with the middle deciles gaining the difference.

Earnings are the standard determinant of welfare in Ireland and inequality in earnings increased in the late 1990s and early 2000s, particularly in the top half of the earnings distribution, reflecting in part increasing returns from higher levels of education and increased demand for skilled labour. Between 1990 and 2000 the earnings share of the top ten per cent of the earnings distribution increased substantially from 33 per cent to 38 per cent, with most of this growth concentrated in the top one per cent. Another factor underlying the distribution of income is the interaction of the tax and social welfare system (see Chapters 4, 5 and 6). As will be seen later in relation to trends in poverty, social welfare payments increased faster than average incomes in the 1980s and early 1990s but from 1994 through 2005, while in excess of inflation, social welfare increases lagged well behind increases in average income.

Section 2 highlighted the sharp increase in income inequality between developed and developing countries but also within most industrialised countries and especially in the UK and the USA. On the basis of the Luxembourg Income Study of the 1980s, income inequality in Ireland was very high vis-à-vis other OECD countries, with only the USA having a higher Gini coefficient. The European Community Household Panel Survey undertaken in 1994 reiterated Ireland's inequality status, although it was lower than Portugal and in the same cluster of countries as the UK, Spain and Greece. The comparative picture provided by the OECD in 2000 showed Ireland having about the same level of income inequality as the UK in the mid-1990s with the level of inequality in the latter having risen dramatically since the mid-1980s.[11] Compared with non-EU countries, it showed Ireland having a higher level of inequality than Canada or Australia but still managing to be more equal than the USA. Table 7.2 shows the Gini coefficient, as reported by Eurostat, for a number of EU member states in 2006.

As usual, inequality is below the EU average in the Scandinavian countries but also, interestingly, in the Czech Republic and Slovenia. Ireland is above the average inequality for the EU as a whole, along with the UK and Spain but is somewhat lower than Portugal, which has the highest inequality in the EU-25. In summary, one can conclude that Ireland, along with a good number of other EU and OECD countries, has had, and continues to have, a high level of income inequality.

Measurement of Wealth
Wealth is a measure of 'net worth', i.e. the sum of physical, financial and human capital assets. The distribution of wealth is much more unequal than the distribution of income. Like income, its measurement is based on data drawn from

household surveys of assets, from taxation records (wealth and estate tax records) and from investment data. The limitations of the data in relation to income also apply to wealth, but the issues of coverage and accuracy are even more pronounced. In particular, the collection of data on wealth suffers from severe under-representation and under-reporting.

Table 7.2

Income Inequality for Selected EU Countries, 2006

Country	Gini coefficient
Czech Republic	0.25
Denmark	0.24
Ireland	*0.32*
Portugal	0.38
Sweden	0.24
Spain	0.31
Slovenia	0.22
UK	0.32
EU-25 Average	0.30

Source: Eurostat, *Population and Social Conditions* (available at http://epp.eurostat.ec.europa.eu/2008)

Household surveys are the main source of information on the distribution of wealth in the USA, Canada, Japan and other countries, but they are not unproblematic. Wealth is more concentrated than income and because of the low participation of respondents at the top end of the wealth distribution, as well as the under-reporting by those that do respond, it is unlikely that the survey will provide a very accurate measure of the distribution of wealth. Some corrections can be made to improve the data, such as over-sampling the very rich or using additional information that is external to the survey. Estate-tax records provide another source of data on wealth. In Ireland this refers to capital acquisitions tax (CAT). Measures of wealth using estate-tax records are derived based on the size of the estates of people who die each year, adjusted to reflect the proportion of adults of each age and gender in the total adult population (referred to as the estate-multiplier method). While these are a good source of information on the very wealthy they are also problematic because small estates are omitted (there is a wealth threshold for taxation purposes); some joint properties (e.g. houses) are omitted; and because there are tax incentives to hide or reduce wealth (e.g. to transfer wealth prior to death). Nevertheless the picture these data provide is useful in illustrating that the form in which people hold their assets changes with the level of wealth. For example, studies in the UK show that the proportion of gross wealth held as interest-bearing assets and household goods falls as wealth grows. Residential property, as well as financial assets, form a significant part of middle-wealth owners while for the very wealthy, shares and assets like land are more important. The importance of housing as a component of wealth for middle-wealth groups is particularly relevant in Ireland in the context of the unprecedented economic growth of the 1990s and early 2000s and the subsequent property boom.

Distribution of Wealth in Ireland

To date, only two studies have been undertaken on wealth inequality in Ireland.[12] A study, by Lyons in 1972, based on 1966 estate-tax records, showed that 66 per cent of the population had a net wealth of zero. The top five per cent of adults held 60 per cent of wealth and the top one per cent of adults held 33 per cent of wealth. The second study, undertaken by the ESRI, was based on data from a 1987 household survey.[13] The data are not comparable as the results of the former are based on individual adults while the latter refers to wealth concentration among households. The latter found that 90 per cent of the population had some form of wealth; about ten per cent held 50 per cent of wealth; and the top one per cent held 20 per cent of wealth.

There are no data available on the current distribution of wealth in Ireland. Against the background of sustained economic growth since the mid-1990s, there have been a number of significant developments in asset holdings and values. The most obvious example is the rise in property values, but other factors include the increase in share ownership, the increase in profits and in employee profit-share schemes and the transfer of public sector housing into tenant purchase agreements. What this translates to in terms of the overall distribution of wealth is difficult to estimate. On the one hand, the massive rise in the value of property is likely to have contributed to a more equal distribution of total wealth with the major caveat that there is now a much wider wealth gap between those with and those without property. Against this trend towards greater wealth equality is the enormous increase in capital income, which one suspects will ensure a greater concentration of wealth at the top of the wealth distribution.

5 POVERTY

Definition

Poverty tends to be a controversial topic. There is debate about its definition, its measurement, its extent and its relationship with other forms of disadvantage or discrimination. There is debate about the appropriateness of absolute poverty or relative conceptions of poverty; which poverty measurement is best or gives the most complete picture; the relationship between poverty and inequality and the relationship between poverty and income, material deprivation, class and education; issues of social exclusion and multiple disadvantage; and finally there is much controversy with respect to the causes and/or consequences of poverty.

At a very broad level two main debates dominate – the issue of poverty versus inequality; and absolute poverty versus relative poverty. Poverty and inequality, while related, are quite distinct concepts. The concepts are usually separated by the notion that poverty refers to living standards whereas inequality relates to the distribution of resources between individuals. The theoretical distinction between the two is clear in that even if there is no poverty, in the sense that no one would be so far below the general standard of living so as to be excluded from participation in the ordinary life of that society, there could still be substantial inequality in the distribution of income between the wealthy and the rest of society. However, there is a view that sees poverty as being effectively synonymous with inequality, especially when using the relative poverty line approach, and this approach would lead to the identification of bottom groups in the income distribution, for example the bottom 20 per cent, as being the 'poor'. In this case the proportion of the population in poverty cannot rise or fall, whereas with the relative poverty line set at, say 50 per cent of mean income, relative poverty can rise, fall or be totally eradicated. In Ireland the emphasis over the last two decades has been on the reduction of poverty rather than on explicitly addressing inequality, and while the rationale for this has been based, to some extent, on pragmatism in terms of inducing a more concrete policy response it is also made on the basis that at an analytical level, poverty is a phenomenon distinct from inequality, that it is not confined to poor countries, and that the extent and especially the experience of it matters in and of itself.

Another debate at the conceptual level is what is referred to as the absolute versus relative one, but the relative approach is, and always has been, the one adopted in practice. The basic question is whether poverty is seen as absolute deprivation or as socially defined (relative) deprivation.[14] Regarding poverty as an absolute concept stems from the time when it was natural to think in subsistence terms, but today in the developed world people, for the most part, live above the subsistence level and the concept of deprivation is more relevantly applied to emotional and cultural standards, as well as physical ones. The core of the debate between absolute and relative definitions is whether standards are to be fixed over time or change with the standard of living. Townsend's definition, when income is so far below average that people are in effect excluded from the normal living patterns of the society to which they belong, makes the relative concept explicit and is probably the most widely adopted definition of poverty. It was the model used for the National Anti-Poverty Strategy's (NAPS) definition of poverty launched in 1997 following the UN Social Summit in Copenhagen, and it underpins most research on poverty in EU countries. Sen dissents somewhat, arguing 'that ultimately poverty must be seen to be primarily an absolute notion' while Piachaud, in a sense, concedes to both views in his definition, which allows that at subsistence level there is some absolute minimum necessary for survival, but beyond this any poverty standard must be relative, i.e. it must reflect prevailing social standards.[15]

Despite the terminology used, the relative view represents actual practice. Rowntree's study of poverty in York in 1899 is classified under the absolute-standard approach based on his compilation of food items deemed necessary for survival. And yet tea, with little or no nutritional value, is included because eating habits are profoundly influenced by social conventions. Similarly, other items included such as newspapers and presents are difficult to justify on an absolute subsistence definition. Sen argues it is in the notion of shame that the core concept of poverty is to be found, which echoes back to Adam Smith's view on linen shirts being a necessity of life in England, so much so that 'the poorest creditable person would be ashamed to appear in public without them'.

Measurement of Poverty

A number of standard quantitative approaches to measuring poverty in industrialised countries can be identified. While all of them employ income to distinguish the poor they use a variety of methods to establish the appropriate income cut-off point, ranging from budget standards (classified under absolute measures but as indicated above only 'relatively absolute'); to income supports offered by the social welfare system (also referred to as official poverty lines); to subjective views on minimum income needs (consensual poverty lines); to mean or median income itself. A less explicitly income-oriented approach is to focus directly on deprivation based on the use of non-monetary deprivation indicators which measure exclusion from normal living patterns. In this chapter we focus on the two approaches, namely relative-income lines and non-monetary deprivation indicators, which underlie most of the research on poverty in Ireland since 1987 and which have also been applied in numerous EU countries.

Relative poverty lines are framed in terms of relative income. Lines are generally set at a particular percentage of mean or median income, for example 60 per cent, and then adjusted for household size and composition using equivalence scales. The choice of cut-off is arbitrary and there is no firm basis for the selection of any particular ratio to serve as the poverty line. For this reason research on poverty undertaken by the ESRI has tended to use more than one cut-off point (at 40, 50, 60 per cent of mean income, or more recently 70 per cent of median income) in order to examine the sensitivity of the results to the choice of cut-off. The rationale behind relative poverty lines is that those falling more than a certain distance below 'normal' income levels in society are unlikely to be able to participate fully in the life of that society. The main advantage of this approach is the ease with which results can be understood and, further, it can be easily applied in cross-country comparisons. The main disadvantage of adopting a purely relative approach is the anomaly highlighted by Sen that any improvement in the living standards of low-income groups which are shared by the rest of the population are discounted, while a general decline in prosperity will not show up as an increase in poverty if the relative picture has not changed. We return to this point later when reviewing trends in Ireland over recent years.

Non-monetary deprivation indicators focus directly on exclusivity from normal living patterns. Townsend pioneered this approach in the late 1970s in his research on Britain. It measures exclusion directly by examining what you do without, by choice, because it is not needed or because it cannot be afforded. Examples of the items in Townsend's deprivation list include certain items of clothing, visits to the doctor, heating, shoes and a television. Table 7.3 shows the set of 11 basic non-monetary indicators used in the CSO's annual Survey on Income and Living Conditions (EU-SILC). These have been revised somewhat from the eight basic deprivation indicators used in the ESRI's Living in Ireland Surveys up until 2003. Two very basic ones (going without a meal, and going into debt for ordinary living expenses) have been dropped and new ones added, such as entertaining and maintaining social relations, in order to reflect a broader conception of deprivation.[16] This revised index underlies the so called 'consistent poverty' measure, discussed below, which is adopted in the National Plan for Social Inclusion 2007–2016. It will become the basis for the calculation of consistent poverty in the EU-SILC from 2007 onwards. Using this measure 6.5 per cent of the population were in consistent poverty in 2006.

Table 7.3

EU-SILC Consistent Poverty Deprivation Indicators

New, not second-hand, clothes
A meal with meat, fish or chicken every second day
A warm waterproof overcoat
Two pairs of strong shoes
A roast or its equivalent once a week
Had to go without heating during last year through lack of money*
Keep the home adequately warm
Presents for friends or family once a year
Replace any worn-out furniture
Have friends or family for a drink or a meal once a month
Have a morning, afternoon or evening out in the last fortnight, for entertainment

Source: CSO, *Measuring Ireland's Progress*, Stationery Office, Dublin 2006.
Note: The asterisk indicates it is presence rather than absence that constitutes deprivation.

The difference between this approach and consensual poverty lines is that this reflects, at least to some extent, social consensus on necessities or actual patterns of possession. The selection of deprivation indicators and the role of choice and differences in tastes is one of the major criticisms of this approach. It has also been argued that the aggregation of deprivation indicators into a single index assumes that poverty is one-dimensional, which may not be an accurate reflection of reality. If poverty is multidimensional, for example, if households can be 'food poor' but not 'house poor', then it is difficult to bring these different facets together to serve as a basis for a cut-off between poor and non-poor. Notwith-standing these criticisms, which have partly been met by more sophisticated approaches to measuring deprivation, explicit analysis of living standards and deprivation gives an important insight into what it means to be poor and the nature of poverty. Combining indicators of deprivation with income lines can produce a very different perspective on trends in poverty than using income poverty lines alone, as we shall see below.

Trends in Poverty

Table 7.4 shows the percentage of households below relative income poverty lines between 1994 and 2006. Up to 2001 the data are based on the Living in Ireland (LII) surveys while from 2003 the data are based on the EU-SILC. Relative-income poverty is measured by calculating the median rather than mean income and setting the line at 60 per cent of the median. Median income is the income level at which half the distribution is to be found above and half below this level of income. People whose incomes fall below this line are said to be at risk of poverty; in 2006 this was an income of below €202.49 a week for an adult. Over the period 1994 to 2001 there was a considerable increase (from 16 to 21 per cent) in the proportion of households below the 60 per cent income line. The main reason for this was that social welfare increases lagged behind the very rapid increases in incomes. In the four years since the EU-SILC began, the risk of poverty rate has been declining. In 2003, the rate was 19.7 per cent; it fell to 18.5 per cent in 2005; and the most recent figure shows a rate of 17.0 per cent in 2006.[17]

Table 7.4

Percentage of Households Below Median Relative Income Poverty Lines

LII Survey	1994	1997	2001
60 per cent	16	18	22

EU-SILC	2003	2005	2006
60 per cent median	20	19	17

Sources: C. Whelan, R. Layte, B. Maître, B. Gannon, B. Nolan, D. Watson and J. Williams, *Monitoring Poverty Trends in Ireland,* Policy Research Series 51, ESRI, Dublin 2003; CSO, *Measuring Ireland's Progress*, Stationery Office, Dublin 2007.

As well as trends in overall poverty, the 1987 Household Budget Survey, the Living in Ireland Surveys 1994–2001, and the subsequent EU-SILC surveys, produce findings on the characteristics of households in poverty, and show how some social groups, including lone-parent families, the unemployed, people with disabilities or long-term illnesses, and immigrants have higher poverty rates than the rest of the population. For example, in 1994, households headed by an unemployed person made up a substantial proportion of the poor or were at high risk of being in poverty, while elderly or retired heads of households represented a small proportion of the poor and had lower than average risk of being poor. By 2000, however, households headed by a retired person were at significantly higher risk; 34 per cent compared to eight per cent in 1994. More recently, there has been a substantial decrease in the 'at risk of poverty' rate for the elderly, with the rate falling from 27 per cent in 2004 to 14 per cent in 2006. One group of particular concern is children, whose position over the period has improved. Notwithstanding this improvement, 20 per cent of children were at risk of poverty in 2006. Parental unemployment is the single biggest factor affecting child poverty, with non-working households accounting for a significant proportion of children in poverty. The level of social welfare payments, especially child income support, is another key factor in determining the proportion of children at risk of poverty.

What is more revealing perhaps than the overall head count is what is called the poverty gap, which refers to how far below the poverty income line households fall. It is a depth of poverty measure and to some extent reflects policy responses to the interaction of factors which underlie poverty such as unemployment and social welfare levels. If we compare poverty measures between different time periods within the 20 years between 1987 and 2007 we get quite different stories. The 1987 poverty figures showed unemployment to be the single most important cause of poverty. Between 1987 and 1994 priority was given to raising the lowest social welfare rates. Means-tested unemployment assistance increased more rapidly than incomes, while support rates for other groups (for example the elderly) rose less rapidly, though they were still ahead of inflation. Not surprisingly, between 1987 and 1994, the poverty gap, using per capita income gap and weighted-gap measures, decreased across all three relative income lines even though the numbers below the lines were rising. In contrast, between 1994 and 1997 the poverty gap widened. Even though unemployment was falling, other groups dependent on social income support did not fare so well in terms of relative-income poverty lines. Between 1994 and 1997 inflation increased by around six per cent; social welfare rates by 12 per cent; but average income rose by 20 per cent. This gap has continued to widen for those who remained reliant on social welfare as these transfers, while still in excess of consumer prices, did not keep pace with income from work or capital (e.g. property). On the other hand, however, more people became employed over the period and even those reliant on social welfare transfers were more likely than before to be in households where other adults were employed.[18]

One of the difficulties of focusing exclusively on relative income poverty lines, especially in a period of rapid growth in average incomes such as that which has characterised the Irish economy for the past decade, is that it can give a misleading picture since the overall improvement in living standards is discounted. As Table 7.4 indicates, more people were below the 60 per cent threshold in 2006 than in 1994, despite unprecedented growth. The non-monetary deprivation approach to measuring poverty can provide a particularly useful complement to relative income lines. The approach, developed at the ESRI, of combining income lines and deprivation indicators, gives a measure of what is termed 'consistently poor' and the trend in these figures shows a steady decline. Using households which are deprived of one or more items on the index, and are below the 60 per cent of mean income threshold, the consistent poverty measure shows a decline from 15.1 per cent in1994 to 8.0 per cent in 1998 and to 5.2 per cent in 2001. While comparison between the LII data and EU-SILC is not possible as different procedures were employed in gathering the data, the results from the EU-SILC reveal a similar picture. In 2004, the EU-SILC found that seven per cent of the population were consistently poor in so far as they were living in households whose net equivalised income was below 60 per cent of the median and they reported enforced absence of two or more of the items on the 11-item index (Table 7.3). Consistent poverty remained at this level in both 2005 and 2006.

6 INCOME SUPPORT AND REDISTRIBUTION

Context

The extent of poverty and inequality in income distribution in Ireland was addressed in the preceding sections. In this section, the focus is on the channels that the state employs to achieve various redistributions.

The main channels through which redistribution is brought about are taxes, cash transfers and the public provision of services. In Ireland, social welfare rather than tax is the more important means of redistributing income, but the interaction between the two is crucial. A tax which takes proportionately more from those on higher incomes is considered to be progressive, while a tax that takes proportionately more from those on lower incomes is termed regressive. In Ireland, the modestly progressive income tax system is largely counterbalanced by the regressive nature of taxes on spending (e.g. excise duties) and of various tax expenditures (e.g. tax relief on pension contributions), giving a broadly neutral overall pattern of redistribution over the tax system as a whole. Redistribution is also dependent on the funding of other public services such as housing, education and health. In Ireland, both welfare payments and non-cash benefits (e.g. medical cards that entitle the holder to free medical care) are skewed towards the poor (mainly through a means-tested system) but are funded through a broadly neutral tax system. Thus the system can be regarded as somewhat progressive overall.

Chapter 4 discusses fiscal policy and taxation and Chapters 11 and 12 examine benefits in kind in terms of health and education. The particular focus in this section is on income support through cash transfers. Social welfare is a huge area of inquiry constituting a vast literature, much of which is beyond the realm of this discussion.[19] The aim here is to outline the main apparatus of social welfare in Ireland, focusing on how the state attempts to redistribute income and how effective it is in achieving that redistribution. It is worth remembering that the welfare state has both redistributive and functional objectives. It seeks not only to enhance social welfare but also to promote a more efficient functioning of the economy in the face of market failures. The implication of this is that the welfare state cannot be judged purely in terms of the extent of redistribution achieved.

Structures and Objectives

The social welfare system is primarily based on dealing with contingencies. The broad structure of Irish social welfare comprises a system of social insurance, a system of social assistance and a system of universal payments. Social insurance payments are made to people who satisfy specific social insurance conditions as well as the necessary circumstantial conditions. Examples of payments based on contributions include jobseekers benefit (previously known as unemployment benefit), maternity benefit, illness benefit, carer's benefit and contributory state pension. The social insurance system is financed through contributions from employers, employees and the state. As well as PAYE (Pay As You Earn) employees, it also includes the self-employed since 1988, part-time employees since 1991 and new civil/public servants since 1995. Social assistance or means-tested payments are primarily designed for people who have insufficient social insurance (PRSI) contributions to qualify for the equivalent social insurance-based payments. 'Means tested' literally means that the relevant government department or agency will examine all sources of income to see whether they fall below a certain level. Universal payments are paid regardless of a person's income or social insurance record. They are only dependent on the claimant satisfying specific personal circumstances. Examples include the medical card for all persons over 70 years of age and child benefit.

Income support measures have various objectives, some of which overlap. These include:

- the prevention of destitution or absolute poverty;
- the reduction of inequality;
- an expression of social solidarity; and
- the protection of usual living standards.

Each of these objectives is pursued within the broad structure outlined above. Policies tend to target different types of individuals or groups or even geographical areas in order to attain particular redistribution outcomes. For example, some income transfers target people living in poverty, others, such as the old age pension or child benefit, target people at different life stages, while some income transfers, such as those from the EU Structural Funds, target on the basis of living in disadvantaged areas. One can distinguish a continuum of objectives, with a narrow conception of social protection primarily concerned with prevention of absolute destitution and a much broader one in terms of its objective of a more substantial redistribution of resources.

Four welfare state models are generally used to describe the member states of the EU. These include the Scandinavian or 'social democratic model', which has a strong focus on social rights, a high degree of universality and is financed through general taxation and social insurance contributions. The 'continental' or 'social capitalism model', where social rights are based on an attachment to the paid labour force and which is financed mainly through work-based social insurance schemes. The Anglo-Saxon/UK model, which is primarily needs-based and combines modest universal schemes and extensive means-tested assistance. The southern European model used to describe the more basic system of income redistribution in Portugal, Spain, Greece and Italy, where, although changing rapidly, the primary source of welfare continues to be a combination of the family, private charity and the Church rather than the state. In terms of typology Ireland is best described as a hybrid comprising various elements from each of the four.

Using indicators of service effort (benefits in kind as a proportion of GDP) and transfer effort (cash benefits as a proportion of GDP), Ireland, along with Greece, Spain and Portugal, can be characterised as having a low-service and transfer effort. Within each category a distinction can be made between expenditure which is means tested and that which is not. Here Ireland fits most comfortably with the Anglo-Saxon model in so far as it aims to provide universal minimum protection with an emphasis on means testing and flat-rate rather than earnings-related provision. Ireland and the UK are both exceptional within the EU for the high proportion of means testing. In Ireland in 2002, 24.5 per cent of all social expenditure was means-tested.

A clear exception is child benefit. A universal child benefit payment was introduced in 1944 and operates alongside relatively small payments made as child-dependent additions to recipients of social-welfare schemes. Child benefit, paid to all parents towards the cost of rearing a child, has been increased significantly in recent years. It rose from six per cent of all social welfare spending to 15 per cent over the ten years from 1993 to 2003. In addition, in 2006 an Early Childcare Supplement payment was introduced and extended to all families in Ireland with children under six years of age.

Disincentives

The key argument against income support is that the income support system, taking into account interactions with the associated PRSI and tax system, may act as a disincentive to people to take up employment or, if in employment, to work more hours and/or seek promotion. In the extreme case, it may create an 'unemployment trap'. This refers to a situation where a person is financially better off remaining unemployed than taking up work. That is, people calculate that unemployment compensation will be higher than the net take-home pay available to them if employed. This disincentive is usually measured by the Replacement Ratio (RR) of unemployment compensation to net take-home pay. In calculating unemployment compensation, not only is the benefit payment itself included but any other allowances, such as a medical card, are also considered. On the other side, the net take-home pay calculation allows for such items as the cost of getting to work. For some types of social welfare recipients this replacement ratio could be very high, i.e. they could receive 80 per cent (or sometimes even over 100 per cent) of what they would get if they were working in the paid labour market.

In evaluating the disincentive effects associated with the interaction between the tax and social welfare system, attention is often focused on the RR facing individuals in various hypothetical scenarios. For example, models that look at the disincentives facing a married couple with four children, living in social housing and in receipt of long-term unemployment assistance often find that their RR is very high. In the examination of real situations, however, only a very small proportion of those currently employed face a high RR. Studies using cross-section analyses suggest that while people with higher RRs may be more likely to be unemployed, this affects the composition of unemployment rather than total unemployment. This is not to say that there are not some people who have little financial incentive to work, but rather that there are few people who are literally caught in an unemployment trap. Further, while there are people working who would be better off in cash terms if they were unemployed, some value is placed on the non-monetary benefits that accrue from employment, such as social status, job satisfaction or social networking. It should also be noted that cross-section measures of the RR exclude dynamic considerations such as long-term employment (e.g. the possibility of future promotions and wage increases) and so understate the full benefits of employment.

Redistributive Effects

From the perspective of equality a key question is whether the social welfare system is effective in meeting its redistribution objective. All countries achieve some redistribution of income through their tax and benefit system, but the extent to which this is achieved differs considerably. Table 7.5 shows the market and disposable income inequality for a number of countries using the Gini index. Market income is the primary source of income for most people and includes wages, salaries, income from self-employment as well as cash income from other sources such as property or private pensions. Disposable income refers to the market income left after income tax and social security contributions have been deducted and after any state transfer payments have been added. All countries show that overall inequality is reduced by the interaction of the tax and benefit system such that disposable-income inequality is less than market-income inequality. The Gini index for market-income inequality ranges from 39 to 50, with Ireland at 42. After tax and income transfers the Gini index for disposable-income inequality ranges from 24 to 37, with Ireland at 32. This implies that income inequality in Ireland is reduced by 24 per cent by taking the interaction between the tax and benefit system into account. This is below that of Belgium, Germany and the Netherlands, about the same as that of Canada, Switzerland and the UK, but more than in the USA. The Netherlands is particularly interesting as it begins with the same level of market-income inequality as Ireland and yet achieves a 40 per cent reduction in inequality through its tax and transfer system.

Similarly, poverty levels are also reduced when taxes and benefits are considered. However, the anti-poverty impact of the tax and benefit system varies considerably depending on the type of programme and policies implemented. Similar to the effects on income distribution, of the countries presented in Table 7.5 the USA shows the least anti-poverty effect with the tax and benefit system reducing poverty measures by only 28 per cent compared with an average reduction of 62 per cent for the group as a whole. Ireland's system performs only slightly better, reducing market-income based poverty by 33 per cent through taxes and social welfare.

Table 7.5

Income Inequality Before and After Taxes and Benefits,
Selected OECD Countries 1999/2000

	Gini index of inequality in market income	Gini index of inequality in disposable income	Percentage reduction in income inequality (%)
Belgium	50	26	48
Canada	41	30	27
Germany	43	25	42
Ireland	*42*	*32*	*24*
Netherlands	42	25	40
Switzerland	39	30	23
UK	45	34	24
USA	45	37	18

Source: B. Nolan and T. Smeeding, 'Ireland's income distribution in comparative perspective', Review of Income and Wealth, Series 51, No. 4, December 2005.

7 CONCLUSIONS

This chapter provided a framework for thinking about equality and distribution. It showed that equality is a complex concept in that people have different conceptions of what it means and of how equality objectives are to be achieved. It also gave an overview of the various institutional and legislative developments in relation to equality over the past ten years in Ireland. While many of these developments must be seen as welcome progress it is still too early to evaluate the long-term implications of their equality objectives or to assess the effectiveness of the different initiatives undertaken.

Cleary there are different views as to whether Ireland has become a fairer society in light of its improved economic circumstances. Focusing on distributional issues, and in particular on the issues of poverty, income inequality and 'quality of life', it is quite difficult to assess Ireland's status from the equality perspectives discussed. In relation to Ireland's global obligations, the picture is fairly positive. Ireland's overseas development aid has increased significantly over the last decade. Within the EU, only Denmark, Luxembourg, the Netherlands and Sweden allocate a greater percentage of national income to aid than Ireland.

Climate change is an issue of both environmental concern and social justice. Current greenhouse gas concentrations in the atmosphere are primarily the responsibility, both historically and currently, of wealthy developed countries (with the more recent exception of China and India) and yet poorer, less developed countries are hardest hit by climate change and the proposed policy responses. According to the UNDP 2007, Ireland's emissions of carbon dioxide amount to 10.5 tonnes per capita per year, which is about the same as the UK and half that of the USA. Under the Kyoto Protocol Ireland must limit its growth in emissions to 13 per cent above the 1990 levels over the 2008–2012 period. To date the effort is not encouraging with figures from the Environmental Protection Agency showing that Ireland is currently polluting at twice the level of its Kyoto target at 24.5 per cent over 1990 levels.

At a national level, the stable environment of rapid economic growth has ensured that the majority of people in Ireland have higher standards of living and higher real incomes than a decade ago, although new pockets of inequality are being created, especially among migrant workers, asylum seekers and refugees. The fact that relative income poverty lines have not decreased illustrates the difficulties of using that measurement approach in times of a rapidly changing economic environment. In contrast, the 'consistent poverty' measure has fallen steadily since the launch of the National Anti-Poverty strategy in 1997. The non-monetary deprivation indicators used as part of this measurement approach have been updated to reflect the huge improvement in living standards and the consequent change in opinion of what is minimally adequate. On the one hand, the unemployment and 'consistent' poverty figures are testament to the general economic improvement. On the other hand, these are not necessarily translating into improved quality of life in some areas, as inadequate childcare supports and over-stretched public services, most notably in health, demonstrate. In terms of distribution, Ireland remains, as it was before the boom, one of the more unequal among the EU in terms of income inequality.

Finally, in relation to social welfare Ireland's redistributive effort is rather poor. By EU standards, Ireland uses a moderate to low proportion of national resources in providing services and a low proportion in providing cash transfers. This is despite the comparative wealth enjoyed by Ireland over the past decade when the gap between Irish national income and average EU income not only closed but was reversed. While some of the gap between wealth and social spending in Ireland compared to the EU is explained by factors such as a relatively young population, a booming economy with near full employment, which allowed real increases in social spending alongside a declining share of GNP, it is also the case that Ireland's level of social protection is poorer than that enjoyed by its fellow EU citizens.

Endnotes

[1] J. Sachs, *The End of Poverty: How Can We Make it Happen in Our Lifetime*, Penguin, London 2005. See also A. Glyn and D. Miliband, *Paying for Inequality – The Economic Cost of Social Injustice*, Rivers Oram Press, London 1994; and R. Wilkinson, *Unhealthy Societies: The Afflictions of Inequalities*, Routledge, London 1996.

199

[2] The statistics presented in this section are taken from UNDP, *UN Human Development Report 2007/2008*, Palgrave Macmillan, New York 2007, and from the OECD website www.oecd.org.

[3] A. Greig, D. Hulme and M. Tuner, *Challenging Global Inequality*, Palgrave Macmillan, New York 2007.

[4] Angel Gurria, OECD Secretary General, 'New Global Economic Challenges', lecture at London School of Economics, March 2007.

[5] This section draws on the framework of equality developed in J. Baker, K. Lynch, S. Cantillon and J. Walsh, *Equality: From Theory to Action*, Palgrave Macmillan, New York 2004.

[6] P. Bourdieu, 'The forms of capital', in J. Richardson (ed.), *Handbook of Theory and Research for the Sociology of Education*, Greenwood Press, Westport CT 1986.

[7] CSO, *Measuring Ireland's Progress*, Stationery Office, Dublin 2007. The calculation of the pay gap is under revision at EU level.

[8] S. O'Rian and P. O'Connell, 'The role of the state in growth and welfare' in B. Nolan, P. O'Connell and C.T. Whelan (eds), *Bust to Boom: the Irish Experience of Growth and Inequality*, Institute of Public Administration, Dublin 2000.

[9] See for example, N. Folbre, *The Economics of the Family*, Edward Elgar, New York 1996.

[10] UNDP, *Human Development Report 2005*, UNDP, New York 2005.

[11] M. Foster, *Trends and Driving Factors in Income Distribution in the OECD Area: Labour Market and Social Policy*, Occasional Papers no 42, OECD, Paris 2000.

[12] A new Luxembourg Wealth Study is under way, which creates for the first time a harmonised cross-national database on household assets and liabilities. Ireland was not one of the eight countries included in the initial phase.

[13] P. Lyons, 'The distribution of personal wealth in Ireland' in J. Bristow and A. Tait (eds), *Ireland: Some Problems of a Developing Economy*, Gill and Macmillan, Dublin 1972; and B. Nolan, *The Wealth of Irish Households*, Combat Poverty Agency, Dublin 1991.

[14] While a discussion of this debate features in all the poverty literature, one of the best sources for a clear overview of both the meaning of, and the various approaches to measuring, poverty remains Chapters 1 and 2 of T. Callan, B. Nolan, B. Whelan, D. Hannan, and S. Creighton, *Poverty Income and Welfare in Ireland*, GRS Paper No. 146, Economic and Social Research Institute, Dublin 1989.

[15] References include A. Sen, 'Poor, relatively speaking', *Oxford Economic Papers*, Vol. 35, No. 2, 1983; D. Piachaud, 'Problems in the definition and measurement of poverty', *Journal of Social Policy*, Vol. 16, No. 2, 1987; P. Townsend, *Poverty in the United Kingdom*, Penguin, Harmondsworth 1979.

[16] B. Maître, B. Nolan and C. Whelan, *Reconfiguring the Measurement of Deprivation and Consistent Poverty in Ireland,* Economic and Social Research Institute, Dublin 2006.

[17] Central Statistics Office, *EU Survey on Income and Living Conditions EU-SILC 2006*, Stationery Office, Dublin 2007.

[18] T. Fahey, H. Russell and C. Whelan, *Best of Times – The Social Impact of the Celtic Tiger*, Institute for Public Administration, Dublin 2007.

[19] See N. Barr, *Economics of the Welfare State* (4th edn), Oxford University Press, Oxford 2004; and National Economic and Social Council, *Developmental Welfare State,* Report No. 113, National Economic and Social Council, Dublin 2005.

POLICY ISSUES IN THE MARKET SECTOR

CHAPTER 8

Manufacturing and Physical Infrastructure

Carol Newman and John O'Hagan

1 INTRODUCTION

Throughout history, economic development has involved a gradual process of structural change whereby a dependence on the agricultural sector in the early stages of development is replaced by a process of industrialisation creating a strong and vibrant manufacturing sector. In recent years, most developed economies have experienced a decline in the share of output and employment attributable to the manufacturing sector and a corresponding increase in the role and importance of services. Ireland is no exception, with the contribution of manufacturing to output declining from 34 per cent in the late 1990s to 27 per cent in recent years. After adjustment is made for outflows of profits from foreign-owned firms, the contribution of the sector could be as low as 13 per cent.[1] Rising costs have led to many firms, including Irish-owned firms, seeking alternative production locations. This has happened to such an extent that recently Ireland has become a net investor abroad. As a result emphasis has shifted away from traditional manufacturing sectors towards high value-added activities such as high-skilled manufacturing and internationally traded services. This structural change will have consequences for Irish economic growth given the historical importance of the manufacturing sector in terms of its contribution to employment, internationally traded activities and aggregate productivity growth. Of particular importance moving forward is improving Ireland's competitive position. Of key concern in this regard is the physical infrastructural deficit that Ireland faces, which represents one of the most significant challenges facing the manufacturing sector and the Irish government over the coming years.

As the physical infrastructure impacts not just on manufacturing but on all aspects of the economy, in terms both of production and consumption, there will be a lengthy discussion later in the chapter on physical infrastructure in general. As such, the chapter is essentially in two parts, the first relating to manufacturing and the second to physical infrastructure. The two of course are closely related, as one of the main concerns in relation to the manufacturing sector relates to deficiencies in the physical infrastructure; such deficiencies, though, impact on all enterprises and indeed all consumers. The discussion is therefore somewhat wider than would be warranted in a chapter solely on manufacturing.

Section 2 begins by discussing the rationale for government supports for the manufacturing sector and discusses the role that direct interventions in the form of fiscal incentives and grants have played in Irish industrial policy over the last few decades. Some discussion of the role of regional policy initiatives and the future policy agenda for Irish government is also provided. Section 3 looks at the nature and importance of the sector by analysing trends in output, employment, exports and productivity and concludes with a case study illustrating the process of structural change that has occurred over the last number of years. A discussion of the emerging importance of internationally traded services is also provided. In Section 4, the role of foreign direct investment (FDI) in the manufacturing sector is explored with emphasis placed on the importance of productivity spillovers for economic growth. The increasing levels of outward direct investment (ODI) are also given some attention. The key policy challenges facing the Irish government in relation to the future of the manufacturing sector are also briefly discussed.

One of the most pressing of these challenges relates to Ireland's infrastructural deficit. Section 5 highlights the importance of physical infrastructure to economic activity, indicating that it is both an input to production and part of final consumption. The role of the state is discussed and the contribution of public-private partnerships (PPPs) examined. Some key political economy issues associated with all large infrastructural projects are also considered. Section 6 outlines some key facts in relation to infrastructure in Ireland and highlights the many challenges to be faced, especially in the light of international comparisons and competition. The National Development Plan 2007–2013 underpins all programmes to remove the infrastructural deficit and the *Annual Competitiveness Reports* of the National Competitiveness Council will be there to remind us of how well the country has done in the past, and will do in years to come, in this regard. Section 7 concludes the chapter.

2 ROLE AND EVOLUTION OF INDUSTRIAL POLICY IN IRELAND

Rationale for Government Intervention

Industrial policy covers all government interventions that affect the activities of firms operating in the industrial sector. As such, the types of policies covered by industrial policy are wide reaching, ranging from policies that affect the ability of firms to trade and compete on world markets to the direct provision of financial assistance to firms in the form of grants or tax incentives. The primary aim of industrial policy is to promote economic growth through creating jobs and facilitating productivity improvements. Regional industrial policy, as shall be discussed later, also plays a role in fulfilling equity objectives through redistributing resources to disadvantaged areas. In particular, promoting industrial activity in rural locations affected by the decline in the importance of the agricultural sector has been a key feature of Irish and EU industrial policy objectives.

Aside from equity considerations, the rationale for state intervention in the manufacturing sector is justifiable where market failure occurs. Thus, the role for government in the provision of infrastructure, the education and training of the labour force and the promotion of research and development (R&D) activities, all of which improve competitiveness and thus the productivity of firms and their ability to compete, is clear and economically justifiable. Infrastructural investments can be justified on public good grounds and this is covered in detail in Section 5. R&D expenditures confer positive external effects in the form of productivity spillovers; as such the social return exceeds the private return, making private investment alone sub-optimal, thus justifying public R&D investments. Investment in education and training are covered by a number of justifications including public good and equity arguments but also information and credit market failures (see Chapter 12).

Direct financial supports to specific firms and industries are more difficult to justify on economic grounds. For example, providing supports to sectors that are in decline as a result of an inability to compete on world markets is not justifiable as no market failure has occurred. In contrast, government intervention to support a particular activity that is not taking place due to information failures is economically justifiable, for example the promotion of environmental awareness. Moreover, the productivity spillovers associated with high-technology activities forms the key rationale for financial supports aimed at promoting R&D investments by the private sector and in attracting technology-intensive multinational corporations (MNCs).

In fulfilling economic growth objectives, industrial policy increasingly focuses on creating favourable economic conditions so that firms can efficiently operate and effectively compete. Both the theoretical and empirical economics literatures posit that a key determinant of growth is the extent of openness of economies in terms of both trade and capital markets. The past two decades have seen an increasingly integrated world economy primarily through the expansion of the World Trade Organisation, both in terms of scope and membership. The role of industrial policy has thus moved away from providing direct financial assistance towards: removing constraints to competition; facilitating productivity improvements through creating a low-cost environment, good physical infrastructure and encouraging R&D investments and productivity spillovers; and promoting trade and foreign investment.

Key Features of Industrial Policy in Ireland
Ireland's approach to industrial policy has involved a combination of direct interventions in the form of capital grants and tax incentives for industry, in

particular for the manufacturing sector, and policies aimed at creating the right conditions for the industrial sector to evolve, including labour market policies, policies aimed at encouraging exports and inward investment, and regional development policies. In fact, the most often cited contributing factor to Ireland's growth performance over the last two decades was the change in policy emphasis, dating back to the 1960s, toward an outward-looking focus, particularly in the manufacturing sector (see Chapters 1 and 6). The key development that changed the nature of industrial policy in Ireland was Ireland's entry into the European Union in 1973 and subsequent commitment to free trade within the EU internal market. Not only did this add to the attractiveness of Ireland as a location for foreign investors, it also expanded the size of the market for domestic firms. Ireland also benefited from the macroeconomic policy discipline imposed by signing up to the Maastricht Treaty in 1992 and by structural and cohesion funds which were invested in the public infrastructure system and rural development initiatives.

These measures were important in improving Ireland's competitiveness and making it an attractive place to do business. The evolution of industrial policy in Ireland is discussed in detail in Chapter 1 and policy issues relating to labour markets, human-capital investments and regulation, all of which fall under the umbrella of industrial policy, are covered elsewhere in the book (see Chapters 5, 9 and 12). Here we focus on two direct policy intervention tools which, despite the lack of a clear economic rationale for their use, have proved instrumental to the success of the manufacturing sector. They are fiscal incentives in the form of corporation profits tax and direct capital grants to firms. We also briefly look at the regional dimension of industrial policy in Ireland and in particular the role of the EU in this regard.

Corporation Taxes

The importance of corporation taxes in attracting FDI is well documented in the literature and is one of the key factors contributing to Ireland's attractiveness as a place to invest.[2] In the early stages of EU membership, in an effort to promote inward foreign investment and indigenous exports, full corporate tax relief on profits generated through export sales was introduced by the Irish government. Coupled with the other favourable conditions for investment, including free access to the large EU market, an English-speaking, relatively low-cost labour supply and strong cultural connections with the USA, Ireland became one of the most FDI-intensive countries in Europe. A strategy of low rates of profit taxes has since been an important feature of Irish industrial policy. However, pressure from the EU Commission to harmonise taxes across all EU countries since the late 1970s has continually threatened to eliminate Ireland's competitive advantage in this regard. In response to changes in EU legislation, in 1978 Export Profit Tax Relief was phased out and replaced by a ten per cent rate for all manufacturing and some internationally traded services. Subsequent pressures to harmonise taxes across sectors led to Ireland introducing a 12.5 per cent rate in

2003 for all sectors. This rate, however, still remains substantially below the average for Western Europe.

Capital Grants

Capital grants have played an important role in the support and evolution of the manufacturing sector in Ireland.[3] Since the 1950s grants have been made available to firms in the manufacturing sector on capital investments. These grants were for all companies producing manufactured goods for export. In the early stages of EU membership financial assistance was also given to domestic companies prepared to restructure following the introduction to free trade. The Industrial Development Authority (IDA), established in 1949, was responsible for the provision of grants. The Authority was later split into IDA Ireland, which became responsible for grant provision to foreign companies, and Enterprise Ireland (formerly Forbairt), which became responsible for supports to Irish companies.

Over time, the awarding of grants became more aligned with strategic priorities for the sector and grants were extended to cover a range of activities including training and R&D as well as loan guarantees, among others. In the 1970s, for example, priority was given to the development of high value-added sectors including electronics, chemicals, pharmaceuticals and healthcare through the process of attracting foreign multinational market leaders in these sectors. These policies were considered a success, particularly given the agglomeration effects observed in these sectors in subsequent years when competition for investment intensified. Ireland was a tried-and-tested location for high value-added sectors which an increasing number of firms wanted to be a part of.

A number of developments over the course of the 1980s and 1990s further changed the way in which grants were awarded. The publication of the Telesis Report in 1984 called for a change in emphasis toward developing domestic industry while the Culliton Report in 1992 called for a reduction in the use of grants and a shift in focus toward policies aimed at improving competitiveness more generally. Furthermore, from 1994, EU state aid rules determined the permissible size of grants awarded. As a result, grants are now awarded on the basis of geographical location, the skill levels of the people employed and the nature of the activities being carried out. Emphasis is placed on activities in the high-tech sector, which increasingly covers service-type activities.

Overall, the role of grant supports has been important to the evolution of the industrial sector in Ireland with strong empirical evidence to support their association with employment generation. However, since 2006, changes to EU limits have further restricted the extent to which state aid can be provided. Consequentially, the government must look to other means of maintaining Ireland's competitive position in terms of attracting FDI and promoting sectors of strategic importance.

Regional Industrial Policy

The decline in the importance of the agricultural sector will generally lead to a gradual outward migration from rural areas to urban centres. The earliest forms of industrial grants in Ireland were given to companies, both foreign and Irish owned, to establish in peripheral locations that were disadvantaged in resources as a result of this process of structural change. An important dimension of the IDA's development strategy has been focused on achieving an even redistribution of manufacturing employment throughout Ireland. Regional industrial policy objectives have also been facilitated to a large extent by EU Structural Funds created to help underdeveloped regions within the EU in a number of different ways aimed at promoting regional industrial development. There is some evidence that these policies were successful given that the levels of migration from rural to urban areas observed in most developing countries did not materialise in Ireland. However, the most successful regional locations are those located around urban centres where industrial clusters, and the benefits that go with them, such as increasing returns to scale and productivity spillovers, were already well developed.

While the regional flavour to industrial policy has diminished considerably, particularly due to the widespread acknowledgement of the benefits of agglomeration, most direct financial supports provided to firms are decided on a case-by-case basis and as such a certain regional dimension still remains in Irish industrial policy. The spatial dimension to economic development is now explicitly incorporated into the National Development Plans 2000–2006, and more recently 2007–2013, under the Rural Social and Economic Development Programme and covers a range of Irish- and EU-funded initiatives such as LEADER, CLÁR and INTERREG, among others (see Chapter 10 for more details).

Future Policy Agenda

The most recent development that will affect the nature of industrial policy in the years to come is Ireland's commitment to achieving the goals set out in the Lisbon Agenda. The Lisbon Agenda was established by the European Council in 2000 with the aim of making the European Union 'the most dynamic and competitive knowledge-based economy in the world capable of sustainable economic growth with more and better jobs and greater social cohesion, and respect for the environment by 2010'. In 2005, the mid-term review of the Agenda highlighted sustainable growth and employment as the most pressing goals of the EU. In October 2007, the National Reform Programme was produced with the aim of bringing together a broad range of policies and initiatives focused on sustaining Ireland's strong economic growth and employment position.[4] The report established 24 guidelines for achieving these aims, covering macroeconomic policy objectives, structural market reforms and employment guidelines. Their successful implementation over the coming years will help ensure the future of the traded sector as it transforms into a knowledge-driven, high value-added entity with less emphasis on manufacturing and an increasing role for services.

Also of importance in the coming years is addressing the key challenges facing the business sector as set out by the Enterprise Strategy Group in their most recent (2004) report.[5] These include: increased globalisation and competition for investment from China and Central and East European countries; the global shift to services, with internationally traded services increasingly becoming the main source for foreign investment and high-skilled jobs; rising costs and the erosion of Ireland's competitiveness; the growing importance of knowledge and the need for increased investments in education and R&D; and the importance of infrastructure.

3 NATURE AND IMPORTANCE OF THE MANUFACTURING SECTOR IN IRELAND[6]

This section reviews the trends in output and employment in the manufacturing sector over the last two decades. A distinction is made between the modern and the traditional manufacturing sectors. The modern manufacturing sector covers all high-technology multinational enterprises (chemicals; computers and instrument engineering; electrical machinery and equipment; and the reproduction of recorded media) with the traditional manufacturing sector including all other sectors. In 2007, the former accounted for 70 per cent of total output of the sector, up from 62 per cent in 2000. Given the emphasis placed on promoting exports in Irish industrial policy over the last number of decades, the export performance of the Irish manufacturing sector is also reviewed.

An important indicator of manufacturing sector performance is productivity. Many studies have documented the link between productivity growth and other indicators of success including employment creation, export status and technology adoption. Ireland's productivity growth between 1990 and 2003 is estimated at approximately 3.3 per cent per annum, a strong performance relative to other countries, but it slowed between 2000 and 2005 to its lowest level since 1980. This is of particular concern given that productivity growth accelerated in the USA during this time and remained strong in the new member states of the EU with whom Ireland competes directly for foreign investment. With this in mind, this section also analyses recent trends in productivity growth, both within the Irish manufacturing sector and in an international context.

Output and Employment
Table 8.1 presents output and employment levels in the manufacturing sector in Ireland for 1995, 2000 and 2005, disaggregated by the modern and traditional sectors. Net output of the manufacturing sector in Ireland amounted to over €58 billion in 2005 and the sector employed approximately 218,000 people. Output has continually grown since 1995 although the pace of growth has slowed.

Between 1995 and 2000 output almost doubled, while between 2000 and 2005 output grew by a much more moderate ten per cent. Since 2000, the increase in output is primarily accounted for by the modern sector which experienced a very high growth rate in output in the early 2000s, but which has also slowed considerably in recent years. Over the course of the 1990s the sector grew by 27 per cent in terms of employment but since 2001 has experienced a decline in employment of over 37,000 people. This loss in employment can be partly attributed to productivity growth (evidenced by the fact that output has simultaneously increased over this period) but also to the off-shoring of manufacturing production to more competitive locations, leading to plant closures and job losses. The decline in employment in traditional sectors such as textiles is common across all OECD countries with low-cost non-OECD countries attracting this kind of investment to their shores. This trend is likely to continue into the future as more and more developing countries sign up to the World Trade Organisation, making them increasingly attractive as locations for labour-intensive manufacturing activities. In contrast, however, Ireland maintains a comparative advantage in certain high-skilled manufacturing activities which are unlikely to be off-shored, particularly if productivity improvements are sustainable. Declines in employment in these sectors have most likely been due to productivity improvements.

Table 8.1

Net Output and Employment in the Manufacturing Sector in Ireland, 1995, 2000 and 2005

	Net Output (€ billions)			Employment (thousands)		
	1995	2000	2005	1995	2000	2005
Manufacturing	19.0	52.7	58.1	221	255	218
Modern[1]	9.4	32.4	34.0	78	107	89
Traditional	9.6	20.3	24.2	142	148	129

Source: CSO, *Census of Industrial Production* (local units), Database Direct. See www.cso.ie.
Value figures are in 2000 prices adjusted using producer price indices.
[1] This excludes NACE 224 for which this disaggregation was not available.

These trends should be interpreted relative to trends in other sectors of the economy. As highlighted in the introduction to this chapter, manufacturing's share in total employment and output of the economy has declined sharply since 1999. An increasing share of economic activity is now attributable to the services sector. The favourable profile of the manufacturing sector in terms of growth prospects implies that this structural change may have implications for future economic growth. First, manufacturing is a high-productivity sector and aggregate productivity growth in Ireland over the last decades has largely been attributable to the manufacturing sector. Second, manufacturing is the main internationally traded activity and as such a weakening of the sector will have implications for exports, a key driver of economic growth. Each of these issues is now addressed.

Productivity

A key driver of economic growth is improvements in the productivity of those at work. Productivity improvements can be attained through a wide variety of means, ranging from decisions made by individual firms in relation to management practices and technology adoption, to government policies which support investment, entrepreneurship, competition and innovation. At near full employment for the last number of years, productivity growth has been a key driver of the Irish economy. Increasing levels of output and declining numbers employed in the manufacturing sector suggest that labour productivity growth in particular has been a key feature of the Irish manufacturing sector over the last decade. Between 1995 and 2005 labour productivity grew by an average of 7.4 per cent per annum for the manufacturing sector as a whole with productivity growth in the modern sector of 9.4 per cent per annum and the traditional sector of 4.3 per cent per annum.[7] In fact, the strong performance of the modern manufacturing sector was a key driver of productivity growth for the economy as a whole during this period, with the highest productivity growth rates recorded in technology-intensive manufacturing and services sectors. This trend mirrors the performance of most OECD countries, which have experienced declining levels of employment in manufacturing over the last two decades, which can in part be attributed to productivity improvements.

While this summary paints a positive picture of the recent productivity performance of the sector, of some concern is that high productivity levels in the modern manufacturing sector include the returns to R&D and improved management practices conducted by multinational companies in other countries, and so these rates may overestimate the actual productivity growth of the sector. With appropriate adjustments, productivity growth may be as little as half of the reported figures. Also of concern is the fact that Ireland's productivity lags behind EU and US levels in traditional manufacturing sectors, suggesting that productivity improvements of the 'home-grown' manufacturing sector are still lagging. With the decline in the relative importance of manufacturing compared with other sectors of the economy, it is unlikely that the same scale of aggregate productivity growth will be attainable in the future given that manufacturing makes up the productive part of the economy. Productivity gains are much more difficult in the more labour-intensive services sectors, particularly given the increasingly high cost of doing business in Ireland.

International Trade

The link between economic growth and export expansion has long been established. Exports fuel economic growth directly through the fact that they bring additional income into the economy that increases domestic demand, and indirectly through the productivity improvements that result from exposure to competitive pressures. The latter may occur through more efficient allocations of resources or the adoption of new technologies required to compete on world markets, for example. While there is much debate in the literature on the direction of causality (are exporting firms more productive a priori or do they become more efficient once exposed to world markets?), there is no doubt that firms that export are more productive than those that do not.

Table 8.2 illustrates the proportion of total gross output attributable to exports of manufacturing firms in Ireland, disaggregated by modern and traditional sectors. In 2005, 83 per cent of output in the manufacturing sector was exported. Of particular note is the fact that for the modern manufacturing sector almost all output is exported (97 per cent). The most significant difference between 2000 and 2005 is that while the proportion of firms who export has declined, the proportion of total output exported has increased. When interpreting this trend it should be borne in mind that the total number of producing units declined by 11 per cent in the manufacturing sector with a decline of over 22 per cent experienced in the modern manufacturing sector. These figures suggest that a large proportion of exporting firms exited between these years. This trend could be explained by the rising cost pressures in Ireland in the 2000s making it an unviable location for export-intensive activities.

Table 8.2

Percentage Contribution of Manufacturing to
Exports and Export Destinations for Ireland, 2000 and 2005

	Firms	Output	UK	Other EU	USA	Elsewhere
			2000			
Manufacturing	62.7	79.0	19.0	50.4	13.9	16.7
Modern[1]	75.6	93.9	15.6	49.5	17.2	17.7
Traditional	60.0	59.2	27.8	52.2	5.6	14.2
			2005			
Manufacturing	49.2	82.8	17.2	53.9	13.5	15.4
Modern[1]	72.6	96.2	13.3	54.6	15.8	16.2
Traditional	43.8	64.0	26.4	52.2	8.6	13.6

Source: CSO, *Census of Industrial Production*, Stationery Office, Dublin 2000 and 2001.
[1] This excludes NACE 224 for which this disaggregation was not available

In terms of the destination of exports, the share going to the UK has declined in all sectors since 2000. This is consistent with the general trend observed throughout the 1990s. The UK still remains an important destination for exports, however, particularly for the traditional manufacturing sector, with one quarter of all exports going to the UK market. Of particular note is the decline in the importance of the USA as a destination for exports of modern manufacturing firms, and the contrasting increase in the importance of the US market to the traditional manufacturing sector. For all sectors, other EU countries (excluding the UK) remain the most important export destinations with their share increasing over time.

The contribution of the Irish manufacturing sector to Ireland's export base is paramount to understanding its economic success story of the last two decades. However, the dependence of the manufacturing sector on export markets leaves it vulnerable to world market conditions. Any international developments that depress demand will have consequences for the Irish manufacturing sector. Furthermore, the declining role of the sector is of concern if the sectors that replace it do not generate significant export activity. Thus a key challenge of Irish policymakers is the promotion of alternative export-based sectors. A sector presenting significant development opportunities in this regard is internationally traded services.

Internationally Traded Services

For most developed economies, the last number of years has seen a significant structural shift away from agricultural and manufacturing production towards service activities. In 2005, almost 62 per cent of total gross value added (GVA) was accounted for by the services sector compared with 55 per cent in 1995 (see Chapters 5 and 9). A number of factors have contributed to the growth of the sector over the last two decades. First, the rapid pace of advancement in information and communications technology (ICT) has made it significantly easier for services companies to trade internationally. Second, the fragmentation of the production process means that an increasing number of services (for example, logistics, IT, etc.) are required to monitor and control the production process within corporations. Third, firms increasingly find it more efficient to outsource many of their service activities, leading to these activities being reclassified from manufacturing to services. Finally, the distinction between manufacturing and services is increasingly blurred, with manufacturing firms often providing services with the products that they sell (for example, products are often sold with training and support services or financial packages provided through the manufacturers themselves). Over 30 per cent of workers in the manufacturing sector are now engaged in service-related activities. There is a great deal of potential for further growth of this sector given that for the OECD as a whole, services account for 68 per cent of GVA. The sector also makes up an increasing proportion of trade in the OECD and is an increasingly important source of high-skilled employment (see Chapter 9).

Process of Structural Change – An Irish Case Study

As illustrated, the manufacturing sector in Ireland is important both in terms of its contribution to output and employment and also in terms of its contribution to exports and aggregate productivity. Over the last five years, however, the sector has undergone a major structural change in terms of the nature of output produced and the type of labour required. This process of structural change can best be illustrated using the example of a key sector in Irish manufacturing up to the turn of the millennium, the computer hardware sector. In this section, the main findings of a recent case study of this sector are presented.[8]

Over the course of the 1990s, Ireland emerged as a major centre for the production of computer hardware and electronics as a result of foreign investment in the area of computer assembly and the manufacture of computer components. With the arrival of companies like Dell, Gateway, AST and most notably Intel, the importance of these sectors to Irish manufacturing in terms of employment and exports grew exponentially. By 2000, the office machinery and computers and the electronic components sectors together accounted for almost 12 per cent of jobs in the manufacturing sector. These sectors were also of significant importance in terms of exports: in 2000 Irish exports of computer hardware and electronic components accounted for five per cent and six per cent, respectively, of total global exports and an estimated one-third of all computer sales in the EU were assembled in Ireland. Since then, however, these sectors have experienced significant decline with the relocation of production to China, the Far East and Central and Eastern Europe, who gained comparative advantage in the production of these goods through offering lower-cost production environments, particularly in terms of labour costs. By 2005, Ireland's share of world exports of computer hardware had fallen to 4.6 per cent while China's share exploded from six per cent to over 28 per cent in the same period. Ireland's losses were even greater in the electronic components sector, with global export shares falling to 2.5 per cent, while China experienced similar gains. Similar losses were experienced in employment: by 2003 the share of total manufacturing employment accounted for by these sectors had fallen to 8.6 per cent, equivalent to a loss of over 10,000 jobs.

The closure of computer assembly firms, though, leads to the establishment of related firms in higher-technology segments offering higher wages. Some assembly firms remained: four of the five major firms are still present in Ireland today. These firms underwent significant change, however. For example, Intel has shifted to producing higher value-added manufacturing output through its establishment of successive wafer fabrication plants while Apple and IBM have transformed their operations from manufacturing to performing high value-added services functions such as technical support and call centres. Undoubtedly favourable economic conditions eased the transition process, but the higher than average levels of educational attainment and lower age profile of workers in these sectors also played an important role. The key lesson to be learnt from this experience is that as the manufacturing sector continues to transform and blur into the boundaries of the high value-added services sector, a highly educated and flexible labour force is essential to facilitate the process of change.

4 FOREIGN DIRECT INVESTMENT

Policies aimed at attracting FDI are based on the premise that FDI brings new investment to the economy that directly boosts national income and leads to the creation of employment. It is also expected that FDI will bring an inflow of knowledge and technology that leads to productivity spillovers to the domestic manufacturing sector. In this section, the importance of FDI to Irish manufacturing relative to other countries in Europe is first examined and the contribution of foreign-owned firms to output and employment in the sector analysed. Second, the extent to which productivity spillovers have materialised is considered. Third, the increasing role of outward direct investment (ODI) and what this means for Ireland is analysed. The section concludes with a brief discussion of future issues facing policymakers in relation to the manufacturing sector.

Inward Foreign Direct Investment
Since the 1960s, Ireland's industrial policy has focused on facilitating inward foreign direct investment. This has yielded substantial rewards for Ireland in terms of economic growth in the latter half of the last century. Of particular importance have been growth-enhancing economic policies such as fiscal stability, labour market flexibility and science-oriented human capital formation as well as a low corporation tax regime.[9] As a result, Ireland has the most FDI-intensive manufacturing sector of all countries in Europe. As illustrated in Table 8.3, in 2006 the stock of inward FDI as a percentage of GDP amounted to 81 per cent compared with an average of 38 per cent for the European Union. Over the course of the 1990s the ratio of inward FDI stock to GDP grew considerably despite rapid increases in GDP over this period. Since 2000, however, the overall stock of inward FDI (relative to GDP) has declined almost to its 1990 levels. This decline is primarily due to the outflow of foreign investors in the early 2000s and is also in line with the decline in the overall importance of the manufacturing sector in terms of output and employment since 2000 (illustrated in Table 8.2). This trend can be explained by the increasing attractiveness of developing countries such as China and India and Central and East European countries as locations for investors in labour-intensive manufacturing sectors. In more recent years, positive inflows have returned but at a more moderate level. These are attributable to an increasing number of investments in higher-tech manufacturing sectors and services.

FDI into Ireland over the last two decades has been on a large scale and this has reshaped the manufacturing sector in Ireland in a significant way. According to IDA Ireland, over 1,000 foreign firms have chosen Ireland as their European base in a variety of different sectors including engineering, financial and international services, information communications technologies, medical technologies and pharmaceuticals. In addition to Intel, Apple and IBM, other overseas companies with large operations in Ireland include Amazon.com, Google, HP, Microsoft and Yahoo. In 2005, foreign-owned firms accounted for almost 50 per cent of employment in the sector and almost 90 per cent of total output, while almost all of the output in the modern manufacturing sector is attributable to foreign-owned firms. Of this output, 94 per cent was exported in

2005 compared with only 33 per cent of output for domestic firms, highlighting the importance of foreign investment to trade flows in Ireland.

Table 8.3
FDI Stocks and Flows for Ireland, the UK and the EU, 1990, 2000 and 2006

	FDI stocks as a percentage of GDP		
	1990	2000	2006
Ireland	79.4	131.9	81.2
United Kingdom	20.6	30.4	47.8
European Union	10.5	26.0	38.0

Source: UNCTAD, *World Investment Report 2007*, UNCTAD, Geneva 2007.

Productivity Spillovers[10]

As discussed in Section 2, a key rationale for industrial policy aimed at promoting FDI is the fact that foreign MNCs establishing in Ireland bring with them knowledge and technology that will spill over into the domestic industrial sector. The extent to which FDI yields benefits to the economy above and beyond the direct contribution to output and employment is an issue that has been extensively debated in the economics literature. The evidence is clear on the fact that foreign-owned firms are larger, have higher labour productivity, higher profits, are more export intensive, employ more skilled workers and spend more on R&D than their domestic counterparts. Thus there is no doubt that the presence of foreign companies in Ireland has contributed to higher aggregate productivity levels and growth rates than would otherwise have been possible.

The measurement of productivity *spillovers* is a more complex matter, however, with no consensus about the most appropriate approach. Productivity spillovers can be horizontal (within a defined sub-sector of manufacturing) or vertical (through backward linkages on the input-supply side). While there is some evidence that the presence of MNCs in Ireland has led to the establishment of an indigenous downstream sector for some industries, most of the empirical literature on the presence of spillovers is concerned with the measurement of horizontal spillovers from MNCs to Irish firms operating in the same sector. The evidence on the presence of horizontal spillovers for Ireland is mixed, however, with positive spillovers only evident when sectors are narrowly defined. The strongest evidence for the importance of spillovers is found in high-technology sectors.

The key to innovation is the improvement of the absorption capacity of firms so that they can benefit from technology spillovers. This can be achieved through appropriate education and training policies to ensure that the labour force is equipped with the necessary skills to innovate effectively. The National Skills Strategy, developed in 2007, aims to address the changing skills needs of the Irish labour force to increase absorption capacity. In addition, as discussed in Section 3, the smooth transition from manufacturing to a knowledge-driven economy will also require a flexible and adaptable labour force. A report published by the Expert

215

Group on Future Skills Needs in 2007, that forms the basis for the National Skills Strategy, calls for the up-skilling of a substantial proportion of the current workforce to ease this transition process and to increase absorption capacity.[11]

Outward Direct Investment[12]

A key concern for many developed economies is the extent to which the manufacturing sector can survive in the face of emerging low-cost economies offering an attractive base for manufacturing investment in terms of low input costs and liberal trade and investment policies. From 2003 to 2005, 35 per cent of global FDI was invested in developing countries, with China accounting for almost half of this. Eastern European countries have also experienced significant growth in inward FDI, with Russia experiencing the greatest gains. In Ireland, the increasing importance of outward direct investment (ODI) is evidenced in Table 8.4. In 2006, the stock of investment by Irish companies abroad amounted to over half of GDP with dramatic increases in the flow of ODI experienced since the early 1990s. While the stock of investment held abroad is still below the UK level, in the last couple of years it has surpassed the EU average and is increasing at a fast pace. The bulk of ODI from Ireland is attributable to a small proportion of long-established Irish companies in the services and traditional industrial sectors (for example, Allied Irish Bank, Bank of Ireland, Cement Roadstone Holdings and Greencore), although Irish-owned high-technology firms have also begun to make their mark, primarily in the USA. Of significance are the overseas investments of companies such as Elan (speciality pharmaceutical company with headquarters in Dublin) and a small number of other technology companies. Outward investment of this kind will most likely continue to increase into the future, particularly from the Irish-owned modern manufacturing sector.

Table 8.4
ODI Stocks and Flows for Ireland, the UK and the EU, 1990, 2000 and 2006

| | ODI stocks as a percentage of GDP | | |
	1990	2000	2006
Ireland	31.2	29.0	56.7
United Kingdom	23.2	62.2	62.6
European Union	11.4	36.4	44.9

Source: As for Table 8.3.

Intuitively, one would expect that, as is the case for foreign-owned firms operating in Ireland, high labour costs make sourcing labour-intensive parts of the production process in Ireland very costly and so sourcing this part of the production chain abroad will improve the competitiveness of Irish producers. Yet Irish ODI flows have been mainly concentrated in the UK and the USA. It is estimated that Irish companies in the USA employed almost 65,000 people in 1999 compared with just over 100,000 workers employed by US companies in

Ireland in the same year. This suggests that low labour costs may not be the only driver of the decision for Irish firms to invest abroad. Portfolio diversification, capacity constraints or a shortage of certain skills are also important factors.

A key concern in the face of rising levels of ODI is that it will have a negative impact on the domestic economy in terms of investment, exports and employment. Evidence from countries with a history of ODI suggests that these concerns are unfounded and that high levels of ODI can lead to economic growth. For example, there is evidence to suggest that high levels of ODI are complementary to a strong export base. Traditional exports of finished goods are replaced with exports of high value-added intermediate goods (as has been the case in Ireland in recent years) and the provision of highly skilled services to overseas foreign affiliates by head offices based in the domestic country. The discussion in Section 3 shows that there is evidence to suggest that this type of restructuring away from low-tech employment to high value-added activities, with corresponding higher wages, is taking place in Ireland. An additional advantage of ODI is that portfolio diversification of this kind may help protect the economy from regional economic downturns at an aggregate level and alleviate some of the pressures associated with export dependence mentioned in the previous section. Finally, high levels of ODI are generally associated with high levels of R&D investment.

Given these advantages, government policy aimed at facilitating outward investments should aim to remove tax and regulatory barriers to investment flows. This can be achieved through an expansion of Ireland's network of international agreements on double taxation and through support for WTO multilateral agreements on investment rules. An expansion of Enterprise Ireland's current supports to companies wishing to invest abroad, such as Overseas Network, Overseas Incubator Facilities, Acquisition Service, Outsourcing Missions, and Foreign Trade and Investment Missions, would also facilitate this process. Ultimately, however, policies aimed at improving Ireland's competitiveness will remain most important, and should aim to re-skill those displaced by these changes and promote high value-added activities in manufacturing and services into the future.

Future Issues

FDI has played a crucial role in the success of the Irish manufacturing sector, not only in terms of output and employment but also in terms of its impact on the domestic industrial sector. Higher than average productivity levels of MNCs has raised aggregate productivity levels for the sector as a whole and productivity spillovers, particularly in the high-tech sector, have also benefited Irish firms. There is also evidence to suggest that the presence of MNCs has increased domestic firm survival rates and encouraged start-up firms in many downstream supply industries. In the face of an increasingly high-cost environment, particularly labour costs, and declining flows of FDI, the challenge for Irish industrial policymakers is not only how to continue to attract foreign investment into Ireland and to hold on to the MNCs that are already here, but how better to develop linkages between MNCs and domestic firms in an attempt to fully exploit productivity spillovers. This is even a greater challenge in the face of increasing pressure from the EU to harmonise corporation tax rates and increased restrictions on the provision of grants: two important policy tool options for the Irish government in the past. Also of importance is the promotion of strategies to facilitate outward direct investment and to ensure that the benefits of ODI are realised in terms of facilitating the shift towards the provision of higher value-added headquarter services to manage foreign affiliates.

Given these trends, and the general decline in the importance of the manufacturing sector, the future competitiveness of all sectors must be pushed to the forefront of the policy agenda. Of critical importance for the manufacturing sector, however, is the need to strengthen the competitive advantages of Ireland's industrial base and the creation of a more competitive business environment. One element of this worth highlighting is the importance of promoting R&D expenditures. The target for the EU, as set out in the Lisbon Agenda, is to increase gross expenditure on R&D as a percentage of GDP from its current level of two per cent to three per cent by 2010, making expenditure levels more comparable with the USA, which spends 2.7 per cent of GDP on R&D, and Japan, which spends 3.1 per cent. While gross expenditure on R&D has been increasing in Ireland in recent times, Ireland still lags behind the European average in terms of R&D expenditures. In response to the Lisbon target, Ireland has set the goal of increasing R&D expenditure to 2.5 per cent of GDP by 2013. The Government Strategy for Science, Technology and Innovation 2006–2013 sets out to transform Ireland into a knowledge economy through substantial increases in R&D investments through third-level education as well as a range of initiatives aimed at promoting enterprise R&D. These will be implemented through the current National Development Plan.

5 PHYSICAL INFRASTRUCTURE: IMPORTANCE AND PROVISION

Input to Production and Final Consumption

Physical infrastructural investment, or physical capital,[13] consists of large capital-intensive projects, mostly, in the case of Ireland, publicly owned or regulated, which provide the core distribution system for production and consumption for any economy. It includes roads, airports and harbours, railways, utility distribution systems, for example for electricity and gas, water and sewerage systems, and communication networks. No economy can exist without large-scale physical infrastructure and it is crucial to the process of economic development in all countries. One of the great successes of the Roman Empire was the construction of major public infrastructure such as roads and basic water and sewerage works. In the case of Ireland a major programme of canal construction took place in the nineteenth century, when water was the main distribution system for goods. Ports were also built and some basic system of roads existed, particularly in towns. This was followed by the construction of major ports and railroads in the first half of the nineteenth century, which greatly increased the opportunities for trade and economic development. Large-scale investment in water and sewerage systems, and electricity and telephone networks, commenced in the twentieth century, greatly facilitating further advances in economic development. By the end of the twentieth century and early twenty-first century, the emphasis was on new communication channels, although in the case of Ireland the majority of infrastructural investment has been on the road networks, in an attempt to make up for a major deficit in this regard from the past and also to accommodate the huge increase in employment and economic activity in the last 20 years (see Chapters 5 and 6).

Thus in a very general sense it is clear that infrastructural investment is crucial to economic growth and living standards. Most industries, not just manufacturing, require a good physical distribution system. Not only is it an input to production but it is also part of direct consumption. Thus, for example, roads are required to transport raw materials and other inputs, plus final goods, for manufacturing industry, retail outlets and most other services industries. They are also required by people when commuting to work and travelling for leisure purposes, for example to take a vacation. Not only does the possibility of taking such trips matter, but safety and time taken also have a large influence on living standards and well-being. Industry needs energy as an input and so do households to heat homes, drive cars and provide the electricity required nowadays to allow all the household and consumer appliances that one needs to function. Industry needs water and waste disposal and they are also vital to household consumption and comfort. Likewise, Internet connections are needed not only by the manufacturing and services industries but also by individuals to access knowledge, to 'shop' and consume different forms of entertainment.

Key Factor in Determining Productivity Growth

As seen in Chapter 6, physical capital has for some time been understood by economists as a key determinant of growth, with the Solow model giving it a particularly significant emphasis. But how important is it and how much do changes in physical infrastructure explain changes in productivity growth? As with so many explanations in economics, there is no consensus on the precise impact, with much written on how the road network in particular impacts, either positively or negatively, on growth.[14] Estimating what forces affect productivity is extremely difficult. For example, public investment in transport networks may allow for increased trade, make profitable continued investment and innovation in the motor industry and eventually allow for the development of efficient and effective supply-chain management techniques that greatly increase productivity in industries. But the marginal impact could decline markedly with increasing road construction and where this happens is very difficult to determine. A further difficulty is that productivity growth and spending on infrastructure are simultaneously determined variables and sometimes it is difficult to isolate the direction of causation. For example, to what extent was the large transport infrastructure investment in Ireland in the last 15 years a cause or consequence of the growing economy? There appears to be a firm consensus, though, based on international comparisons (see below) and everyday experiences for many people, that in Ireland the marginal benefits from increased investment in transport infrastructure are considerable and real, with some way to go before marked reductions in marginal benefits become evident.

The most recent example in relation to this debate is how developments in IT contributed to increased productivity growth in the USA. While increased computing speeds and the huge decrease in the price of computing yielded benefits to consumers and producers alike, the benefits of the computer revolution relate in particular to the advent of the Internet, which in a sense can be thought of as the infrastructure of the computing age. As Gramlich states, 'like other networks the Internet significantly raised the productivity of each and every computer. The more Internet users there are, the more valuable each Internet connection and the more valuable the information that can be disseminated over the Internet. Thus, it seems likely that the synergies between innovations in computing and innovations in communications have yielded great benefits. And like the interstate highway system, the effects of the Internet on productivity growth are likely to wane over time'.[15]

In relation to the productivity impact of increased investment in infrastructure a few general messages appear to apply. First, increased investment is a necessary but not a sufficient condition for increases in productivity. There are many examples of massive wasted investment across the world and over time. Second, the quality and management of the investment are probably more important than its level. Third, the allocation of the total infrastructural budget across the different types of infrastructure listed earlier is an important and difficult policy decision. For example, there is no point in having good IT networks if energy supply cannot be ensured. Last, infrastructure is very costly and that it be provided at lowest cost, for a given quality level, is crucial to its success. This leads to the questions of who should fund large capital projects and whether or not there is a strong competitive environment in the tendering for the construction of such projects. A different question relates to the efficient operation of the various infrastructural networks once constructed and the creation of a strong competitive environment for such provision, a topic which is taken up in Chapter 9.

Role of the State

Many take it as given that the state should largely fund all major infrastructural projects. This appears to be the case in relation to transport infrastructure but it should be remembered that the building of the canals in the nineteenth century in Ireland was sometimes financed by private investors. In the USA, the building of the rail network was financed entirely by private companies, although the federal government heavily subsidised the rail network through land grants. The Channel

Tunnel in Britain was also funded by private investors. Whatever the source of finance, such projects involve huge state involvement, through a strict regulatory environment, subsidies and often major compulsory land purchase.

The first public policy issue revolves around the fact that infrastructure investment has large fixed costs and relatively low marginal costs. In the case of many such projects, the fixed costs are so large that only one firm can feasibly supply the project, hence resulting in monopoly provision. Given the dangers of such provision, with regard to abuse of position in terms of pricing, standards, and so on, the state usually steps in and directly provides the infrastructure itself (although it usually hires private companies to carry out the actual work) or heavily regulates the private providers. Transport infrastructure is a good example of this and as shall be seen later will receive by far the largest allocation of state investment funding in the next ten years in Ireland. Construction of roads and rail networks involves huge fixed costs and up to the point of serious congestion the incremental cost of having an additional car or lorry on the road is tiny. Besides, collecting revenues from users may be costly, particularly in city streets (but also on some motorways, as was the case for the M50 in Dublin with huge costs to commuters in terms of delays at toll booths). As a result, the state pays for most road construction.

A similar issue arises in relation to other infrastructure. It is generally inefficient to have more than one supplier of electricity or water/sewerage. Again, the most efficient solution is monopoly provision, either through state provision or a heavily regulated monopolist, such as the ESB in Ireland.

A second policy issue relates to the network externalities that arise from many large infrastructural projects. A good example here is information technology. There are again large economies of scale in creating information, as once information is created it can be made available to others without any cost. There are also positive network externalities. The larger and more interconnected the road or rail network, the more valuable it is to all, and the same applies to the IT network. Thus the benefits of the whole can be much greater than the sum of its parts and this provides again a strong argument for state intervention to capture such external benefits for all, something a private operator cannot and will not take into account.

It is important, though, not to overstate the value of state intervention. There are cases where government ownership or regulation can actually hamper efficiency and lead to higher prices. State-owned or regulated industries can become entrenched monopolies, innovation can be suppressed and without competition the quality of services can suffer. As will be discussed in Chapter 9, deregulation and privatisation can unleash entrepreneurial forces, leading to such innovations as the hub-and-spoke system following deregulation of the airline industry and the wide variety of IT services following deregulation of the telecommunications sector. This issue relates more to the delivery of services using the infrastructural network than to the initial investment per se and is, as mentioned, the subject matter of Chapter 9.

Whatever the debate about the role of the state in infrastructural projects, the reality in Ireland is that the state *does* provide the vast bulk of funding for such projects. Hence the concern should be with how best such projects are managed by the state and that lowest-cost, high-quality provision is assured. One development of importance in this regard in recent years in Ireland has been the idea of public-private partnerships (PPP) in the provision of large infrastructural projects.

Public-Private Partnership[16]

The involvement of private operators in the funding of large-scale infrastructural projects can lead to many benefits, not least the private operators' administrative and operational efficiencies, increased competition and enhanced services to end-users. Examples of the efficiencies are the technical expertise and the managerial competences of commercial operators. Even where the public sector has access to cheaper funding than private concerns, the efficiency gains from private sector participation can outweigh the extra financing costs.

Some states of course face fiscal burdens giving rise to liquidity constraints or raising funding costs to such an extent where private funding of infrastructure may appear not just the cheapest but the *only* feasible option. Thus the choice in certain cases may be between privately financed infrastructure and no infrastructure. This will be a matter for sound cost-benefit analysis of all costs and risks over the long run, including an assessment of economic, financial and social consequences.

Such an analysis needs to take into account not only individual contracts but also the impact on the full infrastructural system. As seen earlier, in network industries such as transport infrastructure, linkages between different segments of the networks and the 'actors' involved are critical. Thus the knock-on effects throughout the system must be taken into account. Besides, large transport and other infrastructural projects often have major environmental and social repercussions that need to be properly accounted for and independent sustainability impact assessments commissioned. These issues arise not only when the state is involved but must also be taken into account when there is private involvement. The controversy surrounding the construction of the M3 near the Hill of Tara site in County Meath is a good case in point.

Thus there will never likely be private sector provision alone, merely some private sector involvement in funding. As such there will always be a high level of public subsidy and as such there needs to be clear control and management practices put in place for such projects.

The OECD has set out a code of good conduct for private sector funding and management of large infrastructural projects that all countries, including Ireland, can usefully use as guidelines in undertaking PPPs. The first of these is clearly the decision whether or not to involve the private sector at all. The second relates to the enabling institutional environment. Successful private participation in infrastructure depends, like any other business activity, on the quality of the national investment 'climate', with the legal framework transparent and fully applicable. Another issue is that before embarking on large infrastructural projects, but especially where there is private sector involvement, there needs to be extensive consultation with affected parties and communities about the goals of the project. There also needs to be a clear understanding by those involved in the public sector of the realities of commercial life in the private sector.

Further Issues

The above are perhaps issues involving too much detail for a book like this. The main point to make is that the delivery of large infrastructural projects, whether or not private sector financing is involved, is fraught with difficulties. Let us recap on the three discussed already.

The first of these is the huge fixed cost involved and hence the need for monopoly provision, at least of the network, if not the use of it. The second is that there are often significant network externalities, which implies that the total could bring benefits considerably greater than the sum of its parts. Third, there is the issue of whether or not to involve the private sector in the financing and management of the infrastructure. Let us turn now to some other more general problems.

Many of the benefits are very difficult to estimate, such as, for example, in relation to the road network, time savings and reductions in road deaths and accidents. Time savings in travelling for business and leisure purposes is probably the most important benefit of an improved road and rail network in Ireland, yet it can be very difficult to estimate these savings. In particular, the increased future usage of the networks has to be estimated and the problem of severe congestion resulting should usage increase greatly factored in. Likewise, there are considerably fewer road casualties and accidents on wider, multi-carriage roads per kilometre travelled but the valuation of the costs of a life and long-term injuries are almost impossible to measure accurately.

There are many environmental and heritage costs/benefits which are also almost impossible to value yet can be crucial to the debate, in particular in relation to road construction, energy provision and waste disposal. Examples of these are noise and air pollution. There may also be damage to important architectural sites or areas of outstanding beauty or important habitats for birds and other wildlife. How are these costs/benefits to be established, let alone evaluated? The case of the M3 motorway, now under construction in Meath, and the proposed incinerators in Dublin and elsewhere around the country are cases in point.

Many infrastructural projects are long-term in nature, involving huge sums of money, and the choice of a suitable discount rate to take account of the future benefits/costs fraught with difficulty, particularly in relation to the environment. The debate about the economics of global warming hinges fundamentally on the discount rate chosen to apply to the costs and benefits of infrastructural and other measures to deal with expected future losses, 20 to 50 years into the future.

Because the projects are so long-term in nature, there is also often very considerable uncertainty about the benefits/costs into the future, making them difficult to undertake for either the public sector or private sector. For example, estimating future demand for a major transport facility depends on many uncertainties, such as the price of oil and the development of alternative means of transport in the intervening period. In relation to the environment, for decades there was huge disagreement about the actual scientific evidence about global warming into the future and the consequences of global warming for the environment, sea levels and ambient temperatures. The debate surrounding the provision of nuclear energy encapsulates all of the above: it requires huge levels of investment, with a very long time horizon and potentially catastrophic but unknown expected external costs.

There is also the issue of considering alternatives, a process which might never end and/or lead to huge time lags in delivery of major infrastructural projects. Examples of this are roads where even when construction has commenced, after a consultation process of many years, people object that other routes were not considered properly, although some of the costs they complain about can only be realised once construction begins. The building of much-needed airport capacity can often be delayed by many years to take account of the very reasonable concerns of those affected by airport noise and traffic, but these considerations must be set against the benefits to the much larger numbers arising from reduced travel times to/from airports, and better facilities and less crowding and time delays when at the airport.

Finally, there is the huge disruption that can arise during the construction phase. Even where there is broad agreement about the net benefits resulting once the construction phase is completed, there may still be a small number of people so affected during the construction stage that they will, understandably, use every means available to them to prevent the project taking place. Again, though, the possible major benefits to hundreds of thousands of other people must be taken into account.

There is really no scientific way of dealing with all of the issues above arising in relation to large infrastructural projects. At the end of the day they involve major political decisions, which carry many risks to policymakers. There is also an asymmetry in public reaction to such infrastructural projects. Get them right and the outcome is taken as 'expected'; get them 'wrong' and the outcome is there for all to see with the result that politicians face obloquy and public outcry. It is no wonder that politicians sometimes defer decisions on infrastructure for as long as possible. Yet the tough decisions on infrastructure must be taken, for, as argued above, no economy can function without good infrastructure. In particular, the business sector requires its provision, not just to function and produce, but to do so in such a way that it can survive in an intensely competitive international environment. Increasingly the provision of good-quality infrastructure, at lowest cost, can be the factor that makes or breaks the success of an industrial concern, although clearly a host of other competitiveness factors apply, as discussed earlier, such as the quality of the labour force (see Chapter 12) and the regulatory framework applying in product and labour markets (see Chapters 5 and 9).

6 INFRASTRUCTURE: FACTS AND KEY BOTTLENECKS

Overall
National Development Plan 2007–2013
This section turns to more practical issues, namely the key facts and figures relating to the present state and future plans for infrastructure in Ireland. The main reference point for this is the National Development Plan 2007–2013. Besides this, the other main source of information is Forfás,[17] the primary state agency assigned with the task of encouraging enterprise in Ireland.

Table 8.5

Economic Infrastructure Expenditure, 2007–2013 (€ billions)

Programme	Exchequer	PPP	State bodies	Other	Total
Transport	19.9	7.0	2.2	3.8	32.9
Energy	0.3	0.0	8.3	0.0	8.6
Environmental services	4.2	0.3	0.0	1.3	5.8
Other	3.1	2.2	0.0	2.1	7.4
Total	*27.5*	*9.5*	*10.5*	*7.2*	*54.7*

Source: National Competitiveness Council, *Annual Competitiveness Report 2007*, Forfás, Dublin, November 2007 (available at: www.forfas.ie/publications/index.html).

Table 8.5 outlines the main economic infrastructure expenditures under the Plan. As may be seen, expenditure on transport dominates, with over €33 billion of the total of around €55 billion devoted to this sector. It is interesting to note that, of the €33 billion, only €20 billion is to be funded by the Exchequer, €7 billion by PPP and over €2 billion by state bodies. It is planned to spend €8.6 billion on energy infrastructure, most of which is to be funded by state bodies, and €5.8 billion on environmental services. The bulk of this is to be funded by the Exchequer.

Levels of expenditure for the future do not, of course, directly relate to importance to industry. For example, in the 'other' category, less than €0.5 billion is being allocated by the Exchequer to communications and broadband, yet the services provided via this network are crucially important to producers and consumers in the years ahead, with most of the services being provided privately. Thus, while expenditure on IT networks might be relatively small compared to that on transport, the provision of adequate IT networks and the enforcement of strict competition in IT service provision may be just as important to industry and consumers as expenditure on transport infrastructure.

International Comparisons

In the case of Ireland, infrastructural development is required simply to keep pace with the growth in employment and economic development, mainly to maintain productivity levels but also to contribute to enhanced productivity. In this regard the *Annual Competitiveness Report 2007* is clear that expenditure on physical infrastructure has not kept pace and that a very serious infrastructural deficit now exists in Ireland.[18] Drawing on IMF data for 2004 for the OECD countries, the report shows that in terms of public capital stock per person the following held (see Table 8.6):

- The figures for the Netherlands, France, Germany and Denmark (in descending order) were highest, above €14,000 per person in all cases.
- Ireland had a figure of €10,500 per person, similar to the UK and Spain.
- Only Greece and Portugal (not shown in Table 8.6) had significantly lower figures than Ireland, at around €8,000 per person.

Table 8.6

Ireland's Ranking in Terms of Infrastructure

Country	Public capital stock per person (€K)	Perceptions of overall infrastructural quality (score min 0.0, max 7.0)		Perceptions of efficiency of transport network (score min 0.0, max 10.0)	
	2004	2001	2007	2001	2007
Denmark	14.4	6.7	6.4	8.8	9.1
France	15.6	6.8	6.5	8.3	8.0
Germany	14.4	6.8	6.6	8.8	8.8
Hungary	n.a.	4.1	4.2	5.1	7.2
Ireland	*10.5*	*3.7*	*3.9*	*3.7*	*4.9*
Italy	12.8	3.9	3.5	4.0	3.8
Netherlands	17.2	6.2	5.8	7.0	7.7
Poland	n.a.	4.0	2.8	3.2	5.9
Spain	10.3	5.1	5.3	6.1	6.5
UK	10.5	5.6	5.5	5.4	6.4
OECD average	19.1	6.0	5.8	7.6	7.7

Source: National Competitiveness Council, *Annual Competitiveness Report 2007*, Forfás, Dublin, November 2007 (available at: www.forfas.ie/publications/index.html).

The above is as one might expect from general observation when visiting these countries. The picture over time in Ireland, as the report shows, has not improved. The public capital stock *per person*, in real terms, was in 2004 only at 70 per cent of its level in 1987, rising though from just over 60 per cent in 2000 and expected to rise much more since 2004 and on to 2013. The total public capital stock, when expressed as a percentage of GNP, declined from over 90 to around 35 per cent over the period, a quite remarkable decline but mostly explained by the rise in GNP. Ireland, it is true, is now investing more as a percentage of GNP in gross fixed capital formation but this percentage probably needs to be much higher if the gap in public capital stock per person is to be closed in the decade ahead.

Turning now to the quality of the public capital stock, the report draws on a World Economic Forum report which ranks each country in terms of the *perceptions* of business executives regarding the *overall* public capital stock.[19] While such measures have their limitations, nonetheless in many cases it is perhaps perceptions rather than the reality that matter. In any case these perceptions, as can be seen in Table 8.6, correlate closely with the evidence in relation to the value of the public capital stock per person and, besides, there is a reassuring stability in the perception rankings between 2001 and 2007 for the countries which did not undergo much change in this period. The main findings are as follows:

- Denmark, France and Germany got scores greater than 6.0 (max 7.0) in 2007.
- Ireland got a score of 3.9, similar to that for Hungary and, of the countries listed, higher only than Italy and Poland.
- The OECD average in 2007 was 5.8, down from 6.0 in 2001. The figure for Ireland in the same period improved marginally, up from 3.7 to 3.9, well below the OECD average in both years and way below the figures for France, Germany and the Nordic countries.

Thus there appears to be a very serious infrastructural deficit, both real and perceived, and it is this that the National Development Plan is designed to address. The major deficit, again real and perceived, is with the transport system (see Table 8.6), which accounts for the vast bulk of public infrastructure, and to a lesser extent energy and environmental services. With this in mind, the rest of the section will briefly comment on the following main subsectors of economic infrastructure: transport, including road, air and sea; energy; environmental services, such as water provision and waste management; and communications and broadband.

Sectors
Transport
As can be seen in Table 8.6, Ireland ranked very poorly in terms of the perceived efficiency of the public transport infrastructure in 2007, getting a score of 4.9 (max 10.0) compared with an OECD average of 7.7 and figures as high as 9.1 in Denmark and 8.8 in Germany. These are huge differences with the only consoling factor for Ireland being that there was an increase between 2001 and 2007. The UK, where constant complaints about the public transport infrastructure are heard, had a figure of 6.4 in 2007, well above the Irish figure.

227

Any business in Ireland could probably confirm this picture, as indeed could the tens of thousands of commuters, especially in Dublin, who face huge delays on a daily basis getting to work, particularly on the M50 in recent years. Further evidence of the difficult commuting situation in Dublin can be found in the *Annual Competitiveness Report 2007*:

- The average traffic speed in Cologne, a city of similar size to Dublin, was 40kmph, with Helsinki not far behind at 36kmph.
- In Budapest, Copenhagen, Madrid, Rotterdam and Vienna the speeds were above 20kmph.
- Bristol, London and Dublin ranked lowest, with the figure for Dublin being 17 and that for London 15.

These data refer to 2003, though, and things may have improved. Besides, such figures provide only part of the story and in the case of London the slow average traffic speeds do not prevent that city doing very well economically. At least not in the short run, but many predict that the economic success of Dublin and London in recent years, which is due of course to many favourable factors, may be put in jeopardy if the transport infrastructural deficit is not addressed. This is why Dublin gets the main attention in the National Development Plan. As such, there are plans for an outer orbital road and eastern bypass for Dublin: car ownership per thousand of population in Ireland is still below the average of countries with the same level of incomes per head and as such a further large increase in the total number of cars on the road is expected. Having a well-developed and interconnected road network *across* the country is also important, given the relatively dispersed nature of economic activity, partly due to the fact that tourism and agriculture are important sectors of the economy.

While around €18 billion will be allocated to roads, €13 billion will also be allocated to public transport, €2 billion to air transport and around €0.5 billion to seaports. The bulk of the public transport investment is to take place in the Greater Dublin area, with completion of the Metro North line from the city centre to Swords via Dublin Airport planned, as well as a phased development of the Metro West line and extensions to the Luas and a significant expansion of the bus fleet and priority lanes. A key issue is that these systems are integrated, in terms of physical connections, integrated ticketing systems and park-and-ride facilities.

In terms of perceptions of quality of air transport infrastructure, Ireland also comes out badly. Denmark and Germany come out strongly again with scores over 8.3+ (max 10.0) in 2007. The figure for Ireland was 6.2 and even the UK had a higher figure, 6.9, despite the perceived terrible state of its airports, particularly in London. Only Italy and Poland come out worse than Ireland. A new Pier D is under construction at Dublin Airport and a second runway at the planning stage. But it is hard to see how Dublin Airport could match, for decades ahead, the facilities and integrated connecting public and road transport systems at airports such as Copenhagen and Düsseldorf.

Ireland also ranks poorly in terms of port infrastructure, an essential link in the distribution network for industry, with 99 per cent by volume of external trade going through our seaports. The gap with other countries is not as great as for road and rail transport infrastructure, but Ireland still ranked among the lowest in 2007, with no improvement in its ranking between 2001 and 2007. Again, only Italy and Poland were ranked lower.

Energy
The relative rating of the efficiency of Ireland's energy infrastructure mirrors that of perceptions in relation to the quality of the transport infrastructure. Denmark, Germany and France come out near the top again, with scores over 8.0 (max 10.0). Ireland got a score of only 4.3 in 2007, down from 5.9 in 2002, Italy being the only country this time to rank lower than Ireland. The figure for the UK, perhaps Ireland's most comparator country, was 5.5 in 2007 and, like Ireland, down – from 7.6 in 2002. As energy is a major input cost into industry Ireland's very low ranking must be a matter of some concern. Of particular concern is that industrial electricity prices were more than 15 per cent above the EU-15 average and the UK in 2007, almost 60 per cent above those in Denmark and double those in France.[20]

Apart from price, energy supply raises other issues, not least security of supply. Ireland again does badly on this score, with a level of spare capacity over peak demand of only six per cent, compared to figures of around 15 per cent in Germany and the UK, for example. One would expect smaller counties in fact to have a higher spare capacity, although this need could be reduced by interconnectors to larger markets, as is planned between Ireland and the UK.

The other main issue is the very high level of dependence in Ireland on imported fossil fuels for electricity generation, as gas, oil and coal make up over 90 per cent of the total. Partly as a result, Ireland has one of the highest carbon dioxide emissions in Europe. In 2005 only 4.8 per cent of electricity generation in Ireland came from renewable sources such as wind power, compared to a figure of 28 per cent in Denmark. The figure for Ireland is likely to rise significantly, though. For all EU countries the figures will have to rise substantially more in the next decade or so. The alternative is more reliance on nuclear energy (with zero carbon dioxide emissions but other concerns, of course), something that is not yet on the agenda in Ireland. In Denmark, Ireland and Italy there is no nuclear power generation. On the other hand, in the case of France, around 80 per cent of its energy comes from nuclear power, and around 20 per cent in Germany, Spain and the UK.

Other
Continuing the rather worrying 'story' so far in relation to Ireland's relative performance in terms of public infrastructure provision, information and communication technology (ICT), which are essential to modern enterprise, Ireland's investment in both forms of technology, particularly IT, ranks among the lowest in the EU-15.[21]

Broadband affects not just how enterprises work internally or with each other, but also how they interact with consumers. Despite strong growth since 2003, Ireland continues to perform poorly in terms of broadband take-up per 100 of population. The figure for Ireland in 2007 was 15.4, compared to an OECD average of 18.8, and figures of 34.3 in Denmark and 33.5 in the Netherlands. The figure for the UK was around 25.0. These figures can change rapidly, though, as huge increases have been recorded in many countries in the last three to four years and further large changes are likely. The key issue for businesses in Ireland is the limited range and speed of broadband services and their comparatively higher costs.[22]

Environmental services, particularly water and waste disposal, are crucial to the well-being of both industry and households and cannot be taken for granted simply because they have been in existence for so long. Such systems have been put in place over many decades, indeed centuries, but the demands on the systems have intensified greatly in recent years, with the hugely increased level of economic activity and increased environmental and safety concerns. Over the period of the NDP, major investment will be needed to meet: international obligations in relation to climate change; the requirements of the EU Water Framework Directive; the need for a comprehensive system of waste management; and the need for sustainable settlements of people in both urban and rural areas. The scale of the investment here is large, but in terms of exchequer contribution just a little over 20 per cent of that for transport. The bulk of this money will go on upgrading and expanding water and wastewater treatment capacity. The provision of safe drinking water is of course critical to the functioning of any society. The provision of wastewater treatment facilities is crucial to the protection of the environment, especially in wealthy countries such as Ireland. Of no less concern in relation to the environment is the disposal of other non-water waste, with major strides taken in recent years in relation to recycling waste.

7 CONCLUDING COMMENTS

This chapter has brought the reader through a large array of topics and issues. As mentioned at the beginning, in some ways it is a chapter of two quite separate but related halves. The manufacturing sector depends for its competitiveness on many factors and one of the most important concerns in this regard is the much talked-about, and very real, infrastructural deficit in Ireland. There are other challenges of course for policymakers in ensuring that manufacturing, and indeed all businesses in Ireland, remain competitive in the years ahead. In this regard the issue of human capital looms large, especially if the Irish labour force is to have the right labour skills to move up the 'value chain' of production in years to come (see Chapters 5 and 12). This point was emphasised repeatedly throughout this chapter. A strong pro-competition stance must also be maintained in labour markets (see Chapter 5) and product markets (see Chapter 9), for the benefit both of Irish consumers and of Irish business.

Foreign direct investment flows into Ireland have been critical over the last two decades in terms of increased employment and bringing much-needed technological and managerial skills that eventually pass into other sectors of the economy. Such success was based partly on special tax breaks, something which may have to end as other countries become involved in similar competitive tax-cutting exercises. Such a situation will lead to a zero-sum game overall, with national governments the losers and large multinational companies the gainers. There is also now the phenomenon of large investment overseas by Irish companies and this process, as this chapter has emphasised, will have to be managed with care.

There will continue to be a rationale for state support of the manufacturing and business sectors, but the nature of that support is changing and will have to change even more in years to come. The emphasis is shifting from tax breaks and direct grants to providing the correct competitive environment in which businesses can, without any direct state aid or tax breaks, flourish. Top of the list in this regard is the physical infrastructure. As this chapter indicated, the quality of the physical infrastructure impinges on all of our lives, whether in business or as consumers, and very directly so. Physical infrastructure, as seen, relates to the hugely important transport networks, public and private, and also the energy, water, waste-disposal and IT networks. As seen earlier, much work remains to be done to bring this physical infrastructure to best international standards.

Endnotes

[1] E. O'Malley and Y. McCarthy, 'New drivers of economic growth? Sectoral contributions to the Irish economy', *Quarterly Economic Commentary*, ESRI, Dublin 2006.

[2] The discussion here draws from F. Barry, 'Foreign direct investment and institutional co-evolution in Ireland', *Scandinavian Economic History Review*, Vol. 55, No. 3, 2007.

[3] The discussion here draws from M. Cassidy and E. Strobl, 'Subsidizing industry: an empirical analysis of Irish manufacturing', *Journal of Industry, Competition and Trade*, Bank Papers, 2004.

[4] Department of the Taoiseach, *Lisbon Agenda. Integrated Guidelines for Growth and Jobs. Implementation of the National Reform Programme*, Government Publications, Dublin 2006.

[5] Enterprise Strategy Group, *Ahead of the Curve: Ireland's Place in the Global Economy*, Forfás, Dublin 2004.

[6] The statistics and discussion presented in this section are drawn from CSO, *Census of Industrial Production*, Stationery Office, Dublin 2008; Forfás, *Overview of Ireland's Productivity Performance, 1980–2005*, Forfás, Dublin 2006; Forfás, *The Changing Nature of Manufacturing and Services in Ireland*, Forfás, Dublin 2006; and OECD, *OECD in Figures 2007*, OECD, Paris 2007.

[7] J. Sexton, 'Trends in output, employment and productivity in Ireland, 1995–2005', in C. Alyward and R. O'Toole (eds), *Perspectives on Irish Productivity*, Forfás, Dublin 2006.

8   The data and analysis presented in this section are based on F. Barry and C. Van Egeraat, 'The decline of the computer hardware sector: how Ireland adjusted', *Quarterly Economic Commentary*, ESRI, Dublin 2008.

9   F. Barry, 'Export-platform foreign direct investment: the Irish experience', *EIB Papers*, Vol. 9, No. 2, 2004.

10 This section draws on H. Görg, 'Productivity spillovers from multinational companies', in Alyward and O'Toole, op. cit.

11 Expert Group on Future Skills Needs, *Tomorrow's Skills: Towards a National Skills Strategy*, Expert Group on Future Skills Needs, Dublin 2007.

12 This section draws on R. O'Toole, 'Outward direct investment and productivity', in Alyward and O'Toole, op. cit.; and Forfás, *Statement on ODI*, 2007 (available at: www.forfas.ie/publications/outward_direct_invest_01/index.html).

13 There is also investment in human capital, such as education and social capital, e.g. housing and hospitals. These will be looked at in later chapters. There is also the non-built physical capital of a country, such as mountains, rivers and lakes, as well as cultural capital, such as national museums, historical buildings, etc., all of which have importance to the functioning of a successful economy and society.

14 See E. Gramlich, 'Infrastructure and Economic Development', Texas Trade Corridors New Economy Conference, San Antonio, August 2001, available at: www.federalreserve.gov/boarddocs/speeches/2001/20010803/default.htm.

15 Ibid., p. 2.

16 This section draws heavily on H. Christiansen, 'The OECD Principles for Private Sector Participation in Infrastructure', IMF International Seminar on Strengthening Public Investment and Managing Fiscal Risks from Public-Private Partnerships, Budapest, March 2007, available at:
    www.federalreserve.gov/boarddocs/speeches/2001/20010803/default.htm).

17 The National Policy and Advisory Board for Enterprise, Trade, Science, Technology and Innovation. All Forfás publications are available from their website: www.forfas.ie/publications/index.html.

18 National Competitiveness Council, *Annual Competitiveness Report 2007*, Forfás, Dublin, November 2007 (available at: www.forfas.ie/publications/index.html).

19 See National Competitiveness Council, *Review of International Assessments of Ireland's Competitiveness*, Forfás, Dublin 2007 (available at: www.forfas.ie/ncc/reports/ncc071220/index.html). International assessments of Ireland's competitiveness have become very important given that they have such high visibility among international investors and commentators. There are four main international assessments carried out: the World Economic Forum (WEF), *Global Competitiveness Reports*; the Institute for Management Development (IMD), *World Competitiveness Yearbook*; the EU, *Growth and Jobs Strategy*; and Huggins Associates, *European Competitiveness Index*. In the case of the WEF report, which is the one drawn on most in this chapter, 126 indicators of competitiveness are used in total, 69 per cent of which are based on the surveyed opinions of executives. For the 2007–2008 report, over 11,000 business leaders were polled in 131 economies, 42 of whom were from Ireland. The main advantage of an approach based on executive opinions is that they are ultimately what business decisions are based on. They are also timelier than internationally comparable official statistical data, but sample sizes for individual countries can be small.

20 Forfás, *Electricity Benchmarking Analysis and Priorities*, December 2007, and *Review*

of International Assessments of Ireland's Competitiveness, December 2007 (both available at: www.forfas.ie/publications/index.html).

[21] National Competitiveness Council, op. cit.

[22] Forfás, *Ireland's Broadband Performance and Policy Requirements*, December 2007 (available at: www.forfas.ie/publications/index.html).

CHAPTER 9

Services, Competition and Regulation

Francis O'Toole*

1 INTRODUCTION

This chapter examines the related issues of the importance of the services sector and appropriate competition and regulatory policies to Ireland. The importance of the services sector in absolute terms is indicated by the role of the sector with respect to both national output and employment. Well over half of national output stems from the services sector and approximately two-thirds of total employment is located in the services sector (see Chapter 5). The relative importance of the services sector to both national output and employment has been increasing in recent years, generally at the expense of the agriculture, forestry and fishing sector, with the manufacturing sector, notwithstanding the inclusion of the building sub-sector, remaining fairly constant (see Chapter 8). In addition, the value of services to Ireland's trading position is indicated by the likelihood that the value of exports of services from Ireland will exceed the value of exports of goods, or merchandise, from Ireland within the next few years.

The importance of domestic microeconomic policy is increasingly recognised within Ireland. This is partly because of the recognition that the scope for an activist approach to domestic macroeconomic policy has been reduced by the increased role of the EU in monetary and fiscal policies. For example, the adoption of the euro has reduced Ireland's direct and immediate influence over interest rates and exchange rates, while the Stability and Growth Pact imposes significant constraints on domestic budgetary policy (see Chapter 4). However, there has also been an increased realisation that domestic microeconomic policy decisions in their own right can have significant effects, even macroeconomic effects, on the economy. Within the context of microeconomic policies, this chapter focuses particular attention on competition and regulatory policies.

Nature of Services

Products encompass goods and services, both of which provide utility (i.e. satisfaction or happiness) to the consumer. Goods are characterised as being transferable and storable, while services are characterised by their non-transferable and non-storable nature. In general, the consumption of services occurs simultaneously with their production; the services provided by a hair stylist or a tax adviser provide standard examples, although the associated sense of pleasure or displeasure with both of these services can of course live on for a considerable period of time post-production/consumption. In practice, it is often rather difficult to draw exact boundaries between the provision of a good and the provision of a service. A bar or restaurant provides a good (i.e. drink or food) but also, and simultaneously, provides a service (e.g. a certain atmosphere or environment). These two products can be separated into a good and a service, but probably only at a conceptual level. As another example, consider the so-called public utilities such as electricity, telecommunications and water. All of these products are generally classified as being services, notwithstanding the fact that (tap or faucet) water is, at least to some extent, both transferable and storable; indeed, bottled water is classified as a good. More generally, it is becoming increasingly common for the provision of a service to be embedded within the provision of a good. The purchase of a durable product (e.g. software, photocopier), perhaps sold at a small profit or even at a loss, often comes tied to the purchase of an associated servicing contract. Examples of products that are classified unambiguously as services include consulting, child care, contact (or call) centres, gardening, carpentry, arbitration or mediation, teaching, cinema and theatre, laundry, catering and information services (such as data processing and software development).

It can sometimes be useful to distinguish between business services (e.g. software development), consumer services (e.g. hotels and entertainment) and distributive services (e.g. transport and retail/wholesale distribution). Another distinction, and one that is important for the purpose of this chapter, is often drawn between internationally traded services and non-internationally traded services. Certain categories of financial services and tourism provide examples of internationally traded services, e.g. fund management within the Irish Financial Services Centre (IFSC), while the services provided by wholesalers and retailers, as well as the advice and other services provided by doctors, pharmacists, solicitors, bankers, lecturers in economics, etc. to consumers in Ireland constitute, in general, non-internationally traded services. While globalisation implies that some non-internationally traded services may well become internationally traded over time, e.g. Internet or mail-order pharmacy or the purchasing of health services abroad by, or on behalf of, Irish customers, it is also noteworthy that some aspects of what may appear to be internationally traded services are (at least currently) non-internationally traded, e.g. the provision of specific (retail) banking services such as current or checking accounts and residential mortgages.

Policy Dimension
The importance of competition and regulatory policies is felt throughout all sectors of the economy. Within the agriculture, forestry and fishing sector, for example, the

Competition Authority ('the Authority') has in recent years both restricted and facilitated Coillte's (the state-owned forestry company) ability to vertically integrate (i.e. merge); the proposed acquisition of Balcas by Coillte was rejected by the Authority (and the relevant Minister) in 1998 while the proposed acquisition of Weyerhaeuser by Coillte was approved by the Authority in 2006. In addition, various difficulties and delays with respect to the implementation in Ireland of the EU Nitrates Directive, which imposes limits on the amount of nitrogen (e.g. from animal manure/fertiliser) that can be used in farming so as to limit water pollution, highlight the specific importance of regulatory policies to the agriculture sector.

Within the manufacturing sector, it is generally understood that policies with respect to corporation taxes and grants have been responsible for the location of many foreign-owned manufacturing plants in Ireland, for example in the healthcare products and pharmaceutical sub-sectors (see Chapter 8). However, the exact details of these domestic microeconomic policies are, in turn, heavily influenced by EU competition and regulatory policies with respect to, for example, state aids. Indeed, international pressures effectively forced the Irish government to widen the scope of the low corporation tax on the manufacturing and internationally traded services sectors of the economy to all sectors of the economy.

Within the services sector of the economy itself, the potential if not actual importance of competition policy is witnessed by the Authority's recent investigations or studies into certain providers of professional services (e.g. solicitors and barristers) and various insurance and retail-banking markets (e.g. services provided to current account holders and to small companies). In addition, the importance of regulatory polices to the services sector is highlighted by ongoing discussions with respect to the appropriate regulation of both retail and investment banking (e.g. Northern Rock and Bear Stearns, respectively) as well as the appropriate regulation of alcohol sales, both on-trade and off-trade.

Chapter Outline
Section 2 addresses the importance of the services sector to the Irish economy while Section 3 reviews the economic principles that underlie competition policy and provides an overview of European Union and Irish competition law. Section 4 reviews regulatory policy, encompassing both a broad (i.e. regulation of economic and social activities) and a narrow (i.e. regulation of natural monopoly) perspective. Section 4 also reviews Ireland's ongoing regulatory reform experience. Section 5 provides examples of the application of competition and regulatory policies in Ireland, particularly in the services sector, and considers the likely impact of the EU Services Directive. Section 6 offers some concluding comments.

2 THE SERVICES SECTOR

As previously indicated, economic services are essentially characterised by their non-tradeable and non-storable nature, and their growing importance should not be underestimated.[1]

Value Added and Employment

Table 9.1 highlights the importance of the services sector to the economy in terms of the value of output produced, while Table 9.2 focuses attention on the specific importance of the services sector for employment in Ireland.[2] In terms of the total value of output produced in the economy, the importance of the manufacturing or industrial (including building) sector has remained fairly constant since 1991 at approximately 35 per cent, with reduced activity in the agriculture, forestry and fishing sector (down by six percentage points) being offset by increased activity in the services sector (up by over six percentage points). In absolute terms, the services sector accounted for approximately €95 billion of the total gross value added of Irish output at factor cost in 2006, up from approximately €19 billion in 1991.

Table 9.1

Gross Value Added at Factor Cost by Sector of Origin (%)

	1991	2006
Agriculture, forestry and fishing	8.5	2.5
Industry (including building)	35.2	35.1
Services	56.3	62.5

Source: CSO, *National Income and Expenditure*, Stationery Office, Dublin 2000 and 2007, Table 3.

Notwithstanding the above figures, it is noteworthy that the role of the services sector in terms of national output in Ireland is relatively low by EU standards: the services sector accounts for over 70 per cent of EU output. This is due to a combination of the historical importance of the agricultural sector in Ireland and the policy emphasis that was, and continues to be, placed on the manufacturing sector since the 1960s, as well as the more recent boom in residential building, and construction more generally, that has occurred in Ireland. Construction currently accounts for approximately 20 to 25 per cent of the industry sector. Indeed, given that the Irish residential building boom was at its highest in 2006, the above figures over-estimate the importance of the industry (including building) sector, and consequently underestimate the importance of the services sector, to the Irish economy.

In terms of total employment, the relative importance of the industrial and building sector has remained fairly constant since 1991 at approximately 27.5 per cent, with the reduced role of the agriculture, forestry and fishing sector (down by over eight percentage points to 5.5 per cent) being more than offset by the increased importance of the services sector (up by over nine percentage points to over 67 per cent). In absolute terms, the numbers employed in the services sector have increased from approximately 675,000 in 1991 to approximately 1.4 million in 2007.

Again, the figure for industry (including building) for 2007 has been inflated to some extent by the recent residential building boom which only started to ease off in the early part of 2007. For comparison purposes, and using Eurostat data, it is noteworthy that Ireland's employment figures by sector are closer to the equivalent figures for the EU-27 (approximately 6.2 per cent, 25.0 per cent and 68.8 per cent for agriculture, industry and services, respectively) than they are to the equivalent figures for the EU-15 (approximately 3.6 per cent, 23.7 per cent and 72.6 per cent for agriculture, industry and services, respectively).

Table 9.2

Persons at Work in the Main Branches of Economic Activity (%)

	1991	2007
Agriculture, forestry and fishing	13.8	5.5
Industry (including building)	28.1	27.3
Services	58.1	67.2

Sources: CSO, *Quarterly National Household Survey*, Stationery Office, Dublin 2008, Table 3; and CSO, *Labour Force Survey*, Stationery Office, Dublin 2004.

Of the total of approximately 1.4 million employed within the services sector in Ireland, the most important services sub-sectors (in terms of employment) are education and health (354,100), wholesale and retail trade (291,300), financial and other business services (272,700), hotels and restaurants (120,100), transport, storage and communication (123,400) and public administration and defence (105,600). Table 9.3 distinguishes between public services. Approximately 340,000, equivalent to 25 per cent of the services workforce, are employed in the public sector, which encompasses both public services and the commercial state-sponsored bodies (e.g. ESB).

Table 9.3

Public Sector Employment 2007[1]

Department	Numbers Employed
Civil service	37,200
Police	14,115
Defence	11,369
Education	85,777
Non-commercial state-sponsored bodies	12,013
Health services	107,500
Local authorities	34,567
Total public service	*302,541*
Commercial state-sponsored bodies	*39,003*
Public sector	*341,544*

Source: Department of Finance, *Budgetary and Economic Statistics*, Stationery Office, Dublin 2007, Table 57.
[1] Estimates.

Forfás figures, which separate industry (including building) into manufacturing and construction, for the sources of employment growth in Ireland over the period 2000 to 2006, highlight the particular importance of public services such as education and health (approximate 160,000 increase), domestic market services (approximate 60,000 increase), international services (approximate 40,000 increase) and construction (approximate 100,000 increase) compared with agriculture (approximate 10,000 decrease) and manufacturing (approximate 20,000 decrease).

In general, and particularly within the context of the services sector, the output of the public sector is not priced, particularly if general taxation and rationing mechanisms (e.g. hospital beds in A&E units) are not viewed as being proxies for prices, and as such public services are often referred to as non-market services. The output of the private sector is priced, so privately provided services are often referred to as market services. The boundaries of this distinction are increasingly blurred by service charges (e.g. bin charges levied by local authorities as well as by their private sector counterparts/competitors) and by increased contracting out by the public sector (e.g. public health services being provided by private health providers). As such, distinctions between the so-called public and private sectors are becoming somewhat less pronounced.

In addition, the issue of non-marketed, non-priced and non-measured services should also be considered carefully from a policy perspective. For example, housework, childcare and other types of care, that take place outside the domain of the standard market place (either formally/legally within partnerships or informally/illegally within the so-called shadow economy) contribute greatly to the well-being of society and suggest that the contribution of services to the Irish economy is being significantly under-reported and hence under-valued. Indeed, some of the measured increases in output and employment in recent years in Ireland is accounted for by many of these services becoming increasingly marketed. For example, the location of childcare, and care more generally, has to some extent moved from within the (in general, non-priced) household to within (priced) crèches and private nursing homes.

International Role and Policy Importance

Historically, the three sectors of the economy, agriculture, industry or manufacturing, and services, have been regarded, and treated, very differently from a policy perspective. The agricultural and manufacturing sectors were perceived as producing something tangible, being productive and hence important, while the output of the services sector was seen as being somewhat frivolous, non-productive and hence relatively unimportant. The manufacturing sector is still often viewed as being particularly dynamic (e.g. the information and communications technology (ICT), pharmaceutical and chemical sub-sectors), while the services sector is still sometimes viewed as being somewhat of a burden in Ireland, particularly in the context of a discussion of the relative merits of imports and exports.

Balance of Payments: Current Account

From an international trade perspective (see Table 9.4), the manufacturing sector is viewed as 'contributing' very significantly to a large merchandise (i.e. goods) surplus (with the vast majority of the value of merchandise imports and exports being accounted for by manufacturing, as opposed to agricultural, goods), while the services sector (broken down by Eurostat to include: (1) travel, e.g. goods and services acquired by tourists/travellers; and (2) other services, e.g. transportation services, communications, construction, insurance, financial, computer and information, royalties and licence fees and other professional services) is viewed as being responsible for a fairly large trading deficit.

Table 9.4

Balance of International Payments Current
Account Balances (€ million) 2007

	Credit/Exports	Debit/Imports	Surplus (Deficit)
Merchandise ('external trade')	84,311	61,433	22,878
Services	64,770	68,733	(3,963)
Tourism and travel	*4,470*	*6,318*	*(1,848)*
Other services	*60,300*	*62,415*	*(2,115)*

Source: CSO, *Balance of International Payments*, Stationery Office, Dublin 2008, Table 2a.

When income (e.g. with respect to non-resident employees and investment income on external assets and liabilities) and current transfers (e.g. workers' remittances) are incorporated, Ireland's deficit on the current account in 2007 was €9,274m, equivalent to approximately 6.1 per cent of GNP. With respect to the relative importance of goods and services in the current account balance, no other EU-27 country, relative to its GDP, has such a high surplus on goods or such a high deficit on services. However, it should also be noted that the goods or merchandise (or so-called 'external trade') surplus has fallen (even when expressed in current value terms) since 2000 and that the services deficit has fallen very substantially since 2000, i.e. services are becoming much more important with respect to Ireland's current account balance. Indeed, the National Competitiveness Council in its *Annual Report on Competitiveness 2007* noted that by 2006 earnings from services represented approximated 27 per cent of total foreign earnings, up from approximately 16 per cent in 2000.

In Ireland, from the 1960s until relatively recently, this somewhat anti-services perspective, and, in particular, the importance attached to exports, manifested itself in differential tax treatment across sectors. The manufacturing sector (as well as the internationally traded services sector) benefited from a ten per cent corporation tax rate, while the non-internationally traded services sector was taxed at rates of well over 30 per cent for many years (see Chapter 4). The process of increasing European integration, however, forced Irish policymakers to impose a uniform tax rate (currently set at 12.5 per cent) on all sectors in 2003. Grant aid reinforced this discrimination against the services sector with the availability of state aid often being linked to the recipient's likely ability to generate a significant growth in sales, i.e. in practice, implying the need for foreign sales, although it should be acknowledged that state aid was also often granted against the backdrop of attempting to attract foreign investment to Ireland in an environment of high unemployment.

Internationally Traded Services

The Enterprise Strategy Group's Report (July 2004) provides an illustration of the importance of the internationally traded services sector in Ireland. Given the shift towards services as being the primary driver of future economic growth, it is argued that activities complementary to actual manufacturing will become increasingly important in Ireland. In the past, the supply-driven model of manufacturing focused on the production of essentially uniform goods at a competitive price. In the future, the demand-driven model of manufacturing will require that goods (and services) be produced to customers' specific needs. Services will become embedded within the manufacturing process as firms are forced to provide specific solutions to customers' specific requirements. As such, R&D, innovation and sales and marketing will become as important as the actual manufacturing process itself. Specific solutions will, in general, be composed of a good (or service) being complemented by the delivery of ongoing services. This embedding of services within manufacturing is being facilitated by advances in information and communications technology (ICT). (See Chapter 8 for further discussion.)

Non-Internationally Traded Services

It has become increasingly clear that the role of the non-internationally traded services sector is vital for the performance of the whole economy. Firms in the internationally traded sectors depend on the non-internationally traded services sector for many of their essential inputs. For example, all firms, as well as all final consumers, depend on energy (e.g. petroleum products) as well as on communications and transport services. Inefficiencies in the non-internationally traded services sector cause inefficiencies in the internationally traded sectors. In particular, without appropriate policy intervention, firms in the non-internationally traded services sector may be operating in less than competitive environments where inefficiencies can be tolerated and to some extent passed on to customers and ultimately final consumers. In contrast, Irish exporters are in general forced by the presence of international competitors to be competitive while importers in general impose a competitive restraint on Irish-based firms operating in the traded sector.

Within the non-internationally traded services sector, as previously indicated, there has been a distinction drawn between services provided by the private sector, referred to as market services, and services provided by the public sector, referred to as non-market services. Retailing provides an example of the former, while the provision of health and education services provides a standard example of the latter. However, and as previously indicated, the increasing importance of private health insurance, various examples of private education services, the increased usage of various forms of contracting out by the public sector (e.g. administration of the National Car Test (NCT), operation of toll bridges or, more generally, public-private partnerships (PPPs) as well as the possible competitive tendering out of household waste collection services) continues to blur this distinction between market and non-market services (see Chapter 8 for further discussion).

The National Competitiveness Council's *Annual Competitiveness Report 2007* provides an illustration of the growing importance and influence of the non-internationally traded services sector in Ireland. Against the backdrop of Ireland's recently declining competitiveness performance, three main areas of policy concern are highlighted. First, Ireland's recent economic growth was export-led and underpinned by productivity increases. More recently, economic growth has been driven by the construction and public services sectors and has been underpinned by increasing employment, as opposed to increasing productivity. The long-term sustainability of this type of domestically driven growth is questioned. Second, Ireland's price and cost environment has been and remains unfavourable relative to its EU partners. With respect to prices, for example, Ireland is second, behind Denmark, with respect to cost of living. With respect to costs, Ireland performs poorly compared with its trading partners with respect to both pay and non-pay costs. In particular, Ireland performs very poorly with respect to pay in the so-called sheltered sectors of the economy and with respect to non-pay costs in the domestic services sector. Third, and notwithstanding significant amounts of recent public investment, Ireland performs poorly with respect to physical infrastructure, which encompasses transport, energy and information and communications technology (see Chapter 8). All three of these concerns highlight the links between the importance of the non-internationally traded services sector and the need for appropriate competition and regulatory policies.

3 COMPETITION POLICY

The most important economic concept in the area of competition policy is market power and, in particular, significant market power. From the perspective of an individual firm, the presence of significant market power indicates the ability of the firm to raise price significantly above the cost of production. In contrast, the absence of significant market power indicates the presence of a competitive market, and the role of a suitably designed competition policy is to encourage the existence of competitive markets by discouraging the conditions that give rise to the presence of significant market power.[3]

Perfect Competition, Monopoly and Contestable Markets
There are three market structures that are particularly important for an understanding of the economics of competition policy: perfect competition,

monopoly and contestable markets. Perfectly competitive markets have the characteristic of being allocatively efficient, as firms are forced by the pursuit of their own self-interests to price at marginal cost, i.e. $P = MC$. This equality, between price and marginal cost, is regarded as being highly desirable as price represents the economic value placed by society on the marginal or last unit of the product produced, while marginal cost represents the economic cost to society of producing that marginal unit. The primary disadvantage of a (profit-maximising) monopoly is that the monopolist produces a level of output at which price is greater than marginal cost $(P > MC)$, i.e. the monopolist produces too little when viewed from society's perspective. Perfectly competitive markets are also characterised as being productively efficient, as, in the long run, no firm could survive without producing at the lowest point on its average cost curve. In contrast, monopolists restrict output below the technically most productive level in order to raise price. In addition, the monopolist's costs may be higher than the equivalent competitive firm's costs, simply because the monopolist can afford to be at least somewhat inefficient. Finally, it is argued that the monopolist's excess (i.e. above normal) profits do not just represent a transfer from consumer to producer, as profit-seeking (or rent-seeking, as it is generally referred to) activities dissipate these profits over time. In particular, prior to the creation of the monopoly (e.g. markets for various mobile telephony or broadcasting services), firms will involve themselves in socially unproductive activities in order to increase their chances of being the chosen monopolist, while once the monopoly is created, the incumbent will involve itself in unproductive activities, when viewed from society's perspective, in order to sustain its monopoly position.[4]

Notwithstanding the strength of the above arguments against monopoly, there are also arguments in favour of monopoly. First, some economists and other social scientists view monopoly's excess profits as the short-term reward necessary for sustaining the competitive process in the long term. Firms that enter the process of creative destruction that underlies the competitive process are motivated, it is claimed, by the possibility of being a monopolist, albeit only temporarily. Second, it is argued that a monopolistic market structure is more conducive to the pursuit of innovation and research and development which require significant levels of up-front and risky investments. Perfectly competitive firms, it is argued, would not have the level of retained profits required to undertake such activities. Third, in the presence of significant economies of scale, it may be appropriate to place a limit on the number of firms allowed to enter a market; in the extreme case of a natural monopoly (see Section 4 for further details), the appropriate number is one. This latter argument arises continuously in policy debates both at Irish and EU level. For example, in the context of the Irish agri-food sector (e.g. meat processing), it is argued that competition law should be 'clarified' to allow consolidations (i.e. mergers) that are motivated and justified by the need for scale.

More generally, the competitive process is facilitated by the presence of effective and potential competition. Effective competition focuses particular attention on a number of issues, including the degree of inter-brand and intra-brand competition between firms within a particular market. Inter-brand competition refers to competition between sellers of different brands within a given market (e.g. different brands of beer), while intra-brand competition refers to competition between sellers of the same brand (e.g. different pubs or off-licences selling, say, Guinness stout). Potential competition focuses attention on the ability of potential entrants to dissuade incumbent firms from attempting to take advantage of, or abusing, their market position. In the extreme case of a perfectly contestable market, potential competition can simulate perfect competition, even in an apparent monopoly situation. The incumbent firm is forced to price at marginal cost, as any divergence between marginal cost and price would allow an equally efficient entrant to enter with a price below the incumbent's price but above marginal cost and exit when the incumbent reduces its price towards marginal cost. It is claimed that competing on a specific airline route provides such an example, as the entrant's plane and other investments can be withdrawn and used elsewhere at little additional cost. In contrast, it would be difficult for an entrant to withdraw, without incurring substantial sunk costs, after attempting to compete with respect to the provision of a rail network or an electricity grid, for example.

Market Power: Economic Issues
Notwithstanding the core importance of the concept of significant market power to the economics and law of competition policy, there is no generally agreed-upon measure of significant market power and, in practice, economists and more importantly the courts have to proceed on a case-by-case basis.

Own-Price Elasticity of Demand
For example, it seems plausible that the existence, or otherwise, of significant market power could be identified by a close inspection of data on a firm's own-price elasticity of demand. A firm's own-price elasticity of demand measures the percentage decrease (increase) in demand that would follow from a percentage increase (decrease) in the price of the firm's product. Indeed, a low own-price elasticity of demand (in absolute terms) would signal the possession of significant market power as the firm has the ability to significantly increase price without losing significant market share. However, a high own-price elasticity of demand (in absolute terms) does not necessarily imply the absence of significant market power. Such a result would signal that the firm is not able to profitably increase price beyond its current level; it would not, however, signal that the firm has not already increased price significantly above the cost of production. As such, the firm's own-price elasticity of demand does not in general provide definitive evidence with respect to the absence of market power. Typical indicators for competition authorities and courts of the presence or absence of market power include data and information on market shares and market concentration, entry barriers and the competitive environment within the market.

Market Definition

The relevant market, for competition policy purposes, is thought of as representing the minimum set of products over which a (hypothetical) firm would have to have monopoly control before it could be sure of exercising a given degree of market power. In practice, this 'given degree of market power' is perceived of as the ability to profitably raise prices by five or ten per cent above competitive levels for a significant period of time (say, a year). For example, a proposed banana market might be rejected under this test if it can be shown or successfully argued that a sufficient proportion of consumers would switch to other fruits if banana prices increased significantly. In contrast, perhaps a proposed fruit market would be accepted under this test. Significant market power, in turn, is thought of as a position of economic strength enjoyed by a firm that enables it to hinder the maintenance of effective competition on the relevant market by allowing it to behave to an appreciable extent independently of competitors and ultimately of consumers. For example, and as a general rule, a firm with a market share below 40 per cent would not be expected to possess significant market power. It is clear from the insights offered by the new industrial economics (i.e. game theory) and empirical industrial organisation (i.e. applied econometrics in the field of industrial economics) approaches that necessary conditions for the existence of significant market power are the existence of both high market concentration and high barriers to entry.

Market Concentration

Competition authorities have adopted the Herfindahl Hirschman Index (HHI) for the purpose of measuring market concentration. The HHI is defined as the sum of the squared percentage shares of all firms of the relevant variable (e.g. volume or value of sales) in the market. As such, the HHI varies between zero (corresponding to a market with an infinite number of infinitesimally small firms) and 10,000 (corresponding to a market with a single firm, i.e. a pure monopoly). For example, a market consisting of only two equally sized firms would have an HHI of 5,000 ($= 50^2 + 50^2$) whereas a market consisting of five equally sized firms would have an HHI of 2,000. A market with an HHI below 1,000 is generally regarded as a non-concentrated market and, as such, as a market in which market power or competition policy issues are unlikely to arise. In contrast, a market with an HHI above a level of approximately 1,800 to 2,000 is generally regarded as a concentrated market and, as such, as a market in which market power issues may arise.[5] Interactions between market definition and market concentration are crucial with respect to possible competition policy implications. For example, a proposed stout and lager market in Ireland would see Diageo (i.e. Guinness) with a market share below 60 per cent, whereas a proposed stout market in Ireland would increase Diageo's market share to over 85 per cent.

Barriers to Entry

Without entry barriers, any attempt by an incumbent firm to abuse an apparent position of significant market power would attract entry by other firms. The so-called *Chicago School* view entry barriers as being restricted to 'costs that must be borne by an entrant that were not incurred by established firms'. In the extreme, Chicago economists only accept restrictive licensing schemes as being valid examples of entry barriers. In contrast, the so-called *Harvard School* has a much broader definition of entry barriers in mind, 'factors that enable established firms to earn supra-competitive profits without threat of entry'.[6] Economies of scale, excess capacity, lower average costs as a result of experience (i.e. learning-by-doing), brand proliferation, restrictive distributional agreements and product differentiation (perhaps as a result of excessive advertising) represent some of the major examples of entry barriers as justified by this broader definition. In practice, competition authorities and courts appear to feel most comfortable with the approach of the so-called Chicago School towards the formal definition of a barrier to entry, but with the approach of the so-called Harvard School in terms of actually deciding whether or not a specific market feature represents a barrier to entry. In addition, competition authorities and courts appear to distinguish between exogenous or natural barriers to entry (e.g. economies of scale), which tend to arise as a result of the incumbent firm attempting to lower its own costs of production, and endogenous or strategic barriers to entry (e.g. some exclusivity agreements), which tend to arise as a result of the incumbent firm attempting to increase potential entrants' costs.

The Competitive Environment

High market concentration and high barriers to entry are necessary, but not sufficient, conditions for the existence of significant market power. In particular, the existence, or otherwise, of a competitive environment within a market must also be considered. In this regard, economists distinguish between unilateral price effects concerns, which arise particularly in differentiated product markets, perhaps in the context of a proposed merger, and co-ordinated price effects concerns, which arise particularly in homogenous product markets. Unilateral price effects arise where it is in the joint interests of two merging firms to increase their prices, even if their competitors' prices remained constant, i.e. the firms produce relatively close substitutes. A proposed merger of Bank of Ireland and Allied Irish Bank appears to provide a useful hypothetical example. Co-ordinated price effects arise where conditions exist that tend to dampen price competition between all competitors. When reviewing the issue of co-ordinated price effects within a market, the relevant competition authority examines the market for the presence, or absence, of the following features (whose presence would tend to be supportive of tacit collusion): symmetry in market shares; stability in market shares; homogeneity of product and/or firm structure; transparency with respect to trading conditions (and, in particular, transparency with respect to prices), low price elasticity of demand (signalling the absence of a strong temptation to 'cheat', i.e. increase output and lower price); the non-existence of maverick firms; the non-existence of strong buyers; and the non-existence of excess capacity.

Example: Office Supplies Superstores

Notwithstanding the previously mentioned general shortage of suitable data (e.g. price elasticities) for the purpose of ascertaining directly whether or not significant market power exists, competition authorities have recently encouraged the appropriate interrogation of what data may be available in case useful inferences, either positive or negative, can be drawn with respect to the appropriate market definition and the presence, or absence, of significant market power. The most cited case in this regard is the proposed merger of Staples and Office Depot (USA, 1997), where the crucial issue was whether or not, from a competition policy perspective, the three largest office supplies superstores (Staples, Office Depot and OfficeMax) were in a separate product market from the very many remaining relatively small office supplies stores.[7] On the basis of a detailed examination of prices and other data across different geographical locations in which different numbers of office supplies stores were present, the USA Federal Trade Commission was satisfied, as ultimately was the relevant court, that the three office supplies superstores were in a distinct office supplies (superstores) market from the much smaller office supplies stores. Crucially, using a large volume of retailer scanner data across both geography and time, the Federal Trade Commission demonstrated that product prices were significantly higher (all other factors, e.g. wages, land prices and local incomes, held constant) in geographical locations in which fewer than the three largest office supplies stores were present, but were not influenced by the presence, or absence, of the much smaller office supplies stores. As such, econometric interrogation of the data facilitated the drawing of two strong conclusions: (1) the appropriate product market consisted of various services provided by office supplies superstores; and (2) a decrease in the number of superstores from three to two would be expected to significantly increase prices. It must be emphasised, however, that the data interrogation exercise facilitated, as opposed to negated the need for, the examination of data and information on market concentration, barriers to entry and the competitive environment, e.g. from the relevant firms' internal documentation.

Market Power: Legal Issues

Although economists are in general agreement with respect to the use of the above indicators, there is much disagreement with respect to their actual implementation. Witness, for example, the teams of competition economists that have been involved in all sides of the Microsoft cases both in the EU and the USA. In addition, it is ultimately the courts, via the interpretation of competition law, that almost inevitably decide matters of particular importance to competition economists.

Competition law addresses a number of specific concerns. First, and most important, anti-competitive agreements between firms (e.g. price-fixing or market-sharing agreements), are prohibited. In this regard, the courts generally distinguish between horizontal agreements (i.e. agreements between firms at the

247

same level of the production and distribution chain) and vertical agreements (i.e. agreements between firms at different levels of the production and distribution chain). Horizontal agreements are generally discouraged, as the effect of such agreements is to dampen competition, at the almost inevitable expense of final consumers; allowance is made for considering certain classes of potentially beneficial, or pro-competitive, agreements (e.g. research and development joint ventures). In contrast, vertical agreements are treated on a case-by-case basis, as an agreement between, say, a manufacturer and a retailer that enhances the efficiency of their relationship does not necessarily come at the expense of final consumers. Indeed, it may benefit final consumers. For example, service stations are generally restricted to supplying only one brand of motor fuel to their customers. As such, the service station and its customers are restricted with respect to choice, but the distributor will generally have to offer suitable inducements to the service station that may compensate for this, e.g. a lower wholesale price and/or support for improved facilities at the service station, both of which would likely benefit final consumers.

Second, the anti-competitive creation of a position of market power, or what is formally referred to as a dominant position, as well as the abuse of any existing market power (e.g. excessively high prices) is also prohibited via abuse of market power or dominance legislation. Third, competition law also contains a proactive approach to proposed mergers, acquisitions or takeovers, as a reactive approach would require the equivalent of an unscrambling of eggs.

EU Competition Law
EU competition law takes precedence over national competition law, provided that there is a significant effect on inter-state trade. This can be of huge practical and political significance as EU competition law has not one but two policy goals: competition and the pursuit of the single market. Article 81 of the EU Treaty prohibits anti-competitive agreements (e.g. a price-fixing cartel) while Article 82 prohibits abuse of a dominant position (e.g. predation, where an excessively low price, which is used to drive out competition, is expected to be followed by an excessively high price). Mergers with a sufficient 'Community Dimension' are dealt with under the EU Merger Regulation. Cross-border acquisitions are at least implicitly encouraged as they further integration and the pursuit of the single market; in contrast, individual member states may well be less supportive of cross-border acquisitions.

Article 86 of the EU Treaty limits the freedom of member states to intervene in the process of competition, through the actions of public undertakings (e.g. state-owned bodies) or private undertakings granted exclusive rights by member states. Under Article 86, the state has limited exemptions from the application of Article 82 (i.e. abuse of dominance) but only with respect to 'services of general economic interest'. The provision of the traditional postal service (i.e. daily delivery to all addresses) and the standard state pension system offer generally accepted examples of the application of this exemption. Under Articles 87–9 of the EU Treaty, member states are prohibited from granting state aid that would distort competition. As previously mentioned, the continued existence of a special low rate of corporation tax for manufacturing and internationally traded services in Ireland would have fallen foul of these rules on state aids. Any proposed Irish state 'assistance' for Waterford Crystal would also be very likely to come under very serious scrutiny under the EU rules on state aid.

The European Commission enforces EU competition rules, the Court of First Instance hears appeals against Commission competition decisions and the Court of Justice hears further appeals on points of law. However, in the pursuit of a policy of increased subsidiarity, national courts and/or member states' competition authorities have since May 2004 been allowed and encouraged to directly enforce Articles 81 and 82. The increased similarity between national competition laws and Community competition law facilitated this shift. However, it seems inevitable that various practical difficulties will arise with up to 28 different entities (27 member states and the Commission) having rights of interpretation and enforcement of EU competition law.

Irish Competition Law

The Competition Act 1991 introduced a prohibition-based system of competition law to Ireland. Anti-competitive agreements between undertakings (firms) and restrictive trade practices are prohibited under Section 4 and the abuse of a dominant position is prohibited under Section 5. The Competition Authority was established under the Act to play a supportive and advisory role; it had no enforcement powers. However, the passing into legislation of the Competition (Amendment) Bill 1996 represented a significant change in emphasis. The primary aim of this legislation was to provide more effective enforcement of competition policy in Ireland. For example, it became a criminal offence not to comply with the conditions of a licence granted by the Authority. This Act also criminalised certain anti-competitive behaviour and allowed for prison sentences of up to two years and fines of up to ten per cent of a firm's worldwide annual turnover. New powers of search and greater rights of discovery, including the right to conduct a 'dawn raid', were granted to the Competition Authority, along with the ability to initiate prosecutions, both civil and criminal. The Competition Act 2002 transferred responsibility for mergers to the Authority, increased the search powers of the Authority and increased the penalties for business executives in hardcore anti-competitive (e.g. price-fixing cartel) cases. As previously indicated, the Competition Authority's powers are particularly important with respect to activities that do not affect inter-state trade within the EU. However, the Competition Authority also has jurisdictional rights with respect to activities within the EU which affect inter-state trade but which also have a particular effect within Ireland. For example, Heineken's proposed acquisition of Beamish & Crawford was referred back to the Irish Competition Authority by the European Commission. In contrast, Ryanair's proposed acquisition of Aer Lingus was not referred back to the Irish Competition Authority.

4 REGULATORY POLICY

Regulation can be defined as the exercise of control by a public agency over economic and social activities.[8] A set of formal rules, for example with respect to health and safety in the workplace, is an example of regulation, as is the imposition of financial incentives such as taxes and subsidies (e.g. a carbon tax) that aim to alter behaviour or the provision of informational requirements (e.g. with respect to whether or not the seller of a financial product is a tied agent) that aim to inform decisions. At a general level, regulation can be seen as being restrictive and/or facilitating. A regulation limiting the practice of cold calling at home between 9am and 9pm Monday to Saturday is restrictive, at least to the potential seller, while regulations with respect to the various possible uses of the radio frequency spectrum is enabling to both the producer (e.g. a TV broadcaster) and the user (e.g. a mobile telecommunications consumer). Regulations with respect to driving on the left-hand side of the road or with respect to imposing limits on speed and drink-driving are generally regarded as being facilitating notwithstanding their restrictive dimensions. The rest of this section provides an overview of regulation, focuses on the various theories of, and justifications for, regulation; reviews the application of regulation policies to natural monopolies; and addresses the topic of regulatory policy and reform.

Theories of Regulation
There are a number of overlapping theories of regulation. From an economics perspective, it is tempting to focus particular attention upon the distinction between the public-interest approach on the one hand and the interest-group and private-interest approaches on the other hand. The public-interest approach to regulation highlights the claimed equivalence between the regulator's interests and the public interest. As such, the regulator may be said in a sense to be disinterested; the public interest is somehow ascertained (say, with respect to food safety), and the regulator acts in a purely technical manner so as to achieve the desired end-state. In particular, there is no allowance made for any underlying power struggle between, say, the regulated parties (e.g. producers and sellers of food) and the parties for whose benefit the regulations are being put in place (e.g. consumers of food). In contrast, the interest-group and private-interest approaches allow for the private incentives of groups and individuals, respectively. Within the interest-group approach, attention is focused on the relationships between groups and the state. Within the context of these evolving relationships a competition or battle is seen to take place between various different conceptualisations of what is the public interest. Corporatism, for example, can be seen as the process or as the result within this interest-group approach; from an Irish perspective, the evolution of social partnership could be analysed from this perspective. The private-interest approach, often referred to as economic theory of regulation or public choice, goes further and insists that the individual incentives confronting each (rational economic) actor must be considered if regulation is to be understood. For

example, it is claimed that regulatory capture, a process in which regulators over time appear to begin to represent the interests of the regulated, as opposed to society more generally, can only be understood if particular attention is paid to the incentives of the employees of regulatory agencies. It is these employees who interact with, and begin to depend upon, the regulated entities. From the public choice perspective, unless particular safeguards are put in place, it is hardly surprising that implicit understandings between these individuals and even their organisations begin to develop.

In addition to the above interest approaches to regulation, there are other approaches which can be considered on their own merits or in conjunction with the interest approaches. For example, at particular times in history, it is clear that the force of ideas can drive regulatory developments. At a macroeconomic level the Keynesian revolution could be viewed as a prime example of a shift in ideas with significant policy implications, while at a more microeconomic level (albeit one with macroeconomic consequences), there was a shift towards privatisation in the UK and deregulation and market liberalisation in the USA during the early 1980s. Of course, all theories of regulation must be confronted with, and tested against, actual regulatory experiences. For example, the public-interest perspective is hard to reconcile with the high prices that resulted from the air transport regulatory experience up until the late 1970s in the USA and later in Europe and elsewhere. In turn, however, the public choice perspective is itself difficult to reconcile with the actual deregulatory experiences of the 1980s and 1990s, which have reduced the power of at least some groups, unless of course, recourse to the force of ideas approach is added to the mix.

Regulatory Motivations

Under the assumption that the public-interest approach to regulation has some relevance, i.e. regulation is not driven by group or private interests alone, it is necessary to address the issue of the objective need and justification for specific regulations. It is useful to distinguish between two cases. First, specific sectoral regulation is required in the case of natural monopolies, i.e. situations in which competitive markets are not feasible. This represents an extreme form of market failure, in that the relevant market cannot function efficiently or at all without a significant level of regulation; the regulation of natural monopoly is considered separately below. Second, other (and milder) forms of market failure and/or the pursuit of various social objectives independently give rise to regulation. The need for regulation can be understood by considering some or all of the following: externalities, public goods, informational problems, universal service needs and (distributive) justice.

Externalities imply the existence of a divergence between private costs and benefits and social costs and benefits. Externalities, in particular, imply the presence of external and non-priced costs and/or benefits. Within the standard example of pollution – a negative production externality – a producer does not internalise the cost of the pollution that the production process imposes on others.

251

Various options exist with respect to the appropriate form of regulation in the presence of externalities, for example command-and-control (e.g. no smoking indoors in public places), production and/or consumption taxes (e.g. excise duties on motor fuels), pollution quotas, perhaps supported by tradeable permits (e.g. greenhouse gas emissions) or simply naming and shaming (e.g. tax evaders). In contrast to these measures, some market enthusiasts, referencing the Coase Theorem, highlight the need to specify property rights very clearly so as to facilitate negotiations and market-based transactions between affected parties. For example, if anglers have the right to clean water, anglers will be paid by the polluters for any pollution that the anglers choose to allow and if the polluters have the right to pollute the water, the anglers will pay the polluters so as to restrict the level of pollution to the appropriate level.[9] The presence of public goods can to some extent be equated with the presence of positive consumption externalities; for example, your consumption of the flu vaccine also decreases your friend's probability of catching the flu. Again, various regulatory responses to the market failure are feasible, ranging from provision of information to subsidising consumption of the flu vaccine to compulsory flu vaccination.

Many forms of regulation are responses to what are seen as *informational problems*. Markets, it is argued, in general under-provide relevant information. For example, what is the price of an advertised one cent airfare? How can one compare the costs of different loans? The latter question is addressed in the USA by the Truth in Lending Act (2001), which insists that all lenders must quote the annual percentage rate (APR) to potential borrowers; APRs can then be compared across different loan options. Various regulations surrounding information requirements insist that car manufacturers provide fuel efficiency information, brewers of beer provide alcohol content information, cigarette packets carry health warnings, food products carry nutritional information and league tables with respect to school performances are produced and published. In addition, various regulations insist upon what might be termed minimum standards, as opposed to just the provision of information, e.g. travel agencies and operators enter into various forms of travel bonds and retail banks must keep a certain proportion of their retail consumers' deposits in liquid assets.

From a *social policy perspective*, however, many regulations exist that cannot easily fit into the above market failures approach. For example, anti-discrimination legislation and minimum wage legislation are both vitally important forms of regulation that would be difficult to explain on market failure grounds alone. More generally, the taxation of windfall profits (e.g. via a land development tax) or the existence of universal service obligations with respect to say the provision of a fixed-line telephone (at reasonable cost) or a basic daily postal delivery service (at, technically speaking, no direct cost, at least to the recipient) can also be seen as addressing social policy, as opposed to narrowly defined economic policy, objectives. Finally, some regulations that are justified on social policy grounds actually operate against the market-failures approach to regulation. For example, some jurisdictions (e.g. Ireland) actively discourage the publication of school league tables and prohibit private health insurers from offering discounts to non-smokers; most jurisdictions mandate the wearing of safety belts by car drivers and passengers, participation in the social insurance system and regulations against prostitution, ticket touting and the use of so-called recreational drugs; and all jurisdictions mandate against the explicit existence of a market for votes in general elections and against explicit trading in vital organs (e.g. kidneys).

Regulation of Natural Monopoly

Competition policy complements the process of competition as it attempts to facilitate the market conditions that give rise to market outcomes associated with (perfectly) competitive markets. In contrast, regulatory policy, in the context of markets in which a natural monopoly exists, substitutes itself for at least part of the competitive process. A market is said to be a natural monopoly if its total output can be produced more cheaply by a single firm than by two or more firms.[10] The provision of a national electricity or natural gas grid, the provision of a railway network, the provision of a national daily delivery postal service and perhaps the provision of a national broadband network represent some of the standard examples of natural monopolies, many of which have been referred to as public utilities in the past. Other possible examples include the provision of a local, regional or national bus service or the provision of a local household waste collection service. A natural monopoly exists if there are very significant economies of scale. In such a case, an individual firm's marginal cost (MC) and average cost (AC) curves decline continuously and the firm's marginal cost (MC) curve will be below its average cost (AC) curve. The application of competition policy, in terms of attempting to increase the number of competitors, would be inefficient and ineffective. Assuming that the number of firms increased, the average cost of production would also increase, probably dramatically. In addition, it is not clear that firms would enter the market, given the underlying cost conditions.

Marginal/Average Cost Pricing

Regulators can apparently achieve allocative efficiency by insisting that the natural monopolist produces a level of output at which price is equal to marginal cost. There are, however, at least two problems with this proposed solution. First, the regulator may not have enough information to be able to determine the output level at which price would be equal to marginal cost and it would not necessarily be in the natural monopolist's interest to provide the regulator with the appropriate information. Second, if the natural monopolist produces the allocatively efficient level of output, it will sustain losses; pricing at marginal cost implies pricing below average cost as the marginal cost curve lies below the average cost curve in a natural monopoly. One possible solution to this latter problem is for the regulator to provide the natural monopolist with a subsidy to offset the losses associated with achieving allocative efficiency. However, these subsidies must be financed by increased taxation elsewhere, which, in turn, causes inefficiencies. It may also be difficult politically to be seen to provide a monopolist with a subsidy. Setting price at average cost, where the natural monopolist makes neither excess profits nor losses, avoids the problem of having to subsidise the natural monopolist, but at the expense of sacrificing allocative efficiency. Average-cost pricing regulation, however, suffers from the problem of dampening cost-reducing incentives. In practice, average-cost pricing is often adapted so as to encourage cost-reducing innovations by allowing scope for some 'excess' profits. This type of regulation, adjusted average-cost pricing, is referred to as rate of return regulation. More recently, regulators have adopted the so called CPI-X approach, where CPI represents the inflation rate as measured by the consumer price index and X represents the required decrease in real prices within the relevant market. For example, if X was three per cent and inflation was also three per cent, there would be no change in nominal prices but a three per cent decrease in real prices.[11]

Franchise Bidding
Rather than attempting to regulate the natural monopolist on an ongoing basis, it may be preferable to auction the right (franchise) to be the natural monopolist. The auction can be done on the basis of bidders committing to charging a certain price and providing a particular service to customers in the future. The results of this process are likely to be close to the results obtained by average-cost pricing regulation, as bidders would find themselves forced to offer lower and lower (quality-adjusted) prices until almost no net excess profits could be expected. A further possibility is for the auction to be done on the basis of a relatively large number of criteria; bidders would then compete on the basis of quality as well as price and other considerations. This latter possibility is referred to as a 'beauty contest'.

Public Ownership
Rather than the state attempting to regulate the natural monopolist, many governments, particularly within Europe, in the past simply elected to be the natural monopolist. In an Irish context, airport management, airline ownership, electricity, natural gas and transportation provide examples of state ownership of enterprise. The distinctive feature (and advantage or disadvantage depending on one's political perspective) of this approach is that the objective of the natural monopolist is no longer necessarily the maximisation of profits. Management of a public enterprise may be somewhat accountable to voters, usually indirectly via the relevant minister's responsibility for the public enterprise, and, as such, it is possible that the management's goal will be the maximisation of public interest, however defined. Opponents of state ownership of enterprises generally point to the so-called soft budget constraint, with management and workers, it is claimed, being united in their efforts to extract public funds for 'their' enterprises. However, EU restrictions on state aids to public-owned enterprises have removed at least some of the force of this argument.

Privatisation and Market Liberalisation

A movement away from public ownership and towards privatisation began in the early 1980s. The complementary experience in the USA in the late 1970s and early 1980s was one of market liberalisation or deregulation, e.g. in aviation, telecommunications and inter-state trucking. Within a European context, the UK government led by Margaret Thatcher was at the forefront of the privatisation movement, e.g. British Telecom (1984) and British Gas (1986). However, many of the large privatisations within the UK were subsequently followed up by the setting up of specialist independent regulatory agencies (e.g. Oftel, now Ofcom), as the process of competition failed to take off in industries that were still characterised by elements of natural monopolies. The lesson from the UK privatisation experience appears to be that the creation of market conditions conducive for competition is at least as important as the formal ownership structure.

Within an Irish context, the various regulatory agencies have ongoing important decisions to make with respect to pricing and investment decisions within the particular elements of markets that are naturally monopolistic, e.g. Commission for Energy Regulation (CER) and Commission for Aviation Regulation (CAR). In the context of a downstream natural monopoly (e.g. fixed-line telecommunications), the level of the resulting consumer price is highly visible, while in the context of an upstream natural monopoly (e.g. transportation of natural gas or electricity transmission), the level of the access price charged to downstream firms may be less politically sensitive, but still of crucial importance, particularly if the upstream firm itself also operates in various downstream markets. Regulation of prices may also be required in markets that are naturally oligopolistic and the natural number of firms is very low; the regulation of certain mobile telephony charges by ComReg provides an important example.

Ireland only relatively recently started the process of privatisation. After successfully selling its stake in Irish Life, the state privatised Telecom Éireann (later Eircom). Initially, the privatisation proved to be a political success as Eircom's share price increased by over 20 per cent above its flotation price. However, Eircom's share price then fell, and remained, for the rest of its relatively brief (initial) existence as a public limited company, considerably below its flotation price. From a narrow economics perspective, the success, or otherwise, of the privatisation of Eircom should be judged primarily by the effect of the privatisation on the process of competition within the Irish telecommunications market(s). However, from a political perspective, the evolution of Eircom's share price, combined with Ryanair's attempted acquisition of Aer Lingus only days after Aer Lingus's part-privatisation, are likely to have significant repercussions for future possible privatisations in Ireland, e.g. Voluntary Health Insurance.

Regulatory Policy

There has been an internationally based movement towards regulatory reform or what has been more generally referred to as 'better regulation' in recent years.

This movement has been spearheaded by the OECD (Regulatory Reform, 1997), embraced by the EU (EU Action Plan, 2002) and pursued by the UK (e.g. Better Regulation Task Force), Ireland (see www.BetterRegulation.ie) and many other countries. The following five general criteria or tenets of the better regulation movement are considered: legislative mandate; accountability and control; due process; expertise; and efficiency.

Legislative mandate refers to the need for the regime, agency or set of regulations to have a clear legislative mandate. Ideally it should be possible to judge the performance of regulations or agencies against expected results. However, it is also often both desirable and necessary to leave regulators some discretion, as technology, preferences, and interpretations evolve over time. Accountability and control refers to the agencies being under the control of some other democratic institution or at least being restrained by the exercise of some appropriate checks and balances, while due process refers to the need for the existence of fair and transparent procedures. For example, the decisions of many sectoral regulatory agencies in Ireland can be appealed to appeal tribunals and/or the courts. However, the existence of multiple forums for appeals can lead to somewhat wasteful duplication of expertise across different agencies, tribunals and courts as well as an increased level of uncertainty. Expertise refers to the need for the presence of the relevant expertise in the decision-making agency. Efficiency refers to the requirement that the regime be operated or implemented in the most cost-efficient and proportionate manner. Within the Irish context of better regulation, these high-level criteria are implemented in the context of a proposed regulatory initiative as: necessity; effectiveness (i.e. is it well-targeted?); proportionality (i.e. is there a better way of doing the same thing?); transparency; accountability; and consistency.

Proponents of improved regulation have in the past championed the increased usage of international best practice and benchmarking exercises. A best-practice approach to regulation aims to learn from the experiences of other jurisdictions but runs the risk of sample selection bias in that it may be very difficult to pinpoint the exact reasons why some type of regulations perform very well in certain countries. For example, increasing the minimum legal drinking age (e.g. from 18 to 21) may have worked well in some jurisdictions (e.g. in the USA in the late 1980s) but this does not necessarily mean that it would work well in Ireland at the present time. A benchmarking approach to regulation generally involves the setting of targets, perhaps in conjunction with associated rewards and penalties. However, a benchmarking exercise, when used in isolation, can be open to so-called creative compliance. For example, a commitment to reduce a waiting list for a specific operation by a certain date appears to benefit from being unambiguous. However, in the presence of such a commitment, a waiting list for a waiting list may evolve, with the length of the first waiting list being determined solely by the need to meet the formal commitment with respect to the length of the second (and benchmarked) waiting list.

Better regulation champions the use of evidence-based policymaking. In particular, better regulation highlights the need to assess fully all relevant costs, benefits and risks, and regulatory impact assessment (RIA) has become the desired toolkit of better regulation. RIA comes in many formats but it is possible to distinguish between an initial or partial RIA and a full RIA, with the former being conducted during the very early stage of the life of a proposed regulatory policy initiative and the latter only being conducted on proposals that have made it past the initial RIA filtering stage. In keeping with the better regulation criteria, an RIA in general aims to: clarify objectives; consider appropriate alternatives, including that of doing nothing; achieve efficiency; and maximise future compliance. An RIA, perhaps by its very nature, focuses particular attention on those costs and benefits that can be quantified. It is argued that many of the RIAs conducted to date have tended to be weak with respect to: clear statement of the underlying policy objective; analysis of the do-nothing alternative; and realistic consideration of the likely level of compliance. Notwithstanding these initial difficulties, it is clear that RIAs have at least two potentially very significant advantages. First, they can cajole policymakers into revealing their perhaps previously unknown policy goals. Second, and perhaps most important in the context of initial or partial RIAs, they facilitate the early killing off of really inappropriate regulatory initiatives.

5 EXPERIENCES AND EMERGING POLICY ISSUES

This section reviews some recent experiences of competition and regulatory policies, particularly in the non-internationally traded services sector, highlights the contentious issue of parallel imports and addresses the increasing emphasis that has been placed by EU policymakers on opening up the internal market for services via the Services Directive.

Competition Policy and Regulatory Policy Examples
Given the importance of the non-internationally traded services sector for the Irish economy, the general ability of Irish policymakers to influence the development of the sector and the availability of a framework for implementing suitably designed competition and regulatory policies, it is instructive to examine a number of specific case studies. The issues of below-cost selling, regulation of the so-called professions, pharmaceutical retailing and parallel imports are reviewed below. However, there are many other existing Irish regulations that impact on the competitive process, e.g. retail planning guidelines/laws (e.g. with respect to the location and scale of out-of-town shopping centres) and restrictions on off-licences (e.g. the high cost of obtaining a liquor licence). It is crucial to note that competition policy enthusiasts are not claiming or even suggesting that all such guidelines, regulations and laws are anti-competitive, merely highlighting the need for a considered approach to the enacting of such regulations. For example, visions of completely uncontrolled competition between, say, competing

household waste collection trucks in a housing estate, competing buses racing towards the same bus stop and competing hospitals out hunting in ambulances for prospective clients, only highlight the need for a rational policy to, and specific regulatory framework for, competition, and does not imply the more general and inevitable failure of competition in those specific markets.

Below-Cost Selling
To economists interested in competition policy, perhaps the most controversial provision of the Restrictive Practices (Groceries) Order 1987 was the prohibition on retailers selling many grocery products (e.g. bread and milk, but also alcohol) below the relevant suppliers' net invoice price. Fears of predatory pricing by the large retail multiples, where price wars which would eliminate the smaller competitors would be followed by the charging of excessive prices, were used to defend this provision. However, and crucially, off-invoice discounts (e.g. end-of-year rebates) could not be taken into account when defining the net invoice benchmark, i.e. retailers were 'forced' to impose a mark-up that was at least equal in size to off-invoice discounts. Under the Order, the Office of the Director of Consumer Affairs, who was charged with prosecuting breaches of the Groceries Order, fined Dunnes Stores and Tesco over €2,000 for selling baby food products below cost in 2004. The Groceries Order was eventually rescinded in 2006 but only after much debate and recrimination. The Competition Authority, who lobbied against the Order, argued that it could take actions against predatory pricing abuses (albeit perhaps only after the event occurred). Somewhat ironically, the existence of the Groceries Order probably facilitated the discount retailers (e.g. Lidl and Aldi) in increasing their market shares, as they source a significant portion of their produce from foreign suppliers, and thereby, in effect, avoided the Groceries Order, as the practice of large off-invoice discounts by Irish suppliers could be avoided. The rescinding of the Groceries Order remains topical for two reasons. First, comparisons between the current inflation figure for grocery items covered by the Order and the inflation figure for grocery items not covered by the Order are being used to comment on the appropriateness of the rescinding decision and on the effectiveness of competition and competition policy more generally. Second, one of the policy instruments currently being championed by certain parties in the battle against excessive alcohol consumption is a ban on below-cost selling of alcohol, particularly by the multiples.

Professions
The Competition Authority is involved in a long-term professions study, which aims to detail and examine the possible pro-competitive and anti-competitive motivations behind, and effects of, restrictions in the supply of various legal, construction and medical services. For example, the Competition Authority views with some degree of suspicion the principle or practice of self-regulation. Attention has also been paid to barristers, medical practitioners and solicitors with respect to restrictions in advertising, entry and organisational formats. Arguably,

various difficulties with the apparent activities of a small number of solicitors with respect to taking out several mortgages on individual properties has contributed to the apparent general acceptance of the inappropriateness of self-regulation in Ireland.

Pharmaceuticals

The retail pharmacy sector is highly regulated in Ireland, although probably much less so than in many other countries. From a competition policy perspective, apparently excessive restrictions on competition, and arguably unjustified from a public-interest perspective, came in a number of forms. Barriers to entry in terms of access to the relevant profession have existed for many years in terms of the highly restricted access to the required third-level degree course, although this has been relaxed recently with the setting up of some new degree courses. In addition, there is also an arguably justifiable comprehensive ban on mail order and Internet sales. In January 2002, and following a High Court challenge, rather severe pharmacy location restrictions were revoked. Among the location restrictions was a requirement that any new pharmacy had to locate at least 250 metres (5km in rural areas) from the nearest competitor and demonstrate that setting up would not have an adverse effect on the viability of competitors. Given that the state is by far the largest purchaser of medicines, it is not surprising that the state is involved in a process that fixes certain prices in retail pharmacies. However, the extent of the mark-ups agreed (e.g. with respect to the Drugs Payment Scheme or with respect to wholesaling) between the state and various representatives within the pharmaceutical sector (i.e. manufacturers, wholesalers and retailers) has created much tension, particularly between the state, via the HSE, and the retailers.

Parallel Imports and Price Discrimination

Imports, other than through the authorised distribution channels, of genuine products that have been legally marketed in another county are known as parallel imports.[12] Common examples of parallel imports include certain brands of jeans, children's toys and DVDs that are sourced from parts of the Far East. Whether or not parallel imports are legal, in cases where the brand owner has trademark rights in the country of importation, depends on the importing country's trademark regime. The European Economic Area (EEA) retains a policy of regional exhaustion, where parallel imports into the region (e.g. from Hong Kong) are illegal but parallel imports from countries within the region are legal. This policy, which is to at least some extent out of step with international practice, protects EEA-based (and other) producers but penalises EEA consumers, as EU prices tend to be much higher than the prices charged elsewhere for identical products.

More generally, the international pricing of pharmaceuticals, at least some of which would be regarded as essentials (e.g. anti-AIDS drugs), provides an important example of the issue of the appropriate public policy towards international price discrimination. Arguably, pharmaceutical companies should be allowed to practise at least some degree of price discrimination in order to recoup their initial investments. Indeed, the practice of richer countries paying a relatively high price while poorer countries pay a much lower price may not have any detrimental effects on overall societal welfare, as the alternative may be that the product is only sold at the higher price in the richer countries or that it is not produced at all. However, it is also possible that societal welfare declines as a result of price discrimination, as the total output of the product often falls under price discrimination. Notwithstanding the legality of parallel imports within the EEA, very large price differences appear to exist with respect to various pharmaceutical products across member states, e.g. Spain and Ireland.

EU Services Directive

The EU Treaty, with various amendments, facilitated the transition from customs union through single market to economic and monetary union (EMU). With respect to the EU single or internal market, there are two fundamental freedoms: (1) the freedom to offer products in the territories of other member states; and (2) the freedom to establish businesses in the territories of other member states. The single market, and notwithstanding remaining significant issues such as vehicle registration tax and differential pricing (e.g. with respect to pharmaceuticals), essentially exists with respect to goods. However, the European Commission's *Report on the State of the Internal Market for Services* (July 2002) highlighted the continued existence of very significant administrative, legal and practical obstacles to the existence of a single market with respect to services. Examples are unnecessary language requirements or unnecessary residency requirements (e.g. only estate agents or advertising agents actually located in a country can offer their services). As a result of these obstacles, cross-border business opportunities are not being availed of by firms, particularly by small and medium-sized enterprises.

The European Commission published a proposal for a directive on services in the internal market in January 2004. Much controversy surrounded the initially (explicitly) incorporated country of origin principle which arguably would have seen, say, a Polish-based subsidiary of an Irish estate agent being regulated by the relevant Irish, as opposed to Polish, legislation (e.g. with respect to Irish minimum wage, quality or health and safety at work standards) and vice versa. The proposed country of origin principle was subsequently dropped. It is noteworthy, however, that it was not replaced by an explicit country of destination principle. As such, ongoing clarification in this area is likely to stem, as before, from case-by-case decisions of the European Court of Justice.

The Services Directive was subsequently adopted by the European Parliament and Council in December 2006. Member States must transpose (i.e. give effect to) this Directive by the end of 2009. Implementation of the Directive will cut unnecessary red tape, remove discriminatory barriers, simplify and modernise the required administrative and legal frameworks and increase the rights of consumers of services. In addition, and perhaps crucially, each member state will have to provide a one-stop shop for foreign firms so as to facilitate them in dealing with all national, regional and local formalities. Indeed, to the extent that the latter requirement is met in full, it is likely that the foreign firms will find themselves in an advantageous, as opposed to disadvantageous, position relative to the domestic firms.

The Services Directive covers all services which are not explicitly excluded. As such, it covers, for example, professional services provided by those such as architects, engineers, accountants and legal and fiscal advisers; business-related services such as management consultancy; accommodation and food services such as hotels and catering; education services; and real estate services. The Services Directives excludes various public or social services such as childcare; healthcare services, provided that these services are not being provided commercially; and so-called non-economic services of general interest (e.g. national primary and secondary education). The Services Directive also excludes financial services such as mortgages; electronic communications services, but only to the extent that these services are already covered by a package of five sector-specific directives; certain gambling services such as casinos; and private security services. Notwithstanding the importance of excluded public services, it is likely that the Services Directive will cover economic activities in Ireland that account for twice as much economic activity as manufacturing. From an Irish perspective, and against the backdrop of the Services Directive, the Enterprise Strategy Group highlighted specific increased trading opportunities for Irish firms in the provision of education (e.g. e-learning), financial, agriculture (e.g. bloodstock) and professional and consultancy services.

6 CONCLUDING COMMENTS

There are two central themes in this chapter, namely the importance of the Irish services sector and the particular importance of appropriate microeconomic policies to a small open economy such as Ireland. Attention is focused on the policy interactions between these two themes, particularly in the area of competition and regulatory policies in the non-internationally traded services sector. Appropriate competition and regulatory policies in the non-internationally traded services sector (e.g. electricity, natural gas and transportation) reduce inflationary pressures, with respect to both pay and non-pay costs and facilitates efficiencies in the internationally traded sectors. In addition, and against the backdrop of the EU Services Directive, appropriate competition and regulatory policies can in particular encourage the evolving position of internationally traded services as being a key driver of Irish economic growth.

Endnotes

* The author gratefully acknowledges helpful comments and suggestions by Jack Cantillon, Carol Newman and John O'Hagan. Unfortunately the usual disclaimer applies, i.e. any remaining errors and all views expressed remain the sole responsibility of the author.

[1] The following general and specific statistical and informational sources are used in this section: Enterprise Strategy Group, *Ahead of the Curve: Ireland's Place in the Global Economy*, Forfás, Dublin 2004; Central Statistics Office (www.cso.ie) and CSO, *Annual Services Inquiry 2005*, Stationery Office, Dublin 2007; Department of Finance (www.finance.gov.ie) and Department of Finance, *Budgetary and Economic Statistics*, Stationery Office, Dublin 2007; Eurostat (http://epp.eurostat.ec.europa.eu) and Eurostat, *Europe in Figures: Eurostat Yearbook 2006–2007*, Eurostat, Luxembourg 2007; and Forfás (www.forfas.ie) and National Competitiveness Council, *Annual Competitiveness Report 2007*, Forfás, Dublin 2007.

[2] Value added is equal to the difference between the value of output and the value of intermediate consumption. The focus on measures of value added by sector as opposed to measures of output by sector facilitates the elimination of double-counting.

[3] For an overview of microeconomic aspects of competition policy, see S. Bishop and M. Walker, *The Economics of EC Competition Law: Concepts, Application and Measurement* (3rd edn), Sweet & Maxwell, London 2008. In addition, the interested reader should maintain regular contact with a number of online sources for up-to-date information on competition policy and regulatory matters: the Competition Authority's website (www.tca.ie) contains links to many of the relevant national and international regulatory bodies' websites.

[4] The earliest reference to the issue of rent seeking appears to be G. Tullock, 'The welfare cost of tariffs, monopolies and theft', *Western Economic Journal*, Vol. 5, 1967.

[5] The interested reader is directed to the Competition Authority's 'Notice in Respect of Guidelines for Merger Analysis', N/02/004, 2002 (www.tca.ie), for further details of the practical application of the HHI.

[6] For the Chicago School approach, see G. J. Stigler, *The Organisation of Industry*, University of Chicago Press, Chicago 1968. For the Harvard School approach, see J. Bain, *Barriers to New Competition: Their Character and Consequences in Manufacturing Industries*, Harvard University Press, Cambridge MA 1956.

[7] See S. Dalkir and F. Warren-Boulton, 'Prices, market definition and the effects of merger: Staples-Office Depot (1997)', in J. Kwoka and L. White (eds), *The Antitrust Revolution: Economics, Competition and Policy* (3rd edn), Oxford University Press, Oxford 1999, Case 6.

[8] For a review of regulation, see R. Baldwin and M. Cave, *Understanding Regulation: Theory, Strategy and Practice*, Oxford University Press, Oxford 1999. This section draws upon some material from this source.

[9] See R. H. Coase, 'The problem of social cost', *The Journal of Law and Economics*, Vol. 60, 1960.

[10] Technically, a natural monopoly exists if $C(Q) = C(Q_1 + \ldots + Q_N) < C(Q_1) + \ldots + C(Q_N)$, where Q represents total output, $C(Q)$ represents the total cost of producing Q and N represents the relevant number of firms.

[11] More sophisticated versions of regulation allow the firm to engage in two-part pricing, where a fixed fee is used to finance the almost inevitably present large fixed-cost element within the market (e.g. creation or upkeep of the network itself), while an additional per unit user fee is kept close to marginal cost.

[12] For more details, see F. O'Toole and C. Treanor, 'The European Union's trade mark exhaustion regime', *World Competition: Law and Economics Review*, Vol. 6, 2002.

CHAPTER 10

Agriculture and Rural, Conservation and Food Policies

Alan Matthews

1 INTRODUCTION

Agricultural and food policy remains a prominent aspect of economic policy debate in Ireland. This is despite the shrinking economic importance of the sector in GNP and employment. Agriculture no longer has the dominant role in economic activity it once had, although when the contribution of the food industry is factored in, the agri-food sector remains a significant player. In 2006, the agri-food sector accounted for eight per cent of Irish GNP and eight per cent of employment. The agricultural sector remains important in other ways. Together with forestry, it occupies over 70 per cent of the land area of the country; it thus has a significant impact on the physical environment and the protection of biodiversity. It is also the largest contributor to Ireland's greenhouse gas emissions, accounting for 28 per cent of the total in 2006, ahead of transport, which was responsible for 20 per cent. It remains the single most substantial contributor to the economic and social viability of rural areas. Finally, agri-food exports contributed over ten per cent of total merchandise exports in 2006 and food and drink expenditures accounted for 12 per cent of household consumption expenditure. Thus, agricultural and food policy is intimately linked to debates on economic competitiveness, rural development, the environment and consumer well-being.

Another reason for the interest in agricultural and food policy is the decisive influence of government interventions on the fortunes of the industry. This dependence can be highlighted in a single statistic: the income accruing to farmers from agricultural activity arises entirely from public policy transfers from both EU and Irish consumers and taxpayers. Agricultural activity within the EU is highly protected from world market competition. EU tariff levels on agricultural and food imports average around 19 per cent, compared to four per cent for non-agricultural goods, and for some agricultural products exceed 100 per cent. This substantial government intervention in favour of a particular industry raises a series of questions. What objectives is it designed to achieve? Are these objectives justified?

Is the support provided achieving these objectives? Is the support being provided efficiently? These are questions which economists are well placed to answer.

These questions are particularly pertinent at present because agricultural and food policy faces challenges on a number of fronts. Agricultural commodity prices, having fallen steadily in real terms for several decades, have suddenly increased dramatically; the UN Food and Agricultural Organisation's global food price index rose 40 per cent in 2007 compared to nine per cent in 2006. Rising food prices, along with increased energy prices, are now causing a serious headache for central banks trying to prevent inflationary expectations gaining hold. Higher prices, of course, encourage farmers to increase production, but ensuring that this increased production is sustainable in environmental terms will be a major challenge. High prices have also raised again the spectre of food insecurity and focused attention on the appropriate balance between producing food at home and relying on imports from third countries. This debate is central to the ongoing negotiations on agricultural trade liberalisation under the auspices of the World Trade Organisation (WTO). High food prices reflect in part ambitious government mandates to promote the production of renewable energies and, in particular, biofuels. Whether it makes sense to use agricultural land resources to produce food or fuel is a hotly contested issue. Higher food prices also throw into relief the increasing levels of concentration in the food marketing chain and the possible abuse by supermarkets, in particular, of their growing market power. At the same time, there is evidence of growing concern among consumers about the safety and quality of food being produced.

The purpose of this chapter is to describe these challenges in more detail and to discuss the appropriate policy responses. Section 2 provides a brief overview of some salient characteristics of the Irish agricultural sector and describes the main features of recent structural change in the industry. Section 3 discusses the changing policy environment at EU and international levels. Section 4 looks at the rationale for rural development policies, and at the policy framework which has been put in place to encourage balanced regional and rural development. Section 5 addresses some dimensions of the environmental impact of agricultural production. Section 6 examines the growing emphasis given to food safety regulation throughout the food chain. Section 7 concludes the chapter by summarising some of the conflicting tendencies at work as the agriculture and food sector faces into a more market-oriented and uncertain environment.

2 CHARACTERISTICS OF THE AGRICULTURAL SECTOR

Production

The agricultural industry produced food products and raw materials valued at €5.2 billion at producer prices in 2006. Its GNP share was an estimated 2.3 per cent in that year (down from 6.3 per cent in 1996). According to the CSO's Labour Force Survey, around 109,100 persons worked in agriculture in 2006, accounting for just under six per cent of total employment. The discrepancy between the share of the labour force in agriculture and its share of GNP is a first indication that labour productivity and thus farm income might be relatively lower in the sector than in the economy at large.

Climatically, Ireland is more suited to grassland than crop production. Of the total agricultural area of 4.3 million hectares in 2006, over 90 per cent was devoted to grass and rough grazing. Livestock and livestock products accounted for 72 per cent of total output at producers' prices in 2006 (Table 10.1). These figures exclude the direct payments which make a hugely important contribution to farm incomes; in 2006, government payments accounted for 81 per cent of the operating surplus in agriculture, a good proxy for aggregate income from farming. The table also highlights the growing share of material and service inputs as a proportion of gross agricultural output. While this is due partly to the fall in the value of output arising from reform of the EU's Common Agricultural Policy (CAP) (see Section 3), it also reflects the increasing intensification of agricultural production, a phenomenon which has given rise to concern about agriculture's impact on the environment.

Table 10.1
Composition of Agricultural Outputs and Inputs, Selected Years
(per cent of gross agricultural output by value)

	1991	1996	2006
Total Outputs			
Cattle	32.5	28.7	28.6
Milk	27.7	29.8	25.3
Crops	24.8	24.6	27.9
Pigs	5.3	6.9	6.1
Sheep	4.4	4.7	3.6
Other	5.3	5.3	8.4
Gross agricultural output at producer prices	100.0	100.0	100.0
Total Inputs	53.3	60.0	74.4
Feed, fertiliser and seed	22.2	24.4	27.5
Other current inputs	31.1	35.6	46.8

Source: Department of Agriculture, Fisheries and Food, *Compendium of Agricultural Statistics*, Economics and Planning Division, Dublin 2007.

An important characteristic of Irish agriculture is its export orientation. The export market absorbs more than 80 per cent of dairy and beef output. Around 45 per cent of Irish agri-food exports go to the UK, around 30 per cent to the rest of the EU and 25 per cent are exported outside of the EU. Sales to third country markets outside the EU were heavily dependent on export subsidies. This leaves Ireland vulnerable to any changes in agricultural support arrangements which would target these subsidies, even if the higher global commodity prices after

2007, particularly for dairy products, have reduced their importance. The continued use of export subsidies is under challenge from other trading countries in the WTO negotiations on agricultural trade liberalisation (see Section 3).

Price Developments

The real price of agricultural output, measured as the ratio of output prices to the consumer price index, is a good indicator of the purchasing power of farm products relative to consumer goods and services. This ratio more than halved over the period 1980 to 2006. This fall in the relative price of food over time, which is not unique to Ireland but has been a general phenomenon in all industrialised economies, is crucially important in understanding the adjustment pressures on agriculture and hence the reasons for government intervention in the sector.

The fall in relative food prices reflects the interplay of the supply of and demand for farm products. On the one hand, the supply potential of the farm sector has increased as the scientific revolution has gathered pace, making available to farmers a range of productive new inputs such as improved seed varieties, better fertilisers, more powerful machinery, and more effective chemicals and pesticides. Because of this technological innovation, the supply of agricultural products has increased rapidly. However, the market for this increased output did not grow to the same extent. Growth in demand is dependent on growth in population and in per capita incomes. But the rate of population growth in industrialised countries has slowed down and in some cases has virtually ceased. While per capita incomes continue to grow, a smaller and smaller proportion of this increase is spent on food. The consequence has been a downward pressure on the aggregate price level for agricultural products relative to other commodities.

This in turn puts a downward pressure on farm incomes and has encouraged farm family members to take up non-farm job opportunities. In all industrialised countries, the share of the farm workforce in total employment has fallen significantly. In Ireland, the numbers at work in agriculture fell from 330,000 in 1960 to 109,100 in 2006. If this adjustment process proceeds smoothly, the reduction in the numbers engaged in agriculture should ensure that farm incomes, on average, stay in line with average non-farm incomes. For various reasons, however, some farmers may find it difficult to leave farming in the face of this downward pressure on farm incomes. Unemployment may be high in the non-farm sector, or their age and skill profile can make it difficult for them to find off-farm employment. Many farmers appear trapped in agriculture with low incomes. Government transfers to agriculture have been justified in the past as a response to this perceived problem of low average farm incomes relative to the rest of society.

The process of adjustment to falling real farm prices is reflected in ongoing structural change in agriculture. In 2006, there were around 132,700 farms in Ireland. Their average size in terms of land area is 32 hectares although there is considerable diversity around this average. This average area farmed is large in EU terms, but because of the relatively low intensity of land use the average size of farm business in Ireland is at the smaller end of the EU spectrum. There is an important regional dimension to differences in farm size, with a predominance of smaller farms in the west and the northwest, and a greater proportion of larger farms in the south and east. Small farm size is frequently associated with a low-margin farming system (mainly drystock) and a predominance of older farmers, many of whom are unmarried. The number of farms is falling over time, at a rate of about two per cent per annum. A more disaggregated analysis shows that all of the decline is concentrated among smaller farms (less than 20 hectares), whose number fell from 85,000 to 58,000 between 1992 and 2005, while the number of larger farms is stable at around 75,000.

The persistence of this long-term decline in real food prices makes the sudden increase in food prices in 2007 even more striking. The key question is whether this is just a flash in the pan, the outcome of a series of chance events such as drought in major producing countries, or whether it represents the start of a new era in which farmers will receive more for their production. There is much evidence to support the latter view. We can use the same supply and demand framework to understand this phenomenon. On the demand side, rapidly rising per capita incomes in emerging economies are leading to shifts in diet preferences with greater demand for meat and dairy products. Food and energy markets have become increasingly interlinked, not only on the cost side (where modern agriculture is a heavy energy consumer) but also on the output side (as agricultural land is diverted to the production of energy crops for biomass and biofuels). On the supply side, the increasing scarcity of water and land, and in the longer term, the likely impact of climate change, are putting increasing pressure on supply capacity. Public and private investment in agricultural research, which has been behind the productivity growth that has driven the secular decline in food prices in the past, has been cut back or diverted to non-production areas such as the environment, animal welfare or the development of more sophisticated foods. Some of the new technologies available to increase food supply, such as aspects of biotechnology, have met substantial consumer resistance. It is thus very likely that the market environment for the Irish agri-food sector will be very different in the next ten years from what it has been in the past. As a net food exporter, not only farmers but the national economy stands to gain.

Farm Incomes
The changing composition of income sources in farm households can be tracked over time using data from the Household Budget Surveys conducted by the CSO. Whereas in 1973, 70 per cent of farm household income was derived from farming, this had fallen to 34 per cent in 2005 (Table 10.2). Income from farming in this table includes the direct payments which farmers receive under EU agricultural policy (discussed in Section 3). Income from farming compares unfavourably with average industrial earnings, although comparisons are difficult for statistical and conceptual reasons.[1] For example, the average family farm income estimated in 2006 by the Teagasc National Farm Survey was €16,680, compared to average annual male industrial earnings of €32,471. However, this comparison is not comparing like with like. The average family farm income on the 40 per cent of full-time farms in the Teagasc Survey was €34,486 (bear in

mind, however, that this figure must remunerate the capital invested in the farm and that there may be more than one labour unit engaged on full-time farms, so it is not directly comparable to the industrial earnings figure either). Conversely, the average income from farming on the remaining 60 per cent of part-time farms in the Teagasc Survey in 2006 was only €7,899. Clearly, this level of income is inadequate on its own to support a farm family. However, on around 58 per cent of all farms, either the holder and/or the spouse has an off-farm job. The increasing importance of off-farm income means that average farm *household* incomes are now close to average incomes in the non-farm economy.

Table 10.3 compares the average incomes of farm households with those of urban households, other rural households, and the state average.[2] Average household income is a good measure of living standards, although it does not take

Table 10.2
Percentage of Total Farm Household Income from All Sources, 1973–2005

	1973	1980	1987	1994	1999/2000	2005
Farm income	70.1	58.3	54.2	51.3	39.0	34.3
Other direct income	19.1	26.3	17.6	37.0	50.3	49.7
State transfers	10.8	15.2	28.3	11.7	10.6	16.0
Gross income	100.0	100.0	100.0	100.0	100.0	100.0

Source: CSO, *Household Budget Survey,* Stationery Office, Dublin, various issues. 2005 data from the EU Survey of Income and Living Conditions (EU-SILC), 2005.

Table 10.3
Average Annual Household Income, 2005 (€)

Income Source	Farm households	Other rural households	Urban households	State average
Farming income	15,652	-	-	1,170
Non-farm employment	21,512	29,947	44,965	38,693
Other direct income	1,195	714	1,514	1,249
State transfers	7,323	9,953	10,287	9,965
Gross income	45,683	40,613	56,766	51,077
less total direct taxation	6,780	7,246	12,643	10,580
Disposable income	38,903	33,367	44,124	40,496
Persons per household	3.12	2.95	2.93	2.95
Gross income per person in household	14,665	13,752	19,380	17,312
Disposable income per person in household	12,488	11,298	15,064	13,726

Source: EU-SILC (2005 data).

account of differences in the effort or resources required to generate this income. On average, farm household incomes were around ten per cent lower than for the state as a whole in 2005. However, poverty levels among farm households are not that different from those among non-farm households. EU-SILC data for 2005 show that consistent poverty is generally lower among farm households than other household groups, indicating a low rate of enforced deprivation among farm families.

3 POLICY ENVIRONMENT

Common Agricultural Policy (CAP)

At the heart of the original Common Market was an economic deal between France and Germany under which France obtained access to the German market for its agricultural exports in return for opening the French market to German industrial goods. Thus a common agricultural policy had to be included in the Treaty of Rome, which established the European Economic Community in 1958.

The objectives of this common agricultural policy are spelled out in Article 33 (formerly 39) of the Treaty and are worth quoting in full:

- To increase agricultural productivity by promoting technical progress and by ensuring the rational development of agricultural production and the optimum utilisation of all factors of production, in particular labour;
- Thus, to ensure a fair standard of living for the agricultural community, in particular by increasing the individual earnings of persons engaged in agriculture;
- To stabilise markets;
- To provide certainty of supplies;
- To ensure that supplies reach consumers at reasonable prices.

These five objectives of efficient agricultural production, fair incomes for farmers, stable markets, food security and reasonable consumer prices would be broadly acceptable to most people, though the sharp-eyed will note the ambiguity of the wording (what is a fair standard of living for farmers? What is a reasonable price for consumers?) and the potential for conflict between different objectives. However, the mechanisms put in place to achieve these objectives have prioritised the farm income objective at considerable cost to the EU budget and consumers.

These mechanisms have changed over time. We first describe the original mechanisms whose legacy still determines the basic architecture of the CAP despite the reforms which have taken place. For each of the main commodities produced in the EU, each year the Council of Agricultural Ministers established a *target price* (or its equivalent). To maintain the market price around this target level the EU used a number of policy instruments, including import tariffs, market intervention and export subsidies. *Import tariffs* ensure a high domestic price as long as there is a net deficit on the EU market. Originally, the EU's import tariffs took the form of variable levies designed to help stabilise internal EU prices but these were transformed into fixed amounts following the WTO Agreement on Agriculture in 1995 (see below). Price support to producers was further strengthened in the event of excess EU supplies by a guarantee that government agencies would buy farm products at a price (called the *intervention price*) usually set some 10–30 per cent below the target price. Intervention was intended to deal with temporary surpluses of supply. Once the market had recovered and prices had risen, intervention stocks could be sold. As the EU became more than self-sufficient in many temperate-zone foods, greater reliance was placed on *export subsidies or refunds*. These export refunds bridge the gap between the high internal market prices and the lower world prices in most years and make possible the export of higher-priced foodstuffs out of the EU. High import tariffs, intervention purchases and export refunds were the principal means of supporting prices to farmers under the classical CAP.

The operation of the CAP price-support policy ensured a greater degree of internal price stability than in other countries and meant higher per capita incomes for a greater number of farmers than would otherwise have been the case. However, these achievements were bought at a price. The resulting increase in output could not be absorbed by the natural growth in demand, leading to the accumulation of stocks and to dumping on international markets. Thus the EU, which was initially a deficit producer of many agricultural products, became a major net exporter. An obvious consequence of this was the escalating budget cost of purchasing surplus production for intervention storage and of financing export refunds, and growing calls for reform.

Reforms of the CAP

A number of half-hearted attempts were made to limit the budgetary cost of the CAP during the 1980s, of which the introduction of milk quotas in 1984 was the most important. However, the first successful attempt to tackle the malfunctioning CAP was pushed through in 1993 by EU Agriculture Commissioner Ray MacSharry. The MacSharry reform initiated a significant reduction in support prices for the first time, at least for cereals and beef. Supply control measures were extended (through the introduction of 'set-aside' for cereals and oilseeds) and the role of intervention support, particularly in the beef sector, was greatly reduced. Compensation for these price reductions and intensified supply controls was provided by means of arable aid and livestock premia payments. These market regime reforms were accompanied by new agri-environment, forestry and early retirement schemes for farmers, part of an expanded rural development emphasis in the CAP.

A further round of CAP reform was agreed in March 1999 as part of the negotiations on the Agenda 2000 agreement to prepare the EU for eastern enlargement. This pursued the same model of reductions in support prices while compensating farmers by increasing direct payments. For the first time, the dairy sector was included in the reform although implementation was postponed until 2005. As a result of these reforms, the share of direct payments in farm incomes increased. In 1992, the year before the MacSharry reform, direct payments accounted for 22 per cent of Irish farm income. By 2006, direct payments accounted for 81 per cent of farm income. For beef, sheep and cereal farms, in many cases they amounted to more than 100 per cent of farm income, implying that farmers are not covering their costs even when selling at protected EU prices. The Agenda 2000 reform also consolidated various socio-structural measures to encourage farm modernisation as well as agri-environment payments into a single Rural Development Regulation which became known as Pillar 2 of the CAP (see below).

The MacSharry and Agenda 2000 direct payments required that a farmer must plant sufficient arable land (in the case of cereals, oilseeds and protein crops) or keep a sufficient number of animals in order to draw down these payments. Such payments are called *coupled payments* because they are linked to the amount each farmer produces. Because the rules differed for each payments scheme (with respect to payment dates, inspection requirements, etc.), claiming these payments involved farmers (or their advisors) in a great deal of paperwork and administration. A second criticism, as demonstrated by the fact that on many farms the value of income from farming was less than the direct payments received, was that many farmers were keeping livestock or growing crops simply to collect the subsidies, rather than responding to market demand.

Under Franz Fischler, the EU Commissioner for Agriculture in the period 1999 to 2004, the EU embarked on a further CAP reform in 2003 (called the Mid-Term Review (MTR) because it was launched as a mid-term review of the Agenda 2000 reforms). This reform introduced three main changes to the CAP support mechanisms. The most important change was to replace all premia and arable aid payments by a single farm payment to each farmer. This single farm payment is based on the level of assistance received by each farm in the reference period 2000–2002. Farmers are entitled to receive this payment regardless of changes in the area planted to crops or the number of livestock on their farm, or indeed regardless of whether they produce on their farm at all (subject to the conditions specified below). This *decoupling* of the payment from production means that, in future, farmers will make their production decisions based on the relative market returns from each enterprise rather than the size of the subsidy available. The single farm payment is linked to respect for standards in the areas of the environment, food safety, plant health and animal welfare, as well as a requirement to keep all farmland in good agricultural and environmental condition, so called 'cross-compliance' (see Section 4).

Second, the MTR introduced the *modulation* of direct payments. This means that the single farm payment is reduced by three per cent in 2005, four per cent in 2006 and five per cent from 2007 onwards, subject to the exemption of the first €5,000 of direct payments per farm. These funds are transferred for use in financing rural development programmes, with rules ensuring that the bulk of the funds will be returned to the member states that contribute them.

Third, the MTR continued the *reform of the market regimes* by lowering support prices and increasing direct payments in compensation. For Ireland, the most important market reform concerned the milk regime, where a further reduction in support prices, on top of those agreed in the Agenda 2000 package from 2005, was agreed. Subsequently, a rolling programme of reform was implemented which extended the MTR reforms to a variety of other market regimes (cotton, tobacco, olive oil, bananas, sugar). A consequence of the sugar market reform, in which support prices for sugar were reduced and incentives provided to encourage the closure of refining capacity, was that Ireland's only sugar processor, Greencore, ceased production at the end of the 2006 season.

As a consequence of these successive reforms, the CAP is now a very different animal from its classical guise. It now consists of two Pillars: Pillar 1 refers to the market support regimes and single farm payment which contribute to the support of farm incomes, while Pillar 2 refers to rural development measures. Pillar 1 continues to take the lion's share of the CAP budget, accounting for over 75 per cent of the €55 billion included for CAP expenditure in the 2007 EU budget. However, most of Pillar 1 expenditure is now decoupled and does not provide the same incentive to over-production as before. Nonetheless, farmers continue to benefit from high levels of external protection which in normal years keep food prices on the internal EU market considerably higher than world market levels. These high protection levels have come under sustained criticism from the EU's trading partners in negotiations on trade liberalisation under the auspices of the World Trade Organisation, the WTO.

WTO Disciplines on Agricultural Support

The WTO Agreement on Agriculture, which came into force in 1995, establishes rules on the manner and amount of government support to agriculture. All border restrictions, including the EU's variable levies, were converted into fixed tariffs which are bound at a maximum rate. Furthermore, these bound tariffs were reduced by 36 per cent on average compared to their levels in 1986–90 over a six-year period. There is also an obligation to ensure that a minimum of five per cent of the domestic market is open to foreign competition, which is achieved through the use of tariff rate quotas. These allow imports from third countries at a preferential duty rate but only for the quota quantity. For countries which use export subsidies, these subsidies had to be reduced by 36 per cent in value and 21 per cent in volume relative to the average for the period 1986–90; no new export subsidies can be introduced. With regard to domestic support to agriculture, the Agreement distinguishes between permitted and non-permitted forms of support. Support that does not influence, or only minimally influences, farmers' incentives to produce is permitted and there are no disciplines applied (support of this kind is considered decoupled from production and therefore not to cause distortions to trade). Trade distorting support, such as market price support, is capped and had to be reduced by 20 per cent compared to the base period 1986–8.

A new round of negotiations to liberalise agricultural trade began in March 2000 as foreseen in the WTO Agreement on Agriculture. In November 2001, these negotiations were folded into the general round of trade negotiations launched by the WTO Ministerial Council at its meeting in Doha, Qatar, and known as the Doha Round. The negotiations have proved difficult, not least because of disagreements between developed and developing countries over agricultural subsidies. There was an important breakthrough in May 2004 when, for the first time, the EU indicated that it was prepared to negotiate an end date for the elimination of export subsidies provided all other forms of export support used by other countries were eliminated in parallel and provided there was a satisfactory agreement reached in the other areas of the negotiations. However, disagreement on the extent of tariff cuts for both agricultural and non-agricultural products continued, and a new agreement still remained out of reach in April 2008. It is thus too early to evaluate the extent to which a new agreement would require further changes to the CAP beyond those already agreed in the Mid-Term Review in 2003. The fact that the single farm payment has been decoupled from production should protect it if further subsidy cuts are agreed in the Doha Round. However, the significant tariff reductions for beef and dairy products under discussion would certainly mean lower prices for Irish farmers.

CAP Health Check and Beyond
The Commission published proposals for a 'Health Check' of the 2003 MTR reform in November 2007. This was not intended as a major overhaul of the CAP. The Commission's proposals were designed to make the single farm payment simpler and more effective; to rethink the role of market support instruments; and to confront some of the new challenges facing agriculture, such as risk management, climate change, biofuels, water management and the protection of biodiversity. However, the Health Check is a prelude to a more far-reaching review of the CAP scheduled as part of the EU budget review in 2008/09.

The budget review was one outcome of the compromise between the member states required to reach agreement on the 2007–2013 financial perspective, the medium-term budget framework for the EU. Its purpose is to reassess both the revenue and expenditure sides of the EU budget after 2013. Many member states would like to shift the composition of the EU budget to put more emphasis on promoting EU competitiveness, the EU's global role or cohesion spending. As member states are unlikely to agree to a substantial increase in the EU's own resources, the CAP budget, which will still account for around 35 per cent of total EU spending in 2013, will come under greater scrutiny. Particularly problematic is the future justification for the single farm payment. This was introduced originally as compensation for price reductions, then justified as a means of income support, but is increasingly defended as a remuneration to farmers for the provision of public goods and for observing high animal welfare and environmental standards. Whether this will be enough to persuade the member states to continue funding the CAP at its present level remains to be seen. Given the dependence of Irish farm incomes on direct payments, the importance of this debate for Irish agriculture is very clear.

WTO disciplines, along with CAP reform, are slowly changing the focus of government support, from supporting production to supporting the producer, and from paying for surplus food production to paying farmers for the provision of other services which the public values. In the EU, this changing emphasis on the objectives of public support for farming is reflected in the growth of Pillar 2 of the CAP, concerned with rural development, which is described in the following section.

4 RURAL DEVELOPMENT

Pillar 2 of CAP

The price and market support element of the CAP was, from the outset, accompanied by a policy to encourage the modernisation of agriculture through structural improvement. This structural policy initially consisted of measures to promote greater efficiency in agricultural production, processing and marketing. Rural policy gained momentum as a specifically European issue in 1988 when the Commission presented its communication *The Future of Rural Society* which explicitly linked cutbacks in farm support with the need to encourage rural diversification.[3]

In March 1999, as part of the Agenda 2000 CAP reform strategy, EU leaders decided to reinforce rural development policy in several ways. Much preparation had preceded the Agenda 2000 strategy, including an important rural development conference in Cork in 1996. The reform resulted in a clearer statement of the objectives of rural development policy. It aimed to complement reforms in the agricultural market sectors by promoting a competitive, multifunctional agricultural sector, and sought to encourage alternative sources of income in rural areas, while supporting agri-environment measures. The reform also produced a unified system of rural development measures in a single Rural Development Regulation, now Pillar 2 of the CAP. Since then, the resources devoted to Pillar 2 have grown and they now account for 25 per cent of total CAP spending.

This section asks what the implications are for Ireland's rural areas of this increased priority for rural development at EU level. It discusses the meaning of rural development and the justification for rural development measures before describing the current policy framework for Irish rural development.

Definition of Rural Development

Rural development as an *objective* may be defined as seeking to sustain vibrant rural communities with a balanced structure of age, income and occupational groups, capable of adapting to ongoing economic, social and cultural change, enjoying a high standard of living and an attractive quality of life and with sufficient income and employment opportunities to allow individuals and families to live with dignity.[4]

Two issues are raised by this definition. The first is what is meant by 'rural'. In Census terms, rural areas are defined as those areas outside towns and villages with a population of more than 1,500. However, it is now understood that there is a key link between settlement and urban patterns and the well-being of the surrounding hinterland and communities. Counties with strong urban centres retain population while those with the lowest urbanisation rates experience persistent population decline. It is artificial to distinguish between rural areas and their immediate urban centres. The current preferred definition is to define rural areas as all areas outside the Greater Dublin area and the gateways and hubs defined in the National Spatial Strategy (see below). On this definition, 59 per cent of the population are defined as rural. The second issue raised by the definition is the geographical scale against which success should be measured. For example, is it sufficient to achieve balanced economic growth at regional level, or is the objective to be achieved for each county or even each Rural District? Recognition of the intimate link between rural areas and their urban centres suggests that it would be useful to define targets and indicators in terms of 'urban catchments' but there is currently no administrative structure to define or represent these areas.

Rural development can also be defined to mean the *strategy* used to achieve this objective. Here its key characteristic is that it should be multisectoral and multidimensional. Rural development is not confined to a single sector, such as agriculture, but embraces initiatives across a range of natural resource sectors (marine, forestry, mining), the promotion of enterprise, infrastructure, human resources and tourism. Rural development also implies more than economic development, and extends to providing access by rural people to social services, ensuring effective organisational structures and systems of governance to meet collective needs, protection of the physical environment, and strengthening local and regional cultures. As the 1999 White Paper on Rural Development puts it, 'the rural development policy agenda constitutes all Government policies and interventions which are directed towards improving the physical, economic and social conditions of people living ... outside of the five major urban centres'.[5] Of course, this very wide definition of rural development interventions could turn out to be a source of confusion because of the multiplicity of agencies involved in delivering these programmes. To overcome this, the government operates a policy of 'rural proofing' of all national policies to ensure that policymakers are aware of the likely impact of policy proposals on the well-being of rural communities. Rural proofing stands alongside the existing mechanisms of poverty proofing and equality proofing by which policies are assessed at design and review stages for their impact on the areas of concern.

Another way to limit the scope of rural development is to focus on rural development as a *process*. In this sense, rural development is not only concerned with achieving a particular set of outcomes, such as the creation of viable employment opportunities in rural areas, but is also identified with a particular *style* of development characterised by a 'bottom-up' rather than 'top-down' approach. Top-down approaches are associated with mainstream programmes designed and delivered by central agencies and provided uniformly across the country. Bottom-up approaches (also referred to as area-based approaches) are characterised by an emphasis on local participation in the formulation and implementation of development objectives for an area, by a preference for exploiting indigenous skills and resources rather than relying on 'imported' expertise and capital, by the attempt to integrate social as well as economic development and, for some at least, by a concern that development should benefit the more marginal and disadvantaged groups. A key issue here concerns the structures which are put in place to facilitate the coordination of the top-down and bottom-up approaches.

Rationale for Rural Development Policies

It is a relevant question to ask what is the rationale for government support for rural development measures. If people wish to live and work in Dublin or one of the other major cities, why should the government intervene to try to prevent this? As noted above, an important recent justification for rural development measures has been to compensate for cutbacks in farm support. The hope is that it is easier to gain acceptance for reduced agricultural support if offsetting measures to benefit those who might lose out from this process are put in place, but this narrow rationale clearly cannot explain the adoption of the wide-ranging rural development objectives set out in the 1999 White Paper. An important argument is that those who seek to live and work in Dublin are not necessarily doing so from choice and would prefer to remain in a rural area if sufficient employment opportunities were available. In terms of the typology of policy objectives outlined in Chapter 2, this is clearly an equity argument. The implication is that resources should be used to compensate for the competitive disadvantages of rural areas (for example, to provide higher grant-aid levels to assist enterprise start-ups in rural areas) in order to achieve the socially desired objectives of balanced population and economic growth.

This can be complemented by an efficiency argument in terms of market failure. This is often couched in terms of the hidden costs – diseconomies – of urban congestion while rural resources remain underutilised. Long-distance commuting and residential development located at greater and greater distances from where people work resulting from unbalanced development is simply not sustainable in the longer term. There is also an argument that individuals, who might be unwilling to commit to living in rural Ireland if asked to make the decision in isolation, might be very willing to do so if they were aware that there was a concerted plan to build up and support rural communities. This is an example of a network externality where one person's demand (in this case, for living in a rural area) is dependent on the number of people who are also making this decision. In these cases, rural policy is justified over and above any argument based on concepts of equity and balanced distribution of opportunities across geographical areas.

The growing importance of rural development policy at EU level has been reflected in increased funding for and the introduction of new rural development agencies and measures in Ireland. While the rhetoric of rural development is relatively new, there is a long history of rural development initiatives which can be traced back to the establishment of the Congested Districts Board by the British administration in 1898. In the context of the country's poor overall economic performance until the 1960s, these measures failed to stem the fall in the Irish rural population since independence. With improved economic growth, however, this fall was reversed in Leinster in the late 1960s, and the population recovery spread to all provinces during the 1970s. Over the 1996–2006 period, the rural population increased by four per cent, while the urban population increased by 20 per cent.

A simple head count does not tell the whole story. The recovery in the rural population has not been uniform across all districts. About one-quarter of all electoral districts experienced population decline during the 1996–2006 period, with the highest proportionate decrease being recorded in the western part of the country. Rural areas also have higher than average dependency levels, particularly in the western and border counties, where those over 65 years comprise a very high proportion of the population. Many rural areas also have a weak economic structure, with a high dependence on agriculture, the lack of a diversified employment base and the continued out-migration of those with higher levels of education. The low population density and unbalanced demographic structure of many rural areas creates difficulties for both public and private service provision (health, transport, shops) and leads to increasing isolation and social exclusion. But it would be wrong to associate all rural areas with problems arising from remoteness and deprivation. Rural areas today are very heterogeneous, and the problems facing those areas contiguous to urban centres are more often the problems of managing the overspill of urban growth.

Rural Development Policy Framework

In 1999, the government issued a White Paper on Rural Development which, as we noted earlier, set down a clear objective for rural development as well as a set of principles as the basis for strategy. These principles are currently implemented through the National Development Plan (NDP) 2007–2013. This plan, drawn up on the assumption of continued economic growth of 4–4.5 per cent per annum, envisages the expenditure of €184 billion across five investment priorities. A key objective of the NDP is to ensure a better balance in regional development. Ireland's economic success in recent years has been accompanied by spatial patterns of development which have seen employment opportunities becoming more concentrated in some areas, while economic weaknesses remain in others. As part of the previous NDP 2000–2006, the government created two regions at the NUTS2 level, the Border, Midland and Western (BMW) Region and the Southern and Eastern (S&E) Region, respectively.[6] The BMW Region consists of three NUTS3 planning regions which are predominantly rural with a low population density. Although population growth in the BMW region exceeded the national rate in the 2002–2006 period, gross value added per person is only three-quarters of the national level and disposable income per person continues to lag behind the more prosperous S&E Region.

The mechanism to achieve more balanced regional development is the National Spatial Strategy (NSS). This is a 20-year planning framework published in 2002 designed to deliver more balanced social, economic and physical development between regions. The key concept behind the NSS is to focus investment and growth potential around a network of nine competitive national gateways. These are Dublin, Cork, Galway, Limerick/Shannon, Waterford, Sligo, Dundalk, Letterkenny/(Derry) and Athlone/Tullamore/Mullingar. In addition, nine medium-sized hubs to support and be supported by the gateways and to link out to wider rural areas have been identified: Cavan, Ennis, Kilkenny, Mallow, Monaghan, Tuam and Wexford, as well as Ballina/Castlebar and Tralee/Killarney acting as linked hubs. The NSS also identifies an important need to support the role of smaller towns, villages and rural areas at the local level. However, there is some scepticism as to whether the new spatial strategy will be more successful in prioritising investment in a few favoured locations than earlier attempts at a spatial strategy in the 1960s (the Buchanan Report) or the 1970s (the IDA's regional industrial plans). The strong clientelist basis for Irish politics, in which ministers must be seen to deliver for 'their' constituencies, works against a targeted approach. The government's decentralisation programme for the civil service announced in the 2004 Budget, for example, appeared to ignore the NSS guidelines, scattering the 10,000 civil servants to be moved over 53 different locations.

The NDP includes a number of programmes of special relevance to rural development: the agriculture and food development programme; the rural social and economic development programme; the Gaeltacht and Islands development programme; and the marine and coastal communities programme. Some elements of the first two of these programmes are eligible for co-funding under the EU Rural Development Regulation, and a separate CAP Rural Development Plan was prepared to draw down this EU funding for the 2007–2013 period. This plan primarily addresses environmental priorities (see below). In addition, however, the NDP includes many nationally funded rural development measures in its Agriculture and Food Development Programme. These include sectoral on-farm investment support, support for agricultural training, assistance for afforestation, as well as support for investment, marketing, and research and development in the food industry.

A number of other measures which directly target rural communities are funded under the Rural Social and Economic Development Programme of the NDP. One of the more innovative of these is the LEADER programme, launched as an EU-funded initiative. LEADER is a bottom-up process with area-based, local action groups implementing local development programmes. Under LEADER, groups covering defined geographical areas are invited to tender for support on the basis of a development plan each prepares for its area. Activities that can be funded include vocational training, rural tourism, small firms, craft enterprises, local services and marketing local products. Other local development programmes include the CLÁR programme launched in 2001 to provide funding to targeted regions which suffered the most depopulation between 1926 and 1966 and the rural development aspects of the cross-border programmes PEACE and INTERREG. The Department of Community, Rural and Gaeltacht Affairs was established in 2002 with the remit, *inter alia*, of promoting economic and social development in rural communities and is responsible for administering these programmes.

5 AGRI-ENVIRONMENT ISSUES

Agri-environment Policy
In addition to support for agricultural restructuring and rural enterprise development, the other main objective of EU rural development policy is to protect the rural environment. Because agriculture, along with forestry, accounts for over 70 per cent of the country's land use, it has the major responsibility for shaping the rural environment. In this role, it has both negative and positive consequences for environmental protection and rural landscapes. On the one hand, intensive agriculture is associated with a range of environmental risks including water pollution and the loss of biodiversity and valued amenities. Thus, agricultural production is increasingly influenced by environmental regulations designed to minimise these risks. Planning permission is now required for large intensive livestock units. The Nitrates Directive, designed to improve water quality, limits the number of livestock farmers can carry, as well as requiring investment in storage facilities for animal manure to ensure that it is spread only in the months when the land can absorb it. Livestock production is a major contributor to Ireland's greenhouse gas emissions, and reduced livestock numbers may be sought as a way of meeting Ireland's obligations under the Kyoto Protocol (see below). On the other hand, it is increasingly accepted that farmers are managers of our natural resources and provide environmental services as well as foodstuffs, in what is now characterised as a multifunctional agriculture. Farmers are not normally paid by the market to provide such services. Where these services are valued by society, there is a case for public support.

The EU took a big step to integrate environmental considerations into the CAP with the launch of an agri-environment scheme in 1994 as one of the accompanying measures of the MacSharry CAP reform (see Section 3). This is now a major focus of Pillar 2 of the CAP. It is implemented in Ireland as the Rural Environment Protection Scheme (REPS), under which farmers follow environmentally friendly farming practices in return for additional payments. Around 59,000 farmers farming two million hectares participated in the scheme in 2006 and payments under the scheme amounted to €329 million in that year. REPS is now a significant contributor to farm income. Based on 2004 National Farm Survey data, farmers in REPS had an average family farm income (FFI) of €15,990, of which REPS payments contributed €5,638. This compared with an FFI of €12,986 for extensive farmers not in REPS.

Early versions of the REPS scheme were mainly intended to encourage farmers to reduce fertiliser use as a way of avoiding pollution. Over time, the scheme has evolved to put more emphasis on positive actions to promote biodiversity. In REPS3, introduced in 2004, participating farmers were required to choose two from a selection of 16 biodiversity options. Examples of the actions supported include the establishment or rejuvenation of hedgerows, repair and construction of stone walls, establishing nature corridors, and planting species-rich grassland. In addition, farmers could choose from six supplementary measures if they wished. Through these measures, the REPS scheme supports farmers to conserve corncrake habitats and rare breeds, to plant traditional orchards, to grow food for wild birds or to convert to organic farming. REPS4, introduced as part of the CAP Rural Development Plan in the NDP 2007–2013 (see above), continues this emphasis on promoting biodiversity. It increases the number of biodiversity options eligible for support and also makes it easier for more intensive farmers to participate in REPS. €2.1 billion has been set aside to fund REPS payments over the period of the plan.

An important concept introduced as part of the June 2003 CAP reform is cross-compliance. Cross-compliance means that farmers must be in compliance with EU and statutory standards in the field of environmental protection, public health, animal and plant health and animal welfare and are required to keep land in good agricultural and environmental condition to be eligible to receive the single farm payment. Whereas insistence on cross-compliance was optional following the Agenda 2000 CAP reform, member states are now required to ensure that land or production in receipt of direct payments is farmed with appropriate respect for the environment and the other mandatory standards. Payments can be reduced or withheld in the event of non-compliance.

Cross-compliance is now the baseline for payments under Pillar 1 of the CAP. This has had a knock-on effect on the functioning of REPS. We saw that REPS in its early years functioned largely as an extensification scheme. In return for accepting restrictions on fertiliser use, farmers were eligible to receive additional payments under the scheme. But now it is assumed that farmers are compensated for meeting minimum statutory environmental standards with the single farm payment. Payments under the REPS scheme are only justified where farmers make an additional effort to supply environmental benefits which are valued by the public at large, such as the provision of habitats, or the maintenance of hedgerows or stone walls, over and above good environmental practice. As a result, we now see much greater emphasis on positive actions to promote biodiversity in the more recent REPS schemes.

Energy from Agriculture

The significant increase in energy prices (with oil prices increasing from $40 per barrel in mid-2004 to $110 per barrel in early 2008) as well as the need to reduce carbon dioxide emissions has renewed interest in agriculture and forestry as a provider of renewable energy. Ireland is hugely reliant on imported energy to meet over 90 per cent of its requirements and, under prompting from EU legislation, ambitious targets to increase the contribution of renewable energy have been set. Renewable energy includes all non-fossil energy sources such as wind, solar, geothermal, wave, tidal, hydro- and bio-energy. Bio-energy can be derived from agricultural feedstocks, forestry and recycled waste from municipal, agricultural and industrial sources. Renewable energies contributed around 2.5 per cent to Ireland's total primary energy requirement in 2005, with biomass accounting for around one per cent and hydro and wind for most of the remainder. The majority of biomass energy in Ireland is derived from wood products which are converted into heat, although there is growing interest in using wood for electricity production through combined heat and power plants.

The EU has a mandatory 20 per cent target of renewable energies in overall EU energy consumption by 2020. It also agreed a ten per cent binding minimum target to be achieved by all member states for the share of biofuels in overall EU transport petrol and diesel consumption by 2020, provided this can be introduced in a cost-efficient way (this is a reference to the availability by that date of so-called 'second-generation' biofuels presumed to be more cost-effective and sustainable than those currently available). Ireland is bound by both these targets and faces a significant challenge in meeting them. The 2007 Energy White Paper set a target of 15 per cent renewable electricity by 2010 and 33 per cent by 2020, compared to eight per cent in 2006. Ireland's share of biofuels in overall transport fuels was only one per cent in 2005.

Ireland's interventions to meet the biofuels target have been limited to date, restricted to providing excise duty relief for a number of pilot biofuels projects (even though this is estimated to cost some €200m over the 2006–2010 period) and some limited support to farmers for growing energy crops. To meet the biofuels targets, the 2007 Bioenergy Action Plan proposed to develop an obligation scheme that will oblige fuel distributors to achieve an average of 5.75 per cent biofuels (on an energy basis) of their total annual fuel business by 2009. On the production side, additional incentives have been put in place to encourage farmers to grow more energy crops. Also of importance, but of less significance, is the implication of the proposed magnitude of the wind-generated component of renewable energy. An expansion of the agricultural land area devoted to wind farms will likely increase significantly as suitable offshore sites are known to be limited.

The growth in public support for energy production from agriculture has been justified because of its contribution to energy security, to helping meet greenhouse gas reduction targets (see below) and to providing an alternative revenue stream to farmers as traditional forms of agricultural support are wound down. However, the transfer of agricultural resources from food to fuel production has contributed to the recent rise in food prices and has led some voices to question the sustainability of this strategy. Relying on domestic production of feedstock to meet the biofuel targets in the EU, and Ireland, would imply that most of the arable area would be required for fuel rather than food production. The climate change advantages of the first generation of biofuels (largely rapeseed for bio-diesel and sugar beet and wheat for bio-ethanol in Europe) as compared to fossil fuels are increasingly being questioned. Developing countries can produce biofuels much more cheaply than we can in Europe, although there are worries that a large-scale expansion of the land area devoted to biofuels in tropical countries may have other adverse environmental impacts such as the destruction of rainforest. For these reasons, a number of scientific and advocacy bodies have called for the biofuels targets at EU level to be rescinded. In Ireland, solid-fuel energy crops such as willow and miscanthus used for the production of energy and heat are likely to be more economically attractive, have better energy input/output ratios and contribute more to greenhouse gas (GHG) emission savings.

Agriculture and Climate Change
Climate change policy has two consequences for the agricultural and forestry sectors. First, agricultural production will be influenced by climate change. On the assumption of gradual climate change, mean annual temperatures are likely to rise, with greater rainfall in winter but less in the summer months. Increased temperatures and CO_2 levels in the gradual climate change scenario could increase agricultural production potential in Ireland, although this would be hampered by water shortages in summer which could necessitate greater reliance on irrigation, and we would experience greater flooding and more storms. However, the impact of more extreme climate change, perhaps brought on by the melting of the ice caps and the disappearance of the influence of the Gulf Stream on the Irish climate, is much more difficult to predict.

On the other hand, agriculture adds to greenhouse gas (GHG) emissions, although it can also contribute to mitigation strategies through sequestration and through development of renewable energy resources. Because of the importance of cattle production, the agricultural sector contributes around 28 per cent of Ireland's total GHG emissions. This is significantly down from 1990 when agriculture contributed 36 per cent of the total. Emissions are predominantly non-CO_2 gases and arise from enteric fermentation in animals, management of animal manures and agricultural soils.

The EU has adopted a long-term climate protection target to limit global mean temperatures to not more than 2°C above pre-industrial levels. Under the Kyoto Protocol, the EU agreed to reduce its total emissions in the period 2008–2012 by eight per cent below the 1990 level. Ireland's contribution to the EU commitment is to limit its greenhouse gas emissions to no more than 13 per cent above 1990 levels in 2008–2012. In 2007, the EU went further and offered to cut GHG emissions by 30 per cent by 2020 compared to 1990 as its contribution to the negotiation of a post-2012 Kyoto agreement, provided that other developed countries commit themselves to comparable emission reductions. Even in the absence of an international agreement, the EU committed itself to achieve at least a 20 per cent reduction of greenhouse gas emissions by 2020 compared to 1990. The government has recognised that meeting these targets raises very serious economic and social issues for Ireland.

Ireland's National Climate Change Strategy (NCCS) for the 2007–2012 period anticipates that agriculture and forestry will contribute towards GHG reductions partly through a reduction in the national cattle herd stimulated by the decoupling of farm support payments (see above) and partly through an increase in afforestation. Smaller unquantified contributions will be made by reduced fertiliser use, tree and hedgerow planting under the REPS scheme, as well as the production of energy crops. The level of sequestration in Kyoto-eligible forests, which are mainly those newly established since 1990, is not sensitive to the drop in planting which has occurred in recent years, and the NCCS target for forestry will probably be achieved. However, while cattle numbers have been falling, the rate of decline in agricultural emissions may not be sufficiently fast to reach the NCCS target for this sector, particularly if higher milk and livestock prices encourage greater production. This raises the possibility that more vigorous interventions will be needed if the Programme for Government target of a national three per cent fall in emissions annually is to be met.

6 FOOD PROCESSING AND FOOD SAFETY

Food Industry

Very few agricultural products are sold directly to the consumer – vegetables, fruit and eggs in farmers' markets being the main examples. Most agricultural products are purchased by food processors who prepare food for final consumption for either the domestic or export markets. Output of the Irish food industry (including drinks) in 2005 amounted to €24.2 billion or almost five times that of primary agriculture. Gross value added (which subtracts the value of raw materials purchased by the industry and gives a better idea of its contribution to the overall economy) amounted to €8.7 billion in 2005, equivalent to six per cent of GNP at market prices. The industry provides direct employment for around 45,000 people or one-fifth of the total industrial workforce. While there are over 640 individual plants in the industry, the 40 largest firms, each with over 250 employees, account for around 40 per cent of the employment and almost 60 per cent of the output.

The market for food is changing rapidly due to changing consumer demands and market structures. Changing consumer lifestyles are having a decisive influence on food demand. Increased numbers of working women, reduced leisure time and the decline in the traditional family unit are changing eating habits and increasing the demand for convenience foods. Thus important growth areas for the food industry are the food ingredients business (such as dairy ingredients, meat and by-products such as pizza toppings and meat flavourings, and other ingredients such as colourings, flavourings and malt) which produce ingredients for pre-prepared foods, as well as the food service sector (embracing all forms of catering and eating out). Eating out now accounts for 25 per cent of food expenditure in Ireland, though this is still behind the equivalent figure in the USA of 50 per cent. The other important trend is the growing importance of retail concentration, which is shifting market power to the giant retailers. Just 25 retailers in Europe now account for 45 per cent of food sales. In Ireland, three multiples account for over 50 per cent of retail grocery sales. This concentration of buying power gives the large retailers substantial power to dictate terms to their suppliers, including not only price but also quality and safety characteristics.

The Irish food industry has a number of strengths and weaknesses in meeting these market challenges. Production facilities are modern, in part because of generous EU investment aids in the past, and Irish food benefits from a good marketing image abroad. However, the relatively small scale of the industry inhibits cost competitiveness and access to markets. It also makes product and process innovation more difficult. The industry remains reliant on commodity products with limited penetration of value-added markets. The industry has received substantial support in successive National Development Plans designed to enhance its competitiveness and innovative capabilities, while ensuring that development is underpinned by attention to food safety and consumer demands. Food safety issues are considered in more detail in the remainder of this section.

Growing Concern over Food Safety

From earliest times food has been particularly susceptible to exploitation, and there is a long history of food legislation with the purpose of preventing consumers being either cheated or poisoned! Measures for the protection of the consumer against the adulteration of food and drink are among the earliest examples of social legislation. Since then the scope of food law has been greatly widened. Examples of some of the matters now covered by legislation include the produce of diseased animals posing a threat to human health; sanitary conditions in food preparation, packaging and handling; pesticide and hormone residues in food; packaging materials which may pose a threat to health; food additives; the labelling requirements for food products; and weights and measures legislation.

Despite the undoubted improvement in food purity and in merchandising practices brought about by this legislation, consumers are increasingly uneasy about the safety and quality of the modern food supply. Issues of recent concern include agrochemical residues in food, the increasing number and diversity of food additives, the use of illegal substances in livestock production, the presence of nitrates in drinking water and genetically engineered foods. There have been sharp falls in the consumption of particular foods caused by publicity given, for example, to bovine spongiform encephalopathy (BSE) in cattle, listeria in soft cheeses and salmonella in eggs. Consumer concerns also extend beyond the safety of food products to their production methods including genetic modification, animal welfare, and environmental and ethical concerns.

The risk of foodborne diseases has increased for a number of reasons. Best hygiene practices are not always followed in commercial and domestic kitchens. Fewer people are preparing their own food and more eating outside the home means a higher proportion of people at risk in outbreaks. The increasing demand for ready-to-go foods has resulted in food being served in a growing number of non-traditional outlets such as garage forecourts. The global distribution of food has lengthened the food chain. The increased competition and price constraints on food producers has led the food sector to seek cost reductions through ever more complex food processing and may sometimes encourage producers to adopt practices which have adverse health effects. Nutrition is another area of concern. While consumers are preoccupied with food safety at present, food quality issues and the nutritional value of food may re-emerge as a more important policy issue in future.

Fortunately, in Ireland, food problems have not emerged to the dramatic extent reached elsewhere. However, the increase in food poisoning notifications (E. coli, for instance) suggests that vigilance is essential. Food production and tourism are major elements in the economy, and both depend crucially on a favourable international perception of the safety of Irish food. So along with the issue of the health and lives of its own citizens, Ireland has a vital economic interest in becoming a centre of excellence in food safety.

Economic Considerations
In economic terms, the need for governments to regulate for food safety is the result of a market failure. This arises because consumers are not necessarily in a position to determine the safety characteristics of food they consume on the basis of visual inspection alone. There is thus an asymmetry of information between the producer and consumer of food. In this, the market for food safety is like the market for used cars. Sellers have more information than buyers about the quality of the car. Because buyers often cannot tell the difference between a good and a bad used car, both good and bad cars must sell at the same price and the seller of a good car is unable to extract a premium for quality. In the same way, there is a tendency for food safety to be undersupplied by the market because consumers are not always able to distinguish between high and low food standards.

Of course, if we go to a restaurant and subsequently experience illness due to food poisoning, we are unlikely to patronise that restaurant again. Where there is the likelihood of repeat purchases, food businesses have an incentive to maintain high standards in order to maximise the likelihood of retaining our custom. The development of brand names, or supermarkets that monitor quality on our behalf, are other ways in which market institutions can respond to the asymmetry of information. However, sometimes firms themselves may be unaware of, say, the carcinogenic risk associated with a particular additive or production process. There may also be strong externalities that justify government intervention, either on the production side (one rogue producer who fails to meet adequate food standards can put the reputation of an entire national food industry at risk) or on the consumption side (an infectious foodborne illness imposes wider costs on society that transcend those incurred by the individual consumer). This is the economic case for governments to step in to ensure that minimum food standards are maintained.

While the failure to observe adequate food standards can impose economic costs both on individuals and society at large, maintaining and enforcing these standards is also a costly exercise. For economists, this raises the question whether the benefits from a particular food regulation (in terms of the avoided cost of food illnesses or, for an exporting country, the loss of market reputation in export markets) exceed its costs. The idea that we should try to balance benefits and costs in setting food regulations suggests that trying to achieve zero risk is not the optimal strategy. Removing all risk from eating food is likely to be hugely expensive, and the economic benefit from lowering risk from a minimal to a zero risk of contracting an illness may not justify taking this extra step. There may also be an alternative and more efficient instrument available to achieve the same degree of risk reduction, for example by introducing more stringent product liability legislation which allows consumers to claim damages if harmed by consuming unsafe food. Governments, of course, should not take such decisions on the basis of cost benefit studies alone; moral and ethical criteria must also be taken into account. However, the economist's framework of balancing the expected benefits from risk reduction against the costs of achieving such reductions should be an important adjunct to the decision-making process in food safety regulation.

European Union Food Safety Framework

These growing concerns prompted the incoming European Commission in October 1999 to make food safety a top priority. In January 2000, the Irish Commissioner for Health and Consumer Protection, David Byrne, produced a White Paper on Food Safety which outlined a comprehensive strategy to restore consumers' confidence in their food supply.[7] There were three elements to the strategy: new legislation on the safety of food and animal feed; a new agency to offer scientific advice on foodborne threats; and more stringent control and enforcement.

A new General Food Law which brought together the general principles of food and animal feed safety was agreed in 2002. Until then, EU food law had been motivated mainly by the desire to facilitate the free movement of foodstuffs throughout the internal market, by removing technical barriers such as differences in standards. The new law made food safety and consumer protection the cornerstone of the regulatory regime. Including animal feed in its provisions was a major advance as animal feed has been the source of many food scares in the past decade. This was supplemented by new food hygiene legislation passed in 2004 and which has come into effect since 2006. This modernises, consolidates and simplifies the previous EU food hygiene legislation and introduces a 'farm to fork' approach to food safety, by including primary production (that is, farmers and growers) in food hygiene legislation, in the majority of cases for the first time.

The general principles which now underlie food safety policy emphasise a whole food chain approach (food safety must be ensured at all stages of the food chain, from the producer through to the consumer), risk analysis (meaning that the policy is based on a scientific understanding of risk with due account for the need for precaution when scientific opinion is not yet clear), operator liability (all food sector operators are now responsible for ensuring the safety of the products which they import, produce, process or sell), traceability (from 1 January 2005 all foodstuffs, animal feeds and feed ingredients must be traceable right through the food chain) and openness (citizens have the right to clear and accurate information on food and health risks from public authorities). The General Food Law is supplemented by a large number of targeted regulations addressing specific food safety issues, such as the use of pesticides, food supplements, colouring, antibiotics and hormones in food production; rules on hygiene; food labelling; and legislation setting down procedures for the release, marketing, labelling and traceability of crops and foodstuffs containing genetically modified organisms.

The second Commission initiative was the creation of the European Food Safety Authority (EFSA) in 2002 to provide a source of independent, objective scientific advice on food-related risks. The new Authority has responsibility for the EU Rapid Alert System which links EU countries in cases of foodborne threats. The Commission explicitly rejected the option of modelling it on the US Food and Drugs Administration, which has responsibility not only for risk assessment (i.e. quantifying the risk associated with a potential food hazard) but also risk management (i.e. taking the necessary decisions to respond to a perceived foodborne risk such as strengthening existing regulations). The Authority's role is limited to giving its opinion, and it is up to the Commission (in conjunction with the Council and the Parliament) to initiate the required action. The EFSA works through a series of scientific panels composed of independent experts who are responsible for providing scientific opinions to the Authority. Of course, scientists may disagree, and member states in the legislation establishing EFSA were reluctant to grant it the power to act as the ultimate source of food-safety information. In the event of a disagreement between the EFSA and a national food safety agency, for example, it would be up to the courts to resolve this conflict. However, there are encouraging signs that EFSA has developed strong working relationships with national agencies to develop a common approach to risk assessment throughout the Union.

The third initiative was to improve the EU framework for control and enforcement of food safety legislation. Enforcement of food regulations is the responsibility of national governments, albeit under the oversight of the EU. An EU framework directive lays down norms and procedures relating to inspection and enforcement, and the Food and Veterinary Office of the European Commission, which is based in Grange, County Meath, controls the performance of national authorities and makes recommendations aimed at improving national control and inspection systems. The Commission's powers to ensure enforcement in member states have been criticised in the past as slow and unwieldy. An important enforcement change was the extension during 2000 of the EU Product Liability Directive to primary agricultural products such as beef, milk, fruit and vegetables. This will make farmers liable for damages if consumers take legal proceedings against them and if there is proof that they are responsible for putting unsafe food into the food chain.

Irish Responses
In Ireland, the Food Safety Authority was set up in 1999 to ensure that food produced, distributed or marketed in the state meets the highest standards of food safety and hygiene and to co-ordinate food safety activities 'from farm to fork'. The Authority has functions in relation to research, advice, co-ordination of services and certification of food. It operates the national food safety compliance programme by means of service contracts with the agencies involved in the enforcement of food legislation (including government departments, health boards, local authorities, and the Radiological Protection Institute). Around 2,300 persons in total are involved in the inspection and control of food. In addition, the Authority works with industry and training bodies to improve, harmonise and co-ordinate food safety and hygiene training through the country. The Authority is required to operate on the basis of scientific principles and with the primacy of consumer interests in mind.

Initiatives such as the National Beef Assurance Scheme and the National Sheep Identification System have been launched to ensure the identification and traceability of animals/meat. Controls on BSE remain in place to ensure that meat from confirmed cases and from herds in which cases have been located does not enter the food or feed chains. Another priority area concerns residue testing, which is particularly focused on detecting illegal growth promoters in cattle and antibiotic residues in pigs. A new cross-border Food Safety Promotion Board known as Safefood has been established under the Good Friday Agreement to contribute to the improved coordination of food safety activities on the island as a whole. Its functions include food safety promotion; research into food safety; communication of food alerts; surveillance of foodborne diseases; and the promotion of scientific co-operation and links between laboratories.

The growing demand for food safety and improved animal welfare will increasingly impact on farmers. Even in the absence of government regulation, the private sector and particularly the large retail chains are insisting that their suppliers meet stringent hygiene and safety standards. These demands will require farmers to undertake additional investments and will accelerate the process of structural change in the industry. However, they also open up additional marketing opportunities. Instead of selling beef as a commodity product, for example, it becomes possible to produce beef for particular niche markets and to guarantee consumers that their particular requirements have been met. One fast-growing market is for organic produce. Organic production in Ireland is relatively limited, with 1,270 registered producers and 38,000 hectares, or 0.9 per cent of the agricultural land area, in organic production or in conversion in 2006. The 2002 report of the Organic Development Committee had estimated that a target of nine per cent of agricultural land under organic farming by 2006 was a feasible goal. A national steering group has been established to promote marketing and research, and financial assistance for farmers wishing to convert to organic production is available under the REPS agri-environment scheme. The decoupling of direct payments should also give a boost to organic production in future.

7 CONCLUSIONS

The agri-food sector is one of the key sectors of the Irish economy, accounting for around six per cent of GDP and eight per cent of employment. This chapter has emphasised the way in which the sector is heavily influenced by government policies promoting specific objectives. The substantial protection provided to EU agriculture means that almost all the income generated by agricultural production arises because of transfers either from consumers or taxpayers resulting from the operation of the Common Agricultural Policy. The share of budget transfers from taxpayers, which now accounts for 80 per cent of Irish farm income, is particularly striking.

Farming faces both challenges and opportunities in the future. The system of transfers is threatened by further WTO trade commitments, by changing EU budget priorities and by an increasingly powerful environmental lobby concerned about the negative impact of intensive agricultural production on the environment. The future justification for the single farm payment, so important to incomes on many farms, is unclear, with many inequities between farmers themselves. On the other hand, food prices are hardening, driven upwards by growing demand for meat and dairy products in the rapidly growing emerging economies, by the competition between food and fuel for agricultural resources, and by constraints on increasing global supply capacity. There has rarely been a more propitious time to wean farming off protectionism and to encourage a greater market orientation. Over the next decade, more emphasis must be put on strengthening the competitiveness of farm production while ensuring that it lives up to ever higher consumer demands for safety and environmental sustainability.

The relative decline in the importance of food production, given its central importance in rural areas in the past, has stimulated the search for an alternative basis for rural development. In principle, with the publication of the 1999 White Paper on Rural Development informing the investment priorities included in successive National Development Plans, there now exists a coherent and co-ordinated strategy to this end. Advances in our understanding of the dynamics of rural growth have highlighted the importance of dynamic urban centres, or gateways, in underpinning growth in their surrounding rural areas. Hence the importance of the national spatial strategy announced in 2002. Successive National Plans have contained a commitment to balanced regional development, with the implicit objective of encouraging more rapid growth in the less favoured BMW region as compared to the better-endowed S&E region. However, as we noted above, there is a danger that the rhetoric is not yet matched by appropriate resource allocations.

The paradox should be noted that, at a time when government intervention in agricultural markets is being reduced, the demand for greater regulation of food markets has never been greater. While the rationale for continued agricultural support becomes less and less persuasive as food prices increase and farm incomes approach equality with incomes in the non-farm sector, the growing complexity of the food chain and fear of the consequences of new technological advances is fuelling consumer demands for greater food regulation. While a perfectly sound case for regulation can be made, it is important to bear in mind that all regulation imposes costs as well as benefits and that the task of the regulator is to find the appropriate balance. Economists are particularly well trained to assist in finding this balance through assessing the costs and benefits of alternative regulatory policies.

Endnotes

1 A. Matthews, *Farm Incomes: Myths and Reality*, Cork, Cork University Press 2000, contains a discussion of these difficulties.

2 The farm household figures in this section take a broad definition of a farm household as any household with income from farming.

3 Commission of the European Communities, *The Future of Rural Society: Commission Communication to Parliament and the Council*, Office for Official Publications of the European Communities (OOPEC), Luxembourg 1998.

4 Department of Agriculture and Food, *Ensuring the Future – A Strategy for Rural Development in Ireland: A White Paper on Rural Development*, Stationery Office, Dublin 1999, p. 19.

5 Department of Agriculture and Food, op. cit., p. 20.

6 NUTS ('Nomenclature des Unites Territoriales pour Statistiques') is the term given to the EU regional classification system. It is a three-level hierarchical system. NUTS1 regions are normally between three and seven million population in size. Ireland as a whole is a NUTS1 region. Each NUTS1 region contains a number of NUTS2 regions between 800,000 and three million in size, which are in turn divided into a number of NUTS3 regions between 150,000 and 800,000 in size.

7 European Commission, *White Paper on Food Safety*, OOPEC, Brussels January 2000.

POLICY ISSUES IN THE NON-MARKET SECTOR

CHAPTER 11

Health: Funding, Access and Efficiency

*Anne Nolan**

1 INTRODUCTION

This chapter examines the health sector, a key component of Irish economic activity and the subject of much recent policy discussion. In terms of its economic impact, expenditure on the health services accounted for 8.8 per cent of GNI and 9.7 per cent of total employment in 2005.[1] After years of expenditure growth barely in line with inflation during the 1980s and early 1990s, expenditure on the health service in Ireland has increased dramatically, by over 100 per cent in real terms between 1997 and 2007. While Irish health expenditure as a proportion of GNI increased from 7.3 per cent in 2000 to 8.8 per cent in 2005, health expenditure as a proportion of GNI has also risen across the OECD, with the result that Ireland still ranks among the low spenders on health, in terms of health expenditure as a proportion of GNI (see Table 11.1).[2]

The challenges facing the Irish health service today are very different from those of the 1980s and early 1990s. Media commentary highlights the negatives: long waiting lists, A&E overcrowding, spiralling costs and wasteful spending as well as deteriorating outcomes in certain areas (suicide, obesity and binge drinking). While much discussion in Ireland during the 1980s focused on the under-funding of the health services (public expenditure on the health services decreased in real terms in some years during the 1980s), the emphasis has shifted now to consider issues such as the efficiency and effectiveness of increasing levels of spending, quality and patient safety, cost containment and access. While ensuring that increased expenditure delivers a quality service efficiently and with sufficient effectiveness in terms of health outcomes are important concerns, the extent to which access to health services is distributed equitably across the population is a much discussed issue in Ireland and elsewhere. Of crucial concern in Ireland is the extent to which coverage by private health insurance confers faster access to hospital services.

Table 11.1
Health Expenditure as a Percentage of GNI[1], 2000 and 2005

	2000	2005	% aged over 65
Austria	10.2	10.3	15.7
Denmark	8.4	9.0	15.0
Finland	6.6	7.5	15.7
France	9.5	11.0	16.4
Germany	10.4	10.6	19.3
Ireland	*7.3*	*8.8*	*11.1*
Netherlands	7.8	9.0 (2004)	13.8 (2003)
UK	7.2	8.1	16.0
USA	13.2	15.3	12.4

Sources: OECD, *Health Data 2007,* OECD, Paris 2007; European Commission, *AMECO Macro Economic Database 2007* (available at:
http://ec.europa.eu/economy_finance/indicators/annual_macro_economic_database/ameco_en.htm 2008*)*; European Central Bank, Statistical Data Warehouse 2007 (available at:
http://sdw.ecb.europa.eu/home.do 2008).
[1] While health expenditure is usually expressed as a proportion of GDP, the large divergence between Irish GDP and GNP/GNI figures means that, for comparative purposes, it is more appropriate to express health expenditure as a proportion of GNP/GNI (see Chapter 6). Expressing health expenditure as a proportion of GNI makes very little difference to any of the other countries covered but increases Irish health spending, from 7.5 per cent when using GDP to 8.8 per cent when using GNI.

The remainder of this chapter focuses on these themes of access, efficiency and effectiveness in the context of discussions on key issues with regard to the health services in Ireland. Section 2 discusses the rationale for government intervention in the financing and delivery of health services in Ireland (see also Chapter 3 on the role of the state), outlining the various efficiency and equity justifications for government intervention in the sector. Section 3 moves on to outline the structure of the Irish health service, concentrating on the organisation of eligibility for free health services to ensure equity of access to healthcare as well as the interactions between the public and private sectors in both the financing and delivery of health services in Ireland. This section also briefly describes the 2001 Health Strategy and the 2003 Health Service Reform Programme, and the resulting changes in the structure of the healthcare sector in Ireland. Section 4 discusses the four sources of finance in the health sector, concentrating on private health insurance. It also discusses the equity and efficiency concerns surrounding the complex intermix between public and private healthcare in Ireland, in particular in the hospitals sector. Section 5 outlines trends in health expenditure in Ireland, looks at comparisons with other OECD countries and discusses the problem of measuring output from the health sector and making international comparisons at an aggregated level, or at a disaggregated level between different interventions/treatments. Section 6 concludes the chapter.

2 WHY GOVERNMENT INTERVENTION?

Despite the fact that the private sector accounts for approximately 20 per cent of expenditure on the health services (see Section 4) and is heavily involved in the provision of health services in Ireland, the public sector remains the main agent responsible for the finance and delivery of health services in Ireland. Chapter 3 discussed the rationale for government intervention in the economy in general. In terms of the health services, efficiency concerns relating to asymmetric information, uncertainty and the existence of externalities, as well as equity or distributional concerns, motivate government involvement in healthcare. Where the government does not directly involve itself in the provision of healthcare services, it may have a role in terms of financing, regulation, pricing (taxation and subsidies) and information provision.

While asymmetric information, uncertainty and externalities are the most readily identifiable indicators of market failure in the health sector, healthcare markets also suffer from imperfect competition in the sense that many of the conditions for perfectly competitive markets are absent or deficient. Many services, e.g. hospital services, are subject to economies of scale, producers can often influence the level of demand and/or price, and price signals are often absent, particularly where third-party reimbursement systems are in operation. Most importantly, however, the assumptions of perfectly informed consumers, the absence of uncertainty and the absence of externalities are violated in healthcare markets.

Asymmetric Information
The nature of the relationship between producers and consumers in healthcare is distorted by asymmetric information. Patients are essentially buying the doctor's knowledge and/or information when they visit. In comparison with other goods and services, information acquisition on the part of the consumer in healthcare markets is made more difficult by the nature of the product. Learning by experience is complicated by the fact that every illness episode is different and the consumer cannot sample the service before purchase or is unlikely to have had prior experience of the same service. In addition, the information is often technically complex, involving many years of study.

The relationship has often been characterised as a principal agent one: due to the high costs of acquiring such technical information, the patient relies on the doctor to act in their best interests in terms of diagnosis and treatment decisions. While asymmetric information justifies a role for government in regulating the behaviour of doctors and other healthcare professionals through licensing, regulating the pharmaceuticals that can be prescribed to patients and improving consumers' information, it does not follow that government intervention in either the financing or provision of healthcare is necessary.

Uncertainty

Healthcare markets are also characterised by uncertainty, i.e. lack of information about the future. This necessitates a role for insurance in offering the consumer protection against uncertainty. Ill health is inherently unpredictable, both in terms of financial costs and physical and emotional suffering. However, the problems of adverse selection, moral hazard and cream-skimming may arise in a private health insurance market, leading to efficiency and equity failings. Adverse selection arises when the insurer cannot distinguish between low and high risks, because individuals purchasing insurance have better information about their risk status than the insurer. Insurers must therefore base the premium on the risk pool that includes both low and high risks. Low-risk individuals will not purchase insurance because the premium does not reflect their risk status, leaving only high-risk individuals in the risk pool. This can make the fund unsustainable. The solution is to have compulsory insurance or differential premiums. However, due to concerns that certain high-risk individuals would be denied access to healthcare under a private system with differential premiums on the basis of age and health status, most governments intervene to provide compulsory health insurance for most basic health services.

Moral hazard behaviour, where an individual's behaviour is affected by their insurance status, may arise in the form of excessive utilisation of resources on the part of the patient and also providers (as they know that their patients do not bear the full costs). Cost-sharing initiatives, which aim to make both patients and providers more aware of the resource implications of their decisions, are becoming increasingly common. However, to some extent the professional relationship between doctor and patient should limit moral hazard behaviour.

A final problem associated with a private insurance market is that of cream-skimming. Insurers encourage low-risk persons to insure with their company. Once again, due to equity concerns about certain groups being denied medical treatment, governments intervene, either to offer compulsory insurance or to regulate the sector. In Ireland, the government strictly regulates the behaviour of the three major private insurers in an attempt to prevent cream-skimming through the principles of open enrolment (no one can be refused cover), community rating (all individuals face the same premium) and lifetime cover (once insured, an individual's policy cannot be terminated). However, as private insurance in Ireland essentially provides cover for services already available free of charge (or heavily subsidised) in the public sector, the rationale for these restrictions on behaviour, in particular community rating, has been questioned. The continued stability of the community-rating system means that a risk-equalisation scheme (which aims to remove differences in insurers' costs that result from differing risk profiles among members) must be implemented. While the High Court ruled in favour of the risk-equalisation scheme in 2006, there is currently a stay on payments pending further legal proceedings.

Due to concerns over the ability of the private market to deliver insurance efficiently and equitably (in particular, adverse selection, moral hazard and cream-skimming behaviours must be absent), governments in Europe have tended to intervene by providing compulsory insurance for most basic health services (e.g. in France and Germany all individuals are compulsorily insured for most health services and the system is funded through the social insurance scheme with the contributions of those on low incomes or that are economically inactive paid by the state). In Ireland, the state intervenes by providing compulsory insurance for certain services (mainly hospital services) to the full population, providing compulsory insurance for all services to certain vulnerable sections of the population (those on low incomes, the elderly) and strictly regulating conduct in the private insurance market (the Health Insurance Authority was established in 2001 to act as regulator of the private health insurance market in Ireland).

Externalities

The healthcare sector may also be characterised by the presence of externalities when private costs or benefits are out of line with social costs or benefits. For a positive/negative externality, private benefits/costs are less than social benefits/costs, meaning that output is below/above the socially-optimal level. The standard solution to an externality is to levy a Pigouvian tax in the case of goods or services that produce negative externalities or to offer a subsidy in the case of goods or services that produce positive externalities. Free childhood vaccinations against infectious diseases and excise taxes on cigarettes are the most obvious examples of government intervention in the health sector due to the presence of externalities. A vaccinated population confers a positive externality on society while second-hand cigarette smoke confers a negative externality on society; in the absence of government intervention vaccination levels would be lower than the socially optimal level due to higher social benefits than private benefits, while smoking levels would be greater than the socially optimal level due to higher social costs than private costs. Of course, the efficacy of taxes in changing behaviour to reflect the socially optimal level depends on the price elasticity of demand for the good/service, the availability of substitutes, its budget share, etc. (see also Chapter 4).

A related concept is that which regards healthcare as a merit good. While it is commonly assumed that the individual is the best judge of his or her own interests, with merit goods such as education, healthcare or cultural facilities (e.g. museums) this assumption does not necessarily hold. In the absence of government intervention, too little of the good in question will be consumed as individuals are unaware of the long-term benefits. The government therefore intervenes to ensure that all citizens receive free or heavily subsidised basic health services, even if private professionals provide many of these services.

Equity

Apart from efficiency concerns, the desire to ensure that healthcare should be distributed equitably across the population motivates government intervention in the sector. However, there is much discussion over what is meant by equity in the context of the health services (see also Chapter 7). Is the objective equality of opportunity (i.e. access to healthcare) or equality of outcome (i.e. health status)? Many governments intervene to smooth out differences in health outcomes that are not related to need factors such as age, gender or health status, but rather to socio-economic characteristics such as income, area of residence, level of education, etc. For example, a recent study found that women in Ireland from the unskilled manual and unemployed social classes were significantly more likely to give birth to low birth-weight babies than those in the other social classes.[3] However, most governments also subscribe to the notion of equality of opportunity in the sense that access to healthcare should be distributed on the basis of need for care, not on the basis of non-health related attributes, such as ability to pay (which is the case for many other commodities). But how do we define access? Most studies proxy access by utilisation, arguing that access to health services is equitable if utilisation rates are similar, even after controlling for need factors such as age, gender and health status. However, it is obvious that even if everyone enjoys the same access to healthcare, persons in equal need may end up consuming different amounts of care (and types of care) due to differing tastes and preferences.

An additional issue concerns the progressivity of funding sources, i.e. most governments subscribe to the view that health services should be financed in relation to ability to pay (those on higher incomes should pay a higher proportion of their incomes in taxation, social insurance contributions, etc.). Such thinking motivates government involvement in the financing of healthcare services, offering free services to those on low incomes or in particularly vulnerable situations.

In practice, the government uses a variety of instruments to intervene in the health sector. While the government intervenes heavily in terms of regulation, pricing, information provision and financing in Ireland, it mainly leaves the provision of health services to private operators, who consequently receive much of their funding from public sources (e.g. GP services and voluntary hospital services). While government intervention to correct market failures is an accepted feature of modern economies, government failure may itself lead to efficiency or equity failings. In particular, government intervention in terms of provision may lead to inefficiency, as government-owned and operated facilities face a loose budget constraint. In addition, regulatory capture by vested interests may result in regulations that lead to an inefficient level of output, e.g. the restrictions on pharmacy locations which existed prior to the revocation of the 1996 Health Regulations Act in 2001 (see Chapter 9). Ensuring that public funding sources are progressive in their impact is also an important concern.

3 STRUCTURE OF THE IRISH HEALTH SERVICE

The Government, the Minister for Health and Children and the Department of Health and Children are at the head of health service provision in Ireland. The main role of the department is to support the minister in creating and assessing policy for the health services. The department also has a role in the future planning of health services, in consultation with the Health Service Executive (HSE), the voluntary sector, other government departments and other interested parties.

The HSE, which was established in January 2005, is responsible for the actual delivery of health and social care services in Ireland. Prior to its establishment, services were delivered through a complex structure of ten regional Health Boards, the Eastern Regional Health Authority and a number of other different agencies and organisations. The HSE has three core areas of responsibility: population health, which promotes and protects the health of the entire population; primary, community and continuing care (PCCC), which delivers care in the community; and the National Hospitals Office (NHO), which provides acute hospital and ambulance services. It delivers services to the public across four administrative areas – Dublin Mid-East, Dublin North-East, West and South. Each HSE Administrative Area is responsible for the provision of health and social services in its area. They provide many services directly (e.g. district nurses and public nursing homes) and they arrange for the provision of other services by health professionals, private health service providers, voluntary hospitals and voluntary/community organisations. Many other advisory agencies and voluntary organisations under the authority of the HSE play a role in service delivery, regulation and development in the health system, e.g. An Bord Altránais (the Nursing Board) is responsible for the regulation of the nursing profession in Ireland. The HSE is the largest employer in the state, employing 70,000 staff directly and funding a further 36,000 staff. The €12.4 billion budget (in 2006) is the largest of any public sector organisation in Ireland.[4]

Eligibility for Free Public Health Services

All individuals who are ordinarily resident in Ireland are granted either full or limited eligibility for public healthcare services. Individuals with full eligibility, termed 'medical cardholders' or 'public patients', are entitled to receive all health services free of charge, including GP services, prescribed medicines, all dental, ophthalmic and aural services, maternity services, in-patient services in public hospitals and specialist treatment in outpatient clinics of public hospitals. At present just under 30 per cent of the population have a medical card.

The remainder of the population, those with limited eligibility ('non-medical cardholders' or 'private patients'), are entitled to free maternity services, in-patient services in public hospitals (subject to a €66 charge per day), specialist services in outpatient clinics (again, subject to a €66 charge per day), assistance towards the cost of prescribed medicines over a monthly limit (under the Drugs Payment Scheme) and assistance towards the cost of prescribed medicines for certain chronic conditions (under the Long Term Illness Scheme) or high-cost treatments (under the High Tech Drugs Scheme). They must, however, pay for all GP consultations and all dental, ophthalmic and aural treatments. Ireland is unique within the old EU-15 in the extent to which individuals must pay for GP services: only the Netherlands also excludes a significant proportion of the population from eligibility to free GP care.

Delivery of Health Services

While the state is heavily involved in the financing of health services in Ireland (see Section 4), it mainly leaves the delivery of health services to the private sector, with the hospital and primary care sectors providing particularly good examples of the intermix between the public and private sectors in the financing and delivery of health services in Ireland. There are three different types of hospital in Ireland: voluntary hospitals, which are run on a not-for-profit basis by private organisations (usually religious institutions) but which receive most of their funding from the state; HSE hospitals, which are owned and operated by the HSE; and privately owned, operated and funded hospitals. Public hospital services are provided in voluntary and HSE hospitals and most of these hospitals also provide private healthcare, but they must clearly distinguish between public and private beds. In 2006, there were 53 publicly funded acute hospitals, 19 of which were voluntary hospitals located mainly in the Dublin area, and 28 hospitals were entirely privately owned and operated.

Primary care services are mainly provided by independent professionals (e.g. GPs, pharmacists, dentists, etc.) who may be contracted to provide services in the public sector, in addition to services provided to private patients (approximately two-thirds of GPs also have contracts to provide services to medical cardholders). The Primary Care Reimbursement Service (PCRS) undertakes the reimbursement of providers for GP, dental, optical and pharmaceutical services supplied to medical cardholders as well as the reimbursement of pharmacists for services provided to private patients under the various drugs schemes.

The Irish healthcare system therefore is a mixture of a universal public health service and a fee-based private system. Some services are publicly funded and delivered (e.g. treatment as a public patient in a public hospital), some are publicly funded but privately delivered (e.g. GP consultations by medical cardholders), some are privately funded and delivered (e.g. GP consultations by non-medical cardholders, treatment as a private patient in a private hospital) while some are privately funded but publicly delivered (e.g. non-medical cardholders must pay a modest charge for treatment in public hospitals). This complex mixture has implications for the allocation of resources both between the public and the private sector and between different types of care (see Section 4 for further discussion).

2001 Health Strategy and 2003 Health Service Reform Programme

The most recent statement of national health policy is the 2001 Health Strategy, *Quality and Fairness: A Health System for You*. It identifies a wide range of targets in six key areas: primary care services, acute hospital services, funding, workforce, health system structure and health information systems. A subsequent strategy document focused exclusively on the primary care sector (*Primary Care: A New Direction*), and outlined a new model of primary care based on a more integrated approach to the provision of primary care services. It envisaged the creation of primary care teams, with enhanced areas of expertise and opening hours. It was expected that 600–800 of such teams would be in place by 2008, but, of the ten pilot schemes that were established, only six are still in operation.[5]

In June 2003, the government announced its commitment to a major reform of the health service. The Health Service Reform Programme aims to implement the recommendations contained in three major reports on the health system: the *Report of the National Task Force on Medical Staffing* (the Hanly report), the *Report of the Commission on Financial Management and Control Systems in the Health Service* (the Brennan report) and the *Audit of Structures and Functions in the Health System* (the Prospectus report). Issues highlighted for reform included the co-ordination and division of functions between the different agencies involved in planning, managing and delivering health services in Ireland and the degree of financial accountability exercised by those making most resource-using decisions in the health service, in particular hospital consultants. The establishment of the HSE in January 2005 as a single national organisation with responsibility for the management and delivery of health and social care services, leaving the Department of Health and Children free to concentrate on policy formation and issues of strategic development, arose directly out of recommendations contained in the Prospectus report. However, there are concerns that isolating health policy development from budgetary and executive responsibility in this manner may mean that the formulation of health policy becomes less responsive to emerging needs.[6]

Publicly the most contentious aspect of the reform is that relating to the regional organisation of hospital services contained in the Hanly report. As a result of the European Working Time Directive, the hours worked by non-consultant hospital doctors (NCHDs) must be reduced to 48 hours per week by 2009. In response to this directive, the Hanly report recommends a movement away from the current consultant-led service towards a consultant-provided service, with health professionals working in multidisciplinary specialist teams. To this end, the report recommends, for the two pilot areas examined, a reconfiguration of hospital services in each region into a system with one major hospital and a network of local hospitals with certain services still provided on a national (e.g. liver transplant) or supra-regional (e.g. radiation therapy) basis. The most controversial aspects of the report concerned the stipulation that emergency services should be based in major hospitals only. To date, however, little progress has been made on this aspect of the location issue. Negotiations on a new consultant contract, which would allow for the creation of additional consultant posts, concluded in early 2008, although the full details have yet to be announced publicly.

In 2006, the government invited expressions of interest for the co-location of private hospitals on 11 existing public hospital sites, with the aim of 'freeing up' beds in public hospitals allocated to private patients. Generous tax incentives are provided to encourage the establishment of these and other private facilities. However, the fact that many operate on a for-profit basis raises questions over the extent to which they will relieve pressure on the public system, as they are likely to 'cherry-pick' procedures in favour of those that are less complex and less expensive to carry out.

Recent Changes

Continuing changes in the structure of the health sector, combined with recent high-profile revelations in relation to cancer misdiagnoses and hospital-acquired infections, have heightened public awareness regarding patient safety and quality of service. The Health Information and Quality Authority (HIQA), which was first proposed as part of the 2001 Health Strategy, was established as an independent organisation in 2007 to promote quality and safety and to monitor the care provided to users of the health and social care services in Ireland. HIQA incorporates the existing Social Services Inspectorate and Irish Health Services Accreditation Board and has recently published guidelines in relation to nursing home standards and symptomatic breast cancer services, as well as a review of hygiene in acute public hospitals.

Despite a recruitment freeze in operation since September 2007, the Department of Finance continues to express concern over overspending by the HSE. In addition, recent speculation that the new regional hospital for the northeast will be located in Navan has been overshadowed by concerns over the funding of this and other capital projects. The current economic slowdown may further exacerbate this situation, as health will increasingly have to compete with other government departments for public funds.

4 HEALTH SECTOR FINANCE AND ACCESS

Overall Position

Healthcare is generally financed from four main sources, with different countries assigning different levels of importance to each source. Table 11.2 presents the sources of finance for selected OECD countries for 2005. In terms of public sources of finance, countries such as France and Germany rely much more heavily on social insurance contributions than general government sources, e.g. taxation, for their revenue. Social insurance contributions, which are compulsory and generally shared between the employer and employee, tend to be earmarked for specific purposes; in Ireland the 'health levy' amounts to two per cent of taxable income (those earning less than €500 per week in 2008 are exempt). However, it is a minor source of health sector finance in Ireland. As in other countries, revenue from general taxation in Ireland is not earmarked specifically for the health services, which means that it must compete with other areas for public funds.

Table 11.2
Sources of Finance for Total Health Expenditure for Selected EU-15 and OECD Countries (Percentage of Total Health Expenditure, 2005)

Country	General government	Social insurance	Out-of-pocket payments	Private insurance	Other private sources
Austria	30	46	16	5	3
Denmark	84	0	14	2	0
Finland	61	17	18	2	2
France	5	75	7	13	1
Germany	10	67	13	9	1
Ireland	*77*	*1*	*13*	*7*	*2*
Spain	67	5	22	6	1
USA	32	13	13	37	5

Source: OECD, *Health Data 2007*, OECD, Paris 2007.
Note: Data for the Netherlands and the UK are unavailable.

Due to universal eligibility for free public health services in many countries, the share of total expenditure funded through private sources (out-of-pocket payments by individuals and households, private insurance payments and other sources of finance, e.g. voluntary donations) is much smaller than that accounted for by public sources. The exception is the USA, which provides free healthcare only for the old and those on low incomes (through the Medicare and Medicaid schemes, respectively) and consequently relies more heavily on private sources of finance, particularly insurance.

The prevalence of universal entitlement to free public health services across Europe results in monetary costs for healthcare consultations that are effectively zero, meaning that there is little incentive to control utilisation. Cost sharing, either through co-payments, co-insurance or deductibles, can help to control utilisation, although there are concerns that such initiatives may reduce necessary as well as unnecessary utilisation. Nonetheless, most countries levy minimal charges on consumers in an attempt to make them more aware of the resource implications of their behaviour. For example, in Ireland, a charge of €66 per day applies to individuals without medical cards for treatment as an in-patient in the public hospital sector. As Table 11.2 illustrates, out-of-pocket payments are now more important than private insurance as a source of finance for all the countries examined except France and the USA. However, there are concerns that as governments come under increasing pressure to fund public-health programmes and out-of-pocket payments become more important as a source of revenue, a greater share of the funding burden falls on those in ill health (see Chapter 7 for a discussion of equity issues surrounding the social transfer system).[7]

Medical Card and Private Health Insurance Cover

Eligibility for a medical card is dependent upon income and is decided on the basis of a means test with the income thresholds set nationally and updated annually. The intention is that the decision to seek medical care should not be dependent on economic resources/ability to pay. Currently, the weekly income thresholds are €184 for a single person living alone, €267 for a married couple and €343 for a married couple with two children. The limits increase for those aged 66 years and over (e.g. for a single person the limit increases to €202).[8] Since 1 July 2001, all individuals aged 70 years and over are also entitled to a medical card, regardless of income. In special circumstances, such as a cancer diagnosis, an individual who is otherwise ineligible on the basis of income or age may be granted a medical card. In late 2005, the government announced the introduction of a GP Visit Card, which entitles the individual to free GP services only (i.e. it does not cover prescription medicine costs). With income thresholds 50 per cent higher than for the medical card, the aim is to assist those who do not qualify for a medical card on income grounds but for whom the cost of visiting a GP is often prohibitively high.

Table 11.3 shows the change in medical card coverage and private health insurance coverage since 1980. Private health insurance in Ireland is primarily

Table 11.3

Medical Card and Private Health Insurance Coverage
(Percentage of the Population, 1980–2006)

Year	Medical card	GP Visit Card	Private health insurance
1980	35.0	...	26.1
1990	36.7	...	34.4
1995	35.2	...	37.9
2000	30.3	...	45.0
2001	30.6	...	47.7
2002	29.4	...	48.8
2003	28.6	...	49.4
2004	27.8	...	49.7
2005	27.3	0.1	49.9
2006	28.9	1.2	51.4

Sources: Department of Health and Children, *Health Statistics,* Stationery Office, Dublin 2005, 2002, 1986 and 1981; Department of Health and Children, *White Paper: Private Health Insurance*, Stationery Office, Dublin 1999; Primary Care Reimbursement Service (PCRS), *Annual Report and Financial Statements,* PCRS, Dublin 2006; Health Insurance Authority, *Annual Report and Accounts,* Health Insurance Authority, Dublin 2006.

taken out by non-medical cardholders to cover the costs of private or semi-private hospital care in public and private hospitals. At present, just over 50 per cent of the population are covered. Medical card coverage stayed relatively stable at approximately 37 per cent over the 1980s but fell every year during the 1990s as income guidelines failed to increase in line with increases in average incomes. It increased slightly in 2002 after the extension of medical card coverage to all over-70s and again in 2006 as a result of an increase in income thresholds greater than average inflation. Take-up of the GP Visit Card is still considerably lower than anticipated.

Recent studies have confirmed that a primary reason for taking out private health insurance is to ensure speedy access to hospital rather than superior accommodation; as public waiting lists increased in the 1980s and household incomes increased in the 1990s, the demand for insurance grew. In 2005, approximately 22 per cent of the population did not have a medical card or private health insurance; data from the 2005 EU Statistics on Income and Living Conditions (EU-SILC) shows that over 55 per cent of adults without a medical card or private health insurance were aged under 35 years. While these individuals are entitled to receive free public hospital services (subject to the small charges described above), they must pay in full for any primary care consultations or private hospital services. Medical cardholders may take out private health insurance if they wish; however data from EU-SILC for 2005 show that only 5.1 per cent of adults had both a medical card and private health insurance.

Private Health Insurance Market

It is useful to examine the private health insurance system in Ireland in more detail, principally because it is unusual in an international context in the extent to which the system interacts with the public system, particularly in the hospitals sector. Much recent discussion has also focused on regulatory reform in the light of EU regulations regarding competitive behaviour between private insurers. There are three main private health insurance companies in Ireland: VHI, Quinn Healthcare (previously BUPA) and Vivas. As a result of the Third EU Directive on Non-Life Insurance, BUPA entered the market to compete with the VHI in 1996, but withdrew from the market in December 2006 in protest at the announcement of the introduction of risk equalisation payments from January 2007. Quinn Healthcare acquired BUPA in January 2007, while Vivas entered the market in October 2004. There are also a number of smaller employer-provided health insurance schemes such as the St Paul's Garda Medical Aid Society, the Prison Officers' Medical Aid Society and the ESB Medical Provident Fund. Excluding the above schemes, VHI had a 75 per cent market share in September 2006, while BUPA and Vivas had 22 per cent and three per cent respectively.[9]

The VHI, a state-owned non-profit-making company, was originally established in 1957 to provide insurance against hospital expenses for the then 15 per cent of the population who were not entitled to free public hospital services. Despite the extension of entitlement of cover for free public hospital services to the remainder of the population in 1991, the reduction in tax relief from the marginal rate of tax to the standard rate of tax in 1996 and increasing premiums, private insurance coverage in Ireland has grown steadily since 1957 to reach over 50 per cent of the population by 2006. The expansion in private health insurance cover is all the more striking given that private insurance does not generally cover the cost of primary care consultations, except where large deductibles are exceeded (although recently the main insurers have introduced additional plans with partial cover for primary care services). However, factors such as differing waiting times for admission to hospital for those with and without insurance, improved economic conditions and increased incomes, continued policy support for private coverage (principally through the tax code) and an expanding role for employer-provided private health insurance are all important in explaining the growth in coverage.

The profile of those covered by private health insurance is also worth mentioning. There is a strong relationship between private insurance cover and socio-economic characteristics such as income, educational attainment and health status. Interestingly, however, there is no evidence of adverse selection in the market for private health insurance in Ireland, with larger proportions of those in good health having insurance than those in poor health. It is difficult to explain the appeal of private health insurance in Ireland, in the context of universal entitlement to free or heavily subsidised public hospital care. A survey of a random sample of the population in 2000 found that, among both the insured and the not-insured, the most commonly cited reasons for having private health insurance were, in order of importance: to avoid large medical bills; to ensure quick treatment; and to ensure good hospital treatment. Issues such as being able to have a private bed or a private room were perceived as much less important by both sets of respondents.[10]

Access to Hospital Services

Data on waiting lists indicate that public patients face substantially longer waiting times for in-patient and outpatient care than those with private health insurance, although there are obvious differences in age and health status across the two groups that may impact on the types and duration of treatments. Statistics for bed occupancy in public hospitals also led to concerns that access to hospital for elective procedures in Ireland is not distributed by need. Public hospitals in Ireland must allocate a proportion of their beds for private or semi-private use; currently the designations are 20 per cent for in-patient beds and 30 per cent for day beds. However, research on patient discharges shows that for in-patient admissions in 2004, private patients accounted for 25.5 per cent of discharges. For day procedures, discharges were distributed in favour of public patients, with 24.0 per cent of discharges for day procedures classified as private. However, in both cases, the increase in private discharges from 2000 to 2004 was much greater than that for public patients.[11] There are therefore very real concerns that access to hospital for elective procedures in particular is not distributed according to need, but rather by private insurance cover (and by extension, ability to pay, since those with private insurance cover are concentrated in the top levels of income distribution).

However, quite apart from concerns surrounding access to hospital services as a result of this public-private mix, there are also efficiency concerns. Private patients in public hospitals are not charged the full economic cost of their care and treatment; this therefore gives insurers an incentive to encourage the treatment of private patients in public rather than private hospitals and public hospital managers an incentive to encourage the treatment of private patients as they represent an additional income stream for the hospital. The Department of Health and Children, on the other hand, argues that the public-private mix in the hospital sector in Ireland has a number of advantages: it ensures that staff continue to be attracted to the public sector; consultants' time is used more efficiently because public and private patients are on the same site; it facilitates linkage in terms of medical knowledge and facilities; and, probably most important, represents an additional income stream for the public hospital system.

In April 2002, the government established the National Treatment Purchase Fund (NTPF) with the aim of reducing waiting lists for public patients waiting three months or more for in-patient and outpatient care. The NTPF purchases treatment in public and private in hospitals in the Republic, Northern Ireland and the UK. However, there are concerns over the efficiency of the state turning to the private sector to provide care for public patients, while at the same time dedicating 20 per cent of public hospital beds for private use.[12] In addition, the ability of the recently announced co-location hospital policy to 'free up' private beds in public hospitals is questionable given the for-profit nature of many of the new operators in the private sector.

5 HEALTH SECTOR EXPENDITURE AND OUTCOMES

Irish Healthcare Expenditure

Public expenditure on the health services has increased greatly since the mid-1980s, from €3.1 billion in 1990 to €12.3 billion in 2006 (in real 2006 prices). This represents an increase of 295 per cent since 1990, with most of this increase occurring since 1997. This is in contrast to the experience during some years of the 1980s when public health expenditures fell in real terms. Given the share of labour costs in health expenditure, when public sector expenditure is deflated by average industrial wage costs (see Figure 11.1), the increase over the latter part of the 1990s is more modest but still very pronounced, increasing by just over 100 per cent from 1997. While both non-capital and capital public expenditure increased substantially in the late 1990s, capital expenditure increased at a faster pace, increasing its share of total public health expenditure from three per cent in 1990 to five per cent in 2006.

Figure 11.1

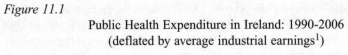

Public Health Expenditure in Ireland: 1990-2006
(deflated by average industrial earnings[1])

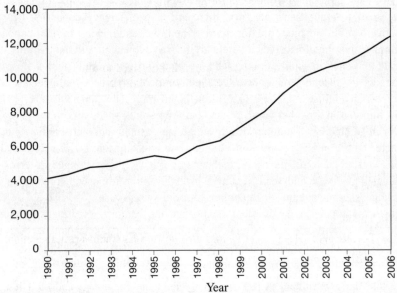

Year

Sources: For expenditure data see Department of Health and Children, *Health Statistics*, Stationery Office, Dublin 2003, 2006, 2007; for consumer price index data see CSO, *Consumer Price Index* (various issues), Stationery Office, Dublin; and for average weekly industrial earnings see CSO, *Industrial Earnings and Hours Worked* (various issues), Stationery Office, Dublin, and CSO, *Statistical Bulletin* (various issues), Stationery Office, Dublin.
[1] While the CSO publish data on public-sector earnings, the data exclude the health sector and are only available back to 1995.

In the non-capital public health expenditure programme, by far the largest component comprises expenditure on the general hospitals service. The remaining components of non-capital public health expenditure are, in order of importance: the community health services programme (which includes expenditure on the provision of primary care services to those on low incomes); the disability programme; the community welfare programme (which includes cash grants to those incapacitated for work);[13] the mental health programme; the general support programme; and the community protection programme (which includes expenditure on the prevention of infectious diseases, food hygiene standards and health promotion).

While no programme has seen its level of expenditure decrease, the proportions allocated to different programmes have changed somewhat over the last number of years (see Table 11.4). In part, this reflects the aspirations of the

307

most recent Health Strategy published in 2001, which envisaged more emphasis on health promotion and prevention rather than on the traditional roles of diagnosis and treatment, in particular through an expanded role for GP and other primary care services as the first point of call for most individuals' contact with the health services.

Table 11.4

Components of Non-Capital Public Expenditure
(percentage of total, 1990–2006)

Programme	1990	2000	2006
Community protection	2	4	3
Community health services	15	18	20
Community welfare	9	8	8
Psychiatric	11	8	7
Handicapped	10	12	13
General hospital	50	46	45
General support	5	5	4

Sources: Department of Health and Children, *Health Statistics* (various issues), Stationery Office, Dublin.

While the government is heavily involved in the financing, and to a lesser extent in the delivery, of health services in Ireland, the private sector plays an important role in both areas. The proportion of total health expenditure accounted for by the private sector has declined slightly over the last decade, from 24.8 per cent in 1990 to 20.3 per cent in 2004, reflecting the proportionately larger increase in public sector expenditure rather than any decrease in private sector expenditure.

Effectiveness of Health Sector Expenditure
Levels of expenditure provide no guidance as to whether this expenditure is efficiently and effectively spent or distributed equitably across different sectors of the population. In terms of the effectiveness of health sector expenditure, it is useful to examine where countries rank in terms of health outcomes and whether there is any correlation between such measures and health expenditure.

The weak association between health spending and health outcome indicators such as life expectancy and infant mortality presented in Table 11.5 highlights the fact that social, environmental and cultural factors such as diet, exercise, genetic inheritance, lifestyle, education, social status, income distribution, social support and housing, and their complex interactions, may be more important in determining the level and distribution of health outcomes than simple health expenditure. The recent increases in resources devoted to health promotion and prevention (e.g. through the smoking in the workplace ban, breast cancer screening, promotion of healthy eating, etc.) reflect this realisation that lifestyle factors are also crucial in influencing population health outcomes.

Table 11.5

Total Health Expenditure Per Capita and Health Outcome Rankings, 2004

Country	Expenditure	Male life expectancy	Female life expectancy	Infant mortality	ESRI
Australia	8	3	4	16	6
Austria	3	13	10	13	8
Belgium	4	12	8	11	14
Canada	7	4	6	18	11
Denmark	10	19	20	14	14
Finland	17	16	9	3	6
France	5	9	2	5	2
Germany	6	15	15	10	9
Greece	13	11	12	9	17
Ireland	*12*	*14*	*18*	*15*	*18*
Italy	15	8	7	8	2
Japan	16	1	1	1	4
Luxembourg	2	18	16	6	n/a
Netherlands	9	7	13	12	10
New Zealand	18	5	11	19	11
Portugal	20	20	17	4	11
Spain	19	6	3	7	4
Sweden	11	2	5	2	1
UK	14	10	14	17	14
USA	1	17	19	20	19

Sources: For data on expenditure (total health expenditure per capita expressed in US$ PPP), male and female life expectancy (at birth) and infant mortality (per 1,000 live births) see OECD, *Health Data 2007,* OECD, Paris 2007. For data on ESRI ranking of countries on overall health system attainment, see A. Nolan, and B. Nolan, *Ireland's Health Care System: Some Issues and Challenges*, Proceedings of ESRI/FFS Budget Perspectives Conference 2004, ESRI, Dublin 2004, Tables 1–4. Rankings are amended to exclude Iceland, Norway and Switzerland, which were included in the original analysis. Luxembourg was excluded from the ESRI analysis.

A related strand of research concentrates on the pitfalls involved in using single measures of health status to assess health sector performance. A recent ESRI report used a methodology developed in Canada to assess overall health system performance by ranking countries on their achievement in relation to 19 broad indicators (such as life expectancy, premature mortality for various conditions and immunisation rates).[14] Of the countries of the old EU-15, Australia, Canada, Japan, New Zealand and the USA (see Table 11.5), the top three performing countries in terms of overall health system performance were Sweden, France and Italy, while their rankings in terms of expenditure were tenth, third and twelfth respectively. While there are countries (such as France) who spend a lot and consequently rank high in terms of health sector performance, there are also exceptions to this trend, namely Denmark and the USA, whose high levels of expenditure are not reflected in health sector performance and, on the other hand, countries such as Japan and Sweden whose spending is in the middle range of countries, yet who perform very well.

Assessing Output of the Health Sector

The above highlights the fact that any assessment of health sector performance is beset with the problem of how to measure the output of the health sector. Cross-country comparisons of performance tend to rely on aggregate indicators such as life expectancy and mortality rates, but at more disaggregated levels (e.g. hospital, GP practice), easily available indicators of output such as hospital admissions, in-patient days, discharges, number of procedures undertaken, number of consultations, etc. are employed. However, these are essentially throughput measures and, in certain cases, they can provide misleading information on the performance of health service providers. For example, an increase in hospital discharges year on year for the same amount of inputs could be construed as an increase in productivity but it could simply be because the hospital is discharging patients 'quicker but sicker'.

Casemix
In the context of hospital services, the need to account for the variety and intensity of treatments undertaken has resulted in the increasing use of the casemix adjustment to monitor output. The casemix measure assigns all in-patient cases exclusively to one category, a diagnosis-related group (DRG), of which there are approximately 500. Each DRG represents a category of cases which may be expected to have the same clinical characteristics, receive similar treatment and use the same amount of hospital resources, i.e. doctor and nursing input, theatre, laboratory, pharmacy, catering and cleaning costs. A casemix-adjusted cost is then estimated for each hospital and hospital group (teaching versus non-teaching). In Ireland, hospitals performing poorly relative to others in the group lose funding whereas those performing better receive extra funding; the casemix adjustment to hospital budgets is therefore budget neutral and aims to increase hospital efficiency. In 1993, the casemix adjustment was applied on a pilot basis to 15 acute public hospitals and was initially used to make adjustments to five per cent of the in-patient budget; the remaining 95 per cent was based on the hospital's historical allocation. The rate of adjustment to hospital budgets (known as the blend rate) has increased over time to 20 per cent of the in-patient and day-case budgets, with all acute public hospitals discharging more than 5,000 patients per annum subject to some degree of casemix adjustment. However, the casemix adjustment is still small relative to the overall size of the hospital budget.[15]

Economic Evaluation of Treatments

Much recent research has concentrated on assessing the efficacy of different treatments. Essentially, there are three different, but related, approaches to assessing efficacy in this context: cost-benefit analysis, cost-effectiveness analysis and cost-utility analysis. In all cases, costs are measured in terms of monetary units. The measurement of benefits or outputs proves more problematic. Cost-benefit analysis is rarely employed as benefits must be converted into monetary units. Cost-effectiveness analysis goes one step further by measuring output in terms of natural units of outcome for the programme being evaluated, e.g. life years gained. It is then possible to calculate a cost-effectiveness ratio, which represents the additional cost per additional unit of output.

Cost-utility analysis attempts to overcome the failing of cost-effectiveness analysis by accounting for the quality of the additional life years gained. Once again, costs are measured in monetary units but outputs are measured in terms of quality-adjusted life years (QALYs), which reflect both the quality and quantity of additional life years gained. Results are presented in terms of a cost per QALY achieved; unlike cost-effectiveness analysis, cross-programme comparisons are possible. Much recent literature has therefore centred on the use of the QALY as a generic measure of output, with the construction of league tables of healthcare interventions, ranking them by cost per QALY achieved. However, the adjustment for quality relies on the subjective evaluations of patients or survey respondents. Different respondents may place different values on outcomes depending on their own situation (e.g. a patient suffering from a certain condition may value a treatment more highly than a healthy individual surveyed as part of a random sample of the population). Despite the advances in such research in recent years, no approach can deal with the thorny problem of defining the appropriate threshold of resources, beyond which the costs are too large relative to the expected benefits.

Controlling Growth in Health Expenditure

What are the factors driving the increase in health expenditure, both in Ireland and across the OECD? On the demand side, such factors include changing demographic structures (particularly ageing populations), increasing incomes, increasing access to free public health services, increasing insurance cover and rising consumer expectations (see the discussion on Wagner's Law in Chapter 3). The role of consumer expectations cannot be underestimated; a recent study highlighted the divergence between the Irish experience in relation to mortality and individuals' perceptions of their own health.[16] Cross-sectional studies attempting to explain the factors driving increases in health sector expenditure across countries typically find that aggregate income is the most important factor with an elasticity of one or greater.

Attention also focuses on supply-side factors such as rising medical prices, technological change, increasing capital stock and labour costs, the regulatory regime governing behaviour in the health sector and the incentive structure facing

311

healthcare providers. Given the labour intensity of the sector, the impact of labour costs on health expenditures cannot be underestimated. In Ireland, labour costs account for approximately 60 per cent of health expenditure; therefore changes in the level and type of employees have implications for spending on health services. Related to this is the concept of Baumol's Disease (see also Chapter 3) whereby public sector employees demand wage increases in line with those of their private sector counterparts. While in the private sector (the 'progressive' sector), wage increases are accompanied by improvements in productivity, in labour intensive sectors such as health, education and public administration (the 'non-progressive' sectors), productivity improvements are harder to implement. Productivity improvements in the health sector are not impossible however; increased use of IT in the operation and management of the health service was recommended by the Brennan report as an aid to increasing productivity in the health service.

Attempts to control the growth in spending across the OECD initially concentrated on macro reforms such as caps on spending or employment freezes. However, 'with little attention paid to the underlying structure of incentives, there is growing doubt about the capacity of purely macroeconomic approaches to sustain overall spending control'.[17] In terms of microeconomic reforms, measures such as: promoting the use of the GP as a gatekeeper to hospital services; remunerating doctors on a capitation (rather than fee-for-service) basis for services provided in the public sector; funding hospitals on a casemix (i.e. adjusting for the nature and intensity of treatments undertaken) or prospective-budget basis with rewards cost savings and sanctions for over-runs rather than on a simple retrospective budget basis; encouraging day surgery over in-patient stays; and encouraging the prescribing of generic drugs are all seen as increasingly important in containing costs.

The way in which doctors are reimbursed for the services that they provide has important implications for healthcare spending. In a fee-for-service regime, doctors receive a fee for each consultation, while in a capitation regime they receive an annual payment per patient that is weighted for characteristics such as the age and gender of the patient. A study of a cross-section of 19 OECD countries in 1987 found that healthcare expenditure was 11 per cent higher in countries where fee-for-service was the dominant form of remuneration for outpatient care in comparison with countries with capitation systems.[18]

On the demand side, implementing some form of cost sharing to make consumers more aware of the resource implications of their behaviour is common. However, there are concerns that charges may reduce 'necessary' as well as 'unnecessary' consultations, thus increasing the tendency to incur higher costs at a later stage of illness. In addition, equity concerns, particularly in relation to fixed charges, have led most countries to exempt lower-income groups or the chronically ill from cost-sharing schemes. In practice, most countries attempt to levy some form of modest charge on consumers, while simultaneously ensuring that the incentives that doctors face do not encourage excessive utilisation.

6 CONCLUDING COMMENTS

In this chapter, an overview of the financing and delivery of health services in Ireland, as well as key policy issues, was provided. The challenges facing the Irish health service today are very different from the concerns of the 1980s when the issue of how to provide services in a climate of real expenditure decreases was paramount. Irish health expenditures have increased steadily since the latter years of the 1990s; the key issues now facing the Irish health services are: how to ensure that access to services is distributed according to need rather than non-need factors such as ability to pay; to ensure that increasing levels of expenditure are spent efficiently and effectively; to ensure quality and safety; and to ensure that costs are contained.

The discussion on the private health insurance system in Ireland highlighted the distributional issues surrounding the complex intermix between the public and private sectors in the Irish health sector, particularly in terms of hospital care. The increasing popularity of private health insurance cover was seen to be in part a response to concerns about access to services and treatment quality between those with and without private insurance cover. Data from a recent household survey support these fears, showing that those with private insurance had shorter waiting times than those without. However, there are concerns that any attempt to adopt a common waiting list would remove the incentive to take out private health insurance and could result in a significant fall in membership, which would increase further the pressure on the public system. In addition, the practice whereby medical consultants treat private patients and junior doctors treat public patients implies differing standards of hospital care between the two groups. On the regulatory side, despite EU regulations on competition between insurers, there has been limited competition between the three insurers in the market, with only three new entrants (and one exit) since the market was opened to competition in 1994.

While access concerns dominate much discussion about the health services in Ireland, the steady growth in health expenditure in recent years has generated increasing concerns as to whether this increased investment is being efficiently and effectively spent. Despite these increases, Ireland still spends less per capita on health than many other OECD countries and performs poorly in terms of aggregate health outcomes such as life expectancy and mortality rates. However, there seems to be little relationship between health expenditure and aggregate measures of performance; such exercises highlight the difficulties involved in proxying health sector performance with such crude measures of output. Measuring the output of the health sector is notoriously difficult; throughput measures such as the number of consultations may lead to misleading conclusions while concepts such as quality-adjusted life years (QALYs) rely heavily on subjective assessments of healthcare benefits. The development of the casemix method in the context of hospital services, however, represents an opportunity to explicitly account for the nature and intensity of treatments undertaken, rather than relying on simplistic measures of throughput. In response to ever-increasing health expenditures, cost-containment measures, which initially concentrated on macro approaches, such as employment freezes, have increasingly considered more micro measures. Measures such as the reimbursement system for doctors and cost-sharing initiatives aim to make both providers and patients more aware of the resource-using implications of their behaviour.

In terms of the overall structure of the public health services in Ireland, progress on the objectives set out in the 2001 Health Strategy and 2003 Health Reform Programme has been slow. Despite recent changes such as the establishment of the HSE and HIQA and the negotiation of a new consultant contract, progress on other issues highlighted for attention, such as the reorganisation of primary care services and the concentration of acute hospital services, has been delayed. Primary care services are still delivered largely by independent professionals working alone, and the complex interaction between public and private healthcare remains in the public hospital sector. Generous tax incentives for the establishment of private medical facilities will further exacerbate the public-private distinction in Irish healthcare. In addition, the private health insurance market faces considerable uncertainty in the face of industry opposition to future risk-equalisation payments. In light of continuing concerns over quality and patient safety, HIQA will fulfil an important role in monitoring and enforcing quality standards in Irish healthcare.

Endnotes

* The author would like to thank Carol Newman and John O'Hagan for comments on an earlier version of the chapter. All views expressed are those of the author and are not necessarily shared by the Economic and Social Research Institute (ESRI).

[1] See Department of Health and Children, *Health in Ireland Key Trends 2007*, Stationery Office, Dublin 2007, Table 6.4; and CSO, *Statistical Yearbook of Ireland*, Stationery Office, Dublin 2007, Table 2.3.

[2] While the proportion of the population aged 65 years and over differs considerably across the countries presented in Table 11.1, there is no significant relationship between expenditure and the age distribution (more important determinants of health expenditure are GDP per capita and institutional arrangements).

[3] J. Barry, H. Sinclair, A. Kelly, R. O'Loughlin, D. Handy and T. O'Dowd, *Inequalities in Health in Ireland – Hard Facts*, Department of Community Health and General Practice, Trinity College Dublin, Dublin 2001.

[4] Health Service Executive, *Annual Report and Financial Statements 2006*, HSE, Dublin 2007.

[5] R. Layte, 'Primary care: the key to healthcare reform', *Public Affairs Ireland Journal*, November 2007.

[6] M. Wiley, 'The Irish health system: developments in strategy, structure, funding and delivery since 1980', *Health Economics*, Vol. 14, No. S1, 2005.

[7] E. Mossialos, A. Dixon, J. Figueras and J. Kutzin (eds), *Funding Healthcare: Options for Europe*, Open University Press, Buckingham 2002.

8   The average weekly industrial wage in Ireland in December 2006 was €620.73 (CSO, *Industrial Earnings and Hours Worked*, Stationery Office, Dublin 2007).

9   Health Insurance Authority, *Competition in the Private Health Insurance Market in Ireland*, Health Insurance Authority, Dublin 2007.

10 D. Watson and J. Williams, *Perceptions of the Quality of Healthcare in the Public and Private Sectors in Ireland*, Report to the Centre for Insurance Studies, Graduate Business School, University College Dublin, Dublin 2001.

11 See Economic and Social Research Institute, *Activity in Acute Public Hospitals in Ireland 2004, Annual Report*, ESRI, Dublin 2004; and J. O'Reilly and M. Wiley, 'The public/private mix in Irish acute public hospitals: trends and implications' (ESRI Working Paper No. 218), ESRI, Dublin 2007.

12 National Economic and Social Forum, *Equity of Access to Hospital Care*, Forum Report No. 25, National Economic and Social Forum, Dublin 2002.

13 Some commentators, including the OECD, have questioned the classification of many of the items under the 'community welfare programme' as health spending, regarding them as instead as social transfers or spending (see also M. Wren, 'Health spending and the black hole', *Quarterly Economic Commentary*, ESRI, Dublin 2004).

14 A. Nolan and B. Nolan, *Ireland's Healthcare System: Some Issues and Challenges* (Proceedings of ESRI/FFS Budget Perspectives Conference 2004), ESRI, Dublin 2004.

15 Wiley, op. cit.

16 R. Layte, A. Nolan and B. Nolan, 'Health and healthcare', in T. Fahey, H. Russell and C. Whelan (eds), *Best of Times? The Social Impact of the Celtic Tiger*, IPA, Dublin 2007.

17 OECD, *Healthcare Reform: Controlling Spending and Increasing Efficiency*, OECD, Paris 1994, p.7.

18 U. Gerdtham, J. Sogaard, F. Andersson and B. Jonsson, 'An econometric analysis of healthcare expenditure: a cross-section study on the OECD countries', *Journal of Health Economics*, Vol. 11, 1992.

CHAPTER 12

Education: Market Failure and Government Interventions

*Colm Harmon and Carol Newman**

1 INTRODUCTION

A key assumption underpinning support for the policymaker for the education system is the belief that education equips individuals with the knowledge and skills necessary to participate in the economy at both an economic and a social level. The role of government is to ensure education provision occurs in an efficient and equitable way. The government may achieve this either through the direct provision of the service or the regulation of some aspects of its provision.

In Ireland, education is largely publicly provided with a small private component. There are three layers to the Irish education system: primary, second level and third level or the tertiary sector. Unlike many other countries, pre-primary education is predominantly privately funded with a minimal role for government.[1] The responsibility for the government's role in the provision of education at primary and second level rests with the Department of Education and Science, while the Higher Education Authority (HEA), an independent statutory body, largely manages provision at third level while remaining answerable to the Minister for Education and Science (unlike many countries Ireland does not have a separate 'ministry' for the higher and further education sector). In 2006, there were 3,160 primary schools and 735 second-level schools aided by the Department and 44 third-level institutions including seven universities and 13 Institutes of Technology (ITs).[2] In total there were just over 927,000 students enrolled in full-time education, 23 per cent of the total population. While the total number of students at primary level declined since the early 1990s this decline halted in 2001 and has increased by over 20,000 (or five per cent) since 2002. The total number at second level has remained relatively stable, illustrating the increase in numbers staying on in school at this level, although the decline in birth rates in the 1980s has fed through somewhat in the recent figures. In addition, overall participation in the tertiary sector has increased over the last decade with an increase of 14,000 (or 20 per cent) since 2001 mainly into the expanded IT sector.

In this chapter we present an analysis of the role and performance of the Irish government in delivering an efficient and equitable education service. We also outline some of the interesting economic policy issues relating to its provision. In Section 2 the economic justifications for government intervention in the provision of education are outlined. Section 3 examines government education policy in an Irish context, focusing on recent policies aimed at promoting growth through various education initiatives, and equity both within the system and as an end goal in the wider distributional context. Before concluding, Section 4 examines the effectiveness of government in delivering an efficient and equitable education service, covering issues relating to the level of expenditure and the allocation of funds across different levels of education, the efficiency of the system in an Irish context and relative to other OECD countries, and the extent to which inequities exist within the system.

2 ECONOMIC PERSPECTIVES OF EDUCATION

In the absence of an education system, citizens will lack the basic social skills necessary to participate in the economy and, more important perhaps, society in general: for example, an illiterate individual may be unable to follow basic rules and regulations imposed by government such as reading road signs or informing themselves on key personal items like medicine dosages or matters relating to their legal and financial position. For these most basic reasons, government intervention in the provision of basic education services is justified. Policy can impact on a range of issues but most governments have focused on easing financial constraints by providing free schooling or creating educational institutions and structures and ensuring their quality. Remedial policies are usually targeted at individuals whose low levels of human capital prevent them from participating in the labour force and integrating into society more generally.

In most developed economies the government requires that all individuals remain in education up to some minimum age: in Ireland education is compulsory up to the age of 16. As such, the state plays a very direct role in the provision and funding of compulsory education.[3] There is no dispute in Ireland or other developed nations about state funding of education up to compulsory levels (indeed, the recommendation of a greater role for state intervention in education provision is a major issue in policy formation for developing countries). There is a vast body of research on this issue with the central conclusion that efficiency in public spending would be enhanced if human-capital investment were directed more toward the young. However, that said, the state increasingly takes a very proactive role in higher education up to and including the postgraduate and postdoctoral research agenda. In this section, the extent to which the government has a necessary role in the provision of education beyond compulsory levels is explored. Government intervention in any market can be justified where the market fails to optimally provide the good or service. Intervention may also be justified on equity grounds to promote distributional objective. The arguments for intervention differ depending on the level of education, a factor also considered in this section.

Education as an Investment: Private and Social Returns

Education is an investment in human capital yielding both private and social returns. The decision to invest in human capital accumulation, like any other investment, will depend on the investor's evaluation of the expected present value of the stream of costs and benefits flowing from that investment. At an aggregate level, the government, in making a decision on whether and how much to invest in the education system, will weigh up the cost of the investment (including the actual cash outlay, the opportunity cost of people not contributing to production while in full-time education and any efficiency losses associated with the financing of education through the tax system) with the aggregate returns to the economy of having a well-educated workforce (such as the extent to which it will contribute to the more productive use of resources, higher levels of output and faster economic growth).

A firm making a decision to invest in training courses to improve the human capital of its workers will undertake the investment if the present value of the expected future returns to that investment, in the form of higher productivity and reduced costs, is greater than the cost of the investment. An individual's decision to invest in personal human capital, such as a third-level degree for example, will involve a comparison of the costs such as tuition fees, books, and foregone earnings and the personal benefits accruing from that investment such as greater employability, higher earnings, greater job satisfaction and social inclusion. The economics of early education relies, to a significant extent, on the complementarity between formal and informal education. Children convert educational inputs into outcomes more effectively if parents reinforce the input by encouraging and motivating them and so the returns realised from investment in early education initiatives will depend to a large extent on family background.

Investment in education may also confer *positive externalities* on the rest of society that will not be taken into account by parents, individuals or firms. These can take the form of productivity improvements which will contribute to economic growth above and beyond those for which an individual/firm is remunerated through higher wages/profits; improvements in the quality of services, for example, the health or legal professions; or other social benefits such as increased political participation and a healthy democratic system. These social returns provide justification for government involvement in education provision beyond compulsory schooling and in particular at third level. This also applies to early education. Indeed the very sizeable returns to early investment programmes cited recently by the current Minister for Education and Science which suggest a ten to one return on investment in children aged zero to four, rely heavily on immediate benefits like better school readiness and cognitive outcomes but also on long-term effects such as lower rates of lone parenthood and lower crime rates.

As already stated, the arguments for government involvement in compulsory education are clear. What is often questioned is the extent to which government involvement in higher levels of schooling is justifiable. As such, much of the empirical literature focuses on the returns, both private and social, from third-level schooling. We review some of this literature here.

Empirical Evidence on Private Returns
Theoretically, the decision for an individual, firm or government to invest in the education system appears quite straightforward. However, in reality an exercise like this is severely hampered by the difficulties faced in quantifying the returns to education.

It is well documented that the accumulation of human capital plays a key role in the growth process (see Chapter 6). Human capital can be considered an input into the production process and its accumulation will lead to faster growth rates and ultimately convergence to some steady-state level of output growth. Others propose that human-capital accumulation contributes even more to growth in the way it facilitates the development and diffusion of new technologies. The OECD estimates that public and private expenditure on educational institutions amounts to approximately six per cent of the collective GDP of OECD member states. It is likely that this figure understates the extent of this investment as it does not take into account earnings foregone by individuals engaged in full-time education.

With such a substantial outlay involved, the importance of understanding and attaining some quantification of the returns to this investment is obvious. Recent studies by the OECD have found empirical evidence of the positive link between human capital accumulation and output growth, estimating that human capital accumulation accounted for more than half of a percentage point acceleration in growth in the 1990s. In Ireland's case, human capital accumulation is often cited as being one of the most important contributing factors to Irish economic growth in the 1990s (see Chapters 5 and 6). The extent to which government involvement in the provision of education is justified on these grounds depends on whether these returns are in excess of those privately yielded by the individuals and firms engaged in human capital accumulation.

There is an extensive literature on quantifying the private individual returns to education and the contribution of educational attainment to productivity at a microeconomic level; and an enormous econometric literature estimating the impact of education on earnings. Studies typically show that the returns to education are around six to eight per cent per school year for men and nine to 11 per cent for women.[4] These so-called Mincer returns (after the pioneering labour economist Jacob Mincer who first formulated the empirical structure for estimating human capital models) apply to all levels of education but are generally larger for higher education.

The earnings return to education has been well documented in the Irish context with evidence suggesting not only a positive relationship between earnings and educational attainment but also that this earnings advantage increases with the length of time spent in the labour market. Higher levels of education are not only associated with higher earnings but also higher levels of labour force participation and lower unemployment risk. Evidence from the ESRI's Living in Ireland Panel Survey supports this result, highlighting the implications of a low level of education attainment on long-term labour market integration.[5] The unemployment rate for early school leavers in the 18 to 24 age group was 19 per cent in 2006 compared with an unemployment rate of 8.2 per cent for all persons in the same age group. The evidence suggests that in the Irish case, like many other OECD countries, the individual returns to education are significant in terms of earnings, labour market participation and unemployment risk.

While findings suggest that education leads to higher private returns, the link between educational attainment and productivity has been more difficult to quantify. An alternative to the human capital view is the screening theory of education, which suggests that there is no link between individual educational attainment and productivity improvements, and that the only purpose of education is to serve as a signalling device to employers as to who the most productive employees are likely to be. This argument is based on the observation that those with the greatest ability, which is determined by unobservable factors such as family background, opportunities, access to quality schools, etc., are more likely to be educated but are also more likely to be productive. Employers will opt to recruit and pay higher salaries to well-educated individuals who by attaining an education have signalled their productive ability.

From an empirical point of view, no consensus has been reached on the link between educational attainment and productivity. One reason for this is that it is statistically very difficult to disentangle the two theories as the end result is the same – more educated persons earn more. In any case, where there are private returns to education, be they a reward for productivity improvements or otherwise (for example, personal fulfilment or satisfaction), the investment should be undertaken by the individual themselves with no justification for government intervention on these grounds. In particular, the private returns to education are higher for third-level compared with compulsory first- and second-level education, making government involvement in the former more difficult to justify in the absence of some quantification of a social return to the investment. While the social returns to education may be significant overall, the extent and scale of the social returns to third-level education remains unresolved.[6] It is to the evidence on social returns that we now turn our attention.

Empirical Evidence on Social Returns
Awareness of the ways in which we all benefit when education opportunities increase (usually through greater government investment) is limited. Given that the social returns to education are more difficult to quantify, awareness of societal

gains from education is limited to an acknowledgment of the increased contributions to the public purse (resulting from the yield from increased earnings) and a decline in the demand for welfare support by those at the higher end of the education spectrum.

An interesting new body of work shows social benefits from investment in education in the form of higher wages for everyone in the labour market. This work compares the proportion of college graduates in the workforce in cities in the USA with the wages of non-graduates, but otherwise similar workers, in the same cities. A positive causal relationship is found between the proportion of university graduates in a city's labour force and average wages: a one per cent increase in the supply of college graduates raises the wages of high-school drop-outs by 1.9 per cent, of high school graduates by 1.6 per cent, and of college graduates by 0.4 per cent. There are two potential explanations for these findings: first, it may be the case that there is poor substitution between high- and low-quality workers; and second, there may be spillover effects (a higher number of more skilled workers in the labour force also raises the general skill levels of other workers in the labour force). Whatever the mechanism, the main finding of this innovative work is that an increase in the supply of graduates to the labour market increases the wages for all workers, thus providing evidence of social returns in excess of private returns (i.e. higher graduate wage levels).

Any further attempts to quantify the social returns to education investment are faced with serious difficulties in establishing causal relationships between education attainment and socially desirable outcomes. Political scientists have highlighted correlations between voter participation and education for many years and have used this to argue that education leads to more informed voters, and hence a more democratic society. However, correlation does not imply causation. There may be unobservable characteristics of people who value schooling which make them more likely to value civic duties and responsibilities. If this is the case, estimates of the correlation between education and civic participation such as voting behaviour may overstate the true civic returns to education. Some of the most rigorous evidence suggests that *entrance* into higher education increases the probability of voter participation by 21 to 30 per cent. As a result of this finding, Irish universities have been developing a variety of programmes geared to promoting and preparing their students for lifetime active civic participation.

The literature on the impact of education on health status again suffers from problems of establishing causation. For example, ability clearly affects an individual's success in schooling and may also affect the productivity of time in the production of health, i.e. those more able may have lower costs of investing in their health. Similarly, initial assets or family wealth may affect an individual's access to both education and health care.

Despite the dearth of empirical evidence, the existence of social returns is the key argument made for government intervention in education provision. There is no doubt that higher levels of education lead to a more skilled and productive labour force, capable of producing greater levels of output, facilitating

321

technological advancement and attracting investment. While the social capital developed at primary and second level (for example, respect for social norms and the rule of law) are fundamental to the functioning of any economy, in developed economies with an advanced compulsory education sector, third-level education often becomes the focus of education policy in fulfilling growth objectives.

Market Failures

While the evidence in support of state involvement in the provision of education on the grounds that the social rate of return exceeds the private rate of return is mixed, certainly for higher education, other market failures may prevent education from being optimally provided in the absence of government intervention.

Education would be, for the most part, unaffordable if privately provided and most people would rely on credit markets to finance their schooling. Credit markets will fail to operate efficiently in this environment for two reasons. First, most students applying for loans to pay for their studies will lack collateral of any kind to guarantee the loan, and second, the benefits of education will vary substantially between individuals, with no guarantee of success and hence no guarantee that the student will be able to repay the loan in the future. In the absence of collateral and a means of repayment, banks will be unwilling to finance individuals to pay for private education. This failure of credit markets to finance private education may warrant government intervention in the provision of education services, especially at third level, where government involvement usually comes in the form of direct financial assistance to students (for example, free tuition fees, government-guaranteed loan schemes, etc.).

Aside from credit market failure, the provision of education itself is characterised by imperfect information at many different levels resulting in sub-optimal outcomes in the absence of government intervention. First, it can be argued that individuals do not have full information on the merits of schooling and will under-invest in education. Furthermore, the extent of this knowledge gap may be unevenly distributed across the population, depending on factors like social class and family background. To overcome this failure, the government can provide incentives to encourage individuals to participate in education, particularly beyond the compulsory level of schooling (for example, maintenance grants for those participating in third-level education who live below a certain income threshold). Second, individuals lack information regarding the quality of the education service being provided. In the case of primary and second-level education where parents can afford to pay fees for their children to attend private schools, market forces will operate in the standard way with higher fees potentially signalling better-quality institutions. However, in most cases parents cannot afford to pay for their children to receive a private education and so the choice of school becomes limited. In the absence of government intervention to ensure certain quality standards are met, there will be no incentive for schools to deliver an efficient service.

An alternative to the regulation of quality standards is to allow schools to be privately run and for the government to regulate the credit markets used to finance education. For example, the government could grant vouchers to all individuals which they can spend as they please, allowing them to choose schools which suit their preferences and meet their standards. A second possibility is for the government to guarantee loans to students which they must repay once their studies have been completed. Of course, this can lead to similar problems to those outlined at the start of this section as there is no guarantee that students will be in a position to repay these loans at a later stage. Many OECD countries operate publicly secured student loans to finance tuition fees or living costs associated with third-level education. In fact, in Australia, Iceland, New Zealand, Norway and Sweden student loans amount to 0.2 per cent of GDP or more.[7]

Equity

Government intervention in the provision of education is also justified on equity grounds. As argued earlier, education is a key determinant of earnings and employment prospects. As such, education plays an important role in determining not only the level of income in society but also the distribution of that income. A key role for government is therefore to promote *equality of opportunity* by attempting to ensure equal access to education for all of its citizens.

The Irish government attempts to achieve this through various different initiatives such as free compulsory education up to a certain age and free fees in third-level institutions. The government also attempts to ensure that discrimination on gender, race, ethnic, disability or any other grounds does not take place within the education system by ensuring equal access to all groups in society. However, since individuals' educational prospects and information on the merits of education are unevenly distributed across the population, it is more likely that specific socio-economic groups, usually those at the lower end of the income distribution, will underachieve in relation to educational attainment. Therefore, on *horizontal equity* grounds it is justified for the government to target education expenditure and programmes at potentially educationally disadvantaged socio-economic groups. In fact, this is also justifiable on efficiency grounds if the extent of the information problems outlined above is more pronounced among these groups, justifying targeted higher levels of expenditure. Intervention on these grounds will also satisfy the principle of *vertical equity*. Since education determines future earnings, by redistributing tax revenues to poorer socio-economic groups in the form of education investments, a more equal outcome will result once the returns to these investments have been realised.

3 EDUCATION POLICY IN IRELAND

Irish education policy was slower to evolve than in many other OECD countries. The seminal development in Irish education policy took place in 1967 with the introduction of free second-level education for all. Since the 1960s, education expenditure as a percentage of national income has doubled and since the early 1990s, the Irish government has recognised the importance of education for economic, social and cultural development, and has demonstrated a real commitment to investment in education and training.

Education policy in Ireland can be divided into two strands, each of which attempts to achieve different objectives for the economy. On the one hand, education policy aims to facilitate the accumulation of human capital in the economy with the aim of fuelling economic growth. On the other hand, education policy aims to aid the government's policy objective of equity by ensuring equal access to, and opportunities within, the system. In addition, there is much co-operation at EU level in the development of education and training policies. For example, most EU countries, including Ireland, signed up to the Bologna Declaration in 1999, under which they agreed to co-operate on achieving a range of objectives for higher education within the EU including comparable degree programmes, a system of credits to aid student mobility and the promotion of inter-institutional co-operation in research.[8] In this section the focus is on specific Irish policy initiatives, but bearing in mind the fact that most are motivated by recommendations made at higher levels of governance.

Policies Aimed at Promoting Economic Growth

As discussed in Section 2, a key rationale for government intervention in education provision (particularly at third level) is the importance of education to the creation of a skilled labour force. Thus, a key role of education is to produce a well-educated workforce that can meet the demands of an expanding economy. A more skilled and productive labour force will produce more output, facilitate the development and diffusion of new technologies, further fuelling growth, and will make the economy a more attractive place to invest, particularly if the skills of the labour force match labour demand. This is the assumption underlying the notion that modern-day economies are both 'knowledge based' and 'knowledge driven', and the ability to innovate is the key to successful economic development.

Acknowledging the fact that a well-educated and skilled labour force is a key determinant of competitiveness, in 1997 the Irish government established an Expert Group on Future Skills Needs to assist in the development of national strategies to ensure a flexible and adaptable labour force. Since its establishment, the Expert Group has produced a range of reports monitoring trends in Ireland's skills supply and making recommendations as to how education and training should best be oriented towards improving labour productivity, minimising unemployment, and developing a labour force that can support high-value knowledge-based industries (see Chapter 8). These have ranged from sector-specific reports (for example, *Future Skills Needs of the Irish Medical Devices Sector* (2008) and the *Future Skills Needs of the International Financial Services Industry* (2007)) to more general reports focusing on the skills needs of the labour market in a broader context. In 2007 the Expert Group published an extensive report outlining a range of measures necessary for Ireland to ensure the transition to a competitive, innovation-driven, knowledge-based economy by 2020.[9] In addition to the upskilling of a substantial proportion of the current workforce they recommend that the proportion of 20- to 24-year- olds completing second-level education should be 94 per cent (compared with 85 per cent today) and an increase in the numbers progressing to third level from 55 per cent to 72 per cent. These recommendations will form the basis of a National Skills Strategy.

We now focus our attention on specific government initiatives within the education system aimed at improving growth prospects through the upskilling of the labour force.

Initiatives at Primary and Second Level
As discussed in Section 2, while the provision of compulsory education sets the foundations for the development of a labour force equipped with the necessary social capital to contribute to the economy and society more generally, the cycle of economic development will generally lead to a shift in focus towards third-level education initiatives to achieve growth objectives, particularly where there is a demand for an adaptable, flexible, high-skilled labour force. An important function of compulsory schooling, however, is to prepare students for third level, so some mention of government initiatives at this level is also warranted.

Aside from ensuring equal access to second-level education so that everyone has an equal opportunity to proceed to third level, the government promotes a number of initiatives at second level which are specifically focused on preparing the future labour force to meet the needs of Ireland's 'knowledge-based' labour market. For example, the decline in the number of students pursuing scientific subjects at second level in the 1990s sparked concern about the ability of the Irish labour force to meet its future skills needs. In response, the Department of Education and Science introduced a range of initiatives to promote science at all levels of the education system. These measures include: introducing science to the curriculum at primary level; better career guidance at second level, particularly in the junior cycle when students begin making career choices; and promoting the application of new technology in teaching methods, among others.

Initiatives at Third Level
The HEA stress the vital role that the higher education sector has to play, not only in educating and training the labour force required for the development and expansion of 'knowledge-based' industry, but also in being the central resource for research, development and innovation.[10] The Irish research environment has changed significantly in recent years as a result of a number of key developments in the provision of funding for third-level research. The most significant development in research was the establishment of Science Foundation Ireland (SFI) in 2000. The role of SFI is to support research in strategic areas that advance the country's technological and economic success and reputation: their aim is to 'enhance Irish science, engineering and economic growth and bring Ireland distinction for its sustained research excellence'.[11] In addition to this, in 1998 the

Programme for Research in Third-level Institutions (PRTLI) provided a new general source of research funding and in 1999 and 2001, respectively, the Irish Research Council for Humanities and Social Sciences and the Irish Research Council for Science, Engineering and Technology were established, providing new and significant sources of funding for individual researchers and research projects in these fields. More recently, the HEA Strategic Innovation Fund (SIF) of €300 million was established in 2006. In addition to these programmes, a programme to develop, reconfigure and refurbish necessary physical facilities has also been established.

Perhaps the greatest shift of policy emphasis can be traced to the 2001 report of the Expert Group on Future Skills Needs, which highlighted the need for Ireland to attract and retain researchers and the need for the higher education system to achieve substantial increases in the output of doctorates (labelled 'fourth level' by policymakers, now in common parlance as referring to doctoral and postdoctoral research activity), particularly in science, engineering and technology; to facilitate undergraduate students to progress into postgraduate research; and to attract international researchers to Ireland. This major policy shift reorients investment in the higher education sector toward investment in research and development (R&D) to be implemented through the third-level sector over the period of the current National Development Plan (2007–2013). This is encapsulated in the announcement of a Strategy for Science, Technology and Innovation (SSTI), which has made clear the government's future commitment to investing in R&D as a key part of economic and education policy.[12] In spending terms, key targets have been established, such as doubling the number of PhD students by 2013. More important, perhaps, is that the SSTI is in effect moving research and higher education spending to the capital or infrastructural portion of government spending and ring-fencing resources on a multi-annual basis.

By refocusing R&D expenditure on spending through the universities the government has implicitly accepted the importance of higher education to economic growth. It is now commonplace to hear politicians claim that university research has the potential to produce breakthrough advances that can fundamentally alter economic growth. Universities are responding to the growing interaction with industry by bolstering their industry liaison and technology transfer offices. Policy infrastructures are also moving to structure their operations to support this core belief in R&D for growth. However, these decisions notwithstanding, there remains a real challenge to show that there is a causal relationship between the different elements of higher education (formation and production of graduates and R&D) and economic growth.

Policies Aimed at Promoting Equity

As discussed in Section 2, an important rationale for government intervention in the provision of education is to promote equality of opportunity by ensuring equal access to the education system for all. While participation rates in education have increased significantly in Ireland over the last number of decades, up to the 1990s education policy in Ireland focused on increasing the overall level of participation in education with little attempts to promote equity in access to the system. Inequalities in education can manifest themselves in two ways, either through inequalities in educational achievement or the level of education attainment across different groups. These inequities are not confined to educational divides on the basis of social class but could manifest themselves as inequities across ethnic, gender or race divides, or against people with disabilities.

With the introduction of free second-level schooling in the 1960s and compulsory education up to the age of 16, participation in schooling is almost universal across all groups in society, with recognition of the core value of this to Irish society motivating strong government investment. However, the problem lies in the extent to which all individuals realise their true potential within the schooling system regardless of circumstances or social background. Increased levels of funding can go some way to alleviating these inequalities in the education system; however, targeting expenditure at the most vulnerable groups will be more effective.

This has been recognised within Irish education policy since 1995 when the Irish government issued a White Paper on Education recognising the need to design education policies to combat directly educational disadvantage. Subsequently, in 1998, the Education Act defined educational disadvantage as the 'impediments to education arising from social or economic disadvantage which prevent students from deriving appropriate benefit from education in schools'. The Act provided for the establishment of an Educational Disadvantage Committee (2002–2005) to advise the Minister for Education on policy issues specifically relating to targeting disadvantage within the education system. In addition, combating educational disadvantage is incorporated into the government's National Anti-Poverty Strategy, which includes as an overall objective the need to ensure that those living in poverty can participate in and benefit from education in a way that will allow them move out of poverty and prevent others from becoming poor. Other inequities are also covered by government policy. In June 2001, the Gender Equality Unit was established in the Department of Education and Science to ensure that the department 'is enabled to integrate a gender dimension into all its services, actions, programmes and measures for children and adults at all levels'.[13] In addition, the Educational Disadvantage Committee's Traveller Education Strategy aims at ensuring equality of outcomes from education for members of the Travelling community.

Initiatives at Primary and Second Level
Specific policy initiatives aimed at promoting equity within the education system have largely targeted compulsory education, since the main determinants of post-compulsory education achievement are educational background and the foundations laid at an early stage of educational development. Two types of policy

initiative have been introduced via the Educational Disadvantage Committee to tackle the inequities apparent in both access and achievement within the Irish education system. First, the school curriculum has been reformed in order to offer alternative, less academic educational routes that allow less academically minded students the opportunity to attain a successful education in areas better suited to them (for example, the Junior Certificate School Programme, the Leaving Certificate Applied Programme and the Leaving Certificate Vocational Programme). Second, expenditure has been targeted at disadvantaged schools or communities, focusing on school inclusion and promoting achievement in education. Such initiatives include, among others, Breaking the Cycle, Early Start programmes and the Home School Community Liaison Scheme. In addition, the government specifically allocates resources to pupils with special educational needs in primary schools.

More recently, the contribution that adult education can make in tackling education disadvantage has also been highlighted, and there has been a sizeable shift in policy considerations of the early childhood care and education (ECCE) agenda. As recently as 2007 the National Economic and Social Forum called for all young children (0–4 years) to have access to, and participate in, a range of quality education and care services and supports of an internationally accepted standard through a plan to be implemented over a ten-year period.

Initiatives at Third Level

By far the most significant development in higher education policy aimed at promoting equality of access to third-level education was the introduction in 1996 of free tuition fees for full-time third-level undergraduate EU students. Over the last number of years the increase in the number of places at third-level institutions has also aimed to improve access to third-level education. The government also provides specific financial incentives to individuals participating in third-level education, such as the Higher Education Grants Scheme and the Vocational Education Committee's Scholarship Scheme (which provide maintenance grants on a means-tested basis). In addition, third-level institutions themselves operate programmes to encourage participation by all groups in society.

The promotion of equal opportunities in third-level education falls under the remit of the HEA, which recognises the promotion of social inclusion as a key national policy objective. In May 2003, a report to government on supporting equity in higher education called for further policy reforms in this regard, including increases in the level and coverage of maintenance grants and an extension of the income threshold at which students are required to pay service charges. They also called for a review of means-testing procedures, the administration of student supports and the free-fees initiatives amidst a gradual move internationally away from a reliance on taxpayers to fund third-level participation toward an increasing role for parents and students. This process was fully recognised in the establishment of the National Office for Equity of Access to Higher Education by the HEA in 2005.

4 LEVEL AND DELIVERY OF EDUCATION SERVICES

Having provided an outline of the specific objectives of various education policy initiatives in Ireland over the last decade, in this section the effectiveness of government in its delivery of education services is evaluated. Evaluating the performance of government in the provision of a service like education is complicated by the fact that many of the returns to education are intangible. This makes traditional cost-benefit analysis very difficult as often the benefits are impossible to quantify. This also creates problems in attempting to compare outcomes across countries. Instead, government involvement in the sector can be evaluated in relation to its delivery of an efficient and equitable service.

In this section, the level of provision of education services is examined by looking at public expenditure on education in Ireland and how this relates to other OECD countries. How funds are allocated at different levels of the education system is also analysed both relative to other OECD countries and within a specifically Irish context. From an efficiency point of view it is important that the government achieves value for money in its spending decisions and so the trade-off between achieving quality outcomes and productivity improvements is discussed. Notwithstanding the difficulties in measuring outcomes in the education sector, how education outcomes in Ireland relate to those in other OECD countries is also analysed. The section concludes with some discussion on the extent to which the system offers equal opportunities or improves the distribution of income by leading to more equal outcomes.

Public Expenditure on Education

Table 12.1 presents statistics on the proportion of education expenditure in GDP (GNI for Ireland) for a selection of OECD countries. In 2004, expenditure on education as a percentage of GNI in Ireland was 5.4 per cent, down from 6.4 per cent in 1995. With a declining birth rate and a reduction in the proportion of the population of school-going age the demand for education expenditure will fall over time. As a result, across most OECD countries a stabilisation or even a fall in spending on education is expected. This was the case for most countries between 1995 and 2000, but since then some increases have been observed. This may in part be explained by slow growth in GDP in many European countries since 2000 but may also be due to increasing expenditure levels in response to new EU targets as set out in the Lisbon Agenda (see Chapter 8). Also illustrated in Table 12.1 is the relatively small level of private expenditure on educational institutions except in the USA.

Education expenditure in Ireland in 2004 accounted for 14 per cent of total government expenditure, up from 12.2 per cent in 1995 compared with an EU average of just below 12 per cent. In Table 12.2 the level of expenditure on educational institutions by student for Ireland and a selection of OECD countries is presented. In all countries spend per student increases across education level with the highest spend per student at third level. European countries lag behind

US investment in education at all levels, but particularly at third level. Ireland lags behind the EU and OECD average on spend per student at primary and second level at $5,422 and $7,110 respectively. Expenditure at third level is at the EU average at $10,211 but is lower than all other EU countries presented in the table. These figures suggest that while Ireland spends more on education in terms of its proportion of total government expenditure it spends less per unit when compared with other countries, particularly on compulsory education. It should be noted, however, that the gap between spend per student in Ireland compared with other countries is closing, particularly at primary and second level: in 2000 spend per student in Ireland was 24 per cent lower for primary and 15 per cent lower for secondary than the OECD average. In contrast, expenditure at third level was at the OECD average in 2000. This suggests a slower pace of growth in third-level education expenditure in Ireland compared with our EU neighbours, and relative to primary and second level within Ireland.

Table 12.1
Expenditure on Educational Institutions as a Percentage of GDP/GNI

	1995 Total	2000 Total	2004 Total	2004 Public	2004 Private
Austria	6.1	5.5	5.4	5.0	0.4
Denmark	6.2	6.6	7.2	6.9	0.3
Finland	6.3	5.6	6.1	6.0	0.1
Germany	5.4	n/a	5.2	4.3	0.9
Ireland[1]	*6.4*	*5.2*	*5.4*	*5.0*	*0.4*
Netherlands	4.8	4.5	5.1	4.6	0.5
UK	5.5	5.0	5.9	5.0	1.0
USA	6.6	7.0	7.4	5.1	2.3
EU-19 Average[2]	...	...	5.4	5.0	0.4
OECD Average[2]	...	...	5.7	5.0	0.7

Source: OECD, *Education at a Glance, OECD Indicators 2007*, OECD, Paris 2007.
Note: Public expenditure includes public expenditure on educational institutions plus public subsidies to households.
[1] Expenditure on educational institutions expressed as a percentage of GNI.
[2] Averages are not available for 1995 and 2000.

Given the difficulties in measuring the effectiveness of investment at all levels of education in terms of outcomes, it is difficult to evaluate whether it is more efficient for the government to allocate funds to one level of education over another. While Ireland allocates a greater proportion of its education budget to third level compared with most other EU countries (the proportion of total government expenditure spent on third level in 2004 was 3.3 per cent compared with an EU average of 2.9 per cent), as the previous discussion has shown, expenditure at all levels has increased over the last five years with first and second level experiencing a proportionally greater increase in spend per student terms than third level.

Table 12.2
Expenditure on Educational Institutions per Student by Level of Education, 2004 (expressed in equivalent US$ converted using PPPs)

	Primary level	Second level	Third level
Austria	7,669	9,446	13,959
Denmark	8,081	8,849	15,225
Finland	5,581	7,441	12,505
France	5,082	8,737	10,668
Germany	4,948	7,576	12,255
Ireland	*5,422*	*7,110*	*10,211*
Netherlands	6,222	7,541	13,846
UK	5,941	7,090	11,484
USA	8,805	9,938	22,476
EU-19 Average	5,788	7,236	10,191
OECD Average	5,832	7,276	11,100

Source: As for Table 12.1.
Note: Figures include expenditure on both public and private institutions.

Allocation of Funds at Primary and Second Level
The government adopts a centralised approach to allocating resources to primary and second-level schools with some variation across different types of school, such as vocational, community and comprehensive schools. Private fee-paying schools are allocated resources to cover teachers' salaries. The allocation of teachers to schools is also important given the government's commitment to lowering student-teacher ratios. Currently, teachers are allocated on the basis of student enrolment. There may also be a number of ex-quota posts, such as guidance teachers, deputy principals or home-school liaison officers allocated on the basis of school size or need (for example, if the school is located in a disadvantaged area they may qualify for more ex-quota posts). In some cases there may also be lower student-teacher ratios linked to certain programmes aimed at tackling disadvantage. Overall, student-teacher ratios have been reduced at both primary and second level over the 1990s but still remain above the EU average. In 2005, the number of students to teaching staff in primary schools in Ireland was 17.9 compared with an EU average of 14.9, while for secondary schools the student-teacher ratio was 15.5, also above the EU average of 12.2.[14]

The most significant component of government expenditure on education at this level is wages and salaries. Capital expenditure also makes up a large proportion of the education spend at both primary and second level at eight and seven per cent respectively in 2004. In addition to the allocation of resources to schools, some resources are allocated directly to students for primary and secondary education such as book grants, free school meals, Back to School Clothing Allowances, etc. However, these types of individual transfers play a much more significant role in the third-level sector in the form of maintenance grants to third-level students (discussed below).

Allocation of Funds at Third Level

The higher education system in Ireland is predominantly publicly funded. The HEA is responsible for the allocation of funding to universities and some other institutions, while the Department of Education and Science is responsible for funding the ITs (although from 2006 a transition of management and governance of the IT sector to the HEA has been initiated). As already mentioned, in 1996 free tuition fees were introduced for eligible full-time undergraduate EU students. These fees are paid to higher education institutions by the state. Prior to the launch of the PRTLI (see above) state funding for research was low. The PRTLI scheme is managed by the HEA and awards funding for research on a competitive basis across universities based on the quality and merit of the proposed research. Up to 2008 approximately €850 million was allocated under the programme. Other capital funding is allocated on a case-by-case basis. In total, capital expenditure, at 13 per cent, makes up a greater proportion of the overall budget compared with primary and second level. When all income is taken into account state funding as a percentage of total funding amounts to 80 per cent for universities and 90 per cent for ITs.[15]

While there have been major investments at third level through R&D programmes, there has not been the corresponding investment in the core budget of higher education institutions. This could rapidly lead to the phenomenon of 'overtrading' where universities take on more and more R&D funding without the necessary core funding to support the additional activity associated with these projects. While there will be continued increase in the quality and quantity of research output this cannot be to the detriment of other activities, notably the output of high-quality undergraduate students.

By far the most contentious issue in relation to the allocation of third-level funding is government expenditure on student transfers, both in the form of tuition fees and maintenance grants, which form a significant component of tertiary-sector state expenditure compared with primary and second-level education. As discussed in Section 2, the private returns to third-level education are significant in terms of higher earnings, higher labour force participation rates and lower unemployment risk. In addition, statistics show a high correlation between third-level participation and social class of parents. It is therefore difficult to justify the use of taxation income, collected from the general public, to finance individual participation in the accumulation of human capital, which may yield significant private returns in the future. In addition, the effectiveness of such schemes is questionable. Alternative mechanisms such as offering state-guaranteed student loans, voucher systems, etc. have been explored by the HEA in the 2002/2003 review of third-level tuition fees and student supports and revisited by the OECD and in countless submissions by the Irish Universities Association (the umbrella organisation for the seven universities), but no specific policy move has been made or seems likely for the foreseeable future.

Efficiency of Education Expenditure[16]

It is difficult to draw conclusions on the performance of the sector on the basis of the level of government expenditure alone as higher levels of government expenditure do not automatically imply a higher-quality service. In fact, the empirical evidence is mixed on whether increased expenditure per pupil positively impacts student achievement. In contrast with other sectors of the economy where productivity improvements are often associated with using fewer labour inputs to achieve the same level of output, in the education sector, where the objective is achieving a higher-quality service, increasing the number of labour inputs (i.e. reducing student-teacher ratios) is inevitable as over time the public demand higher-quality education services (Wagner's law, see Chapter 3). There is much debate, however on whether reduced student-teacher ratios result in improved academic achievement, with many empirical studies supporting the notion that class sizes matter but many others providing little evidence of such a relationship. Achieving productivity improvements (or value for money) is further impeded by the phenomenon known as Baumol's Disease (see Chapters 3 and 11) where inflationary cost increases lead to high wages in the non-productive sectors (primarily public services) of the economy. This is particularly the case for education because it is such a labour-intensive service. As a result, in the Irish case, the majority of the budget is absorbed by salaries and wages.

At first and second level, salaries and wages account for almost 84 per cent of current education expenditure in Ireland with the salaries of Irish teachers among some of the highest in the EU. Coupled with declining teacher-student ratios the only possibility for improvements in productivity is to improve outcomes. However, while schools are required to undergo a range of evaluations, such as school inspections and self-evaluations, this information is not publicly available nor is it used at higher administrative levels in making school funding decisions.

In 2004, compensation of staff in the tertiary sector in Ireland accounted for 74 per cent of all current expenditure, well above the OECD average of 66 per cent. Given that spend per student at third level is below the OECD average (see Table 12.2), it appears that more resources are allocated to salaries and wages in Ireland compared with elsewhere. Of particular note is the fact that expenditure per student at third level in Ireland is 12 per cent below that of the UK, where only 58 per cent of current expenditure is absorbed by salaries and wages. While average class sizes are slightly smaller in the tertiary sector in Ireland compared with the UK (17.4 compared with 18.2), they are higher than the OECD and EU-19 averages (at 15.8 and 16.4, respectively). Notwithstanding the important role that government funding plays for R&D at third level, the extent to which the government achieves value for money in terms of *education* at this level, as with primary and second level, is therefore also questionable. One recent development

333

which presents an opportunity for productivity improvements in the sector in the future is the increase in e-learning, particularly at third level. The debate on the extent to which this may affect the quality of education services provided, however, is ongoing.

Benchmarking Education Performance

The previous analysis highlights the fact that Ireland still invests less in education compared with other EU countries, particularly when the proportion of expenditure on salaries and wages at all levels is taken into account. Overall, Ireland was late to make any substantial investments in the education sector, with free second-level education only introduced in the 1960s. However, investment levels have increased significantly over time and while it may take some time for the returns to higher investment levels to be realised there are some early indicators of success. The proportion of the 20–24 year-old population with upper second-level education is now above the Lisbon Agenda target of 85 per cent. According to the OECD Programme for International Student Assessment (PISA) combined reading literacy scale conducted in 2003, Ireland ranks sixth in the OECD in terms of reading literacy and second in the EU-15 after Finland.[17] Ireland does not perform as well in relation to mathematics and science, however, ranking thirteenth in scientific literacy, a fall of four places since 2000, and sixteenth in terms of mathematical literacy. These trends are worrying given the importance for future employment and economic growth of building a knowledge-based economy, and the recent policy emphasis on the promotion of science, mathematics and engineering at all levels of the education system (see Section 3).

Table 12.3

Upper Second-Level and Tertiary-Level Graduates as a
Percentage of Population at Typical Age of Graduation[1]

	Second level		Third level	
	2000	2005	2000	2005
Denmark	90	86	37	46
Finland[2]	91	95	41	47
Germany	92	100	18	19
Ireland	*74*	*91*	*30*	*39*
UK[3]	...	86	37	39
USA	74	76	34	34
EU-19 Average	78	86	27	35
OECD Average	77	82	28	36

Source: As for Table 12.1.

[1] Data are not available for Austria, France and the Netherlands.

[2] Figures for Finland are for 2000 and 2004.

[3] Data for second-level graduation rates for the UK in 2000 are not available.

Overall, however, there is evidence that education outcomes are improving in Ireland. In Table 12.3 the percentage of upper secondary and tertiary graduates of the population at the typical age of graduation are presented. The most remarkable improvement for Ireland was the increase in the proportion of the population aged 17 to 18 that graduated from upper secondary level, from only 74 per cent in 2000 (below the EU average) to 91 per cent in 2005, well above the EU average of 82 per cent. Ireland also performs well on the proportion of the population aged 21 with a tertiary-level qualification at 39 per cent in 2005, above the EU average of 35 per cent and up from 30 per cent in 2000.

Equity

Since earnings are a key determinant of well-being, a lower probability of participating in the labour force, a higher probability of unemployment and lower average earnings of those with lower levels of education attainment together imply that inequalities in educational opportunities will have serious implications for the distribution of income in the economy. This does not take into account the other negative welfare effects associated with early school leavers such as social exclusion or crime, for example, which exacerbate the need for government education policies that target such inequities.

Across countries, evidence suggests that those who fail to complete upper second-level education are more likely to come from disadvantaged backgrounds.[18] In an Irish context research has shown that those from working-class and unemployed families are more likely to underperform in Junior and Leaving Certificate examinations relative to their initial ability compared with other social groups. In addition, participation in tertiary education is highly correlated with the educational attainment and social background of parents, with those from unskilled-manual backgrounds less likely to stay on in full-time education compared with those from professional backgrounds.[19]

At primary and second level, government policy has focused on the retention and achievement of students, particularly from disadvantaged backgrounds. Declining student-teacher ratios are part of these measures but there are also targeted initiatives aimed at tackling educational disadvantage (see Section 3). However, it will be a number of years before the benefits of these measures are fully realised. At second level, there have been substantial increases in the provision of, and numbers taking, the special Junior Certificate School Programme and the Applied Leaving Certificate Programme, which were introduced to target equality in second-level education for all. The benefits of interventions of this kind are evidenced by the increasing rates of second-level completion: by 2006, 85.4 per cent of the population aged 20–24 had completed second-level education compared with 77.3 per cent a decade before.[20]

Of more significance, however, is the extent to which this follows through to equality of access and achievement at third level. In May 2003, a report to the Minister for Education and Science on Supporting Equity in Higher Education provided an analysis of the extent to which equality of access to third level has improved in Ireland over the last number of years. Between 1980 and 1998, participation in third level by students whose fathers are semi-skilled or unskilled workers increased from nine per cent and three per cent to 23 and 21 per cent respectively. However, overall participation rates of this age cohort increased from 20 per cent to 44 per cent over this period. The majority of the increase was accounted for by increased participation by students whose fathers are in higher socio-economic groupings. For example, participation rates of students whose fathers are higher professionals increased from 59 per cent to 97 per cent. Similar increases in participation rates were observed for students whose fathers are employers and managers or farmers. Despite some evidence of an increase in participation rates by lower socio-economic groups, they continue to be under-represented at third level (the bottom three groupings account for 20 per cent of all participants compared with 43 per cent by the top three groupings). In addition, students from higher socio-economic backgrounds are highly represented in universities while students from lower socio-economic backgrounds have higher representation in the non-university sector. Furthermore, the rate of non-completion in the non-university sector is more than twice that found in universities. These trends highlight the need for continued government efforts to promote equity at all levels of the education system.

5 CONCLUSION

Education plays a vitally important role in the economic, social and cultural development of all economies. Not only is education a key to economic development in the contribution it makes to enhancing the skill level, productivity and competitiveness of the economy, it also plays a vital role in determining the income level and social status of individuals and will directly impact on the distribution of income in an economy. Due to the failure of private markets to provide education optimally, the government has a crucial role to play in ensuring education services are provided in such a way as optimally to meet these objectives.

In an Irish context, education policy attempts to ensure the delivery of an efficient and equitable service. Evidence suggests that Ireland performs well in achieving desired educational outcomes such as high achievement in terms of reading literacy, and high education participation and attainment rates (see Section 4). The government has a long way to go in its delivery of an equitable service which ensures that individuals from all groups in society realise their true potential within the system. However, the outcome of the government's bottom-up approach to tackling educational disadvantage may not be realised for a number of years.

Looking to the future, education policy will continue to focus on initiatives aimed at improving Ireland's competitiveness, primarily through the promotion of lifelong learning and reform of the tertiary sector. Higher education is now an internationally traded service providing both teaching and research services nationally and internationally. In order for Irish higher education institutions to be in a position to compete internationally it is well recognised that change and reform is both necessary and inevitable. The OECD review of higher education in Ireland called for a 'step change' in funding for higher education institutions and in particular presented strong arguments in favour of investment in education at this level. However, what form this investment should take is another question entirely. Simply handing out money to universities with no national development strategies does not guarantee that the expected benefits will be delivered. Government policy therefore plays a critical role in the successful development of a country's international education industry.

Endnotes

* We would like to thank John O'Hagan, Liam Delaney and Martin Ryan for helpful comments and assistance on this chapter.

1 The establishment of the Office of the Minister for Children and the associated Ministry puts a greater emphasis on the planning and initiation of services in pre-formal education – the so-called early childhood care and education agenda. See www.dohc.ie for further information.

2 A new category of higher education sector emerged in the late 1990s consisting of private sector colleges which are fully funded by student fees but, by virtue of their provision of state-admitted degree programmes, are classified in these data.

3 The recent increase in the range of private sector education institutions in Ireland has led to a very significant rise in the number of parents who choose to send their children to private education at primary and second levels. This is perhaps a function of greater wealth, but may also be attributable to the fact that the private sector is grant aided by the Department of Education and Science, unlike many other countries, so the fees applicable are much lower than, say, comparable schools in the UK. Furthermore, with free tuition fees at third level, parents may choose instead to invest in their children's education at an earlier stage. This may also reflect, as with health choices, an expectation of greater service or quality from the private sector.

4 See C. Harmon, H. Oosterbeek and I. Walker, 'The returns to education: micro-economics', *Journal of Economic Surveys*, Vol. 17, No. 2, 2003; and J. Heckman, L. Lochner and P. Todd, 'Fifty years of Mincer earnings regressions' (NBER Working Paper 9732), National Bureau of Economics Research, 2003.

5 For examples, see A. Barrett, J. FitzGerald and A. Nolan, 'Earnings inequality, returns to education and immigration into Ireland', *Labour Economics*, Vol. 9, No. 5, 2002; OECD, 'Investment in human capital through upper-secondary and tertiary education', *OECD Economic Studies No. 34*, OECD, Paris 2002; and S. McCoy and S. Smyth, 'Educational expenditure: implications for equality', *Budget Perspectives 2004*, ESRI, Dublin 2004.

6 See OECD, 'Growth Effects of Education and Social Capital in the OECD Countries' (Economics Department Working Papers No. 263), OECD, Paris 2000 (available at: www.oecd.org), for an overview of recent literature in this area.

[7] OECD, *OECD Economic Survey of the United Kingdom: Graduate Contributions for Higher Education,* OECD, Paris 2004.

[8] See http://europa.eu.int for further details.

[9] Expert Group on Future Skills Needs, *Tomorrow's Skills: Towards a National Skills Strategy*, Forfás, Dublin 2007.

[10] Higher Education Authority, *Strategy Statement 2004–2007*, HEA, Dublin 2004.

[11] Science Foundation Ireland, *Vision 2003–2007: People, Ideas and Partnerships for a Globally Competitive Irish Research System*, SFI, Dublin 2003.

[12] Department of Enterprise, Trade and Employment, *Strategy for Science Technology and Innovation (SSTI) 2006–2013*, DETE, Dublin 2006.

[13] The department has also recently published a report investigating gender and education in Ireland that provides an overview of education statistics disaggregated by gender (Department of Education and Science, *Sé Sí Gender in Irish Education*, DES, Dublin 2007).

[14] OECD, *Education at a Glance 2007*, OECD, Paris 2007.

[15] See the Higher Education Authority, *Financial Management in Irish Institutions of Higher Education*, Higher Education Authority, Dublin 2003, for more detail on the allocation of funding to third-level institutions.

[16] Statistics used in this section are drawn from OECD, op. cit., 2007.

[17] Expert Group on Future Skills Needs, *Monitoring Ireland's Skills Supply. Trends in Education/Training Outputs*, Forfás, Dublin 2007.

[18] Examples taken from OECD, op. cit., 2002.

[19] McCoy and Smyth, op. cit.

[20] CSO, *Education Statistics*, Stationery Office, Dublin, various years (accessed at: www.cso.ie)

Index